Constitutional Law

2002 Supplement

2002 Supplement

Constitutional Law

Erwin Chemerinsky
Sydney M. Irmas Professor of Public Interest Law, Legal
Ethics, and Political Science
University of Southern California

ASPEN LAW & BUSINESS
A Division of Aspen Publishers, Inc.
New York   Gaithersburg

Printed in the United States of America

ISBN 0-7355-2856-6

1 2 3 4 5 6 7 8 9 0

Library of Congress Cataloging-in-Publication Data

Chemerinsky, Erwin.
    Constitutional law / Erwin Chemerinsky.
      p. cm.
    Includes index.
    ISBN 0-7355-2061-5 (casebound)
    ISBN 0-7355-2856-6 (supplement)
      1. Constitutional law—United States—Cases. I. Title.

KF4549 .C44 2001
342.73—dc21   2001018911

About Aspen Law & Business Legal Education Division

With a dedication to preserving and strengthening the long-standing tradition of publishing excellence in legal education, Aspen Law & Business continues to provide the highest quality teaching and learning resources for today's law school community. Careful development, meticulous editing, and an unmatched responsiveness to the evolving needs of today's discerning educators combine in the creation of our outstanding casebooks, coursebooks, textbooks, and study aids.

ASPEN LAW & BUSINESS
A Division of Aspen Publishers, Inc.
A Wolters Kluwer Company
www.aspenpublishers.com

Contents*

---

*Major cases are indicated in italics. Cases without italics are presented much more briefly.

Preface

This Supplement covers the October 2000 and October 2001 Terms. That is, the Supplement covers the developments since the publication of the casebook, which is complete through the October 1999 Term, which ended on June 28, 2000.

I know that many teachers will want to begin their classes with a discussion of some of the constitutional issues arising from the government's reaction to the tragedy of September 11. Therefore, the introduction to this Supplement presents materials on the constitutionality of military tribunals. (Obviously, it also might be considered in Chapter 3, as part of a discussion of presidential power and separation of powers.) The material from last year's Supplement on Bush v. Gore is included in Chapter 8 of this Supplement.

The remainder of the Supplement follows the organization of the casebook. I tried to be clear about where the new cases would fit within the organization of the casebook. The Supplement follows the same approach as the casebook. There generally are brief explanations to help students understand the context and law surrounding the case. In editing cases, as in the casebook, I omitted most internal citations and did not use ellipses to indicate deletions. All additions, however minor, are indicated by brackets.

I have begun work on the second edition of the casebook, which is scheduled for publication in the spring of 2004. I very much appreciate the many useful suggestions that I have received from users of the book and encourage professors and students to send me suggestions for future annual supplements and the next edition.

I want to thank Jennifer Fercovich, Jorge Luna, David Swift, and Anieko Webb for their excellent research assistance. I also am grateful to everyone at Aspen for their continual support and help.

Erwin Chemerinsky

July 2002

Constitutional Law

2002 Supplement

Introduction*

Are Military Tribunals Constitutional?

The tragic events of September 11, 2001, have led to many government actions that will raise important difficult constitutional questions: Is the indefinite detention of "unlawful combatants" constitutional? Are secret deportation proceedings constitutional? Is it permissible for the government to hold individuals indefinitely as "material witnesses"? Are provisions of the USA Patriot Act, which include expanded authorization for electronic eavesdropping by the government, constitutional? Although many of these questions are beyond the scope of a traditional constitutional law course (many are more commonly covered in Criminal Procedure or other classes), one important issue likely to be discussed in constitutional law classes is whether President George W. Bush's order for military tribunals is constitutional.

The order for military tribunals raises many basic questions: Does the President, as Commander-in-Chief, have the authority to create military tribunals or is creating courts entirely a Congressional power under the Constitution? Can the government suspend provisions of the Bill of Rights in trying noncitizens accused of terrorism or supporting terrorism? More generally, how should the Constitution be interpreted during war time?

To facilitate discussion of these issues, below is President Bush's Executive Order for military tribunals, followed by a summary of the "Procedures for Trials by Military Commissions," promulgated by the Department of Defense in March 2002. After these materials, the only Supreme Court case on the issue of military tribunals is presented: Ex parte Quirin, from 1942. A crucial question will be whether *Quirin* provides adequate authority for President Bush's action or whether it is distinguishable. Also, the underlying issue is whether *Quirin* was properly decided in allowing military tribunals.

---

*Last year's introductory material on Bush v. Gore has been moved to Chapter 8 in this Supplement, under the right to vote.

DETENTION, TREATMENT, AND TRIAL OF CERTAIN NON-CITIZENS IN THE WAR AGAINST TERRORISM
November 13, 2001
66 FR 57833

By the authority vested in me as President and as Commander in Chief of the Armed Forces of the United States by the Constitution and the laws of the United States of America, including the Authorization for Use of Military Force Joint Resolution and sections 821 and 836 of title 10, United States Code, it is hereby ordered as follows:

SECTION 1.   FINDINGS

(a) International terrorists, including members of al Qaida, have carried out attacks on United States diplomatic and military personnel and facilities abroad and on citizens and property within the United States on a scale that has created a state of armed conflict that requires the use of the United States Armed Forces.

(b) In light of grave acts of terrorism and threats of terrorism, including the terrorist attacks on September 11, 2001, on the headquarters of the United States Department of Defense in the national capital region, on the World Trade Center in New York, and on civilian aircraft such as in Pennsylvania, I proclaimed a national emergency on September 14, 2001.

(c) Individuals acting alone and in concert involved in international terrorism possess both the capability and the intention to undertake further terrorist attacks against the United States that, if not detected and prevented, will cause mass deaths, mass injuries, and massive destruction of property, and may place at risk the continuity of the operations of the United States Government.

(d) The ability of the United States to protect the United States and its citizens, and to help its allies and other cooperating nations protect their nations and their citizens, from such further terrorist attacks depends in significant part upon using the United States Armed Forces to identify terrorists and those who support them, to disrupt their activities, and to eliminate their ability to conduct or support such attacks.

(e) To protect the United States and its citizens, and for the effective conduct of military operations and prevention of terrorist attacks, it is necessary for individuals subject to this order pursuant to section 2 hereof to be detained, and, when tried, to be tried for violations of the laws of war and other applicable laws by military tribunals.

(f) Given the danger to the safety of the United States and the nature of international terrorism, and to the extent provided by and under this order, I find consistent with section 836 of title 10, United States Code, that it is not practicable to apply in military commissions under this order the principles of law and the rules of evidence generally recognized in the trial of criminal cases in the United States district courts.

(g) Having fully considered the magnitude of the potential deaths, injuries, and property destruction that would result from potential acts of terrorism against the United States, and the probability that such acts will occur, I have determined that an extraordinary emergency exists for national defense 57834 purposes, that this emergency constitutes an urgent and compelling government interest, and that issuance of this order is necessary to meet the emergency.

SECTION 2.   DEFINITION AND POLICY

(a) The term "individual subject to this order" shall mean any individual who is not a United States citizen with respect to whom I determine from time to time in writing that:

    (1) there is reason to believe that such individual, at the relevant times,

        (i) is or was a member of the organization known as al Qaida;

        (ii) has engaged in, aided or abetted, or conspired to commit, acts of international terrorism, or acts in preparation therefor, that have caused, threaten to cause, or have as their aim to cause, injury to or adverse effects on the United States, its citizens, national security, foreign policy, or economy; or

        (iii) has knowingly harbored one or more individuals described in subparagraphs (i) or (ii) of subsection 2(a)(1) of this order; and

    (2) it is in the interest of the United States that such individual be subject to this order.

(b) It is the policy of the United States that the Secretary of Defense shall take all necessary measures to ensure that any individual subject to this order is detained in accordance with section 3, and, if the individual is to be tried, that such individual is tried only in accordance with section 4.

(c) It is further the policy of the United States that any individual subject to this order who is not already under the control of the Secretary of Defense but who is under the control of any other officer or agent of the United States or any State shall, upon delivery of a copy of such written determination to such officer or agent, forthwith be placed under the control of the Secretary of Defense.

SECTION 3.   DETENTION AUTHORITY OF THE SECRETARY OF DEFENSE

Any individual subject to this order shall be—

(a) detained at an appropriate location designated by the Secretary of Defense outside or within the United States;

(b) treated humanely, without any adverse distinction based on race, color, religion, gender, birth, wealth, or any similar criteria;

(c) afforded adequate food, drinking water, shelter, clothing, and medical treatment;

(d) allowed the free exercise of religion consistent with the requirements of such detention; and

(e) detained in accordance with such other conditions as the Secretary of Defense may prescribe.

SECTION 4.   AUTHORITY OF THE SECRETARY OF DEFENSE REGARDING TRIALS OF INDIVIDUALS SUBJECT TO THIS ORDER

(a) Any individual subject to this order shall, when tried, be tried by military commission for any and all offenses triable by military commission that such individual is alleged to have committed, and may be punished in accordance with the penalties provided under applicable law, including life imprisonment or death.

(b) As a military function and in light of the findings in section 1, including subsection (f) thereof, the Secretary of Defense shall issue such orders and regulations, including orders for the appointment of one or more military commissions, as may be necessary to carry out subsection (a) of this section.

(c) Orders and regulations issued under subsection (b) of this section shall include, but not be limited to, rules for the conduct of the proceedings of military commissions, including pretrial, trial, and post-trial procedures, modes of proof, issuance of process, and qualifications of attorneys, which shall at a minimum provide for—

(1) military commissions to sit at any time and any place, consistent with such guidance regarding time and place as the Secretary of Defense may provide;

(2) a full and fair trial, with the military commission sitting as the triers of both fact and law;

(3) admission of such evidence as would, in the opinion of the presiding officer of the military commission (or instead, if any other member of the commission so requests at the time the presiding officer renders that opinion, the opinion of the commission rendered at that time by a majority of the commission), have probative value to a reasonable person;

(4) in a manner consistent with the protection of information classified or classifiable under Executive Order 12958 of April 17, 1995, as amended, or any successor Executive Order, protected by statute or rule from unauthorized disclosure, or otherwise protected by law, (A) the handling of, admission into evidence of, and access to materials and information, and (B) the conduct, closure of, and access to proceedings;

(5) conduct of the prosecution by one or more attorneys designated by the Secretary of Defense and conduct of the defense by attorneys for the individual subject to this order;

(6) conviction only upon the concurrence of two-thirds of the members of the commission present at the time of the vote, a majority being present;

(7) sentencing only upon the concurrence of two-thirds of the members of the commission present at the time of the vote, a majority being present; and

(8) submission of the record of the trial, including any conviction or sentence, for review and final decision by me or by the Secretary of Defense if so designated by me for that purpose.

SECTION 5. OBLIGATION OF OTHER AGENCIES TO ASSIST THE SECRETARY OF DEFENSE

Departments, agencies, entities, and officers of the United States shall, to the maximum extent permitted by law, provide to the Secretary of Defense such assistance as he may request to implement this order.

SECTION 6. ADDITIONAL AUTHORITIES OF THE SECRETARY OF DEFENSE

(a) As a military function and in light of the findings in section 1, the Secretary of Defense shall issue such orders and regulations as may be necessary to carry out any of the provisions of this order.

(b) The Secretary of Defense may perform any of his functions or duties, and may exercise any of the powers provided to him under this order (other than under section 4(c)(8) hereof) in accordance with section 113(d) of title 10, United States Code.

SECTION 7. RELATIONSHIP TO OTHER LAW AND FORUMS

(a) Nothing in this order shall be construed to—

(1) authorize the disclosure of state secrets to any person not otherwise authorized to have access to them;

(2) limit the authority of the President as Commander in Chief of the Armed Forces or the power of the President to grant reprieves and pardons; or

(3) limit the lawful authority of the Secretary of Defense, any military commander, or any other officer or agent of the United States or of any State to detain or try any person who is not an individual subject to this order.

(b) With respect to any individual subject to this order—

(1) military tribunals shall have exclusive jurisdiction with respect to offenses by the individual; and

(2) the individual shall not be privileged to seek any remedy or maintain any proceeding, directly or indirectly, or to have any such remedy or 57836 proceeding sought on the individual's behalf, in (i) any court of the United States, or any State thereof, (ii) any court of any foreign nation, or (iii) any international tribunal.

(c) This order is not intended to and does not create any right, benefit, or privilege, substantive or procedural, enforceable at law or equity by any party, against the United States, its departments, agencies, or other entities, its officers or employees, or any other person.

(d) For purposes of this order, the term "State" includes any State, district, territory, or possession of the United States.

(e) I reserve the authority to direct the Secretary of Defense, at any time hereafter, to transfer to a governmental authority control of any individual subject to this order. Nothing in this order shall be construed to limit the authority of any such governmental authority to prosecute any individual for whom control is transferred.

On March 21, 2002, the Department of Defense issued Military Commission Order No. 1, "Procedures for Trials by Military Commissions of Certain Non-United States Citizens in the War Against Terrorism." The order provides that military commissions shall have between three and seven judges, each of whom "shall be a commissioned officer of the United States Armed Forces." Additionally, both prosecutors and defense counsel shall be military officers, though the order also provides that the accused "may also retain the services of a civilian attorney of the Accused's own choosing and at no expense to the United States."

The procedures provide that the accused shall have notice of the charges and "be presumed innocent until proven guilty." A Commission member may vote for a guilty verdict "if and only if that member is convinced beyond a reasonable doubt, based on the evidence admitted at trial that the Accused is guilty of the crime." An accused cannot be required to testify at trial and no adverse inference can be drawn from a defendant's choice not to testify. The accused may obtain witnesses and documents and may present evidence and cross-examine adverse witnesses. There is a presumption of openness for trials, but the Presiding Officer may close them when deemed necessary.

If there is a conviction, the Secretary of Defense shall designate a review panel consisting of three military officers. The review panel makes a recommendation to the Secretary of Defense who makes the final decision, unless the matter is referred to the President for the final decision. The order provides: "After review by the Secretary of Defense, the record of trial and recommendations will be forwarded to the President for review and final decision (unless the President has designated the Secretary of Defense to perform this function.)." No judicial review in any court is provided for or authorized.

There is one major Supreme Court decision concerning military tribunals: Ex parte Quirin, from World War II:

EX PARTE QUIRIN
317 U.S. 1 (1942)

Chief Justice STONE delivered the opinion of the Court.

The question for decision is whether the detention of petitioners by respondent for trial by Military Commission, appointed by Order of the President of

July 2, 1942, on charges preferred against them purporting to set out their violations of the law of war and of the Articles of War, is in conformity to the laws and Constitution of the United States.

After denial of their applications by the District Court, petitioners asked leave to file petitions for habeas corpus in this Court. In view of the public importance of the questions raised by their petitions and of the duty which rests on the courts, in time of war as well as in time of peace, to preserve unimpaired the constitutional safeguards of civil liberty, and because in our opinion the public interest required that we consider and decide those questions without any avoidable delay, we directed that petitioners' applications be set down for full oral argument at a special term of this Court, convened on July 29, 1942.

The following facts appear from the petitions or are stipulated. Except as noted they are undisputed. All the petitioners were born in Germany; all have lived in the United States. All returned to Germany between 1933 and 1941. All except petitioner Haupt are admittedly citizens of the German Reich, with which the United States is at war. Haupt came to this country with his parents when he was five years old; it is contended that he became a citizen of the United States by virtue of the naturalization of his parents during his minority and that he has not since lost his citizenship. The Government, however, takes the position that on attaining his majority he elected to maintain German allegiance and citizenship or in any case that he has by his conduct renounced or abandoned his United States citizenship. For reasons presently to be stated we do not find it necessary to resolve these contentions.

After the declaration of war between the United States and the German Reich, petitioners received training at a sabotage school near Berlin, Germany, where they were instructed in the use of explosives and in methods of secret writing. Thereafter petitioners, with a German citizen, Dasch, proceeded from Germany to a seaport in Occupied France, where petitioners Burger, Heinck and Quirin, together with Dasch, boarded a German submarine which proceeded across the Atlantic to Amagansett Beach on Long Island, New York. The four were there landed from the submarine in the hours of darkness, on or about June 13, 1942, carrying with them a supply of explosives, fuses and incendiary and timing devices. While landing they wore German Marine Infantry uniforms or parts of uniforms. Immediately after landing they buried their uniforms and the other articles mentioned and proceeded in civilian dress to New York City.

The remaining four petitioners at the same French port boarded another German submarine, which carried them across the Atlantic to Ponte Vedra Beach, Florida. On or about June 17, 1942, they came ashore during the hours of darkness wearing caps of the German Marine Infantry and carrying with them a supply of explosives, fuses, and incendiary and timing devices. They immediately buried their caps and the other articles mentioned and proceeded in civilian dress to Jacksonville, Florida, and thence to various points in the United States. All were taken into custody in New York or Chicago by agents of the Federal Bureau of Investigation. All had received instructions in Germany from an officer of the German High Command to destroy war industries and war facilities in the United States, for which they or their relatives in Germany were to receive salary payments from the German Government. They also had been paid by the German Government during their course of training at the sabotage school and had received substantial sums in United States currency, which were in their possession when arrested. The currency had been handed to them by an officer of the German High Command, who had instructed them to wear their German uniforms while landing in the United States.

The President, as President and Commander in Chief of the Army and Navy, by Order of July 2, 1942, appointed a Military Commission and directed it to try petitioners for offenses against the law of war and the Articles of War, and prescribed regulations for the procedure on the trial and for review of the record of the trial and of any judgment or sentence of the Commission. On the same day, by Proclamation, the President declared that "all persons who are subjects, citizens or residents of any nation at war with the United States or who give obedience to or act under the direction of any such nation, and who during time of war enter or attempt to enter the United States . . . through coastal or boundary defenses, and are charged with committing or attempting or preparing to commit sabotage, espionage, hostile or warlike acts, or violations of the law of war, shall be subject to the law of war and to the jurisdiction of military tribunals."

The Proclamation also stated in terms that all such persons were denied access to the courts. Pursuant to direction of the Attorney General, the Federal Bureau of Investigation surrendered custody of petitioners to respondent, Provost Marshal of the Military District of Washington, who was directed by the Secretary of War to receive and keep them in custody, and who thereafter held petitioners for trial before the Commission.

On July 3, 1942, the Judge Advocate General's Department of the Army prepared and lodged with the Commission the following charges against petitioners, supported by specifications:

1. Violation of the law of war.
2. Violation of Article 81 of the Articles of War, defining the offense of relieving or attempting to relieve, or corresponding with or giving intelligence to, the enemy.
3. Violation of Article 82, defining the offense of spying.
4. Conspiracy to commit the offenses alleged in charges 1, 2 and 3.

The Commission met on July 8, 1942, and proceeded with the trial, which continued in progress while the causes were pending in this Court. On July 27th, before petitioners' applications to the District Court, all the evidence for the prosecution and the defense had been taken by the Commission and the case had been closed except for arguments of counsel. It is conceded that ever since petitioners' arrest the state and federal courts in Florida, New York, and the District of Columbia, and in the states in which each of the petitioners was arrested or detained, have been open and functioning normally.

Petitioners' main contention is that the President is without any statutory or constitutional authority to order the petitioners to be tried by military tribunal for offenses with which they are charged; that in consequence they are entitled to be tried in the civil courts with the safeguards, including trial by jury, which the Fifth and Sixth Amendments guarantee to all persons charged in such courts with criminal offenses. In any case it is urged that the President's Order, in prescribing the procedure of the Commission and the method for review of its findings and sentence, and the proceedings of the Commission under the Order, conflict with Articles of War adopted by Congress and are illegal and void.

The Government challenges each of these propositions. But regardless of their merits, it also insists that petitioners must be denied access to the courts, both because they are enemy aliens or have entered our territory as enemy belligerents, and because the President's Proclamation undertakes in terms to deny such access to the class of persons defined by the Proclamation, which aptly describes the character and conduct of petitioners. It is urged that if they are enemy aliens or if the Proclamation has force no court may afford the petitioners a hearing. But there is certainly nothing in the Proclamation to preclude access to the courts for determining its applicability to the particular case. And neither the Proclamation nor the fact that they are enemy aliens forecloses consideration by the courts of petitioners' contentions that the Constitution and laws of the United States constitutionally enacted forbid their trial by military commission. [W]e have resolved those questions by our conclusion that the Commission has jurisdiction to try the charge preferred against petitioners. There is therefore no occasion to decide contentions of the parties unrelated to this issue. We pass at once to the consideration of the basis of the Commission's authority.

We are not here concerned with any question of the guilt or innocence of petitioners. Constitutional safeguards for the protection of all who are charged with offenses are not to be disregarded in order to inflict merited punishment on some who are guilty. But the detention and trial of petitioners—ordered by the President in the declared exercise of his powers as Commander in Chief of the Army in time of war and of grave public danger—are not to be set aside by the courts without the clear conviction that they are in conflict with the Constitution or laws of Congress constitutionally enacted.

Congress and the President, like the courts, possess no power not derived from the Constitution. But one of the objects of the Constitution, as declared by its preamble, is to "provide for the common defence." As a means to that end the Constitution gives to Congress the power to "provide for the common Defence," Art. I, § 8, cl. 1; "To raise and support Armies," "To provide and maintain a Navy," Art. I, § 8, cls. 12, 13; and "To make Rules for the Government and Regulation of the land and naval Forces," Art. I, § 8, cl. 14. Congress is given authority "To declare War, grant Letters of Marque and Reprisal, and make Rules concerning Captures on Land and Water," Art. I, § 8, cl. 11; and "To define and punish Piracies and Felonies committed on the high Seas, and Offenses against the Law of Nations," Art. I, § 8, cl. 10. And finally the Constitution authorizes Congress "To make all Laws which shall be necessary and proper for carrying into Execution the foregoing Powers, and all other Powers vested by this Constitution in the Government of the United States, or in any Department or Officer thereof." Art. I, § 8, cl. 18.

The Constitution confers on the President the "executive Power," Art II, § 1, cl. 1, and imposes on him the duty to "take Care that the Laws be faithfully executed." Art. II, § 3. It makes him the Commander in Chief of the Army and Navy, Art. II, § 2, cl. 1, and empowers him to appoint and commission officers of the United States. Art. II, § 3, cl. 1.

By the Articles of War, Congress has provided rules for the government of the Army. It has provided for the trial and punishment, by courts martial, of violations of the Articles by members of the armed forces and by specified classes of persons associated or serving with the Army. Arts. 1, 2. But the Articles also recognize the "military commission" appointed by military command as an appropriate tribunal for the trial and punishment of offenses against the law of war not ordinarily tried by court martial. See Arts. 12, 15. Articles 38 and 46 authorize the President, with certain limitations, to prescribe the procedure for military commissions. Articles 81 and 82 authorize trial, either by court martial or military commission, of those charged with relieving, harboring or corresponding with the enemy and those charged with spying. And Article 15 declares that "the provisions of these articles conferring jurisdiction upon courts-martial shall not be construed as depriving military commissions . . . or other military tribunals of concurrent jurisdiction in respect of offenders or offenses that by statute or by the law of war may be triable by such military commissions . . . or other military tribunals." Article 2 includes among those persons subject to military law the personnel of our own military establishment. But this, as Article 12 provides, does not exclude from that class "any other person who by the law of war is subject to trial by military tribunals" and who under Article 12 may be tried by court martial or under Article 15 by military commission.

Similarly the Espionage Act of 1917, which authorizes trial in the district courts of certain offenses that tend to interfere with the prosecution of war, provides that nothing contained in the act "shall be deemed to limit the jurisdiction of the general courts-martial, military commissions, or naval courts-martial."

From the very beginning of its history this Court has recognized and applied the law of war as including that part of the law of nations which prescribes, for the conduct of war, the status, rights and duties of enemy nations as well as of enemy individuals. By the Articles of War, and especially Article 15, Congress has explicitly provided, so far as it may constitutionally do so, that military tribunals shall have jurisdiction to try offenders or offenses against the law of war in appropriate cases. Congress, in addition to making rules for the government of our Armed Forces, has thus exercised its authority to define and punish offenses against the law of nations by sanctioning, within constitutional limitations, the jurisdiction of military commissions to try persons for offenses which, according to the rules and precepts of the law of nations, and more particularly the law of war, are cognizable by such tribunals. And the President, as Commander in Chief, by his Proclamation in time of war his invoked that law. By his Order creating the present Commission he has undertaken to exercise the authority conferred upon him by Congress, and also such authority as the Constitution itself gives the Commander in Chief, to direct the performance of those functions which may constitutionally be performed by the military arm of the nation in time of war.

An important incident to the conduct of war is the adoption of measures by the military command not only to repel and defeat the enemy, but to seize and subject to disciplinary measures those enemies who in their attempt to thwart or impede our military effort have violated the law of war. It is unnecessary for present purposes to determine to what extent the President as Commander in Chief has constitutional power to create military commissions without the support of Congressional legislation. For here Congress has authorized trial of offenses against the law of war before such commissions. We are concerned only with the question whether it is within the constitutional power of the national government to place petitioners upon trial before a military commission for the offenses with which they are charged. We must therefore first inquire whether any of the acts charged is an offense against the law of war cognizable before a military tribunal, and if so whether the Constitution prohibits the trial. We may assume that there are acts regarded in other countries, or by some writers on international law, as offenses against the law of war which would not be triable by military tribunal here, either because they are not recognized by our courts as violations of the law of war or because they are of that class of offenses constitutionally triable only by a jury. It was upon such grounds that the Court denied the right to proceed by military tribunal in Ex parte Milligan, supra. But as we shall show, these petitioners were charged with an offense against the law of war which the Constitution does not require to be tried by jury.

It is no objection that Congress in providing for the trial of such offenses has not itself undertaken to codify that branch of international law or to mark its precise boundaries, or to enumerate or define by statute all the acts which that law condemns. An Act of Congress punishing "the crime of piracy as defined by the law of nations" is an appropriate exercise of its constitutional authority, Art. I, § 8, cl. 10, "to define and punish" the offense since it has adopted by reference the sufficiently precise definition of international law. Similarly by the reference in the 15th Article of War to "offenders or offenses that . . . by the law of war may be triable by such military commissions," Congress has incorporated by reference, as within the jurisdiction of military commissions, all offenses which are defined as such by the law of war and which may constitutionally be included within that jurisdiction. Congress had the choice of crystallizing in permanent form and in minute detail every offense against the law of war, or of adopting the system of common law applied by military tribunals so far as it should be recognized and deemed applicable by the courts. It chose the latter course.

By universal agreement and practice the law of war draws a distinction between the armed forces and the peaceful populations of belligerent nations and also between those who are lawful and unlawful combatants. Lawful combatants are subject to capture and detention as prisoners of war by opposing military forces. Unlawful combatants are likewise subject to capture and detention, but in addition they are subject to trial and punishment by military tribunals for acts which render their belligerency unlawful. The spy who secretly and without uniform passes the military lines of a belligerent in time of war, seeking to gather military information and communicate it to the enemy, or an enemy combatant who without uniform comes secretly through the lines for the purpose of waging war by destruction of life or property, are familiar examples of belligerents who are generally deemed not to be entitled to the status of prisoners of war, but to be offenders against the law of war subject to trial and punishment by military tribunals.

Such was the practice of our own military authorities before the adoption of the Constitution, and during the Mexican and Civil Wars. During the Civil War the military commission was extensively used for the trial of offenses against the law of war. By a long course of practical administrative construction by its military authorities, our Government has likewise recognized that those who during time of war pass surreptitiously from enemy territory into our own, discarding their uniforms upon entry, for the commission of hostile acts involving destruction of life or property, have the status of unlawful combatants punishable as such by military commission. This precept of the law of war has been so recognized in practice both here and abroad, and has so generally been accepted as valid by authorities on international law that we think it must be regarded as a rule or principle of the law of war recognized by this Government by its enactment of the Fifteenth Article of War.

Specification 1 of the First charge is sufficient to charge all the petitioners with the offense of unlawful belligerency, trial of which is within the jurisdiction of the Commission, and the admitted facts affirmatively show that the charge is not merely colorable or without foundation. Specification 1 states that petitioners "being enemies of the United States and acting for . . . the German Reich, a belligerent enemy nation, secretly and covertly passed, in civilian dress, contrary to the law of war, through the military and naval lines and defenses of the United States . . . and went behind such lines, contrary to the law of war, in civilian dress . . . for the purpose of committing . . . hostile acts, and, in particular, to destroy certain war industries, war utilities and war materials within the United States."

This specification so plainly alleges violation of the law of war as to require but brief discussion of petitioners' contentions. As we have seen, entry upon our territory in time of war by enemy belligerents, including those acting under the direction of the armed forces of the enemy, for the purpose of destroying property used or useful in prosecuting the war, is a hostile and war-like act. It subjects those who participate in it without uniform to the punishment prescribed by the law of war for unlawful belligerents. It is without significance that petitioners were not alleged to have borne conventional weapons or that their proposed hostile acts did not necessarily contemplate collision with the Armed Forces of the United States. Paragraphs 351 and 352 of the Rules of Land Warfare, already referred to, plainly contemplate that the hostile acts and purposes for which unlawful belligerents may be punished are not limited to assaults on the Armed Forces of the United States. Modern warfare is directed at the destruction of enemy war supplies and the implements of their production and transportation quite as much as at the armed forces. Every consideration which makes the unlawful belligerent punishable is equally applicable whether his objective is the one or the other. The law of war cannot rightly treat those agents of enemy armies who enter our territory, armed with explosives intended for the destruction of war industries and supplies, as any the less belligerent enemies than are agents similarly entering for the purpose of destroying fortified places or our Armed Forces. By passing our boundaries for such purposes without uniform or other emblem signifying their belligerent status, or by discarding that means of identification after entry, such enemies become unlawful belligerents subject to trial and punishment.

Citizenship in the United States of an enemy belligerent does not relieve him from the consequences of a belligerency which is unlawful because in violation of the law of war. Citizens who associate themselves with the military arm of the enemy government, and with its aid, guidance and direction enter this country bent on hostile acts are enemy belligerents within the meaning of the Hague Convention and the law of war. It is as an enemy belligerent that petitioner Haupt is charged with entering the United States, and unlawful belligerency is the gravamen of the offense of which he is accused.

Nor are petitioners any the less belligerents if, as they argue, they have not actually committed or attempted to commit any act of depredation or entered the theatre or zone of active military operations. The argument leaves out of account the nature of the offense which the Government charges and which the Act of Congress, by incorporating the law of war, punishes. It is that each petitioner, in circumstances which gave him the status of an enemy belligerent, passed our military and naval lines and defenses or went behind those lines, in civilian dress and with hostile purpose. The offense was complete when with that purpose they entered—or, having so entered, they remained upon—our territory in time of war without uniform or other appropriate means of identification. For that reason, even when committed by a citizen, the offense is distinct from the crime of

treason defined in Article III, § 3 of the Constitution, since the absence of uniform essential to one is irrelevant to the other.

But petitioners insist that even if the offenses with which they are charged are
offenses against the law of war, their trial is subject to the requirement of the
Fifth Amendment that no person shall be held to answer for a capital or otherwise infamous crime unless on a presentment or indictment of a grand jury, and
that such trials by Article III, § 2, and the Sixth Amendment must be by jury in a
civil court. Before the Amendments, § 2 of Article III, the Judiciary Article, had
provided: "The Trial of all Crimes, except in Cases of Impeachment, shall be by
Jury," and had directed that "such Trial shall be held in the State where the said
Crimes shall have been committed."

Presentment by a grand jury and trial by a jury of the vicinage where the
crime was committed were at the time of the adoption of the Constitution familiar parts of the machinery for criminal trials in the civil courts. But they were
procedures unknown to military tribunals, which are not courts in the sense of
the Judiciary Article, and which in the natural course of events are usually called
upon to function under conditions precluding resort to such procedures. As this
Court has often recognized, it was not the purpose or effect of § 2 of Article III,
read in the light of the common law, to enlarge the then existing right to a jury
trial. The object was to preserve unimpaired trial by jury in all those cases in
which it had been recognized by the common law and in all cases of a like nature as they might arise in the future, but not to bring within the sweep of the
guaranty those cases in which it was then well understood that a jury trial could
not be demanded as of right. The Fifth and Sixth Amendments, while guaranteeing the continuance of certain incidents of trial by jury which Article III, § 2
had left unmentioned, did not enlarge the right to jury trial as it had been established by that Article.

All these are instances of offenses committed against the United States, for
which a penalty is imposed, but they are not deemed to be within the provisions
of the Fifth and Sixth Amendments relating to "crimes" and "criminal prosecutions." In the light of this long-continued and consistent interpretation we must
conclude that § 2 of Article III and the Fifth and Sixth Amendments cannot be
taken to have extended the right to demand a jury to trials by military commission, or to have required that offenses against the law of war not triable by jury
at common law be tried only in the civil courts. It has not hitherto been challenged, and so far as we are advised it has never been suggested in the very extensive literature of the subject that an alien spy, in time of war, could not be
tried by military tribunal without a jury.

The exception from the Amendments of "cases arising in the land or naval
forces" was not aimed at trials by military tribunals, without a jury, of such offenses against the law of war. Its objective was quite different—to authorize the
trial by court martial of the members of our Armed Forces for all that class of
crimes which under the Fifth and Sixth Amendments might otherwise have been
deemed triable in the civil courts. The cases mentioned in the exception are not

restricted to those involving offenses against the law of war alone, but extend to trial of all offenses, including crimes which were of the class traditionally triable by jury at common law.

Since the Amendments, like § 2 of Article III, do not preclude all trials of offenses against the law of war by military commission without a jury when the offenders are aliens not members of our Armed Forces, it is plain that they present no greater obstacle to the trial in like manner of citizen enemies who have violated the law of war applicable to enemies. Under the original statute authorizing trial of alien spies by military tribunals, the offenders were outside the constitutional guaranty of trial by jury, not because they were aliens but only because they had violated the law of war by committing offenses constitutionally triable by military tribunal.

We cannot say that Congress in preparing the Fifth and Sixth Amendments intended to extend trial by jury to the cases of alien or citizen offenders against the law of war otherwise triable by military commission, while withholding it from members of our own armed forces charged with infractions of the Articles of War punishable by death. It is equally inadmissible to construe the Amendments—whose primary purpose was to continue unimpaired presentment by grand jury and trial by petit jury in all those cases in which they had been customary—as either abolishing all trials by military tribunals, save those of the personnel of our own armed forces, or what in effect comes to the same thing, as imposing on all such tribunals the necessity of proceeding against unlawful enemy belligerents only on presentment and trial by jury. We conclude that the Fifth and Sixth Amendments did not restrict whatever authority was conferred by the Constitution to try offenses against the law of war by military commission, and that petitioners, charged with such an offense not required to be tried by jury at common law, were lawfully placed on trial by the Commission without a jury.

Accordingly, we conclude that Charge I, on which petitioners were detained for trial by the Military Commission, alleged an offense which the President is authorized to order tried by military commission; that his Order convening the Commission was a lawful order and that the Commission was lawfully constituted; that the petitioners were held in lawful custody and did not show cause for their discharge.

Chapter 1

The Federal Judicial Power

B. Limits on the Federal Judicial Power

3. Justiciability Limits

c. Ripeness (casebook, p. 66)

In Palazzolo v. Rhode Island, 121 S. Ct. 2448 (2001), the Supreme Court considered when a claim under the Takings Clause becomes ripe for review. *Palazzolo*, including its discussion of the ripeness issue, is presented below under Chapter 5. Simply stated, the Supreme Court ruled that the takings claim was ripe for review, even though there had not been a request for permission for the specific development, because it was clear from many previous denials that the request would be refused.

d. Mootness (casebook, p. 71)

The following decision illustrates the Court's finding that a case is moot and not within the exceptions to the mootness doctrine.

CITY NEWS AND NOVELTY, INC. v. CITY OF WAUKESHA, 121 S. Ct. 743 (2001). Justice Ginsburg wrote the opinion for the Court. [The issue in the case concerns the meaning of the requirement for prompt judicial review of denials of licenses when the government requires a license or a permit for speech.] The City of Waukesha, Wisconsin (City), requires sellers of sexually explicit materials to obtain and annually renew adult business licenses.

In letters sent to Waukesha two months after petitioning for review in this Court, City News gave notice that it would withdraw its renewal application and close its business upon the City's grant of a license to another corporation, B. J. B., Inc., "a larger and more modern business" with which City News felt "it could not effectively compete."

Observing that City News neither now pursues nor currently expresses an intent to pursue a license under Waukesha law, Waukesha asserts that the case has become moot, for City News no longer has "a legally cognizable interest in the outcome." We agree that the case no longer qualifies for judicial review.

City News [argues that the case remains justiciable and] appears to rely on the general rule that voluntary cessation of a challenged practice rarely moots a federal case. That principle does not aid City News. For it is City News, not its adversary, whose conduct saps the controversy of vitality, and City News can gain nothing from our dismissal.

City News also urges that it experiences ongoing injury because it is conclusively barred by Waukesha's ordinance from reopening as an adult business until 2005. It is far from clear, however, whether City News actually suffers that disability. [A] live controversy is not maintained by speculation that City News might be temporarily disabled from reentering a business that City News has left and currently asserts no plan to reenter.

e.   The Political Question Doctrine

ii.   The Political Question Doctrine Applied: Congressional Self-Governance (casebook, p. 81)

In United States Term Limits, Inc. v. Thornton (1995) (casebook, p. 83), the Supreme Court declared unconstitutional a state law that prevented candidates for the United States Senate or House of Representatives from being listed on the ballot after they served a specified number of terms. In Cook v. Gralike, 121 S. Ct. 1029 (2001), the Supreme Court declared unconstitutional a Missouri law that "instruct[s]" each Member of Missouri's congressional delegation "to use all of his or her delegated powers to pass a Congressional Term Limits Amendment" that would limit service in the United States Congress to three terms in the House of Representatives and two terms in the Senate.

Additionally, the law requires that the statement "DISREGARDED VOTERS' INSTRUCTION ON TERM LIMITS" be printed on all primary and general ballots adjacent to the name of a Senator or Representative who fails to take any one of eight legislative acts in support of the proposed amendment. The law required that the statement "DECLINED TO PLEDGE TO SUPPORT TERM LIMITS" be printed on all primary and general election ballots next to the name of every nonincumbent congressional candidate who refuses to take a "Term Limit" pledge that commits the candidate, if elected, to performing the legislative acts enumerated in the law. Also, candidates could have next to their name the following statement: "I support term limits and pledge to use all my legislative powers to enact the proposed Constitutional Amendment set forth in the Term Limits Act of 1996. If elected, I pledge to vote in such a way that the designation 'DISREGARDED VOTERS' INSTRUCTION ON TERM LIMITS' will not appear adjacent to my name."

The Supreme Court, in an opinion by Justice Stevens, declared this unconstitutional. The Court explained that states may regulate the procedures for conducting federal elections, but this was an additional requirement for election to Congress and thus exceeded the scope of the state's permissible authority.

Chapter 2
The Federal Legislative Power

B. The Commerce Power

4. 1990s-???: Narrowing of the Commerce Power and Revival of the Tenth Amendment as a Constraint on Congress

a. What Is Congress's Authority to Regulate "Commerce Among the States"? (casebook, p. 143)

In Solid Waste Agency of Northern Cook County v. United States Army Corps of Engineers, below, the Supreme Court used its recent decisions restricting the scope of the Commerce Clause as the basis for narrowly interpreting a federal law. In reading the case, notice that the Court does not declare the federal law unconstitutional. Instead, to avoid serious questions about its constitutionality, the Court narrowly interpreted the federal statute.

SOLID WASTE AGENCY OF NORTHERN COOK COUNTY v.
UNITED STATES ARMY CORPS OF ENGINEERS
121 S. Ct. 675 (2001)

Chief Justice REHNQUIST delivered the opinion of the Court.

Section 404(a) of the Clean Water Act (CWA or Act), regulates the discharge of dredged or fill material into "navigable waters." The United States Army Corps of Engineers (Corps), has interpreted § 404(a) to confer federal authority over an abandoned sand and gravel pit in northern Illinois which provides habitat for migratory birds. We are asked to decide whether the provisions of § 404(a) may be fairly extended to these waters, and, if so, whether Congress could exercise such authority consistent with the Commerce Clause. We answer the first question in the negative and therefore do not reach the second.

Petitioner, the Solid Waste Agency of Northern Cook County (SWANCC), is a consortium of 23 suburban Chicago cities and villages that united in an effort to locate and develop a disposal site for baled nonhazardous solid waste. The

Chicago Gravel Company informed the municipalities of the availability of a 533-acre parcel, bestriding the Illinois counties Cook and Kane, which had been the site of a sand and gravel pit mining operation for three decades up until about 1960. Long since abandoned, the old mining site eventually gave way to a successional stage forest, with its remnant excavation trenches evolving into a scattering of permanent and seasonal ponds of varying size (from under one-tenth of an acre to several acres) and depth (from several inches to several feet).

The municipalities decided to purchase the site for disposal of their baled nonhazardous solid waste. By law, SWANCC was required to file for various permits from Cook County and the State of Illinois before it could begin operation of its balefill project. In addition, because the operation called for the filling of some of the permanent and seasonal ponds, SWANCC contacted federal respondents (hereinafter respondents), including the Corps, to determine if a federal landfill permit was required under § 404(a) of the CWA.

Section 404(a) grants the Corps authority to issue permits "for the discharge of dredged or fill material into the navigable waters at specified disposal sites." The term "navigable waters" is defined under the Act as "the waters of the United States, including the territorial seas." The Corps has issued regulations defining the term "waters of the United States" to include "waters such as intrastate lakes, rivers, streams (including intermittent streams), mudflats, sandflats, wetlands, sloughs, prairie potholes, wet meadows, playa lakes, or natural ponds, the use, degradation or destruction of which could affect interstate or foreign commerce. . . ." 33 CFR § 328.3(a)(3) (1999).

In 1986, in an attempt to "clarify" the reach of its jurisdiction, the Corps stated that § 404(a) extends to intrastate waters: "a. Which are or would be used as habitat by birds protected by Migratory Bird Treaties; or b. Which are or would be used as habitat by other migratory birds which cross state lines; or c. Which are or would be used as habitat for endangered species; or d. Used to irrigate crops sold in interstate commerce." This last promulgation has been dubbed the "Migratory Bird Rule."

[A]fter the Illinois Nature Preserves Commission informed the Corps that a number of migratory bird species had been observed at the site, the Corps asserted jurisdiction over the site pursuant to subpart (b) of the "Migratory Bird Rule." The Corps found that approximately 121 bird species had been observed at the site, including several known to depend upon aquatic environments for a significant portion of their life requirements. Thus, on November 16, 1987, the Corps formally "determined that the seasonally ponded, abandoned gravel mining depressions located on the project site, while not wetlands, did qualify as 'waters of the United States' . . . based upon the following criteria: (1) the proposed site had been abandoned as a gravel mining operation; (2) the water areas and spoil piles had developed a natural character; and (3) the water areas are used as habitat by migratory bird [sic] which cross state lines."

Despite SWANCC's securing the required water quality certification from the Illinois Environmental Protection Agency, the Corps refused to issue a § 404(a) permit. The Corps found that SWANCC had not established that its proposal was the "least environmentally damaging, most practicable alternative" for disposal of nonhazardous solid waste; that SWANCC's failure to set aside sufficient funds to remediate leaks posed an "unacceptable risk to the public's drinking water supply"; and that the impact of the project upon area-sensitive species was "unmitigatable since a landfill surface cannot be redeveloped into a forested habitat."

Congress passed the CWA for the stated purpose of "restor[ing] and maintain[ing] the chemical, physical, and biological integrity of the Nation's waters." In so doing, Congress chose to "recognize, preserve, and protect the primary responsibilities and rights of States to prevent, reduce, and eliminate pollution, to plan the development and use (including restoration, preservation, and enhancement) of land and water resources, and to consult with the Administrator in the exercise of his authority under this chapter." Relevant here, § 404(a) authorizes respondents to regulate the discharge of fill material into "navigable waters," which the statute defines as "the waters of the United States, including the territorial seas." Respondents have interpreted these words to cover the abandoned gravel pit at issue here because it is used as habitat for migratory birds. We conclude that the "Migratory Bird Rule" is not fairly supported by the CWA.

In order to rule for respondents here, we would have to hold that the jurisdiction of the Corps extends to ponds that are not adjacent to open water. We decline respondents' invitation to hold that isolated ponds, some only seasonal, wholly located within two Illinois counties, fall under § 404(a)'s definition of "navigable waters" because they serve as habitat for migratory birds. As counsel for respondents conceded at oral argument, such a ruling would assume that "the use of the word navigable in the statute . . . does not have any independent significance." We cannot agree that Congress' separate definitional use of the phrase "waters of the United States" constitutes a basis for reading the term "navigable waters" out of the statute. The term "navigable" has at least the import of showing us what Congress had in mind as its authority for enacting the CWA: its traditional jurisdiction over waters that were or had been navigable in fact or which could reasonably be so made.

Respondents contend that, at the very least, it must be said that Congress did not address the precise question of § 404(a)'s scope with regard to nonnavigable, isolated, intrastate waters, and that, therefore, we should give deference to the "Migratory Bird Rule." See, e.g., Chevron U.S.A. Inc. v. Natural Resources Defense Council, Inc. (1984). We find § 404(a) to be clear, but even were we to agree with respondents, we would not extend *Chevron* deference here.

Where an administrative interpretation of a statute invokes the outer limits of Congress' power, we expect a clear indication that Congress intended that result. This requirement stems from our prudential desire not to needlessly reach constitutional issues and our assumption that Congress does not casually authorize administrative agencies to interpret a statute to push the limit of congressional authority. This concern is heightened where the administrative interpretation alters the federal-state framework by permitting federal encroachment upon a traditional state power. Thus, "where an otherwise acceptable construction of a statute would raise serious constitutional problems, the Court will construe the statute to avoid such problems unless such construction is plainly contrary to the intent of Congress."

Twice in the past six years we have reaffirmed the proposition that the grant of authority to Congress under the Commerce Clause, though broad, is not unlimited. See United States v. Morrison (2000); United States v. Lopez (1995). Respondents argue that the "Migratory Bird Rule" falls within Congress' power to regulate intrastate activities that "substantially affect" interstate commerce. They note that the protection of migratory birds is a "national interest of very nearly the first magnitude," Missouri v. Holland (1920), and that, as the Court of Appeals found, millions of people spend over a billion dollars annually on recreational pursuits relating to migratory birds. These arguments raise significant constitutional questions. For example, we would have to evaluate the precise object or activity that, in the aggregate, substantially affects interstate commerce. This is not clear, for although the Corps has claimed jurisdiction over petitioner's land because it contains water areas used as habitat by migratory birds, respondents now focus upon the fact that the regulated activity is petitioner's municipal landfill, which is "plainly of a commercial nature." But this is a far cry, indeed, from the "navigable waters" and "waters of the United States" to which the statute by its terms extends.

These are significant constitutional questions raised by respondents' application of their regulations, and yet we find nothing approaching a clear statement from Congress that it intended § 404(a) to reach an abandoned sand and gravel pit such as we have here. Permitting respondents to claim federal jurisdiction over ponds and mudflats falling within the "Migratory Bird Rule" would result in a significant impingement of the States' traditional and primary power over land and water use. We thus read the statute as written to avoid the significant constitutional and federalism questions raised by respondents' interpretation, and therefore reject the request for administrative deference.

Justice STEVENS, with whom Justice SOUTER, Justice GINSBURG, and Justice BREYER join, dissenting.

In 1969, the Cuyahoga River in Cleveland, Ohio, coated with a slick of industrial waste, caught fire. Congress responded to that dramatic event, and to others like it, by enacting the Federal Water Pollution Control Act (FWPCA) Amendments of 1972. It is fair to characterize the Clean Water Act as "watershed" legislation. The statute endorsed fundamental changes in both the purpose and the scope of federal regulation of the Nation's waters.

In § 13 of the Rivers and Harbors Appropriation Act of 1899 (RHA), Congress had assigned to the Army Corps of Engineers (Corps) the mission of regulating discharges into certain waters in order to protect their use as highways for the transportation of interstate and foreign commerce; the scope of the Corps' jurisdiction under the RHA accordingly extended only to waters that were "navigable." In the CWA, however, Congress broadened the Corps' mission to include the purpose of protecting the quality of our Nation's waters for esthetic, health, recreational, and environmental uses. The scope of its jurisdiction was therefore redefined to encompass all of "the waters of the United States, including the territorial seas." That definition requires neither actual nor potential navigability.

In its decision today, the Court draws a new jurisdictional line, one that invalidates the 1986 migratory bird regulation as well as the Corps' assertion of jurisdiction over all waters except for actually navigable waters, their tributaries, and wetlands adjacent to each. Its holding rests on two equally untenable premises: (1) that when Congress passed the 1972 CWA, it did not intend "to exert anything more than its commerce power over navigation"; and (2) that in 1972 Congress drew the boundary defining the Corps' jurisdiction at the odd line on which the Court today settles.

Contrary to the Court's suggestion, the Corps' interpretation of the statute does not "encroac[h]" upon "traditional state power" over land use. "Land use planning in essence chooses particular uses for the land; environmental regulation, at its core, does not mandate particular uses of the land but requires only that, however the land is used, damage to the environment is kept within prescribed limits." California Coastal Comm'n v. Granite Rock Co. (1987). The CWA is not a land-use code; it is a paradigm of environmental regulation. Such regulation is an accepted exercise of federal power. Hodel v. Virginia Surface Mining & Reclamation Assn., Inc. (1981).

It is particularly ironic for the Court to raise the specter of federalism while construing a statute that makes explicit efforts to foster local control over water regulation. Faced with calls to cut back on federal jurisdiction over water pollution, Congress rejected attempts to narrow the scope of that jurisdiction and, by incorporating § 404(g), opted instead for a scheme that encouraged States to supplant federal control with their own regulatory programs. Because Illinois could have taken advantage of the opportunities offered to it through § 404(g), the federalism concerns to which the majority adverts are misplaced. The Corps' interpretation of the statute as extending beyond navigable waters, tributaries of navigable waters, and wetlands adjacent to each is manifestly reasonable and therefore entitled to deference.

Because I am convinced that the Court's miserly construction of the statute is incorrect, I shall comment briefly on petitioner's argument that Congress is without power to prohibit it from filling any part of the 31 acres of ponds on its property in Cook County, Illinois. The Corps' exercise of its § 404 permitting power over "isolated" waters that serve as habitat for migratory birds falls well within the boundaries set by this Court's Commerce Clause jurisprudence. In United States v. Lopez (1995), this Court identified "three broad categories of activity that Congress may regulate under its commerce power": (1) channels of interstate commerce; (2) instrumentalities of interstate commerce, or persons and things in interstate commerce; and (3) activities that "substantially affect" interstate commerce. The migratory bird rule at issue here is properly analyzed under the third category. In order to constitute a proper exercise of Congress' power over intrastate activities that "substantially affect" interstate commerce, it is not necessary that each individual instance of the activity substantially affect commerce; it is enough that, taken in the aggregate, the class of activities in question has such an effect.

The activity being regulated in this case (and by the Corps' § 404 regulations in general) is the discharge of fill material into water. The Corps did not assert jurisdiction over petitioner's land simply because the waters were "used as habitat by migratory birds." It asserted jurisdiction because petitioner planned to discharge fill into waters "used as habitat by migratory birds." Had petitioner intended to engage in some other activity besides discharging fill (i.e., had there been no activity to regulate), or, conversely, had the waters not been habitat for migratory birds (i.e., had there been no basis for federal jurisdiction), the Corps would never have become involved in petitioner's use of its land. There can be no doubt that, unlike the class of activities Congress was attempting to regulate in United States v. Morrison (2000) ("[g]ender-motivated crimes"), and *Lopez* (possession of guns near school property), the discharge of fill material into the Nation's waters is almost always undertaken for economic reasons.

Moreover, no one disputes that the discharge of fill into "isolated" waters that serve as migratory bird habitat will, in the aggregate, adversely affect migratory bird populations. Nor does petitioner dispute that the particular waters it seeks to fill are home to many important species of migratory birds, including the second-largest breeding colony of Great Blue Herons in northeastern Illinois, and several species of waterfowl protected by international treaty and Illinois endangered species laws.

In addition to the intrinsic value of migratory birds, see Missouri v. Holland (1920) (noting the importance of migratory birds as "protectors of our forests and our crops" and as "a food supply"), it is undisputed that literally millions of people regularly participate in birdwatching and hunting and that those activities generate a host of commercial activities of great value. The causal connection between the filling of wetlands and the decline of commercial activities associated with migratory birds is not "attenuated," it is direct and concrete.

Finally, the migratory bird rule does not blur the "distinction between what is truly national and what is truly local." Justice Holmes cogently observed in Missouri v. Holland that the protection of migratory birds is a textbook example of a national problem. The destruction of aquatic migratory bird habitat, like so many other environmental problems, is an action in which the benefits (e.g., a new landfill) are disproportionately local, while many of the costs (e.g., fewer migratory birds) are widely dispersed and often borne by citizens living in other States. In such situations, described by economists as involving "externalities," federal regulation is both appropriate and necessary. Identifying the Corps' jurisdiction by reference to waters that serve as habitat for birds that migrate over state lines also satisfies this Court's expressed desire for some "jurisdictional element" that limits federal activity to its proper scope.

The power to regulate commerce among the several States necessarily and properly includes the power to preserve the natural resources that generate such commerce. Moreover, the protection of migratory birds is a well-established federal responsibility. As Justice Holmes noted in Missouri v. Holland, the federal interest in protecting these birds is of "the first magnitude." Because of their transitory nature, they "can be protected only by national action."

Whether it is necessary or appropriate to refuse to allow petitioner to fill those ponds is a question on which we have no voice. Whether the Federal Government has the power to require such permission, however, is a question that is easily answered. If, as it does, the Commerce Clause empowers Congress to regulate particular "activities causing air or water pollution, or other environmental hazards that may have effects in more than one State," it also empowers Congress to control individual actions that, in the aggregate, would have the same effect. There is no merit in petitioner's constitutional argument.

E. Congress's Power to Authorize Suits Against State Governments

1. Background on the Eleventh Amendment and State Sovereign Immunity (casebook, p. 201)

The Supreme Court long has held that state governments may waive their sovereign immunity and may be sued in federal court. In Lapides v. University of Georgia, below, the Supreme Court confronted the issue of whether a state government's removal of a case from state to federal court is a waiver of its sovereign immunity. Actually, the Court decided only a more limited question, presented before it: Is removal from state to federal court a waiver as to state law claims for which the state has waived its sovereign immunity in state court?

LAPIDES v. BOARD OF REGENTS OF THE UNIVERSITY SYSTEM OF GEORGIA, 122 S. Ct. 1640 (2002)   Justice Breyer delivered the opinion of the Court.

The issue before the Court was "whether the State's act of removing a lawsuit from state court to federal court waives this immunity." The Court declared: "We hold that it does." The case involved a suit by a professor in the Georgia state university system filed in state court. The state removed the case from state to federal court and then moved to dismiss based on the Eleventh Amendment. There were no viable federal claims because state governments cannot be sued under 42 U.S.C. § 1983 and all that remained were state claims. Georgia had waived sovereign immunity for these state claims in state court.

The Supreme Court ruled that the state's choice to remove the case to federal court was a waiver of its sovereign immunity. The Court's actual holding was narrow: a State's choice to remove a case from state to federal court is a removal when there are state law claims and the state has waived its immunity as to these claims in state court. The Court declared: "It has become clear that we must limit our answer to the context of state-law claims, in respect to which the State has explicitly waived immunity from state-court proceedings. That is because Lapides' only federal claim against the State arises under 42 U.S.C. § 1983, that claim seeks only monetary damages, and we have held that a State is not a person against whom a § 1983 claim for money damages might be asserted. Will v. Michigan Dept. of State Police (1989). Hence this case does not present a valid federal claim against the State. Nor need we address the scope of waiver by removal in a situation where the State's underlying sovereign immunity from suit has not been waived or abrogated in state court."

But the Court's reasoning means that the case likely has broader implications: if the state removes a case from state to federal court, it has made the choice to invoke federal jurisdiction, and thus waives its sovereign immunity. The Court explained: "It would seem anomalous or inconsistent for a State both (1) to invoke federal jurisdiction, thereby contending that the 'Judicial power of the United States' extends to the case at hand, and (2) to claim Eleventh Amendment immunity, thereby denying that the 'Judicial power of the United States' extends to the case at hand. And a Constitution that permitted States to follow their litigation interests by freely asserting both claims in the same case could generate seriously unfair results. Thus, it is not surprising that more than a century ago this Court indicated that a State's voluntary appearance in federal court amounted to a waiver of its Eleventh Amendment immunity." Clark v. Barnard, 108 U.S. 436 (1883).

In this case, the State was brought involuntarily into the case as a defendant in the original state-court proceedings. But the State then voluntarily agreed to remove the case to federal court. In doing so, it voluntarily invoked the federal court's jurisdiction. And unless we are to abandon the general principle just stated, or unless there is something special about removal or about this case, the general legal principle requiring waiver ought to apply."

2. Congress's Power to Authorize Suits Against State Governments (casebook, p. 203)

Over the last few years, the Supreme Court repeatedly has considered the scope of Congress's section 5 power in deciding whether a particular law can be used to sue a state government. In Seminole Tribe v. Florida (1996) (casebook, p. 205), the Court held that Congress only may override the Eleventh Amendment and authorize suits against state governments pursuant to section 5 of the

Fourteenth Amendment. In City of Boerne v. Flores (1997) (casebook p. 196), the Court ruled that Congress could not use its section 5 power to create new rights or to expand the scope of rights. Rather, Congress only could enact laws to prevent or remedy the violations of rights recognized by the courts and such laws had to be "proportionate" and "congruent" to the problem. Thus, in Florida Prepaid v. College Savings Bank (1999) (casebook, p. 210), the Court ruled that state governments could not be sued for patent infringement, despite a federal law expressly authorizing this. In Kimel v. Florida Board of Regents (2000) (casebook, p. 215), the Court ruled that state governments could not be sued for violating the Age Discrimination in Employment Act.

In 2001, in University of Alabama v. Garrett, below, the Court considered whether state governments may be sued for violating Title I of the Americans with Disabilities Act, which prohibits employment discrimination against the disabled and requires reasonable accommodation for disabilities by employers. The plaintiff's key argument to the Court was that the elaborate legislative history documenting government discrimination against the disabled made the Americans with Disabilities Act different from other laws the Court had considered in the last few years. In reading the case, notice the Court's rejection of this argument and consider what would be a sufficient legislative history, after *Garrett*, to justify a federal law under section 5 of the Fourteenth Amendment.

UNIVERSITY OF ALABAMA v. GARRETT
121 S. Ct. 955 (2001)

Chief Justice REHNQUIST delivered the opinion of the Court.

We decide here whether employees of the State of Alabama may recover money damages by reason of the State's failure to comply with the provisions of Title I of the Americans with Disabilities Act of 1990 (ADA or Act).[1] We hold that such suits are barred by the Eleventh Amendment.

The ADA prohibits certain employers, including the States, from "discriminat[ing] against a qualified individual with a disability because of the disability of such individual in regard to job application procedures, the hiring, advancement, or discharge of employees, employee compensation, job training, and other terms, conditions, and privileges of employment." To this end, the Act

---

1. Respondents' complaints in the United States District Court alleged violations of both Title I and Title II of the ADA, and petitioners' "Question Presented" can be read to apply to both sections. Though the briefs of the parties discuss both sections in their constitutional arguments, no party has briefed the question whether Title II of the ADA, dealing with the "services, programs, or activities of a public entity," is available for claims of employment discrimination when Title I of the ADA expressly deals with that subject. We are not disposed to decide the constitutional issue whether Title II, which has somewhat different remedial provisions from Title I, is appropriate legislation under section 5 of the Fourteenth Amendment when the parties have not favored us with briefing on the statutory question. [Footnote by the Court.]

requires employers to "mak[e] reasonable accommodations to the known physical or mental limitations of an otherwise qualified individual with a disability who is an applicant or employee, unless [the employer] can demonstrate that the accommodation would impose an undue hardship on the operation of the [employer's] business."

Respondent Patricia Garrett, a registered nurse, was employed as the Director of Nursing, OB/Gyn/Neonatal Services, for the University of Alabama in Birmingham Hospital. In 1994, Garrett was diagnosed with breast cancer and subsequently underwent a lumpectomy, radiation treatment, and chemotherapy. Garrett's treatments required her to take substantial leave from work. Upon returning to work in July 1995, Garrett's supervisor informed Garrett that she would have to give up her Director position. Garrett then applied for and received a transfer to another, lower paying position as a nurse manager.

I

The Eleventh Amendment provides: "The Judicial power of the United States shall not be construed to extend to any suit in law or equity, commenced or prosecuted against one of the United States by Citizens of another State, or by Citizens or Subjects of any Foreign State." Although by its terms the Amendment applies only to suits against a State by citizens of another State, our cases have extended the Amendment's applicability to suits by citizens against their own States. The ultimate guarantee of the Eleventh Amendment is that nonconsenting States may not be sued by private individuals in federal court.

We have recognized, however, that Congress may abrogate the States' Eleventh Amendment immunity when it both unequivocally intends to do so and "act[s] pursuant to a valid grant of constitutional authority." The first of these requirements is not in dispute here. See 42 U.S.C. § 12202 ("A State shall not be immune under the eleventh amendment to the Constitution of the United States from an action in [a] Federal or State court of competent jurisdiction for a violation of this chapter"). The question, then, is whether Congress acted within its constitutional authority by subjecting the States to suits in federal court for money damages under the ADA.

Congress may not, of course, base its abrogation of the States' Eleventh Amendment immunity upon the powers enumerated in Article I. In Fitzpatrick v. Bitzer (1976), however, we held that "the Eleventh Amendment, and the principle of state sovereignty which it embodies, are necessarily limited by the enforcement provisions of § 5 of the Fourteenth Amendment." As a result, we concluded, Congress may subject nonconsenting States to suit in federal court when it does so pursuant to a valid exercise of its § 5 power. Our cases have adhered to this proposition. Accordingly, the ADA can apply to the States only to the extent that the statute is appropriate § 5 legislation.

Congress is not limited to mere legislative repetition of this Court's constitutional jurisprudence. "Rather, Congress' power 'to enforce' the Amendment includes the authority both to remedy and to deter violation of rights guaranteed thereunder by prohibiting a somewhat broader swath of conduct, including that which is not itself forbidden by the Amendment's text."

City of Boerne v. Flores also confirmed, however, the long-settled principle that it is the responsibility of this Court, not Congress, to define the substance of constitutional guarantees. Accordingly, § 5 legislation reaching beyond the scope of § 1's actual guarantees must exhibit "congruence and proportionality between the injury to be prevented or remedied and the means adopted to that end."

II

The first step in applying these now familiar principles is to identify with some precision the scope of the constitutional right at issue. Here, that inquiry requires us to examine the limitations § 1 of the Fourteenth Amendment places upon States' treatment of the disabled. We look to our prior decisions under the Equal Protection Clause dealing with this issue.

In Cleburne v. Cleburne Living Center, Inc. (1985), we considered an equal protection challenge to a city ordinance requiring a special use permit for the operation of a group home for the mentally retarded. We conclud[ed] that such legislation incurs only the minimum "rational-basis" review applicable to general social and economic legislation. In a statement that today seems quite prescient, we explained that "if the large and amorphous class of the mentally retarded were deemed quasi-suspect for the reasons given by the Court of Appeals, it would be difficult to find a principled way to distinguish a variety of other groups who have perhaps immutable disabilities setting them off from others, who cannot themselves mandate the desired legislative responses, and who can claim some degree of prejudice from at least part of the public at large. One need mention in this respect only the aging, the disabled, the mentally ill, and the infirm. We are reluctant to set out on that course, and we decline to do so."

Under rational-basis review, where a group possesses "distinguishing characteristics relevant to interests the State has the authority to implement," a State's decision to act on the basis of those differences does not give rise to a constitutional violation. "Such a classification cannot run afoul of the Equal Protection Clause if there is a rational relationship between the disparity of treatment and some legitimate governmental purpose." Heller v. Doe (1993).

Thus, the result of *Cleburne* is that States are not required by the Fourteenth Amendment to make special accommodations for the disabled, so long as their actions towards such individuals are rational. They could quite hardheadedly— and perhaps hardheartedly—hold to job-qualification requirements which do not make allowance for the disabled. If special accommodations for the disabled are to be required, they have to come from positive law and not through the Equal Protection Clause.[2]

III

Once we have determined the metes and bounds of the constitutional right in question, we examine whether Congress identified a history and pattern of unconstitutional employment discrimination by the States against the disabled. Just as § 1 of the Fourteenth Amendment applies only to actions committed "under color of state law," Congress' § 5 authority is appropriately exercised only in response to state transgressions. The legislative record of the ADA, however, simply fails to show that Congress did in fact identify a pattern of irrational state discrimination in employment against the disabled.

Respondents contend that the inquiry as to unconstitutional discrimination should extend not only to States themselves, but to units of local governments, such as cities and counties. All of these, they say, are "state actors" for purposes of the Fourteenth Amendment. This is quite true, but the Eleventh Amendment does not extend its immunity to units of local government. See Lincoln County v. Luning (1890). These entities are subject to private claims for damages under the ADA without Congress' ever having to rely on § 5 of the Fourteenth Amendment to render them so. It would make no sense to consider constitutional violations on their part, as well as by the States themselves, when only the States are the beneficiaries of the Eleventh Amendment.

Congress made a general finding in the ADA that "historically, society has tended to isolate and segregate individuals with disabilities, and, despite some improvements, such forms of discrimination against individuals with disabilities continue to be a serious and pervasive social problem." The record assembled by Congress includes many instances to support such a finding. But the great majority of these incidents do not deal with the activities of States. Respondents in their brief cite half a dozen examples from the record that did involve States. A department head at the University of North Carolina refused to hire an applicant for the position of health administrator because he was blind; similarly, a student at a state university in South Dakota was denied an opportunity to practice teach because the dean at that time was convinced that blind people could not teach in public schools. A microfilmer at the Kansas Department of Transportation was fired because he had epilepsy; deaf workers at the University of Oklahoma were paid a lower salary than those who could hear. The Indiana State Personnel Office informed a woman with a concealed disability that she should not disclose it if she wished to obtain employment.

Several of these incidents undoubtedly evidence an unwillingness on the part of state officials to make the sort of accommodations for the disabled required by the ADA. Whether they were irrational under our decision in *Cleburne* is

2. It is worth noting that by the time that Congress enacted the ADA in 1990, every State in the Union had enacted such measures. [Footnote by the Court.]

more debatable, particularly when the incident is described out of context. But even if it were to be determined that each incident upon fuller examination showed unconstitutional action on the part of the State, these incidents taken together fall far short of even suggesting the pattern of unconstitutional discrimination on which § 5 legislation must be based. Congress, in enacting the ADA, found that "some 43,000,000 Americans have one or more physical or mental disabilities." In 1990, the States alone employed more than 4.5 million people. It is telling, we think, that given these large numbers, Congress assembled only such minimal evidence of unconstitutional state discrimination in employment against the disabled.

Justice Breyer maintains that Congress applied Title I of the ADA to the States in response to a host of incidents representing unconstitutional state discrimination in employment against persons with disabilities. A close review of the relevant materials, however, undercuts that conclusion. Justice Breyer's Appendix C consists not of legislative findings, but of unexamined, anecdotal accounts of "adverse, disparate treatment by state officials."[3] Of course, as we have already explained, "adverse, disparate treatment" often does not amount to a constitutional violation where rational-basis scrutiny applies. These accounts, moreover, were submitted not directly to Congress but to the Task Force on the Rights and Empowerment of Americans with Disabilities, which made no findings on the subject of state discrimination in employment. And, had Congress truly understood this information as reflecting a pattern of unconstitutional behavior by the States, one would expect some mention of that conclusion in the Act's legislative findings. There is none.

Even were it possible to squeeze out of these examples a pattern of unconstitutional discrimination by the States, the rights and remedies created by the ADA against the States would raise the same sort of concerns as to congruence and proportionality as were found in *City of Boerne.* For example, whereas it would be entirely rational (and therefore constitutional) for a state employer to conserve scarce financial resources by hiring employees who are able to use existing facilities, the ADA requires employers to "mak[e] existing facilities used by employees readily accessible to and usable by individuals with disabilities." The ADA does except employers from the "reasonable accommodatio[n]" requirement where the employer "can demonstrate that the accommodation would impose an undue hardship on the operation of the business of such covered entity." However, even with this exception, the accommodation duty far exceeds what is constitutionally required in that it makes unlawful a range of alternate responses that would be reasonable but would fall short of imposing an "undue burden" upon the employer. The Act also makes it the employer's duty to prove that it would suffer such a burden, instead of requiring (as the Consti-

---

3. Justice Breyer attached a 39-page appendix to his opinion (Appendix C) that listed references in the legislative history to government discrimination against the disabled. [Footnote by casebook author.]

tution does) that the complaining party negate reasonable bases for the employer's decision.

The ADA also forbids "utilizing standards, criteria, or methods of administration" that disparately impact the disabled, without regard to whether such conduct has a rational basis. Although disparate impact may be relevant evidence of racial discrimination, see Washington v. Davis (1976), such evidence alone is insufficient even where the Fourteenth Amendment subjects state action to strict scrutiny.

The ADA's constitutional shortcomings are apparent when the Act is compared to Congress' efforts in the Voting Rights Act of 1965 to respond to a serious pattern of constitutional violations. In South Carolina v. Katzenbach (1966), we considered whether the Voting Rights Act was "appropriate" legislation to enforce the Fifteenth Amendment's protection against racial discrimination in voting. Concluding that it was a valid exercise of Congress' enforcement power under § 2 of the Fifteenth Amendment, we noted that "[b]efore enacting the measure, Congress explored with great care the problem of racial discrimination in voting."

In that Act, Congress documented a marked pattern of unconstitutional action by the States. State officials, Congress found, routinely applied voting tests in order to exclude African-American citizens from registering to vote. Congress also determined that litigation had proved ineffective and that there persisted an otherwise inexplicable 50-percentage-point gap in the registration of white and African-American voters in some States. Congress' response was to promulgate in the Voting Rights Act a detailed but limited remedial scheme designed to guarantee meaningful enforcement of the Fifteenth Amendment in those areas of the Nation where abundant evidence of States' systematic denial of those rights was identified.

The contrast between this kind of evidence, and the evidence that Congress considered in the present case, is stark. Congressional enactment of the ADA represents its judgment that there should be a "comprehensive national mandate for the elimination of discrimination against individuals with disabilities." Congress is the final authority as to desirable public policy, but in order to authorize private individuals to recover money damages against the States, there must be a pattern of discrimination by the States which violates the Fourteenth Amendment, and the remedy imposed by Congress must be congruent and proportional to the targeted violation. Those requirements are not met here, and to uphold the Act's application to the States would allow Congress to rewrite the Fourteenth Amendment law laid down by this Court in *Cleburne*. Section 5 does not so broadly enlarge congressional authority.[4]

---

4. Our holding here that Congress did not validly abrogate the States' sovereign immunity from suit by private individuals for money damages under Title I does not mean that persons with disabilities have no federal recourse against discrimination. Title I of the ADA still prescribes standards applicable to the States. Those standards can be enforced by the United States in actions for money damages, as well as by private individuals in actions for injunctive relief under Ex parte

Justice KENNEDY, with whom Justice O'CONNOR joins, concurring.

One of the undoubted achievements of statutes designed to assist those with impairments is that citizens have an incentive, flowing from a legal duty, to develop a better understanding, a more decent perspective, for accepting persons with impairments or disabilities into the larger society. The law works this way because the law can be a teacher. So I do not doubt that the Americans with Disabilities Act of 1990 will be a milestone on the path to a more decent, tolerant, progressive society.

It is a question of quite a different order, however, to say that the States in their official capacities, the States as governmental entities, must be held in violation of the Constitution on the assumption that they embody the misconceived or malicious perceptions of some of their citizens. It is a most serious charge to say a State has engaged in a pattern or practice designed to deny its citizens the equal protection of the laws, particularly where the accusation is based not on hostility but instead on the failure to act or the omission to remedy. States can, and do, stand apart from the citizenry. States act as neutral entities, ready to take instruction and to enact laws when their citizens so demand. The failure of a State to revise policies now seen as incorrect under a new understanding of proper policy does not always constitute the purposeful and intentional action required to make out a violation of the Equal Protection Clause. See Washington v. Davis (1976).

For the reasons explained by the Court, an equal protection violation has not been shown with respect to the several States in this case. If the States had been transgressing the Fourteenth Amendment by their mistreatment or lack of concern for those with impairments, one would have expected to find in decisions of the courts of the States and also the courts of the United States extensive litigation and discussion of the constitutional violations. This confirming judicial documentation does not exist. That there is a new awareness, a new consciousness, a new commitment to better treatment of those disadvantaged by mental or physical impairments does not establish that an absence of state statutory correctives was a constitutional violation.

It must be noted, moreover, that what is in question is not whether the Congress, acting pursuant to a power granted to it by the Constitution, can compel the States to act. What is involved is only the question whether the States can be subjected to liability in suits brought not by the Federal Government (to which the States have consented) but by private persons seeking to collect moneys from the state treasury without the consent of the State. The predicate for money damages against an unconsenting State in suits brought by private persons must be a federal statute enacted upon the documentation of patterns of constitutional violations committed by the State in its official capacity. That predicate, for rea-

---

Young (1908). In addition, state laws protecting the rights of persons with disabilities in employment and other aspects of life provide independent avenues of redress. [Footnote by Court.]

sons discussed here and in the decision of the Court, has not been established. With these observations, I join the Court's opinion.

Justice BREYER, with whom Justice STEVENS, Justice SOUTER, and Justice GINSBURG join, dissenting.

Reviewing the congressional record as if it were an administrative agency record, the Court holds the statutory provision before us unconstitutional. The Court concludes that Congress assembled insufficient evidence of unconstitutional discrimination, that Congress improperly attempted to "re-write" the law we established in Cleburne v. Cleburne Living Center, Inc. (1985), and that the law is not sufficiently tailored to address unconstitutional discrimination.

Section 5, however, grants Congress the "power to enforce, by appropriate legislation" the Fourteenth Amendment's equal protection guarantee. As the Court recognizes, state discrimination in employment against persons with disabilities might "run afoul of the Equal Protection Clause" where there is no "rational relationship between the disparity of treatment and some legitimate governmental purpose." In my view, Congress reasonably could have concluded that the remedy before us constitutes an "appropriate" way to enforce this basic equal protection requirement. And that is all the Constitution requires.

I

The Court says that its primary problem with this statutory provision is one of legislative evidence. It says that "Congress assembled only . . . minimal evidence of unconstitutional state discrimination in employment." In fact, Congress compiled a vast legislative record documenting "'massive, society-wide discrimination'" against persons with disabilities. S. Rep. No. 101-116, pp. 8-9 (1989). In addition to the information presented at 13 congressional hearings (see Appendix A, infra), and its own prior experience gathered over 40 years during which it contemplated and enacted considerable similar legislation (see Appendix B, infra), Congress created a special task force to assess the need for comprehensive legislation. That task force held hearings in every State, attended by more than 30,000 people, including thousands who had experienced discrimination first-hand. The task force hearings, Congress' own hearings, and an analysis of "census data, national polls, and other studies" led Congress to conclude that "people with disabilities, as a group, occupy an inferior status in our society, and are severely disadvantaged socially, vocationally, economically, and educationally." As to employment, Congress found that "[t]wo-thirds of all disabled Americans between the age of 16 and 64 [were] not working at all," even though a large majority wanted to, and were able to, work productively. S. Rep. No. 101-116, at 9. And Congress found that this discrimination flowed in significant part from "stereotypic assumptions" as well as "purposeful unequal treatment."

The powerful evidence of discriminatory treatment throughout society in general, including discrimination by private persons and local governments, implicates state governments as well, for state agencies form part of that same larger society. There is no particular reason to believe that they are immune from the "stereotypic assumptions" and pattern of "purposeful unequal treatment" that Congress found prevalent. The Court claims that it "make[s] no sense" to take into consideration constitutional violations committed by local governments. But the substantive obligation that the Equal Protection Clause creates applies to state and local governmental entities alike. Local governments often work closely with, and under the supervision of, state officials, and in general, state and local government employers are similarly situated. Nor is determining whether an apparently "local" entity is entitled to Eleventh Amendment immunity as simple as the majority suggests—it often requires a "'detailed examination of the relevant provisions of [state] law.'"

In any event, there is no need to rest solely upon evidence of discrimination by local governments or general societal discrimination. There are roughly 300 examples of discrimination by state governments themselves in the legislative record. See, e.g., Appendix C, infra. I fail to see how this evidence "fall[s] far short of even suggesting the pattern of unconstitutional discrimination on which § 5 legislation must be based."

The congressionally appointed task force collected numerous specific examples, provided by persons with disabilities themselves, of adverse, disparate treatment by state officials. They reveal, not what the Court describes as "half a dozen" instances of discrimination, but hundreds of instances of adverse treatment at the hands of state officials—instances in which a person with a disability found it impossible to obtain a state job, to retain state employment, to use the public transportation that was readily available to others in order to get to work, or to obtain a public education, which is often a prerequisite to obtaining employment. State-imposed barriers also frequently made it difficult or impossible for people to vote, to enter a public building, to access important government services, such as calling for emergency assistance, and to find a place to live due to a pattern of irrational zoning decisions similar to the discrimination that we held unconstitutional in *Cleburne*.

As the Court notes, those who presented instances of discrimination rarely provided additional, independent evidence sufficient to prove in court that, in each instance, the discrimination they suffered lacked justification from a judicial standpoint. Perhaps this explains the Court's view that there is "minimal evidence of unconstitutional state discrimination." But a legislature is not a court of law. And Congress, unlike courts, must, and does, routinely draw general conclusions—for example, of likely motive or of likely relationship to legitimate need—from anecdotal and opinion-based evidence of this kind, particularly when the evidence lacks strong refutation. In reviewing § 5 legislation, we have never required the sort of extensive investigation of each piece of evidence that the Court appears to contemplate.

Regardless, Congress expressly found substantial unjustified discrimination against persons with disabilities. The evidence in the legislative record bears out Congress' finding that the adverse treatment of persons with disabilities was often arbitrary or invidious in this sense, and thus unjustified. For example, one study that was before Congress revealed that "most . . . governmental agencies in [one State] discriminated in hiring against job applicants for an average period of five years after treatment for cancer," based in part on coworkers' misguided belief that "cancer is contagious." A school inexplicably refused to exempt a deaf teacher, who taught at a school for the deaf, from a "listening skills" requirement. A State refused to hire a blind employee as director of an agency for the blind—even though he was the most qualified applicant. Certain state agencies apparently had general policies against hiring or promoting persons with disabilities. A zoo turned away children with Downs Syndrome "because [the zookeeper] feared they would upset the chimpanzees." There were reports of numerous zoning decisions based upon "negative attitudes" or "fear," such as a zoning board that denied a permit for an obviously pretextual reason after hearing arguments that a facility would house "'deviants'" who needed "'room to roam.'" A complete listing of the hundreds of examples of discrimination by state and local governments that were submitted to the task force is set forth in Appendix C, infra. Congress could have reasonably believed that these examples represented signs of a widespread problem of unconstitutional discrimination.

II

The Court's failure to find sufficient evidentiary support may well rest upon its decision to hold Congress to a strict, judicially created evidentiary standard, particularly in respect to lack of justification. Justice Kennedy's empirical conclusion—which rejects that of Congress—rests heavily upon his failure to find "extensive litigation and discussion of constitutional violations," in "the courts of the United States." And the Court itself points out that, when economic or social legislation is challenged in court as irrational, hence unconstitutional, the "burden is upon the challenging party to negative any reasonably conceivable state of facts that could provide a rational basis for the classification." Or as Justice Brandeis, writing for the Court, put the matter many years ago, "'if any state of facts reasonably can be conceived that would sustain'" challenged legislation, then "'there is a presumption of the existence of that state of facts, and one who assails the classification must carry the burden of showing . . . that the action is arbitrary.'" Imposing this special "burden" upon Congress, the Court fails to find in the legislative record sufficient indication that Congress has "negative[d]" the presumption that state action is rationally related to a legitimate objective.

The problem with the Court's approach is that neither the "burden of proof" that favors States nor any other rule of restraint applicable to judges applies to Congress when it exercises its § 5 power. "Limitations stemming from the nature of the judicial process . . . have no application to Congress." Oregon v. Mitchell (1970). Rational-basis review—with its presumptions favoring constitutionality—is "a paradigm of judicial restraint." And the Congress of the United States is not a lower court.

Indeed, the Court in *Cleburne* drew this very institutional distinction. We emphasized that "courts have been very reluctant, as they should be in our federal system and with our respect for the separation of powers, to closely scrutinize legislative choices." Our invocation of judicial deference and respect for Congress was based on the fact that "[§] 5 of the [Fourteenth] Amendment empowers Congress to enforce [the equal protection] mandate." Indeed, we made clear that the absence of a contrary congressional finding was critical to our decision to apply mere rational-basis review to disability discrimination claims—a "congressional direction" to apply a more stringent standard would have been "controlling." In short, the Court's claim that "to uphold the Act's application to the States would allow Congress to rewrite the Fourteenth Amendment law laid down by this Court in *Cleburne*," is repudiated by *Cleburne* itself.

There is simply no reason to require Congress, seeking to determine facts relevant to the exercise of its § 5 authority, to adopt rules or presumptions that reflect a court's institutional limitations. Unlike courts, Congress can readily gather facts from across the Nation, assess the magnitude of a problem, and more easily find an appropriate remedy. Unlike courts, Congress directly reflects public attitudes and beliefs, enabling Congress better to understand where, and to what extent, refusals to accommodate a disability amount to behavior that is callous or unreasonable to the point of lacking constitutional justification. Unlike judges, Members of Congress can directly obtain information from constituents who have first-hand experience with discrimination and related issues.

Moreover, unlike judges, Members of Congress are elected. When the Court has applied the majority's burden of proof rule, it has explained that we, i.e., the courts, do not "'sit as a superlegislature to judge the wisdom or desirability of legislative policy determinations.'" To apply a rule designed to restrict courts as if it restricted Congress' legislative power is to stand the underlying principle—a principle of judicial restraint—on its head. But without the use of this burden of proof rule or some other unusually stringent standard of review, it is difficult to see how the Court can find the legislative record here inadequate. Read with a reasonably favorable eye, the record indicates that state governments subjected those with disabilities to seriously adverse, disparate treatment. And Congress could have found, in a significant number of instances, that this treatment violated the substantive principles of justification—shorn of their judicial-restraint-related presumptions—that this Court recognized in *Cleburne*.

III

The Court argues in the alternative that the statute's damage remedy is not "congruent" with and "proportional" to the equal protection problem that Congress found. The Court suggests that the Act's "reasonable accommodation" requirement, and disparate impact standard, "far excee[d] what is constitution-ally required." But we have upheld disparate impact standards in contexts where they were not "constitutionally required."

And what is wrong with a remedy that, in response to unreasonable employer behavior, requires an employer to make accommodations that are reasonable? Of course, what is "reasonable" in the statutory sense and what is "unreason-able" in the constitutional sense might differ. In other words, the requirement may exceed what is necessary to avoid a constitutional violation. But it is just that power—the power to require more than the minimum that § 5 grants to Congress, as this Court has repeatedly confirmed.

For the reasons stated, I respectfully dissent.

5. Congress's Power to Authorize Suits Against State Governments in Federal Administrative Proceedings (new, to be inserted after casebook p. 230)

In Alden v. Maine (casebook, p. 220), the Supreme Court held that state govern-ments cannot be sued in state court, even on federal claims, without their con-sent. Although the Eleventh Amendment only bars suits against states in *federal* court, the Supreme Court held that sovereign immunity is broader than the Elev-enth Amendment and bars suits against unconsenting states in state court.

In Federal Maritime Commission v. South Carolina Port Authority, the Supreme Court considered whether federal administrative proceedings against state governments are permitted. In reading the case, it is important to note how Justice Thomas's majority opinion justifies the broad scope of sovereign im-munity and also to note, Justice Breyer's dissenting opinion, which emphasizes that administrative proceedings should be regarded as executive, not judicial, and thus not affected by sovereign immunity.

FEDERAL MARITIME COMMISSION v. SOUTH CAROLINA STATE PORT AUTHORITY
122 S. Ct. 1864 (2002)

Justice THOMAS delivered the opinion of the Court.

This case presents the question whether state sovereign immunity precludes petitioner Federal Maritime Commission (FMC or Commission) from adjudi-cating a private party's complaint that a state-run port has violated the Shipping Act of 1984, 46 U.S.C. App. § 1701. We hold that state sovereign immunity bars such an adjudicative proceeding.

I

On five occasions, South Carolina Maritime Services, Inc. (Maritime Services), asked respondent South Carolina State Ports Authority (SCSPA) for permission to berth a cruise ship, the M/V Tropic Sea, at the SCSPA's port facilities in Charleston, South Carolina. Maritime Services intended to offer cruises on the M/V Tropic Sea originating from the Port of Charleston. Some of these cruises would stop in the Bahamas while others would merely travel in international waters before returning to Charleston with no intervening ports of call. On all of these trips, passengers would be permitted to participate in gambling activities while on board.

The SCSPA repeatedly denied Maritime Services' requests, contending that it had an established policy of denying berths in the Port of Charleston to vessels whose primary purpose was gambling. As a result, Maritime Services filed a complaint with the FMC, contending that the SCSPA's refusal to provide berthing space to the M/V Tropic Sea violated the Shipping Act. Maritime Services alleged in its complaint that the SCSPA had implemented its antigambling policy in a discriminatory fashion by providing berthing space in Charleston to two Carnival Cruise Lines vessels even though Carnival offered gambling activities on these ships. Maritime Services therefore complained that the SCSPA had unduly and unreasonably preferred Carnival over Maritime Services in violation of 46 U.S.C. App. § 1709(d)(4) and unreasonably refused to deal or negotiate with Maritime Services in violation of § 1709(b)(10). It further alleged that the SCSPA's unlawful actions had inflicted upon Maritime Services a "loss of profits, loss of earnings, loss of sales, and loss of business opportunities."

To remedy its injuries, Maritime Services prayed that the FMC: (1) seek a temporary restraining order and preliminary injunction in the United States District Court for the District of South Carolina "enjoining [the SCSPA] from utilizing its discriminatory practice to refuse to provide berthing space and passenger services to Maritime Services"; (2) direct the SCSPA to pay reparations to Maritime Services as well as interest and reasonable attorneys' fees; (3) issue an order commanding, among other things, the SCSPA to cease and desist from violating the Shipping Act; and (4) award Maritime Services "such other and further relief as is just and proper."

Consistent with the FMC's Rules of Practice and Procedure, Maritime Services' complaint was referred to an administrative law judge (ALJ). The SCSPA then filed an answer, maintaining, inter alia, that it had adhered to its antigambling policy in a nondiscriminatory manner. It also filed a motion to dismiss, asserting, as relevant, that the SCSPA, as an arm of the State of South Carolina, was "entitled to Eleventh Amendment immunity" from Maritime Services' suit. The ALJ agreed, concluding that recent decisions of this Court "interpreting the 11th Amendment and State sovereign immunity from private suits . . . require[d] that [Maritime Services'] complaint be dismissed."

II

Dual sovereignty is a defining feature of our Nation's constitutional blueprint. States, upon ratification of the Constitution, did not consent to become mere appendages of the Federal Government. Rather, they entered the Union "with their sovereignty intact." An integral component of that "residuary and inviolable sovereignty," The Federalist No. 39, (C. Rossiter ed. 1961) (J. Madison), retained by the States is their immunity from private suits. Reflecting the widespread understanding at the time the Constitution was drafted, Alexander Hamilton explained, "It is inherent in the nature of sovereignty not to be amenable to the suit of an individual without its consent. This is the general sense and the general practice of mankind; and the exemption, as one of the attributes of sovereignty, is now enjoyed by the government of every State of the Union. Unless, therefore, there is a surrender of this immunity in the plan of the convention, it will remain with the States. . . ." Id., No. 81.

States, in ratifying the Constitution, did surrender a portion of their inherent immunity by consenting to suits brought by sister States or by the Federal Government. Nevertheless, the Convention did not disturb States' immunity from private suits, thus firmly enshrining this principle in our constitutional framework. "The leading advocates of the Constitution assured the people in no uncertain terms that the Constitution would not strip the States of sovereign immunity."

The States' sovereign immunity, however, fell into peril in the early days of our Nation's history when this Court held in Chisholm v. Georgia (1793), that Article III authorized citizens of one State to sue another State in federal court. The "decision 'fell upon the country with a profound shock.'" In order to overturn *Chisholm,* Congress quickly passed the Eleventh Amendment and the States ratified it speedily. The Amendment clarified that "[t]he judicial Power of the United States shall not be construed to extend to any suit in law or equity, commenced or prosecuted against one of the United States by Citizens of another State, or by Citizens or Subjects of any Foreign State." We have since acknowledged that the *Chisholm* decision was erroneous. See, e.g., Alden v. Maine (1999).

Instead of explicitly memorializing the full breadth of the sovereign immunity retained by the States when the Constitution was ratified, Congress chose in the text of the Eleventh Amendment only to "address the specific provisions of the Constitution that had raised concerns during the ratification debates and formed the basis of the *Chisholm* decision." As a result, the Eleventh Amendment does not define the scope of the States' sovereign immunity; it is but one particular exemplification of that immunity.

III

We now consider whether the sovereign immunity enjoyed by States as part of our constitutional framework applies to adjudications conducted by the FMC.

Petitioner FMC and respondent United States initially maintain that the Court of Appeals erred because sovereign immunity only shields States from exercises of "judicial power" and FMC adjudications are not judicial proceedings. For purposes of this case, we will assume, arguendo, that in adjudicating complaints filed by private parties under the Shipping Act, the FMC does not exercise the judicial power of the United States. Such an assumption, however, does not end our inquiry as this Court has repeatedly held that the sovereign immunity enjoyed by the States extends beyond the literal text of the Eleventh Amendment. [W]e must determine whether the sovereign immunity embedded in our constitutional structure and retained by the States when they joined the Union extends to FMC adjudicative proceedings.[1]

A

"[L]ook[ing] first to evidence of the original understanding of the Constitution," as well as early congressional practice, we find a relatively barren historical record. Because formalized administrative adjudications were all but unheard of in the late 18th century and early 19th century, the dearth of specific evidence indicating whether the Framers believed that the States' sovereign immunity would apply in such proceedings is unsurprising. This Court, however, has applied a presumption—first explicitly stated in Hans v. Louisiana (1890)—that the Constitution was not intended to "rais[e] up" any proceedings against the States that were "anomalous and unheard of when the Constitution was adopted." We therefore attribute great significance to the fact that States were not subject to private suits in administrative adjudications at the time of the founding or for many years thereafter. For instance, while the United States asserts that "state entities have long been subject to similar administrative enforcement proceedings," the earliest example it provides did not occur until 1918.

B

To decide whether the *Hans* presumption applies here, however, we must examine FMC adjudications to determine whether they are the type of proceedings from which the Framers would have thought the States possessed immunity when they agreed to enter the Union. In another case asking whether an immunity present in the judicial context also applied to administrative adjudications, this Court considered whether administrative law judges share the same absolute

1. To the extent that Justice Breyer, looking to the text of the Eleventh Amendment, suggests that sovereign immunity only shields States from the "'the judicial power of the United States,'" he "engage[s] in the type of ahistorical literalism we have rejected in interpreting the scope of the States' sovereign immunity since the discredited decision in *Chisholm*," Alden v. Maine (1999). Furthermore, it is ironic that Justice Breyer adopts such a textual approach in defending the conduct of an independent agency that itself lacks any textual basis in the Constitution. [Footnote by Justice Thomas.]

immunity from suit as do Article III judges. See Butz v. Economou (1978). Examining in that case the duties performed by an ALJ, this Court observed: "There can be little doubt that the role of the modern federal hearing examiner or administrative law judge . . . is 'functionally comparable' to that of a judge. His powers are often, if not generally, comparable to those of a trial judge: He may issue subpoenas, rule on proffers of evidence, regulate the course of the hearing, and make or recommend decisions. More importantly, the process of agency adjudication is currently structured so as to assure that the hearing examiner exercises his independent judgment on the evidence before him, free from pressures by the parties or other officials within the agency." Beyond the similarities between the role of an ALJ and that of a trial judge, this Court also noted the numerous common features shared by administrative adjudications and judicial proceedings: This Court therefore concluded in *Butz* that administrative law judges were "entitled to absolute immunity from damages liability for their judicial acts."

Turning to FMC adjudications specifically, neither the Commission nor the United States disputes the Court of Appeals' characterization below that such a proceeding "walks, talks, and squawks very much like a lawsuit." Nor do they deny that the similarities identified in *Butz* between administrative adjudications and trial court proceedings are present here. A review of the FMC's Rules of Practice and Procedure confirms that FMC administrative proceedings bear a remarkably strong resemblance to civil litigation in federal courts. For example, the FMC's Rules governing pleadings are quite similar to those found in the Federal Rules of Civil Procedure. In short, the similarities between FMC proceedings and civil litigation are overwhelming. In fact, to the extent that situations arise in the course of FMC adjudications "which are not covered by a specific Commission rule," the FMC's own Rules of Practice and Procedure specifically provide that "the Federal Rules of Civil Procedure will be followed to the extent that they are consistent with sound administrative practice."

C

The preeminent purpose of state sovereign immunity is to accord States the dignity that is consistent with their status as sovereign entities. Given both this interest in protecting States' dignity and the strong similarities between FMC proceedings and civil litigation, we hold that state sovereign immunity bars the FMC from adjudicating complaints filed by a private party against a nonconsenting State. Simply put, if the Framers thought it an impermissible affront to a State's dignity to be required to answer the complaints of private parties in federal courts, we cannot imagine that they would have found it acceptable to compel a State to do exactly the same thing before the administrative tribunal of an agency, such as the FMC. The affront to a State's dignity does not lessen when an adjudication takes place in an administrative tribunal as opposed to an Article III court. In both instances, a State is required to defend itself in an adversarial proceeding against a private party before an impartial federal officer. Moreover, it would be quite strange to prohibit Congress from exercising its Article I powers to abrogate state sovereign immunity in Article III judicial proceedings, see Seminole Tribe v. Florida (1996), but permit the use of those same Article I powers to create court-like administrative tribunals where sovereign immunity does not apply.[2]

D

The United States suggests two reasons why we should distinguish FMC administrative adjudications from judicial proceedings for purposes of state sovereign immunity. Both of these arguments are unavailing. The United States first contends that sovereign immunity should not apply to FMC adjudications because the Commission's orders are not self-executing. Whereas a court may enforce a judgment through the exercise of its contempt power, the FMC cannot enforce its own orders. Rather, the Commission's orders can only be enforced by a federal district court. For purposes of this case, however, it is a distinction without a meaningful difference. To the extent that the United States highlights this fact in order to suggest that a party alleged to have violated the Shipping Act is not coerced to participate in FMC proceedings, it is mistaken. The relevant statutory scheme makes it quite clear that, absent sovereign immunity, States would effectively be required to defend themselves against private parties in front of the FMC. A State seeking to contest the merits of a complaint filed against it by a private party must defend itself in front of the FMC or substantially compromise its ability to defend itself at all. Should a party choose to ignore an order issued by the FMC, the Commission may impose monetary penalties for each day of noncompliance. The Commission may then request that the Attorney General of the United States seek to recover the amount assessed by the Commission in federal district court, and a State's sovereign immunity would not extend to that action, as it is one brought by the United States.

The United States next suggests that sovereign immunity should not apply to FMC proceedings because they do not present the same threat to the financial integrity of States as do private judicial suits. The Government highlights the fact that, in contrast to a nonreparation order, for which the Attorney General may seek enforcement at the request of the Commission, a reparation order may be enforced in a United States district court only in an action brought by the private party to whom the award was made. The United States then points out that a State's sovereign immunity would extend to such a suit brought by a private party. This argument, however, reflects a fundamental misunderstanding of the purposes of sovereign immunity. While state sovereign immunity serves the

2. One, in fact, could argue that allowing a private party to haul a State in front of such an administrative tribunal constitutes a greater insult to a State's dignity than requiring a State to appear in an Article III court presided over by a judge with life tenure nominated by the President of the United States and confirmed by the United States Senate. [Footnote by Justice Thomas.]

important function of shielding state treasuries and thus preserving "the States' ability to govern in accordance with the will of their citizens," the doctrine's central purpose is to "accord the States the respect owed them as" joint sovereigns. It is for this reason, for instance, that sovereign immunity applies regardless of whether a private plaintiff's suit is for monetary damages or some other type of relief. Sovereign immunity does not merely constitute a defense to monetary liability or even to all types of liability. Rather, it provides an immunity from suit. The statutory scheme, as interpreted by the United States, is thus no more permissible than if Congress had allowed private parties to sue States in federal court for violations of the Shipping Act but precluded a court from awarding them any relief.

It is also worth noting that an FMC order that a State pay reparations to a private party may very well result in the withdrawal of funds from that State's treasury. A State subject to such an order at the conclusion of an FMC adjudicatory proceeding would either have to make the required payment to the injured private party or stand in violation of the Commission's order.

While some might complain that our system of dual sovereignty is not a model of administrative convenience, see, e.g., (Breyer, J., dissenting), that is not its purpose. Rather, "[t]he 'constitutionally mandated balance of power' between the States and the Federal Government was adopted by the Framers to ensure the protection of 'our fundamental liberties.'" By guarding against encroachments by the Federal Government on fundamental aspects of state sovereignty, such as sovereign immunity, we strive to maintain the balance of power embodied in our Constitution and thus to "reduce the risk of tyranny and abuse from either front." Although the Framers likely did not envision the intrusion on state sovereignty at issue in today's case, we are nonetheless confident that it is contrary to their constitutional design.

Justice STEVENS, dissenting.

Justice Breyer has explained why the Court's recent sovereign immunity jurisprudence does not support today's decision. I join his opinion without reservation, but add these words to emphasize the weakness of the two predicates for the majority's holding. Those predicates are, first, the Court's recent decision in Alden v. Maine (1999), and second, the "preeminent" interest in according States the "dignity" that is their due.

Justice Souter has already demonstrated that *Alden*'s creative "conception of state sovereign immunity . . . is true neither to history nor to the structure of the Constitution." And I have previously explained that the "dignity" rationale is "'embarrassingly insufficient,'" in part because "Chief Justice Marshall early on laid to rest the view that the purpose of the Eleventh Amendment was to protect a State's dignity," (citing Cohens v. Virginia (1821)).

This latter point is reinforced by the legislative history of the Eleventh Amendment. It is familiar learning that the Amendment was a response to this Court's decision in Chisholm v. Georgia (1793). Less recognized, however, is that *Chisholm* necessarily decided two jurisdictional issues: that the Court had personal jurisdiction over the state defendant, and that it had subject-matter jurisdiction over the case. The first proposed draft of a constitutional amendment responding to *Chisholm*—introduced in the House of Representatives in February, 1793, on the day after *Chisholm* was decided—would have overruled the first holding, but not the second. That proposal was not adopted. Rather, a proposal introduced the following day in the Senate, which was "cast in terms that we associate with subject matter jurisdiction," provided the basis for the present text of the Eleventh Amendment.

This legislative history suggests that the Eleventh Amendment is best understood as having overruled *Chisholm*'s subject-matter jurisdiction holding, thereby restricting the federal courts' diversity jurisdiction. However, the Amendment left intact *Chisholm*'s personal jurisdiction holding: that the Constitution does not immunize States from a federal court's process. If the paramount concern of the Eleventh Amendment's framers had been protecting the so-called "dignity" interest of the States, surely Congress would have endorsed the first proposed amendment granting the States immunity from process, rather than the later proposal that merely delineates the subject matter jurisdiction of courts. Moreover, as Chief Justice Marshall recognized, a subject-matter reading of the Amendment makes sense, considering the states' interest in avoiding their creditors. The reasons why the majority in *Chisholm* concluded that the "dignity" interests underlying the sovereign immunity of English Monarchs had not been inherited by the original 13 States remain valid today. By extending the untethered "dignity" rationale to the context of routine federal administrative proceedings, today's decision is even more anachronistic than *Alden*.

Justice BREYER, with whom Justice STEVENS, Justice SOUTER, and Justice GINSBURG join, dissenting.

The Court holds that a private person cannot bring a complaint against a State to a federal administrative agency where the agency (1) will use an internal adjudicative process to decide if the complaint is well founded, and (2) if so, proceed to court to enforce the law. Where does the Constitution contain the principle of law that the Court enunciates? I cannot find the answer to this question in any text, in any tradition, or in any relevant purpose. In saying this, I do not simply reiterate the dissenting views set forth in many of the Court's recent sovereign immunity decisions. For even were I to believe that those decisions properly stated the law—which I do not—I still could not accept the Court's conclusion here.

I

At the outset one must understand the constitutional nature of the legal proceeding before us. The legal body conducting the proceeding, the Federal Maritime Commission, is an "independent" federal agency. Constitutionally speaking, an "independent" agency belongs neither to the Legislative Branch nor to the Judicial Branch of Government. Although Members of this Court have referred to agencies as a "fourth branch" of Government, the agencies, even "independent" agencies, are more appropriately considered to be part of the Executive Branch. The President appoints their chief administrators, typically a Chairman and Commissioners, subject to confirmation by the Senate. The agencies derive their legal powers from congressionally enacted statutes. And the agencies enforce those statutes, i.e., they "execute" them, in part by making rules or by adjudicating matters in dispute. The Court long ago laid to rest any constitutional doubts about whether the Constitution permitted Congress to delegate rulemaking and adjudicative powers to agencies. Consequently, in exercising those powers, the agency is engaging in an Article II, Executive Branch activity. And the powers it is exercising are powers that the Executive Branch of Government must possess if it is to enforce modern law through administration.

The case before us presents a fairly typical example of a federal administrative agency's use of agency adjudication. Congress has enacted a statute, the Shipping Act of 1984 (Act or Shipping Act), which, among other things, forbids marine terminal operators to discriminate against terminal users. The Act grants the Federal Maritime Commission the authority to administer the Act. The law grants the Commission the authority to enforce the Act in a variety of ways, for example, by making rules and regulations, by issuing or revoking licenses, and by conducting investigations and issuing reports.

The upshot is that this case involves a typical Executive Branch agency exercising typical Executive Branch powers seeking to determine whether a particular person has violated federal law. The particular person in this instance is a state entity, the South Carolina State Ports Authority, and the agency is acting in response to the request of a private individual. But at first blush it is difficult to see why these special circumstances matter. After all, the Constitution created a Federal Government empowered to enact laws that would bind the States and it empowered that Federal Government to enforce those laws against the States. It also left private individuals perfectly free to complain to the Federal Government about unlawful state activity, and it left the Federal Government free to take subsequent legal action. Where then can the Court find its constitutional principle—the principle that the Constitution forbids an Executive Branch agency to determine through ordinary adjudicative processes whether such a private complaint is justified? As I have said, I cannot find that principle anywhere in the Constitution.

II

The Court's principle lacks any firm anchor in the Constitution's text. The Eleventh Amendment cannot help. It says: "The Judicial power of the United States shall not . . . extend to any suit . . . commenced or prosecuted against one of the . . . States by Citizens of another State." Federal administrative agencies do not exercise the "[j]udicial power of the United States."

The Constitution has "delegated to the United States" the power here in question, the power "[t]o regulate Commerce with foreign Nations, and among the several States." The Court finds within this delegation a hidden reservation, a reservation that, due to sovereign immunity, embodies the legal principle the Court enunciates. But the text of the Tenth Amendment says nothing about any such hidden reservation, one way or the other. Indeed, the Court refers for textual support only to an earlier case, namely Alden v. Maine (1999) (and, through *Alden*, to the texts that *Alden* mentioned. These textual references include: (1) what Alexander Hamilton described as a constitutional "postulate," namely that the States retain their immunity from "suits, without their consent," unless there has been a "surrender" of that immunity "in the plan of the convention"; (2) what the *Alden* majority called "the system of federalism established by the Constitution"; and (3) what the *Alden* majority called "the constitutional design."

Considered purely as constitutional text, these words—"constitutional design," "system of federalism," and "plan of the convention"—suffer several defects. Their language is highly abstract, making them difficult to apply. They invite differing interpretations at least as much as do the Constitution's own broad liberty-protecting phrases, such as "due process of law" or the word "liberty" itself. And compared to these latter phrases, they suffer the additional disadvantage that they do not actually appear anywhere in the Constitution. Regardless, unless supported by considerations of history, of constitutional purpose, or of related consequence, those abstract phrases cannot support today's result.

III

Conceding that its conception of sovereign immunity is ungrounded in the Constitution's text, the Court attempts to support its holding with history. But this effort is similarly destined to fail, because the very history to which the majority turned in *Alden* here argues against the Court's basic analogy—between a federal administrative proceeding triggered by a private citizen and a private citizen's lawsuit against a State.

In any event, the 18th-century was not totally silent. The Framers enunciated in the "plan of the convention," the principle that the Federal Government may sue a State without its consent. They also described in the First Amendment the right of a citizen to petition the Federal Government for a redress of grievances. The first principle applies here because only the Federal Government, not the private party, can—in light of this Court's recent sovereign immunity jurisprudence, bring the ultimate court action necessary legally to force a State to comply with the relevant federal law. The second principle applies here because a private citizen has asked the Federal Government to determine whether the State has complied with federal law and, if not, to take appropriate legal action in court.

Of course these two principles apply only through analogy. (The Court's decision also relies on analogy—one that jumps the separation-of-powers boundary that the Constitution establishes.) Yet the analogy seems apt. A private citizen, believing that a State has violated federal law, seeks a determination by an Executive Branch agency that he is right; the agency will make that determination through use of its own adjudicatory agency processes; and, if the State fails to comply, the Federal Government may bring an action against the State in federal court to enforce the federal law.

Twentieth-century legal history reinforces the appropriateness of this description. The growth of the administrative state has led this Court to determine that administrative agencies are not Article III courts, that they have broad discretion to proceed either through agency adjudication or through rulemaking, and that they may bring administrative enforcement proceedings against States. At a minimum these historically established legal principles argue strongly against any effort to analogize the present proceedings to a lawsuit brought by a private individual against a State in a state court or to an Eleventh Amendment type lawsuit brought by a private individual against a State in a federal court.

This is not to say that the analogy (with a citizen petitioning for federal intervention) is, historically speaking, a perfect one. As the Court points out, the Framers may not have "anticipated the vast growth of the administrative state," and the history of their debates "does not provide direct guidance." But the Court is wrong to ignore the relevance and importance of what the Framers did say. And it is doubly wrong to attach "great" legal "significance" to the absence of 18th- and 19th-century administrative agency experience. Even if those alive in the 18th century did not "anticipat[e] the vast growth of the administrative state," they did write a Constitution designed to provide a framework for Government across the centuries, a framework that is flexible enough to meet modern needs. And we cannot read their silence about particular means as if it were an instruction to forbid their use.

IV

The Court argues that the basic purpose of "sovereign immunity" doctrine—namely preservation of a State's "dignity"—requires application of that doctrine here. It rests this argument upon (1) its efforts to analogize agency proceedings to court proceedings, and (2) its claim that the agency proceedings constitute a form of "compulsion" exercised by a private individual against the State. As I have just explained, I believe its efforts to analogize agencies to courts are, constitutionally speaking, too frail to support its conclusion. Neither can its claim of "compulsion" provide the necessary support.

Viewed from a purely legal perspective, the "compulsion" claim is far too weak. That is because the private individual lacks the legal authority to compel the State to comply with the law. For as I have noted, in light of the Court's recent sovereign immunity decisions, if an individual does bring suit to enforce the Commission's order, the State would arguably be free to claim sovereign immunity. Only the Federal Government, acting through the Commission or the Attorney General, has the authority to compel the State to act.

V

The Court cannot justify today's decision in terms of its practical consequences. The decision, while permitting an agency to bring enforcement actions against States, forbids it to use agency adjudication in order to help decide whether to do so. Consequently the agency must rely more heavily upon its own informal staff investigations in order to decide whether a citizen's complaint has merit. The natural result is less agency flexibility, a larger federal bureaucracy, less fair procedure, and potentially less effective law enforcement. And at least one of these consequences, the forced growth of unnecessary federal bureaucracy, undermines the very constitutional objectives the Court's decision claims to serve.

These consequences are not purely theoretical. The Court's decision may undermine enforcement against state employers of many laws designed to protect worker health and safety. See, e.g., 42 U.S.C. § 7622 (Clean Air Act); 33 U.S.C. § 1367 (Clean Water Act); 15 U.S.C. § 2622 (Toxic Substances Control Act); 42 U.S.C. § 6971 (Solid Waste Disposal Act). And it may inhibit the development of federal fair, rapid, and efficient, informal non-judicial responses to complaints, for example, of improper medical care (involving state hospitals).

The Court's decision threatens to deny the Executive and Legislative Branches of Government the structural flexibility that the Constitution permits and which modern government demands. The Court derives from the abstract notion of state "dignity" a structural principle that limits the powers of both Congress and the President. Its reasoning rests almost exclusively upon the use of a formal analogy, which, as I have said, jumps ordinary separation-of-powers bounds. It places "great significance" upon the 18th century absence of 20th century administrative proceedings. And its conclusion draws little support from considerations of constitutional purpose or related consequence. In its readiness to rest a structural limitation on so little evidence and in its willingness to interpret that limitation so broadly, the majority ignores a historical lesson, reflected in a constitutional understanding that the Court adopted long ago: An overly restrictive judicial interpretation of the Constitution's structural constraints (unlike its protections of certain basic liberties) will undermine the Constitution's own efforts to achieve its far more basic structural aim, the creation of a representative form of government capable of translating the people's will into effective public action.

This understanding, underlying constitutional interpretation since the New Deal, reflects the Constitution's demands for structural flexibility sufficient to adapt substantive laws and institutions to rapidly changing social, economic, and technological conditions. It reflects the comparative inability of the Judiciary to understand either those conditions or the need for new laws and new administrative forms they may create. It reflects the Framers' own aspiration to write a document that would "constitute" a democratic, liberty-protecting form of government that would endure through centuries of change. This understanding led the New Deal Court to reject overly restrictive formalistic interpretations of the Constitution's structural provisions, thereby permitting Congress to enact social and economic legislation that circumstances had led the public to demand. And it led that Court to find in the Constitution authorization for new forms of administration, including independent administrative agencies, with the legal authority flexibly to implement, i.e., to "execute," through adjudication, through rulemaking, and in other ways, the legislation that Congress subsequently enacted.

Today's decision reaffirms the need for continued dissent—unless the consequences of the Court's approach prove anodyne, as I hope, rather than randomly destructive, as I fear.

Chapter 3

The Federal Executive Power

C. The Constitutional Problems of the Administrative State

1. The Non-Delegation Doctrine and Its Demise (casebook, p. 252)

As the casebook indicates (p. 254), since 1936, not a single federal law has been declared unconstitutional by the Supreme Court as an excessive delegation of powers. However, the United States Court of Appeals for the District of Columbia Circuit found that the Clean Air Act was an impermissible delegation of powers to the Environmental Protection Agency. In a unanimous decision, below, the Supreme Court reversed the D.C. Circuit and upheld the delegation. The issue remains open as to whether there is any limit, and if so what, on the ability of Congress to delegate its legislative powers.

WHITMAN v. AMERICAN TRUCKING ASSOCIATION, INC.
121 S. Ct. 903 (2001)

Justice SCALIA delivered the opinion of the Court.

These cases present the question [w]hether § 109(b)(1) of the Clean Air Act (CAA) delegates legislative power to the Administrator of the Environmental Protection Agency (EPA).[1]

Section 109(a) of the CAA requires the Administrator of the EPA to promulgate [National Ambient Air Quality Standards] NAAQS for each air pollutant for which "air quality criteria" have been issued. Once a NAAQS has been promulgated, the Administrator must review the standard (and the criteria on

---

1. There also were statutory questions presented in this case, including "[w]hether the Administrator may consider the costs of implementation in setting national ambient air quality standards (NAAQS) under § 109(b)(1); [w]hether the Court of Appeals had jurisdiction to review the EPA's interpretation of Part D of Title I of the CAA, with respect to implementing the revised ozone NAAQS; [i]f so, whether the EPA's interpretation of that part was permissible." The Court's discussion of these issues is not included because these are statutory and not constitutional questions. [Footnote by casebook author.]

which it is based) "at five-year intervals" and make "such revisions . . . as may
be appropriate." These cases arose when, on July 18, 1997, the Administrator
revised the NAAQS for particulate matter (PM) and ozone.

The District of Columbia Circuit agreed with the respondents that § 109(b)(1)
delegated legislative power to the Administrator in contravention of the United
States Constitution, Art. I, § 1, because it found that the EPA had interpreted the
statute to provide no "intelligible principle" to guide the agency's exercise of
authority. The court thought, however, that the EPA could perhaps avoid the
unconstitutional delegation by adopting a restrictive construction of § 109(b)(1),
so instead of declaring the section unconstitutional the court remanded the
NAAQS to the agency.

[I]

In Lead Industries Assn., Inc. v. EPA, the District of Columbia Circuit held that
"economic considerations [may] play no part in the promulgation of ambient air
quality standards under Section 109" of the CAA. In the present cases, the court
adhered to that holding, as it had done on many other occasions. Respondents
argue that these decisions are incorrect. We disagree; and since the first step in
assessing whether a statute delegates legislative power is to determine what authority the statute confers, we address that issue of interpretation first and reach
respondents' constitutional arguments in Part [II].

Section 109(b)(1) instructs the EPA to set primary ambient air quality standards "the attainment and maintenance of which . . . are requisite to protect the
public health" with "an adequate margin of safety." Here were it not for the
hundreds of pages of briefing respondents have submitted on the issue, one
would have thought it fairly clear that this text does not permit the EPA to consider costs in setting the standards. The language, as one scholar has noted, "is
absolute." D. Currie, Air Pollution: Federal Law and Analysis 4-15 (1981). The
EPA, "based on" the information about health effects contained in the technical
"criteria" documents compiled under § 108(a)(2), is to identify the maximum
airborne concentration of a pollutant that the public health can tolerate, decrease
the concentration to provide an "adequate" margin of safety, and set the standard
at that level. Nowhere are the costs of achieving such a standard made part of
that initial calculation. The text of § 109(b), interpreted in its statutory and historical context and with appreciation for its importance to the CAA as a whole,
unambiguously bars cost considerations from the NAAQS-setting process, and
thus ends the matter for us as well as the EPA.

III

Section 109(b)(1) of the CAA instructs the EPA to set "ambient air quality standards the attainment and maintenance of which in the judgment of the Administrator, based on [the] criteria [documents of § 108] and allowing an adequate

margin of safety, are requisite to protect the public health." The Court of Appeals held that this section as interpreted by the Administrator did not provide an "intelligible principle" to guide the EPA's exercise of authority in setting NAAQS. "[The] EPA," it said, "lack[ed] any determinate criteria for drawing lines. It has failed to state intelligibly how much is too much." The court hence found that the EPA's interpretation (but not the statute itself) violated the nondelegation doctrine. We disagree.

In a delegation challenge, the constitutional question is whether the statute has delegated legislative power to the agency. Article I, § 1, of the Constitution vests "[a]ll legislative Powers herein granted . . . in a Congress of the United States." This text permits no delegation of those powers, and so we repeatedly have said that when Congress confers decisionmaking authority upon agencies Congress must "lay down by legislative act an intelligible principle to which the person or body authorized to [act] is directed to conform." We have never suggested that an agency can cure an unlawful delegation of legislative power by adopting in its discretion a limiting construction of the statute. The idea that an agency can cure an unconstitutionally standardless delegation of power by declining to exercise some of that power seems to us internally contradictory. The very choice of which portion of the power to exercise—that is to say, the prescription of the standard that Congress had omitted—would itself be an exercise of the forbidden legislative authority. Whether the statute delegates legislative power is a question for the courts, and an agency's voluntary self-denial has no bearing upon the answer.

We agree with the Solicitor General that the text of § 109(b)(1) of the CAA at a minimum requires that "[f]or a discrete set of pollutants and based on published air quality criteria that reflect the latest scientific knowledge, [the] EPA must establish uniform national standards at a level that is requisite to protect public health from the adverse effects of the pollutant in the ambient air." Requisite, in turn, "mean[s] sufficient, but not more than necessary." These limits on the EPA's discretion are strikingly similar to the ones we approved in Touby v. United States (1991), which permitted the Attorney General to designate a drug as a controlled substance for purposes of criminal drug enforcement if doing so was "necessary to avoid an imminent hazard to the public safety." They also resemble the Occupational Safety and Health Act provision requiring the agency to "set the standard which most adequately assures, to the extent feasible, on the basis of the best available evidence, that no employee will suffer any impairment of health"—which the Court upheld in Industrial Union Dept., AFL-CIO v. American Petroleum Institute (1980), and which even then-Justice Rehnquist, who alone in that case thought the statute violated the nondelegation doctrine, would have upheld if, like the statute here, it did not permit economic costs to be considered.

The scope of discretion § 109(b)(1) allows is in fact well within the outer limits of our nondelegation precedents. In the history of the Court we have found the requisite "intelligible principle" lacking in only two statutes, one of which provided literally no guidance for the exercise of discretion, and the other of which conferred authority to regulate the entire economy on the basis of no more precise a standard than stimulating the economy by assuring "fair competition." See Panama Refining Co. v. Ryan (1935); A.L.A. Schechter Poultry Corp. v. United States (1935). We have, on the other hand, upheld the validity of § 11(b)(2) of the Public Utility Holding Company Act of 1935, which gave the Securities and Exchange Commission authority to modify the structure of holding company systems so as to ensure that they are not "unduly or unnecessarily complicate[d]" and do not "unfairly or inequitably distribute voting power among security holders." American Power & Light Co. v. SEC (1946). We have approved the wartime conferral of agency power to fix the prices of commodities at a level that "will be generally fair and equitable and will effectuate the [in some respects conflicting] purposes of th[e] Act." Yakus v. United States (1944). And we have found an "intelligible principle" in various statutes authorizing regulation in the "public interest." See, e.g., National Broadcasting Co. v. United States (1943) (FCC's power to regulate airwaves); New York Central Securities Corp. v. United States (1932) (ICC's power to approve railroad consolidations). In short, we have "almost never felt qualified to second-guess Congress regarding the permissible degree of policy judgment that can be left to those executing or applying the law."

[E]ven in sweeping regulatory schemes we have never demanded, as the Court of Appeals did here, that statutes provide a "determinate criterion" for saying "how much [of the regulated harm] is too much." It is therefore not conclusive for delegation purposes that, as respondents argue, ozone and particulate matter are "nonthreshold" pollutants that inflict a continuum of adverse health effects at any airborne concentration greater than zero, and hence require the EPA to make judgments of degree. "[A] certain degree of discretion, and thus of lawmaking, inheres in most executive or judicial action." Mistretta v. United States (Scalia, J., dissenting). Section 109(b)(1) of the CAA, which to repeat we interpret as requiring the EPA to set air quality standards at the level that is "requisite"—that is, not lower or higher than is necessary—to protect the public health with an adequate margin of safety, fits comfortably within the scope of discretion permitted by our precedent. We therefore reverse the judgment of the Court of Appeals.

D.   Separation of Powers and Foreign Policy
   (casebook, p. 281)

Material on this topic is presented in the Introduction to this Supplement, in the discussion of the constitutionality of President Bush's order for military tribunals.

Chapter 4

Limits on State Regulatory and Taxing Power

A. Preemption of State and Local Laws

1. Express Preemption (casebook, p. 306)

The casebook uses Cipolone v. Liggett Group, Inc. to illustrate the issue of express preemption. *Cipollone* concerns whether federal regulation of cigarettes, and especially cigarette advertising, preempts liability for cigarette manufacturers under state law. In Lorillard Tobacco Co. v. Reilly, below, the Court considered the constitutionality of Massachusetts regulations of the advertising of tobacco products. The regulations prevented advertising of tobacco products—cigarettes, cigars, and smokeless tobacco—within 1,000 feet of a school or a playground. Also, the regulations limited advertising in stores selling such products—called "point of sale" advertising—by requiring that the ads be at least five feet above the ground so as to not be at the eye level of children.

The Court, in a 5-4 decision, declared that the regulation of cigarette advertising was preempted by federal law. This part of the opinion is presented below, along with Justice Stevens' dissenting opinion on this issue. The federal law, however, only applies to cigarettes, not to cigars or smokeless tobacco products. Therefore, preemption did not apply to the latter products. The Court then considered whether the restrictions on advertising of these products violated the First Amendment and concluded that the limits on commercial speech were unconstitutional. The part of the opinion dealing with commercial speech, and the concurring opinions concerning that issue, are presented in Chapter 9.

LORILLARD TOBACCO CO. v. REILLY
121 S. Ct. 2404 (June 28, 2001)

O'CONNOR, J., delivered the opinion of the Court, Parts I, II-C, and II-D of which were unanimous; Parts II-A, II-B of which were joined by REHNQUIST, C.J., and SCALIA, KENNEDY, and THOMAS, JJ.

In January 1999, the Attorney General of Massachusetts promulgated comprehensive regulations governing the advertising and sale of cigarettes, smokeless tobacco, and cigars. The first question presented for our review is whether certain cigarette advertising regulations are pre-empted by the Federal Cigarette Labeling and Advertising Act (FCLAA).

I

In November 1998, Massachusetts, along with over 40 other States, reached a landmark agreement with major manufacturers in the cigarette industry. The signatory States settled their claims against these companies in exchange for monetary payments and permanent injunctive relief. At the press conference covering Massachusetts' decision to sign the agreement, then-Attorney General Scott Harshbarger announced that as one of his last acts in office, he would create consumer protection regulations to restrict advertising and sales practices for tobacco products. He explained that the regulations were necessary in order to "close holes" in the settlement agreement and "to stop Big Tobacco from recruiting new customers among the children of Massachusetts."

In January 1999, pursuant to his authority to prevent unfair or deceptive practices in trade, the Massachusetts Attorney General (Attorney General) promulgated regulations governing the sale and advertisement of cigarettes, smokeless tobacco, and cigars. The purpose of the regulations is "to eliminate deception and unfairness in the way tobacco products are marketed, sold and distributed in Massachusetts in order to address the incidence of tobacco use by children under legal age . . . [and] in order to prevent access to such products by underage consumers."

The cigarette and smokeless tobacco regulations being challenged before this Court provide:

> (2) Retail Outlet Sales Practices.   Except as otherwise provided, it shall be an unfair or deceptive act or practice for any person who sells or distributes cigarettes or smokeless tobacco products through a retail outlet located within Massachusetts to engage in any of the following retail outlet sales practices:
>> (c) Using self-service displays of cigarettes or smokeless tobacco products;
>> (d) Failing to place cigarettes and smokeless tobacco products out of the reach of all consumers, and in a location accessible only to outlet personnel.
>
> (5) Advertising Restrictions.   Except as provided, it shall be an unfair or deceptive act or practice for any manufacturer, distributor or retailer to engage in any of the following practices:
>> (a) Outdoor advertising, including advertising in enclosed stadiums and advertising from within a retail establishment that is directed toward or visible from the outside of the establishment, in any location that is within a 1,000 foot radius of any public playground, playground area in a public park, elementary school or secondary school;
>> (b) Point-of-sale advertising of cigarettes or smokeless tobacco products any portion of which is placed lower than five feet from the floor of any retail establishment which is located within a one thousand foot radius of any

public playground, playground area in a public park, elementary school or secondary school, and which is not an adult-only retail establishment.

II

Before reaching the First Amendment issues, we must decide to what extent federal law pre-empts the Attorney General's regulations. The cigarette petitioners contend that the FCLAA pre-empts the Attorney General's cigarette advertising regulations.

A

In the FCLAA, Congress has crafted a comprehensive federal scheme governing the advertising and promotion of cigarettes. The FCLAA's pre-emption provision provides:

> (a) Additional statements
> No statement relating to smoking and health, other than the statement required by section 1333 of this title, shall be required on any cigarette package.
> (b) State regulations
> No requirement or prohibition based on smoking and health shall be imposed under State law with respect to the advertising or promotion of any cigarettes the packages of which are labeled in conformity with the provisions of this chapter.

The FCLAA's pre-emption provision does not cover smokeless tobacco or cigars.

In this case, our task is to identify the domain expressly pre-empted, because "an express definition of the pre-emptive reach of a statute . . . supports a reasonable inference . . . that Congress did not intend to pre-empt other matters." Congressional purpose is the "ultimate touchstone" of our inquiry. Because "federal law is said to bar state action in [a] fiel[d] of traditional state regulation," namely, advertising, we "wor[k] on the assumption that the historic police powers of the States [a]re not to be superseded by the Federal Act unless that [is] the clear and manifest purpose of Congress." In the pre-emption provision, Congress unequivocally precludes the requirement of any additional statements on "cigarette packages beyond those provided in [the statute]." Congress further precludes States or localities from imposing any requirement or prohibition based on smoking and health with respect to the advertising and promotion of cigarettes. Without question, the second clause is more expansive than the first; it employs far more sweeping language to describe the state action that is pre-empted. We must give meaning to each element of the pre-emption provision. We are aided in our interpretation by considering the predecessor pre-emption provision and the circumstances in which the current language was adopted.

In 1964, the groundbreaking Report of the Surgeon General's Advisory Committee on Smoking and Health concluded that "[c]igarette smoking is a health hazard of sufficient importance in the United States to warrant appropriate remedial action." In 1965, Congress enacted the FCLAA as a proactive measure in the face of impending regulation by federal agencies and the States. The purpose of the FCLAA was twofold: to inform the public adequately about the hazards of cigarette smoking, and to protect the national economy from interference due to diverse, nonuniform, and confusing cigarette labeling and advertising regulations with respect to the relationship between smoking and health. The FCLAA prescribed a label for cigarette packages. Section 5 of the FCLAA included a pre-emption provision in which "Congress spoke precisely and narrowly." Subsection 5(a) prohibited any requirement of additional statements on cigarette packaging. Subsection 5(b) provided that "[n]o statement relating to smoking and health shall be required in the advertising of any cigarettes the packages of which are labeled in conformity with the provisions of this Act."

In 1969, House and Senate committees held hearings about the health effects of cigarette smoking and advertising by the cigarette industry. The bill that emerged from the House of Representatives strengthened the warning and maintained the pre-emption provision. The Senate amended that bill, adding the ban on radio and television advertising, and changing the pre-emption language to its present form.

The final result was the Public Health Cigarette Smoking Act of 1969, in which Congress, following the Senate's amendments, made three significant changes to the FCLAA. First, Congress drafted a new label that read: "Warning: The Surgeon General Has Determined That Cigarette Smoking Is Dangerous to Your Health." Second, Congress declared it unlawful to advertise cigarettes on any medium of electronic communication subject to the jurisdiction of the FCC. Finally, Congress enacted the current pre-emption provision, which proscribes any "requirement or prohibition based on smoking and health . . . imposed under State law with respect to the advertising or promotion" of cigarettes. The new subsection 5(b) did not pre-empt regulation by federal agencies, freeing the FTC to impose warning requirements in cigarette advertising. The new pre-emption provision, like its predecessor, only applied to cigarettes, and not other tobacco products.

In 1984, Congress again amended the FCLAA in the Comprehensive Smoking Education Act. The purpose of the Act was to "provide a new strategy for making Americans more aware of any adverse health effects of smoking, to assure the timely and widespread dissemination of research findings and to enable individuals to make informed decisions about smoking." The Act established a series of warnings to appear on a rotating basis on cigarette packages and in cigarette advertising, and directed the Health and Human Services Secretary to create and implement an educational program about the health effects of cigarette smoking.

The FTC has continued to report on trade practices in the cigarette industry. In 1999, the first year since the master settlement agreement, the FTC reported that the cigarette industry expended $8.24 billion on advertising and promotions, the largest expenditure ever. Substantial increases were found in point-of-sale promotions, payments made to retailers to facilitate sales, and retail offers such as buy one, get one free, or product giveaways. Substantial decreases, however, were reported for outdoor advertising and transit advertising.

The scope and meaning of the current pre-emption provision become clearer once we consider the original pre-emption language and the amendments to the FCLAA. Without question, "the plain language of the pre-emption provision in the 1969 Act is much broader." Rather than preventing only "statements," the amended provision reaches all "requirement[s] or prohibition[s] . . . imposed under State law." And, although the former statute reached only statements "in the advertising," the current provision governs "with respect to the advertising or promotion" of cigarettes. Congress expanded the pre-emption provision with respect to the States, and at the same time, it allowed the FTC to regulate cigarette advertising. Congress also prohibited cigarette advertising in electronic media altogether. Viewed in light of the context in which the current pre-emption provision was adopted, we must determine whether the FCLAA pre-empts Massachusetts' regulations governing outdoor and point-of-sale advertising of cigarettes.

B

The Court of Appeals acknowledged that the FCLAA pre-empts any "requirement or prohibition based on smoking and health . . . with respect to the advertising or promotion of . . . cigarettes," but concluded that the FCLAA does not nullify Massachusetts' cigarette advertising regulations. The court concentrated its analysis on whether the regulations are "with respect to" advertising and promotion, relying on two of its sister Circuits to conclude that the FCLAA only pre-empts regulations of the content of cigarette advertising. The Court of Appeals also reasoned that the Attorney General's regulations are a form of zoning, a traditional area of state power; therefore the presumption against pre-emption applied.

The cigarette petitioners maintain that the Court of Appeals' "with respect to" analysis is inconsistent with the FCLAA's statutory text and legislative history, and gives the States license to prohibit almost all cigarette advertising. Petitioners also maintain that there is no basis for construing the pre-emption provision to prohibit only content-based advertising regulations.

Turning first to the language in the pre-emption provision relied upon by the Court of Appeals, we reject the notion that the Attorney General's cigarette advertising regulations are not "with respect to" advertising and promotion. We disagree with the Court of Appeals' analogy to the Employee Retirement Income Security Act of 1974 (ERISA). In some cases concerning ERISA's pre-emption of state law, the Court has had to decide whether a particular state law "relates to" an employee benefit plan covered by ERISA even though the state law makes no express reference to such a plan. Here, however, there is no question about an indirect relationship between the regulations and cigarette advertising because the regulations expressly target cigarette advertising.

Before this Court, the Attorney General focuses on a different phrase in the pre-emption provision: "based on smoking and health." The Attorney General argues that the cigarette advertising regulations are not "based on smoking and health," because they do not involve health-related content in cigarette advertising but instead target youth exposure to cigarette advertising. To be sure, Members of this Court have debated the precise meaning of "based on smoking and health," but we cannot agree with the Attorney General's narrow construction of the phrase.

As Congress enacted the current pre-emption provision, Congress did not concern itself solely with health warnings for cigarettes. In the 1969 amendments, Congress not only enhanced its scheme to warn the public about the hazards of cigarette smoking, but also sought to protect the public, including youth, from being inundated with images of cigarette smoking in advertising. In pursuit of the latter goal, Congress banned electronic media advertising of cigarettes. And to the extent that Congress contemplated additional targeted regulation of cigarette advertising, it vested that authority in the FTC.

The context in which Congress crafted the current pre-emption provision leads us to conclude that Congress prohibited state cigarette advertising regulations motivated by concerns about smoking and health. Massachusetts has attempted to address the incidence of underage cigarette smoking by regulating advertising, much like Congress' ban on cigarette advertising in electronic media. At bottom, the concern about youth exposure to cigarette advertising is intertwined with the concern about cigarette smoking and health. Thus the Attorney General's attempt to distinguish one concern from the other must be rejected.

The Attorney General next claims that the State's outdoor and point-of-sale advertising regulations for cigarettes are not pre-empted because they govern the location, and not the content, of advertising. This is also Justice STEVENS' main point with respect to pre-emption.

The content versus location distinction has some surface appeal. The pre-emption provision immediately follows the section of the FCLAA that prescribes warnings. The pre-emption provision itself refers to cigarettes "labeled in conformity with" the statute. But the content/location distinction cannot be squared with the language of the pre-emption provision, which reaches all "requirements" and "prohibitions" "imposed under State law." A distinction between the content of advertising and the location of advertising in the FCLAA also cannot be reconciled with Congress' own location-based restriction, which bans advertising in electronic media, but not elsewhere. We are not at liberty to pick and choose which provisions in the legislative scheme we will consider, but must examine the FCLAA as a whole.

Justice Stevens maintains that Congress did not intend to displace state regulation of the location of cigarette advertising. There is a critical distinction, however, between generally applicable zoning regulations, and regulations targeting cigarette advertising. The latter type of regulation, which is inevitably motivated by concerns about smoking and health, squarely contradicts the FCLAA. The FCLAA's comprehensive warnings, advertising restrictions, and pre-emption provision would make little sense if a State or locality could simply target and ban all cigarette advertising.

In sum, we fail to see how the FCLAA and its pre-emption provision permit a distinction between the specific concern about minors and cigarette advertising and the more general concern about smoking and health in cigarette advertising, especially in light of the fact that Congress crafted a legislative solution for those very concerns. We also conclude that a distinction between state regulation of the location as opposed to the content of cigarette advertising has no foundation in the text of the pre-emption provision. Congress pre-empted state cigarette advertising regulations like the Attorney General's because they would upset federal legislative choices to require specific warnings and to impose the ban on cigarette advertising in electronic media in order to address concerns about smoking and health. Accordingly, we hold that the Attorney General's outdoor and point-of-sale advertising regulations targeting cigarettes are pre-empted by the FCLAA.

C

Although the FCLAA prevents States and localities from imposing special requirements or prohibitions "based on smoking and health" "with respect to the advertising or promotion" of cigarettes, that language still leaves significant power in the hands of States to impose generally applicable zoning regulations and to regulate conduct. Although Congress has taken into account the unique concerns about cigarette smoking and health in advertising, there is no indication that Congress intended to displace local community interests in general regulations of the location of billboards or large marquee advertising, or that Congress intended cigarette advertisers to be afforded special treatment in that regard. Restrictions on the location and size of advertisements that apply to cigarettes on equal terms with other products appear to be outside the ambit of the pre-emption provision. Such restrictions are not "based on smoking and health."

The FCLAA also does not foreclose all state regulation of conduct as it relates to the sale or use of cigarettes. The FCLAA's pre-emption provision explicitly governs state regulations of "advertising or promotion." Accordingly, the FCLAA does not pre-empt state laws prohibiting cigarette sales to minors. To the contrary, there is an established congressional policy that supports such laws; Congress has required States to prohibit tobacco sales to minors as a condition of receiving federal block grant funding for substance abuse treatment activities.

Justice STEVENS, with whom Justices SOUTER, GINSBURG, and BREYER join, dissenting [on the preemption issue]:

This suit presents two separate sets of issues. The first—involving preemption—is straightforward. The second—involving the First Amendment—is more complex. Because I strongly disagree with the Court's conclusion that the Federal Cigarette Labeling and Advertising Act of 1965 (FCLAA or Act), precludes States and localities from regulating the location of cigarette advertising, I dissent from Parts II-A and II-B of the Court's opinion.

I

As the majority acknowledges, under prevailing principles, any examination of the scope of a preemption provision must "'start with the assumption that the historic police powers of the States [are] not to be superseded by . . . Federal Act unless that [is] the clear and manifest purpose of Congress.'" Cipollone v. Liggett Group, Inc. (1992). As the regulations at issue in this suit implicate two powers that lie at the heart of the States' traditional police power—the power to regulate land usage and the power to protect the health and safety of minors—our precedents require that the Court construe the preemption provision "narrow[ly]." If Congress' intent to preempt a particular category of regulation is ambiguous, such regulations are not preempted.

The text of the preemption provision must be viewed in context, with proper attention paid to the history, structure, and purpose of the regulatory scheme in which it appears. An assessment of the scope of a preemption provision must give effect to a "reasoned understanding of the way in which Congress intended the statute and its surrounding regulatory scheme to affect business, consumers, and the law."

This task, properly performed, leads inexorably to the conclusion that Congress did not intend to preempt state and local regulations of the location of cigarette advertising when it adopted the provision at issue in this suit. In both 1965 and 1969, Congress made clear the purposes of its regulatory endeavor, explaining with precision the federal policies motivating its actions. According to the acts, Congress adopted a "comprehensive Federal program to deal with cigarette labeling and advertising with respect to any relationship between smoking and health," for two reasons: (1) to inform the public that smoking may be hazardous to health and (2) to ensure that commerce and the interstate economy not be "impeded by diverse, nonuniform, and confusing cigarette labeling and advertising regulations with respect to any relationship between smoking and health."

In order to serve the second purpose it was necessary to preempt state regulation of the content of both cigarette labels and cigarette advertising. If one State required the inclusion of a particular warning on the package of cigarettes while another State demanded a different formulation, cigarette manufacturers would have been forced into the difficult and costly practice of producing different packaging for use in different States. To foreclose the waste of resources that would be entailed by such a patchwork regulatory system, Congress expressly precluded other regulators from requiring the placement on cigarette packaging of any "statement relating to smoking and health." Similar concerns applied to cigarette advertising. If different regulatory bodies required that different warnings or statements be used when cigarette manufacturers advertised their products, the text and layout of a company's ads would have had to differ from locale to locale. The resulting costs would have come with little or no health benefit. Moreover, given the nature of publishing, it might well have been the case that cigarette companies would not have been able to advertise in national publications without violating the laws of some jurisdictions. In response to these concerns, Congress adopted a parallel provision preempting state and local regulations requiring inclusion in cigarette advertising of any "statement relating to smoking and health."

There was, however, no need to interfere with state or local zoning laws or other regulations prescribing limitations on the location of signs or billboards. Laws prohibiting a cigarette company from hanging a billboard near a school in Boston in no way conflict with laws permitting the hanging of such a billboard in other jurisdictions. Nor would such laws even impose a significant administrative burden on would-be advertisers, as the great majority of localities impose general restrictions on signage, thus requiring advertisers to examine local law before posting signs whether or not cigarette-specific laws are preempted.

All signs point inescapably to the conclusion that Congress only intended to preempt content regulations in the 1969 Act. It is of crucial importance that, in making modifications of the preemption provision, Congress did not alter the statement laying out the federal policies the provision was intended to serve. To this day, the stated federal policies in this area are (1) to inform the public of the dangers of cigarette smoking and (2) to protect the cigarette companies from the burdens of confusing and contradictory state regulations of their labels and advertisements. The retention of this provision unchanged is strong evidence that Congress' only intention in expanding the preemption clause was to capture forms of content regulation that had fallen through the cracks of the prior provision—for example, state laws prohibiting cigarette manufacturers from making particular claims in their advertising or requiring them to utilize specified layouts or include particular graphics in their marketing.

The legislative history of the provision also supports such a reading. The record does not contain any evidence that Congress intended to expand the scope of preemption beyond content restrictions. To the contrary, the Senate Report makes it clear that the changes merely "clarified" the scope of the original provision. Even as amended, Congress perceived the provision as "narrowly phrased" and emphasized that its purpose is to "avoid the chaos created by a multiplicity of conflicting regulations." According to the Senate Report, the changes "in no way affect the power of any state or political subdivision of any state with respect to . . . the sale of cigarettes to minors . . . or similar police regulations."

I am firmly convinced that, when Congress amended the preemption provision in 1969, it did not intend to expand the application of the provision beyond content regulations. I, therefore, find the conclusion inescapable that the zoning regulation at issue in this suit is not a "requirement or prohibition . . . with respect to . . . advertising" within the meaning of the 1969 Act. Even if I were not so convinced, however, I would still dissent from the Court's conclusion with regard to preemption, because the provision is, at the very least, ambiguous. The historical record simply does not reflect that it was Congress' "'clear and manifest purpose,'" to preempt attempts by States to utilize their traditional zoning authority to protect the health and welfare of minors. Absent such a manifest purpose, Massachusetts and its sister States retain their traditional police powers.

Chapter 5

The Structure of the Constitution's Protection of Civil Rights and Civil Liberties

B. The Application of the Bill of Rights to the States

3. The Incorporation of the Bill of Rights into the Due Process Clause of the Fourteenth Amendment

THE CONTENT OF INCORPORATED RIGHTS (casebook, p. 400)

In Zelman v. Simmons-Harris, 122 S. Ct. 2460 (2002), Justice Thomas, in a concurring opinion, argued that the Establishment Clause of the First Amendment should not have the same content when applied to the states as applied to the federal government. Justice Thomas's concurring opinion, and the decision in *Zelman* approving vouchers, is presented at length in Chapter 10 below. As to incorporation, Justice Thomas said:*

> The Establishment Clause of the First Amendment states that "Congress shall make no law respecting an establishment of religion." On its face, this provision places no limit on the States with regard to religion. The Establishment Clause originally protected States, and by extension their citizens, from the imposition of an established religion by the Federal Government. Whether and how this Clause should constrain state action under the Fourteenth Amendment is a more difficult question.
>
> When rights are incorporated against the States through the Fourteenth Amendment they should advance, not constrain, individual liberty. Consequently, in the context of the Establishment Clause, it may well be that state action should be evaluated on different terms than similar action by the Federal Government. "States, while bound to observe strict neutrality, should be freer to experiment with involvement [in religion]—on a neutral basis—than the Federal Government." Thus, while the Federal Government may "make no law respecting an establish-

---

*Justice Thomas's concurring opinion, including the excerpt here, is presented below in Chapter 10. The discussion on incorporation is also presented here because it might be useful as part of discussing the issue of incorporation, apart from other aspects of the constitutionality of voucher programs that can be used in parochial schools.

ment of religion," the States may pass laws that include or touch on religious matters so long as these laws do not impede free exercise rights or any other individual religious liberty interest. By considering the particular religious liberty right alleged to be invaded by a State, federal courts can strike a proper balance between the demands of the Fourteenth Amendment on the one hand and the federalism prerogatives of States on the other.

Whatever the textual and historical merits of incorporating the Establishment Clause, I can accept that the Fourteenth Amendment protects religious liberty rights. But I cannot accept its use to oppose neutral programs of school choice through the incorporation of the Establishment Clause. There would be a tragic irony in converting the Fourteenth Amendment's guarantee of individual liberty into a prohibition on the exercise of educational choice.

C.   The Application of the Bill of Rights and the Constitution to Private Conduct

2.   The Exceptions to the State Action Doctrine (casebook, p. 405)

As the casebook indicates, the Supreme Court has recognized two narrow exceptions to the state action requirement: the public functions exception, which provides that private conduct must comply with the Constitution when it is performing a task that has been traditionally, exclusively done by the government; and the entanglement exception, in which the government affirmatively authorizes, encourages, or facilitates unconstitutional conduct. In Brentwood Academy v. Tennessee Secondary School Athletic Association, the Court finds that a private entity is a state actor based on its "entwinement" with the government. The key question, not answered by the Court, is how "entwinement" relates to "entanglement." Is this a new exception to the state action requirement? If so, how is it different? Is it that entanglement requires government encouragement, but entwinement does not? None of these questions are addressed by the Court, but they undoubtedly are ones that will be litigated in the future and thus are ones to consider as you read this decision.

BRENTWOOD ACADEMY v. TENNESSEE SECONDARY SCHOOL ATHLETIC ASSOCIATION
121 S. Ct. 924 (2001)

Justice SOUTER delivered the opinion of the Court.

The issue is whether a statewide association incorporated to regulate interscholastic athletic competition among public and private secondary schools may be regarded as engaging in state action when it enforces a rule against a member school. The association in question here includes most public schools located within the State, acts through their representatives, draws its officers from them, is largely funded by their dues and income received in their stead, and has historically been seen to regulate in lieu of the State Board of Education's exercise of its own authority. We hold that the association's regulatory activity may and should be treated as state action owing to the pervasive entwinement of state school officials in the structure of the association, there being no offsetting reason to see the association's acts in any other way.

I

Respondent Tennessee Secondary School Athletic Association (Association) is a not-for-profit membership corporation organized to regulate interscholastic sport among the public and private high schools in Tennessee that belong to it. No school is forced to join, but without any other authority actually regulating interscholastic athletics, it enjoys the memberships of almost all the State's public high schools (some 290 of them or 84% of the Association's voting membership), far outnumbering the 55 private schools that belong. A member school's team may play or scrimmage only against the team of another member, absent a dispensation.

The Association's rulemaking arm is its legislative council, while its board of control tends to administration. The voting membership of each of these nine-person committees is limited under the Association's bylaws to high school principals, assistant principals, and superintendents elected by the member schools, and the public school administrators who so serve typically attend meetings during regular school hours. Although the Association's staff members are not paid by the State, they are eligible to join the State's public retirement system for its employees. Member schools pay dues to the Association, though the bulk of its revenue is gate receipts at member teams' football and basketball tournaments, many of them held in public arenas rented by the Association.

The constitution, bylaws, and rules of the Association set standards of school membership and the eligibility of students to play in interscholastic games. Each school, for example, is regulated in awarding financial aid, most coaches must have a Tennessee state teaching license, and players must meet minimum academic standards and hew to limits on student employment. Under the by-laws, "in all matters pertaining to the athletic relations of his school," the principal is responsible to the Association, which has the power "to suspend, to fine, or otherwise penalize any member school for the violation of any of the rules of the Association or for other just cause."

Ever since the Association was incorporated in 1925, Tennessee's State Board of Education (State Board) has (to use its own words) acknowledged the corporation's functions "in providing standards, rules and regulations for inter-scholastic competition in the public schools of Tennessee." Specifically, in

1972, it went so far as to adopt a rule expressly "designat[ing]" the Association as "the organization to supervise and regulate the athletic activities in which the public junior and senior high schools in Tennessee participate on an interscholastic basis." [O]n several occasions over the next 20 years, the State Board reviewed, approved, or reaffirmed its approval of the recruiting Rule at issue in this case. In 1996, however, the State Board dropped the original Rule expressly designating the Association as regulator; it substituted a statement "recogniz[ing] the value of participation in interscholastic athletics and the role of [the Association] in coordinating interscholastic athletic competition," while "authoriz[ing] the public schools of the state to voluntarily maintain membership in [the Association]."

The action before us responds to a 1997 regulatory enforcement proceeding brought against petitioner, Brentwood Academy, a private parochial high school member of the Association. The Association's board of control found that Brentwood violated a rule prohibiting "undue influence" in recruiting athletes, when it wrote to incoming students and their parents about spring football practice. The Association accordingly placed Brentwood's athletic program on probation for four years, declared its football and boys' basketball teams ineligible to compete in playoffs for two years, and imposed a $3,000 fine. When these penalties were imposed, all the voting members of the board of control and legislative council were public school administrators.

Brentwood sued the Association and its executive director in federal court under 42 U.S.C. § 1983, claiming that enforcement of the Rule was state action and a violation of the First and Fourteenth Amendments.

II

A

Our cases try to plot a line between state action subject to Fourteenth Amendment scrutiny and private conduct (however exceptionable) that is not. The judicial obligation is not only to "'preserv[e] an area of individual freedom by limiting the reach of federal law' and avoi[d] the imposition of responsibility on a State for conduct it could not control," but also to assure that constitutional standards are invoked "when it can be said that the State is responsible for the specific conduct of which the plaintiff complains." If the Fourteenth Amendment is not to be displaced, therefore, its ambit cannot be a simple line between States and people operating outside formally governmental organizations, and the deed of an ostensibly private organization or individual is to be treated sometimes as if a State had caused it to be performed. Thus, we say that state action may be found if, though only if, there is such a "close nexus between the State and the challenged action" that seemingly private behavior "may be fairly treated as that of the State itself."

What is fairly attributable is a matter of normative judgment, and the criteria lack rigid simplicity. From the range of circumstances that could point toward the State behind an individual face, no one fact can function as a necessary condition across the board for finding state action; nor is any set of circumstances absolutely sufficient, for there may be some countervailing reason against attributing activity to the government.

Our cases have identified a host of facts that can bear on the fairness of such an attribution. We have, for example, held that a challenged activity may be state action when it results from the State's exercise of "coercive power," when the State provides "significant encouragement, either overt or covert," or when a private actor operates as a "willful participant in joint activity with the State or its agents." We have treated a nominally private entity as a state actor when it is controlled by an "agency of the State," when it has been delegated a public function by the State, when it is "entwined with governmental policies" or when government is "entwined in [its] management or control."

Amidst such variety, examples may be the best teachers, and examples from our cases are unequivocal in showing that the character of a legal entity is determined neither by its expressly private characterization in statutory law, nor by the failure of the law to acknowledge the entity's inseparability from recognized government officials or agencies.

NCAA v. Tarkanian (1989) arose when an undoubtedly state actor, the University of Nevada, suspended its basketball coach, Tarkanian, in order to comply with rules and recommendations of the National Collegiate Athletic Association (NCAA). The coach charged the NCAA with state action, arguing that the state university had delegated its own functions to the NCAA, clothing the latter with authority to make and apply the university's rules, the result being joint action making the NCAA a state actor.

To be sure, it is not the strict holding in *Tarkanian* that points to our view of this case, for we found no state action on the part of the NCAA. We could see, on the one hand, that the university had some part in setting the NCAA's rules, and the Supreme Court of Nevada had gone so far as to hold that the NCAA had been delegated the university's traditionally exclusive public authority over personnel. But on the other side, the NCAA's policies were shaped not by the University of Nevada alone, but by several hundred member institutions, most of them having no connection with Nevada, and exhibiting no color of Nevada law. Since it was difficult to see the NCAA, not as a collective membership, but as surrogate for the one State, we held the organization's connection with Nevada too insubstantial to ground a state action claim.

But dictum in *Tarkanian* pointed to a contrary result on facts like ours, with an organization whose member public schools are all within a single State. "The situation would, of course, be different if the [Association's] membership consisted entirely of institutions located within the same State, many of them public institutions created by the same sovereign."

B

Just as we foresaw in *Tarkanian*, the "necessarily fact-bound inquiry," leads to the conclusion of state action here. The nominally private character of the Association is overborne by the pervasive entwinement of public institutions and public officials in its composition and workings, and there is no substantial reason to claim unfairness in applying constitutional standards to it.

The Association is not an organization of natural persons acting on their own, but of schools, and of public schools to the extent of 84% of the total. Under the Association's bylaws, each member school is represented by its principal or a faculty member, who has a vote in selecting members of the governing legislative council and board of control from eligible principals, assistant principals and superintendents.

Although the findings and prior opinions in this case include no express conclusion of law that public school officials act within the scope of their duties when they represent their institutions, no other view would be rational, the official nature of their involvement being shown in any number of ways. Interscholastic athletics obviously play an integral part in the public education of Tennessee, where nearly every public high school spends money on competitions among schools. Since a pickup system of interscholastic games would not do, these public teams need some mechanism to produce rules and regulate competition. The mechanism is an organization overwhelmingly composed of public school officials who select representatives (all of them public officials at the time in question here), who in turn adopt and enforce the rules that make the system work. Thus, by giving these jobs to the Association, the 290 public schools of Tennessee belonging to it can sensibly be seen as exercising their own authority to meet their own responsibilities. Unsurprisingly, then, the record indicates that half the council or board meetings documented here were held during official school hours, and that public schools have largely provided for the Association's financial support. A small portion of the Association's revenue comes from membership dues paid by the schools, and the principal part from gate receipts at tournaments among the member schools. Unlike mere public buyers of contract services, whose payments for services rendered do not convert the service providers into public actors, the schools here obtain membership in the service organization and give up sources of their own income to their collective association. The Association thus exercises the authority of the predominantly public schools to charge for admission to their games; the Association does not receive this money from the schools, but enjoys the schools' moneymaking capacity as its own.

In sum, to the extent of 84% of its membership, the Association is an organization of public schools represented by their officials acting in their official capacity to provide an integral element of secondary public schooling. There would be no recognizable Association, legal or tangible, without the public school officials, who do not merely control but overwhelmingly perform all but the purely ministerial acts by which the Association exists and functions in practical terms. Only the 16% minority of private school memberships prevents this entwinement of the Association and the public school system from being total and their identities totally indistinguishable.

To complement the entwinement of public school officials with the Association from the bottom up, the State of Tennessee has provided for entwinement from top down. State Board members are assigned ex officio to serve as members of the board of control and legislative council, and the Association's ministerial employees are treated as state employees to the extent of being eligible for membership in the state retirement system.

Justice THOMAS, with whom the Chief Justice, Justice SCALIA, and Justice KENNEDY join, dissenting.

We have never found state action based upon mere "entwinement." Until today, we have found a private organization's acts to constitute state action only when the organization performed a public function; was created, coerced, or encouraged by the government; or acted in a symbiotic relationship with the government. The majority's holding—that the Tennessee Secondary School Athletic Association's (TSSAA) enforcement of its recruiting rule is state action —not only extends state-action doctrine beyond its permissible limits but also encroaches upon the realm of individual freedom that the doctrine was meant to protect. I respectfully dissent.

I

Like the state-action requirement of the Fourteenth Amendment, the state-action element of 42 U.S.C. § 1983 excludes from its coverage "merely private conduct, however discriminatory or wrongful." "Careful adherence to the 'state action' requirement" thus "preserves an area of individual freedom by limiting the reach of federal law and federal judicial power." The state-action doctrine also promotes important values of federalism, "avoid[ing] the imposition of responsibility on a State for conduct it could not control." Although we have used many different tests to identify state action, they all have a common purpose. Our goal in every case is to determine whether an action "can fairly be attributed to the State."

A

Regardless of these various tests for state action, common sense dictates that the TSSAA's actions cannot fairly be attributed to the State, and thus cannot constitute state action. The TSSAA was formed in 1925 as a private corporation to organize interscholastic athletics and to sponsor tournaments among its member schools. Any private or public secondary school may join the TSSAA by signing a contract agreeing to comply with its rules and decisions. Although public schools currently compose 84% of the TSSAA's membership, the TSSAA does not require that public schools constitute a set percentage of its membership, and, indeed, no public school need join the TSSAA. The TSSAA's rules are enforced not by a state agency but by its own board of control, which comprises high school principals, assistant principals, and superintendents, none of whom must work at a public school. Of course, at the time the recruiting rule was enforced in this case, all of the board members happened to be public school officials. However, each board member acts in a representative capacity on behalf of all the private and public schools in his region of Tennessee, and not simply his individual school.

The State of Tennessee did not create the TSSAA. The State does not fund the TSSAA and does not pay its employees. In fact, only 4% of the TSSAA's revenue comes from the dues paid by member schools; the bulk of its operating budget is derived from gate receipts at tournaments it sponsors. The State does not permit the TSSAA to use state-owned facilities for a discounted fee, and it does not exempt the TSSAA from state taxation. No Tennessee law authorizes the State to coordinate interscholastic athletics or empowers another entity to organize interscholastic athletics on behalf of the State. The only state pronouncement acknowledging the TSSAA's existence is a rule providing that the State Board of Education permits public schools to maintain membership in the TSSAA if they so choose.

Moreover, the State of Tennessee has never had any involvement in the particular action taken by the TSSAA in this case: the enforcement of the TSSAA's recruiting rule prohibiting members from using "undue influence" on students or their parents or guardians "to secure or to retain a student for athletic purposes." There is no indication that the State has ever had any interest in how schools choose to regulate recruiting. In fact, the TSSAA's authority to enforce its recruiting rule arises solely from the voluntary membership contract that each member school signs, agreeing to conduct its athletics in accordance with the rules and decisions of the TSSAA.

B

Even approaching the issue in terms of any of the Court's specific state-action tests, the conclusion is the same: The TSSAA's enforcement of its recruiting rule against Brentwood Academy is not state action. The TSSAA has not performed a function that has been "traditionally exclusively reserved to the State." Jackson v. Metropolitan Edison Co. (1974). The organization of interscholastic sports is neither a traditional nor an exclusive public function of the States. Widespread organization and administration of interscholastic contests by schools did not begin until the 20th century. Indeed, no one claims that the State of Tennessee played any role in the creation of the TSSAA as a private corporation in 1925. The TSSAA was designed to fulfill an objective—the organization of interscholastic athletic tournaments—that the government had not contemplated, much less pursued. And although the board of control currently is composed of public school officials, and although public schools currently account for the majority of the TSSAA's membership, this is not required by the TSSAA's constitution.

In addition, the State of Tennessee has not "exercised coercive power or . . . provided such significant encouragement [to the TSSAA], either overt or covert," that the TSSAA's regulatory activities must in law be deemed to be those of the State. The State has not promulgated any regulations of inter-scholastic sports, and nothing in the record suggests that the State has en-couraged or coerced the TSSAA in enforcing its recruiting rule. To be sure, public schools do provide a small portion of the TSSAA's funding through their membership dues, but no one argues that these dues are somehow conditioned on the TSSAA's enactment and enforcement of recruiting rules. Likewise, even if the TSSAA were dependent on state funding to the extent of 90%, instead of less than 4%, mere financial dependence on the State does not convert the TSSAA's actions into acts of the State.

Finally, there is no "symbiotic relationship" between the State and the TSSAA. Contrary to the majority's assertion, the TSSAA's "fiscal relationship with the State is not different from that of many contractors performing services for the government." The TSSAA provides a service—the organization of athletic tournaments—in exchange for membership dues and gate fees, just as a vendor could contract with public schools to sell refreshments at school events. Certainly the public school could sell its own refreshments, yet the existence of that option does not transform the service performed by the contractor into a state action. Also, there is no suggestion in this case that, as was the case in *Burton,* the State profits from the TSSAA's decision to enforce its recruiting rule.

Because I do not believe that the TSSAA's action of enforcing its recruiting rule is fairly attributable to the State of Tennessee, I would affirm.

II

Although the TSSAA's enforcement activities cannot be considered state action as a matter of common sense or under any of this Court's existing theories of state action, the majority presents a new theory. Under this theory, the majority holds that the combination of factors it identifies evidences "entwinement" of the State with the TSSAA, and that such entwinement converts private action into state action. The majority does not define "entwinement," and the meaning of the term is not altogether clear. But whatever this new "entwinement" theory may entail, it lacks any support in our state-action jurisprudence. There is no case in which we have rested a finding of state action on entwinement alone.

Because the majority never defines "entwinement," the scope of its holding is unclear. If we are fortunate, the majority's fact-specific analysis will have little bearing beyond this case. But if the majority's new entwinement test develops in future years, it could affect many organizations that foster activities, enforce rules, and sponsor extracurricular competition among high schools—not just in athletics, but in such diverse areas as agriculture, mathematics, music, marching bands, forensics, and cheerleading. Indeed, this entwinement test may extend to other organizations that are composed of, or controlled by, public officials or public entities, such as firefighters, policemen, teachers, cities, or counties. I am not prepared to say that any private organization that permits public entities and public officials to participate acts as the State in anything or everything it does, and our state-action jurisprudence has never reached that far. The state-action doctrine was developed to reach only those actions that are truly attributable to the State, not to subject private citizens to the control of federal courts hearing § 1983 actions. I respectfully dissent.

Chapter 6

Economic Liberties

D. The Takings Clause

2. Is There a "Taking"? (casebook, p. 498)

REGULATORY TAKINGS (casebook, p. 501)

In the last two years, the Supreme Court has decided two significant takings cases. In Palazzolo v. Rhode Island, below, the Supreme Court addressed two important issues concerning regulatory takings under the Takings Clause: When does a takings claim become ripe for review; and may an owner of property challenge regulations that existed when he or she purchased the property? The Court also reviewed the law concerning the Takings Clause, especially as to the requirements for a regulatory taking.

In Tahoe-Sierra Presentation Council, Inc. v. Tahoe Regional Planning Agency, the Court considered when a moratorium on development is a taking.

PALAZZOLO v. RHODE ISLAND
121 S. Ct. 2448 (June 28, 2001)

Justice KENNEDY delivered the opinion of the Court.

Petitioner Anthony Palazzolo owns a waterfront parcel of land in the town of Westerly, Rhode Island. Almost all of the property is designated as coastal wetlands under Rhode Island law. After petitioner's development proposals were rejected by respondent Rhode Island Coastal Resources Management Council (Council), he sued in state court, asserting the Council's application of its wetlands regulations took the property without compensation in violation of the Takings Clause of the Fifth Amendment, binding upon the State through the Due Process Clause of the Fourteenth Amendment. Petitioner sought review in this Court, contending the Supreme Court of Rhode Island erred in rejecting his takings claim.

I

The town of Westerly is on an edge of the Rhode Island coastline. In 1959 petitioner, a lifelong Westerly resident, decided to invest in three undeveloped, adjoining parcels. To purchase and hold the property, petitioner and associates formed Shore Gardens, Inc. (SGI). After SGI purchased the property petitioner bought out his associates and became the sole shareholder. In the first decade of SGI's ownership of the property the corporation submitted a plat to the town subdividing the property into 80 lots; and it engaged in various transactions that left it with 74 lots, which together encompassed about 20 acres. During the same period SGI also made initial attempts to develop the property and submitted intermittent applications to state agencies to fill substantial portions of the parcel. Most of the property was then, as it is now, salt marsh subject to tidal flooding. The wet ground and permeable soil would require considerable fill— as much as six feet in some places—before significant structures could be built. SGI's proposal, submitted in 1962 to the Rhode Island Division of Harbors and Rivers (DHR), sought to dredge from Winnapaug Pond and fill the entire property. The application was denied for lack of essential information.

A second, similar proposal followed a year later. A third application, submitted in 1966 while the second application was pending, proposed more limited filling of the land for use as a private beach club. These latter two applications were referred to the Rhode Island Department of Natural Resources, which indicated initial assent. The agency later withdrew approval, however, citing adverse environmental impacts. SGI did not contest the ruling.

No further attempts to develop the property were made for over a decade. Two intervening events, however, become important to the issues presented. First, in 1971, Rhode Island enacted legislation creating the Council, an agency charged with the duty of protecting the State's coastal properties. Regulations promulgated by the Council designated salt marshes like those on SGI's property as protected "coastal wetlands." Second, in 1978 SGI's corporate charter was revoked for failure to pay corporate income taxes; and title to the property passed, by operation of state law, to petitioner as the corporation's sole shareholder.

In 1983 petitioner, now the owner, renewed the efforts to develop the property. An application to the Council, resembling the 1962 submission, requested permission to construct a wooden bulkhead along the shore of Winnapaug Pond and to fill the entire marsh land area. The Council rejected the application, noting it was "vague and inadequate for a project of this size and nature." The agency also found that "the proposed alteration . . . will conflict with the Coastal Resources Management Plan presently in effect." Petitioner did not appeal the agency's determination.

Petitioner went back to the drawing board, this time hiring counsel and preparing a more specific and limited proposal for use of the property. The new application, submitted to the Council in 1985, echoed the 1966 request to build a private beach club. The details do not tend to inspire the reader with an idyllic coastal image, for the proposal was to fill 11 acres of the property with gravel to accommodate "50 cars with boat trailers, a dumpster, port-a-johns, picnic tables, barbecue pits of concrete, and other trash receptacles."

The application fared no better with the Council than previous ones. Under the agency's regulations, a landowner wishing to fill salt marsh on Winnapaug Pond needed a "special exception" from the Council. In a short opinion the Council said the beach club proposal conflicted with the regulatory standard for a special exception. To secure a special exception the proposed activity must serve "a compelling public purpose which provides benefits to the public as a whole as opposed to individual or private interests." This time petitioner appealed the decision to the Rhode Island courts, challenging the Council's conclusion as contrary to principles of state administrative law. The Council's decision was affirmed.

Petitioner filed an inverse condemnation action in Rhode Island Superior Court, asserting that the State's wetlands regulations, as applied by the Council to his parcel, had taken the property without compensation in violation of the Fifth and Fourteenth Amendments. The suit alleged the Council's action deprived him of "all economically beneficial use" of his property, resulting in a total taking requiring compensation under Lucas v. South Carolina Coastal Council (1992). He sought damages in the amount of $3,150,000, a figure derived from an appraiser's estimate as to the value of a 74-lot residential subdivision. The State countered with a host of defenses. After a bench trial, a justice of the Superior Court ruled against petitioner, accepting some of the State's theories. The Rhode Island Supreme Court affirmed. Like the Superior Court, the State Supreme Court recited multiple grounds for rejecting petitioner's suit. The court held, first, that petitioner's takings claim was not ripe; second, that petitioner had no right to challenge regulations predating 1978, when he succeeded to legal ownership of the property from SGI; and third, that the claim of deprivation of all economically beneficial use was contradicted by undisputed evidence that he had $200,000 in development value remaining on an upland parcel of the property.

We disagree with the Supreme Court of Rhode Island as to the first two of these conclusions; and, we hold, the court was correct to conclude that the owner is not deprived of all economic use of his property because the value of upland portions is substantial. We remand for further consideration of the claim under the principles set forth in *Penn Central*.

II

The Takings Clause of the Fifth Amendment, applicable to the States through the Fourteenth Amendment, prohibits the government from taking private property for public use without just compensation. The clearest sort of taking occurs when the government encroaches upon or occupies private land for its own proposed use. Our cases establish that even a minimal "permanent physical occupation of real property" requires compensation under the Clause. Loretto v. Teleprompter Manhattan CATV Corp. (1982). In Pennsylvania Coal Co. v. Mahon (1922), the Court recognized that there will be instances when government actions do not encroach upon or occupy the property yet still affect and limit its use to such an extent that a taking occurs. In Justice Holmes' well-known, if less than self-defining, formulation, "while property may be regulated to a certain extent, if a regulation goes too far it will be recognized as a taking."

Since *Mahon*, we have given some, but not too specific, guidance to courts confronted with deciding whether a particular government action goes too far and effects a regulatory taking. First, we have observed, with certain qualifications, that a regulation which "denies all economically beneficial or productive use of land" will require compensation under the Takings Clause. Where a regulation places limitations on land that fall short of eliminating all economically beneficial use, a taking nonetheless may have occurred, depending on a complex of factors including the regulation's economic effect on the landowner, the extent to which the regulation interferes with reasonable investment-backed expectations, and the character of the government action. These inquiries are informed by the purpose of the Takings Clause, which is to prevent the government from "forcing some people alone to bear public burdens which, in all fairness and justice, should be borne by the public as a whole."

Petitioner seeks compensation under these principles. At the outset, however, we face the two threshold considerations invoked by the state court to bar the claim: ripeness, and acquisition which postdates the regulation.

A

In Williamson County Regional Planning Comm'n v. Hamilton Bank of Johnson City (1985), the Court explained the requirement that a takings claim must be ripe. The Court held that a takings claim challenging the application of land-use regulations is not ripe unless "the government entity charged with implementing the regulations has reached a final decision regarding the application of the regulations to the property at issue." A final decision by the responsible state agency informs the constitutional determination whether a regulation has deprived a landowner of "all economically beneficial use" of the property, or defeated the reasonable investment-backed expectations of the landowner to the extent that a taking has occurred. These matters cannot be resolved in definitive terms until a court knows "the extent of permitted development" on the land in question. Drawing on these principles, the Rhode Island Supreme Court held that petitioner had not taken the necessary steps to ripen his takings claim.

The central question in resolving the ripeness issue, under *Williamson County* and other relevant decisions, is whether petitioner obtained a final decision from the Council determining the permitted use for the land. As we have noted, SGI's early applications to fill had been granted at one point, though that assent was later revoked. Petitioner then submitted two proposals: the 1983 proposal to fill the entire parcel, and the 1985 proposal to fill 11 of the property's 18 wetland acres for construction of the beach club. The court reasoned that, notwithstanding the Council's denials of the applications, doubt remained as to the extent of development the Council would allow on petitioner's parcel. We cannot agree.

The court based its holding in part upon petitioner's failure to explore "any other use for the property that would involve filling substantially less wetlands." The suggestion is that while the Council rejected petitioner's effort to fill all of the wetlands, and then rejected his proposal to fill 11 of the wetland acres, perhaps an application to fill (for instance) 5 acres would have been approved. Thus, the reasoning goes, we cannot know for sure the extent of permitted development on petitioner's wetlands.

This is belied by the unequivocal nature of the wetland regulations at issue, [which require] a special exception from the Council to engage in a prohibited use [and] the Council is permitted to allow the exception only where a "compelling public purpose" is served, and by the Council's application of the regulations to the subject property. There is no indication the Council would have accepted the application had petitioner's proposed beach club occupied a smaller surface area. To the contrary, it ruled that the proposed activity was not a "compelling public purpose."

Williamson County's final decision requirement "responds to the high degree of discretion characteristically possessed by land-use boards in softening the strictures of the general regulations they administer." While a landowner must give a land-use authority an opportunity to exercise its discretion, once it becomes clear that the agency lacks the discretion to permit any development, or the permissible uses of the property are known to a reasonable degree of certainty, a takings claim is likely to have ripened.

With respect to the wetlands on petitioner's property, the Council's decisions make plain that the agency interpreted its regulations to bar petitioner from engaging in any filling or development activity on the wetlands, a fact reinforced by the Attorney General's forthright responses to our questioning during oral argument in this case. The rulings of the Council interpreting the regulations at issue, and the briefs, arguments, and candid statements by counsel for both sides, leave no doubt on this point: On the wetlands there can be no fill for any ordinary land use. There can be no fill for its own sake; no fill for a beach club, either rustic or upscale; no fill for a subdivision; no fill for any likely or foreseeable use. And with no fill there can be no structures and no development on the wetlands. Further permit applications were not necessary to establish this point.

B

We turn to the second asserted basis for declining to address petitioner's takings claim on the merits. When the Council promulgated its wetlands regulations, the disputed parcel was owned not by petitioner but by the corporation of which he was sole shareholder. When title was transferred to petitioner by operation of law, the wetlands regulations were in force. The state court held the postregulation acquisition of title was fatal to the claim for deprivation of all economic use and to the *Penn Central* claim. [The state court's] holdings together amount to a single, sweeping, rule: A purchaser or a successive title holder like petitioner is deemed to have notice of an earlier-enacted restriction and is barred from claiming that it effects a taking.

The theory underlying the argument that postenactment purchasers cannot challenge a regulation under the Takings Clause seems to run on these lines: Property rights are created by the State. So, the argument goes, by prospective legislation the State can shape and define property rights and reasonable investment-backed expectations, and subsequent owners cannot claim any injury from lost value. After all, they purchased or took title with notice of the limitation.

The State may not put so potent a Hobbesian stick into the Lockean bundle. The right to improve property, of course, is subject to the reasonable exercise of state authority, including the enforcement of valid zoning and land-use restrictions. The Takings Clause, however, in certain circumstances allows a landowner to assert that a particular exercise of the State's regulatory power is so unreasonable or onerous as to compel compensation. Just as a prospective enactment, such as a new zoning ordinance, can limit the value of land without effecting a taking because it can be understood as reasonable by all concerned, other enactments are unreasonable and do not become less so through passage of time or title. Were we to accept the State's rule, the postenactment transfer of title would absolve the State of its obligation to defend any action restricting land use, no matter how extreme or unreasonable. A State would be allowed, in effect, to put an expiration date on the Takings Clause. This ought not to be the rule. Future generations, too, have a right to challenge unreasonable limitations on the use and value of land.

Nor does the justification of notice take into account the effect on owners at the time of enactment, who are prejudiced as well. Should an owner attempt to challenge a new regulation, but not survive the process of ripening his or her claim (which, as this case demonstrates, will often take years), under the proposed rule the right to compensation may not by asserted by an heir or successor, and so may not be asserted at all. The State's rule would work a critical alteration to the nature of property, as the newly regulated landowner is stripped of the ability to transfer the interest which was possessed prior to the regulation. The State may not by this means secure a windfall for itself. The proposed rule is, furthermore, capricious in effect. The young owner contrasted with the older owner, the owner with the resources to hold contrasted with the owner with the need to sell, would be in different positions. The Takings Clause is not so quixotic. A blanket rule that purchasers with notice have no compensation right when a claim becomes ripe is too blunt an instrument to accord with the duty to compensate for what is taken.

We have no occasion to consider the precise circumstances when a legislative enactment can be deemed a background principle of state law or whether those circumstances are present here. It suffices to say that a regulation that otherwise would be unconstitutional absent compensation is not transformed into a background principle of the State's law by mere virtue of the passage of title.

III

As the case is ripe, and as the date of transfer of title does not bar petitioner's takings claim, we have before us the alternative ground relied upon by the Rhode Island Supreme Court in ruling upon the merits of the takings claims. It held that all economically beneficial use was not deprived because the uplands portion of the property can still be improved. On this point, we agree with the court's decision. Petitioner accepts the Council's contention and the state trial court's finding that his parcel retains $200,000 in development value under the State's wetlands regulations. He asserts, nonetheless, that he has suffered a total taking and contends the Council cannot sidestep the holding in *Lucas* "by the simple expedient of leaving a landowner a few crumbs of value."

Assuming a taking is otherwise established, a State may not evade the duty to compensate on the premise that the landowner is left with a token interest. This is not the situation of the landowner in this case, however. A regulation permitting a landowner to build a substantial residence on an 18-acre parcel does not leave the property "economically idle."

In his brief submitted to us petitioner attempts to revive this part of his claim by reframing it. He argues, for the first time, that the upland parcel is distinct from the wetlands portions, so he should be permitted to assert a deprivation limited to the latter. This contention asks us to examine the difficult, persisting question of what is the proper denominator in the takings fraction. Some of our cases indicate that the extent of deprivation effected by a regulatory action is measured against the value of the parcel as a whole; but we have at times expressed discomfort with the logic of this rule. Whatever the merits of these criticisms, we will not explore the point here. Petitioner did not press the argument in the state courts, and the issue was not presented in the petition for certiorari. The case comes to us on the premise that petitioner's entire parcel serves as the basis for his takings claim, and, so framed, the total deprivation argument fails.

Justice O'CONNOR, concurring.

I join the opinion of the Court but with my understanding of how the issues discussed in Part II-B of the opinion must be considered on remand. Part II-B of the Court's opinion addresses the circumstance, present in this case, where a takings claimant has acquired title to the regulated property after the enactment of the regulation at issue. As the Court holds, the Rhode Island Supreme Court erred in effectively adopting the sweeping rule that the preacquisition enactment of the use restriction ipso facto defeats any takings claim based on that use restriction.

The more difficult question is what role the temporal relationship between regulatory enactment and title acquisition plays in a proper *Penn Central* analysis. Today's holding does not mean that the timing of the regulation's enactment relative to the acquisition of title is immaterial to the *Penn Central* analysis. Indeed, it would be just as much error to expunge this consideration from the takings inquiry as it would be to accord it exclusive significance. Our pole-star instead remains the principles set forth in *Penn Central* itself and our other cases that govern partial regulatory takings. Under these cases, interference with investment-backed expectations is one of a number of factors that a court must examine. Further, the regulatory regime in place at the time the claimant acquires the property at issue helps to shape the reasonableness of those expectations.

Justice SCALIA, concurring.

I write separately to make clear that my understanding of how the issues discussed in Part II-B of the Court's opinion must be considered on remand is not Justice O'Connor's.

The principle that underlies her separate concurrence is that it may in some (unspecified) circumstances be "[un]fai[r]," and produce unacceptable "wind-falls," to allow a subsequent purchaser to nullify an unconstitutional partial taking (though, inexplicably, not an unconstitutional total taking) by the government. The polar horrible, presumably, is the situation in which a sharp real estate developer, realizing (or indeed, simply gambling on) the unconstitutional exces-siveness of a development restriction that a naive landowner assumes to be valid, purchases property at what it would be worth subject to the restriction, and then develops it to its full value (or resells it at its full value) after getting the unconstitutional restriction invalidated.

This can, I suppose, be called a windfall—though it is not much different from the windfalls that occur every day at stock exchanges or antique auctions, where the knowledgeable (or the venturesome) profit at the expense of the ignorant (or the risk averse). There is something to be said (though in my view not much) for pursuing abstract "fairness" by requiring part or all of that wind-fall to be returned to the naive original owner, who presumably is the "rightful" owner of it. But there is nothing to be said for giving it instead to the govern-ment—which not only did not lose something it owned, but is both the cause of the miscarriage of "fairness" and the only one of the three parties involved in the miscarriage (government, naive original owner, and sharp real estate developer) which acted unlawfully—indeed unconstitutionally. Justice O'Connor would eliminate the windfall by giving the malefactor the benefit of its malefaction. It is rather like eliminating the windfall that accrued to a purchaser who bought property at a bargain rate from a thief clothed with the indicia of title, by making him turn over the "unjust" profit to the thief.

In my view, the fact that a restriction existed at the time the purchaser took title (other than a restriction forming part of the "background principles of the State's law of property and nuisance") should have no bearing upon the determination of whether the restriction is so substantial as to constitute a taking. The "investment-backed expectations" that the law will take into account do not include the assumed validity of a restriction that in fact deprives property of so much of its value as to be unconstitutional. Which is to say that a *Penn Central* taking, no less than a total taking, is not absolved by the transfer of title.

Justice STEVENS, concurring in part and dissenting in part.

In an admirable effort to frame its inquiries in broadly significant terms, the majority offers six pages of commentary on the issue of whether an owner of property can challenge regulations adopted prior to her acquisition of that property without ever discussing the particular facts or legal claims at issue in this case. While I agree with some of what the Court has to say on this issue, an examination of the issue in the context of the facts of this case convinces me that the Court has oversimplified a complex calculus and conflated two separate questions. Therefore, while I join Part II-A of the opinion, I dissent from the judgment and, in particular, from Part II-B.

I

If a regulating body fails to adhere to its procedural or substantive obligations in developing land use restrictions, anyone adversely impacted by the restrictions may challenge their validity in an injunctive action if the application of such restriction to a property owner would cause her a "direct and substantial injury." It by no means follows, however, that, as the Court assumes, a succeeding owner may obtain compensation for a taking of property from her predecessor in interest. A taking is a discrete event, a governmental acquisition of private property for which the state is required to provide just compensation. Like other transfers of property, it occurs at a particular time, that time being the moment when the relevant property interest is alienated from its owner.

Precise specification of the moment a taking occurred and of the nature of the property interest taken is necessary in order to determine an appropriately compensatory remedy. For example, the amount of the award is measured by the value of the property at the time of taking, not the value at some later date. Similarly, interest on the award runs from that date. Most importantly for our purposes today, it is the person who owned the property at the time of the taking that is entitled to the recovery.

II

Much of the difficulty of this case stems from genuine confusion as to when the taking Palazzolo alleges actually occurred. If it is the regulations themselves of which petitioner complains, and if they did, in fact, diminish the value of his property, they did so when they were adopted. To the extent that the adoption of the regulations constitute the challenged taking, petitioner is simply the wrong party to be bringing this action. If the regulations imposed a compensable injury on anyone, it was on the owner of the property at the moment the regulations were adopted. Given the trial court's finding that petitioner did not own the property at that time, in my judgment it is pellucidly clear that he has no standing to claim that the promulgation of the regulations constituted a taking of any part of the property that he subsequently acquired. His lack of standing does not depend, as the Court seems to assume, on whether or not petitioner "is deemed to have notice of an earlier-enacted restriction." If those early regulations changed the character of the owner's title to the property, thereby diminishing its value, petitioner acquired only the net value that remained after that diminishment occurred.

Of course, if, as respondent contends, even the prior owner never had any right to fill wetlands, there never was a basis for the alleged takings claim in the first place. But accepting petitioner's theory of the case, he has no standing to complain that preacquisition events may have reduced the value of the property that he acquired. If the regulations are invalid, either because improper procedures were followed when they were adopted, or because they have somehow gone "too far," petitioner may seek to enjoin their enforcement, but he has no right to recover compensation for the value of property taken from someone else. A new owner may maintain an ejectment action against a trespasser who has lodged himself in the owner's orchard but surely could not recover damages for fruit a trespasser spirited from the orchard before he acquired the property.

Justice GINSBURG, with whom Justice SOUTER and Justice BREYER join, dissenting.

A regulatory takings claim is not ripe for adjudication, this Court has held, until the agency administering the regulations at issue, proceeding in good faith, "has arrived at a final, definitive position regarding how it will apply [those regulations] to the particular land in question." Williamson County Regional Planning Comm'n v. Hamilton Bank of Johnson City (1985). Absent such a final decision, a court cannot "kno[w] the nature and extent of permitted development" under the regulations, and therefore cannot say "how far the regulation[s] g[o]," as regulatory takings law requires. Therefore, even when a landowner seeks and is denied permission to develop property, if the denial does not demonstrate the effective impact of the regulations on the land, the denial does not represent the "final decision" requisite to generate a ripe dispute.

As the Rhode Island Supreme Court saw the case, Palazzolo's claim was not ripe for several reasons, among them, that Palazzolo had not sought permission for "development only of the upland portion of the parcel." The Rhode Island court emphasized the "undisputed evidence in the record that it would be possible to build at least one single-family home on the existing upland area, with no need for additional fill."

Today, the Court rejects the Rhode Island court's determination that the case is unripe, finding no "uncertainty as to the [uplands'] permitted use." The Court's conclusion is, in my view, both inaccurate and inequitable. It is inaccurate because the record is ambiguous. And it is inequitable because, given the claim asserted by Palazzolo in the Rhode Island courts, the State had no cause to pursue further inquiry into potential upland development. In sum, as I see this case, we still do not know "the nature and extent of permitted development" under the regulation in question. I would therefore affirm the Rhode Island Supreme Court's judgment.

Justice BREYER, dissenting.

I agree with Justice Ginsburg that Palazzolo's takings claim is not ripe for adjudication, and I join her opinion in full. Ordinarily I would go no further. But because the Court holds the takings claim to be ripe and goes on to address some important issues of substantive takings law, I add that, given this Court's precedents, I would agree with Justice O'Connor that the simple fact that a piece of property has changed hands (for example, by inheritance) does not always and automatically bar a takings claim. Here, for example, without in any way suggesting that Palazzolo has any valid takings claim, I believe his post-regulatory acquisition of the property (through automatic operation of law) by itself should not prove dispositive.

As Justice O'Connor explains, under Penn Central Transp. Co. v. New York City (1978), much depends upon whether, or how, the timing and circumstances of a change of ownership affect whatever reasonable investment-backed expectations might otherwise exist. Ordinarily, such expectations will diminish in force and significance—rapidly and dramatically—as property continues to change hands over time. I believe that such factors can adequately be taken into account within the *Penn Central* framework.

[F]or the sake of clarity it is worth emphasizing that, on my view, even a newly adopted regulation that diminishes the value of property does not produce a significant Takings Clause issue if it (1) is generally applicable and (2) is directed at preventing a substantial public harm. It is quite likely that a regulation prohibiting the filling of wetlands meets those criteria.

When is a moratorium on development a taking?

TAHOE-SIERRA PRESERVATION COUNCIL, INC.
v. TAHOE REGIONAL PLANNING AGENCY
122 S. Ct. 1465 (2002)

Justice STEVENS delivered the opinion of the Court.

The question presented is whether a moratorium on development imposed during the process of devising a comprehensive land-use plan constitutes a per se taking of property requiring compensation under the Takings Clause of the United States Constitution. This case actually involves two moratoria ordered by respondent Tahoe Regional Planning Agency (TRPA) to maintain the status quo while studying the impact of development on Lake Tahoe and designing a strategy for environmentally sound growth. The first, Ordinance 81-5, was effective from August 24, 1981, until August 26, 1983, whereas the second more restrictive Resolution 83-21 was in effect from August 27, 1983, until April 25, 1984. As a result of these two directives, virtually all development on a substantial portion of the property subject to TRPA's jurisdiction was prohibited for a period of 32 months. Although the question we decide relates only to that 32-month period, a brief description of the events leading up to the moratoria and a comment on the two permanent plans that TRPA adopted thereafter will clarify the narrow scope of our holding.

I

The relevant facts are undisputed. All agree that Lake Tahoe is "uniquely beautiful," that President Clinton was right to call it a "'national treasure that must be protected and preserved,'" and that Mark Twain aptly described the clarity of its waters as "'not merely transparent, but dazzlingly, brilliantly so.'" Lake Tahoe's exceptional clarity is attributed to the absence of algae that obscures the waters of most other lakes. Historically, the lack of nitrogen and phosphorous, which nourish the growth of algae, has ensured the transparency of its waters. Unfortunately, the lake's pristine state has deteriorated rapidly over the past 40 years; increased land development in the Lake Tahoe Basin (Basin) has threatened the "'noble sheet of blue water'" beloved by Twain and countless others. As the District Court found, "[d]ramatic decreases in clarity first began to be noted in the 1950's/early 1960's, shortly after development at the lake began in earnest." The lake's unsurpassed beauty, it seems, is the wellspring of its undoing.

The upsurge of development in the area has caused "increased nutrient loading of the lake largely because of the increase in impervious coverage of land in the Basin resulting from that development." Given this trend, the District Court predicted that "unless the process is stopped, the lake will lose its clarity and its trademark blue color, becoming green and opaque for eternity."

Those areas in the Basin that have steeper slopes produce more runoff; therefore, they are usually considered "high hazard" lands. Moreover, certain areas near streams or wetlands known as "Stream Environment Zones" (SEZs) are especially vulnerable to the impact of development because, in their natural state, they act as filters for much of the debris that runoff carries. Because "[t]he most obvious response to this problem . . . is to restrict development around the lake—especially in SEZ lands, as well as in areas already naturally prone to runoff," conservation efforts have focused on controlling growth in these high hazard areas.

In combination, Ordinance 81-5 and Resolution 83-21 effectively prohibited all construction on sensitive lands in California and on all SEZ lands in the entire Basin for 32 months, and on sensitive lands in Nevada (other than SEZ lands) for eight months. It is these two moratoria that are at issue in this case.

II

Approximately two months after the adoption of the 1984 Plan, petitioners filed parallel actions against TRPA and other defendants in federal courts in Nevada and California that were ultimately consolidated for trial in the District of Nevada. The petitioners include the Tahoe Sierra Preservation Council, a nonprofit membership corporation representing about 2,000 owners of both improved and unimproved parcels of real estate in the Lake Tahoe Basin, and a class of some 400 individual owners of vacant lots located either on SEZ lands or in other parts of districts 1, 2, or 3. Those individuals purchased their properties prior to the effective date of the 1980 Compact, primarily for the purpose of constructing "at a time of their choosing" a single-family home "to serve as a permanent, retirement or vacation residence." When they made those purchases, they did so with the understanding that such construction was authorized provided that "they complied with all reasonable requirements for building."

III

Petitioners make only a facial attack on Ordinance 81-5 and Resolution 83-21. They contend that the mere enactment of a temporary regulation that, while in effect, denies a property owner all viable economic use of her property gives rise to an unqualified constitutional obligation to compensate her for the value of its use during that period. Hence, they "face an uphill battle," Keystone Bituminous Coal Assn. v. DeBenedictis (1987), that is made especially steep by their desire for a categorical rule requiring compensation whenever the government imposes such a moratorium on development. Under their proposed rule, there is no need to evaluate the landowners' investment-backed expectations, the actual impact of the regulation on any individual, the importance of the public interest served by the regulation, or the reasons for imposing the temporary restriction. For petitioners, it is enough that a regulation imposes a temporary deprivation—no matter how brief—of all economically viable use to trigger a per se rule that a taking has occurred. Petitioners assert that our opinions in *First English* and *Lucas* have already endorsed their view, and that it is a logical application of the principle that the Takings Clause was "designed to bar Government from forcing some people alone to bear burdens which, in all fairness and justice, should be borne by the public as a whole."

We shall first explain why our cases do not support their proposed categorical rule—indeed, fairly read, they implicitly reject it. In our view the answer to the abstract question whether a temporary moratorium effects a taking is neither "yes, always" nor "no, never"; the answer depends upon the particular circumstances of the case. Resisting "[t]he temptation to adopt what amount to per se rules in either direction," we conclude that the circumstances in this case are best analyzed within the *Penn Central* framework.

IV

The text of the Fifth Amendment itself provides a basis for drawing a distinction between physical takings and regulatory takings. Its plain language requires the payment of compensation whenever the government acquires private property for a public purpose, whether the acquisition is the result of a condemnation proceeding or a physical appropriation. But the Constitution contains no comparable reference to regulations that prohibit a property owner from making certain uses of her private property. Our jurisprudence involving condemnations and physical takings is as old as the Republic and, for the most part, involves the straightforward application of per se rules. Our regulatory takings jurisprudence, in contrast, is of more recent vintage and is characterized by "essentially ad hoc, factual inquiries," designed to allow "careful examination and weighing of all the relevant circumstances."

When the government physically takes possession of an interest in property for some public purpose, it has a categorical duty to compensate the former owner, United States v. Pewee Coal Co. (1951), regardless of whether the interest that is taken constitutes an entire parcel or merely a part thereof. Thus, compensation is mandated when a leasehold is taken and the government occupies the property for its own purposes, even though that use is temporary. Similarly, when the government appropriates part of a rooftop in order to provide cable TV access for apartment tenants, Loretto v. Teleprompter Manhattan CATV Corp. (1982); or when its planes use private airspace to approach a government airport, United States v. Causby (1946), it is required to pay for that share no matter how small. But a government regulation that merely prohibits landlords from evicting tenants unwilling to pay a higher rent, Block v. Hirsh (1921); that bans certain private uses of a portion of an owner's property, Village of Euclid v. Ambler Realty Co., (1926); Keystone Bituminous Coal Assn. v. DeBenedictis (1987); or that forbids the private use of certain airspace, Penn Central Transp. Co. v. New York City (1978), does not constitute a categorical taking. "The first category of cases requires courts to apply a clear rule; the second necessarily entails complex factual assessments of the purposes and economic effects of government actions."

This longstanding distinction between acquisitions of property for public use, on the one hand, and regulations prohibiting private uses, on the other, makes it inappropriate to treat cases involving physical takings as controlling precedents for the evaluation of a claim that there has been a "regulatory taking," and vice versa. For the same reason that we do not ask whether a physical appropriation advances a substantial government interest or whether it deprives the owner of all economically valuable use, we do not apply our precedent from the physical takings context to regulatory takings claims. Land-use regulations are ubiquitous and most of them impact property values in some tangential way—often in completely unanticipated ways. Treating them all as per se takings would transform government regulation into a luxury few governments could afford. By contrast, physical appropriations are relatively rare, easily identified, and usually represent a greater affront to individual property rights.

"This case does not present the 'classi[c] taking' in which the government directly appropriates private property for its own use"; instead the interference with property rights "arises from some public program adjusting the benefits. . . ." Perhaps recognizing this fundamental distinction, petitioners wisely do not place all their emphasis on analogies to physical takings cases. Instead, they rely principally on our decision in Lucas v. South Carolina Coastal Council (1992)—a regulatory takings case that, nevertheless, applied a categorical rule —to argue that the *Penn Central* framework is inapplicable here.

[W]e have "generally eschewed" any set formula for determining how far is too far, choosing instead to engage in "'essentially ad hoc, factual inquiries.'" Indeed, we still resist the temptation to adopt per se rules in our cases involving partial regulatory takings, preferring to examine "a number of factors" rather than a simple "mathematically precise" formula. Justice Brennan's opinion for the Court in *Penn Central* did, however, make it clear that even though multiple factors are relevant in the analysis of regulatory takings claims, in such cases we must focus on "the parcel as a whole."

In *First English,* the Court unambiguously and repeatedly characterized the issue to be decided as a "compensation question" or a "remedial question." And the Court's statement of its holding was equally unambiguous: "We merely hold that where the government's activities have already worked a taking of all use of property, no subsequent action by the government can relieve it of the duty to provide compensation for the period during which the taking was effective." In fact, *First English* expressly disavowed any ruling on the merits of the takings issue because the California courts had decided the remedial question on the assumption that a taking had been alleged. After our remand, the California courts concluded that there had not been a taking, and we declined review of that decision.

To the extent that the Court in *First English* referenced the antecedent takings question, we identified two reasons why a regulation temporarily denying an owner all use of her property might not constitute a taking. First, we recognized that "the county might avoid the conclusion that a compensable taking had occurred by establishing that the denial of all use was insulated as a part of the State's authority to enact safety regulations." Second, we limited our holding "to the facts presented" and recognized "the quite different questions that would arise in the case of normal delays in obtaining building permits, changes in zoning ordinances, variances, and the like which [were] not before us." Thus, our decision in *First English* surely did not approve, and implicitly rejected, the categorical submission that petitioners are now advocating.

Similarly, our decision in *Lucas* is not dispositive of the question presented. Although *Lucas* endorsed and applied a categorical rule, it was not the one that petitioners propose. Lucas purchased two residential lots in 1988 for $975,000. These lots were rendered "valueless" by a statute enacted two years later. The trial court found that a taking had occurred and ordered compensation of $1,232,387.50, representing the value of the fee simple estate, plus interest. As the statute read at the time of the trial, it effected a taking that "was unconditional and permanent."

The categorical rule that we applied in *Lucas* states that compensation is required when a regulation deprives an owner of "all economically beneficial uses" of his land. Under that rule, a statute that "wholly eliminated the value" of Lucas' fee simple title clearly qualified as a taking. But our holding was limited to "the extraordinary circumstance when no productive or economically beneficial use of land is permitted." The emphasis on the word "no" in the text of the opinion was, in effect, reiterated in a footnote explaining that the categorical rule would not apply if the diminution in value were 95% instead of 100%. Anything less than a "complete elimination of value," or a "total loss," the Court acknowledged, would require the kind of analysis applied in *Penn Central*.

Certainly, our holding that the permanent "obliteration of the value" of a fee simple estate constitutes a categorical taking does not answer the question whether a regulation prohibiting any economic use of land for a 32-month period has the same legal effect. Petitioners seek to bring this case under the rule announced in *Lucas* by arguing that we can effectively sever a 32-month segment from the remainder of each landowner's fee simple estate, and then ask whether that segment has been taken in its entirety by the moratoria. Of course, defining the property interest taken in terms of the very regulation being challenged is circular. With property so divided, every delay would become a total ban; the moratorium and the normal permit process alike would constitute categorical takings. Petitioners' "conceptual severance" argument is unavailing because it ignores *Penn Central*'s admonition that in regulatory takings cases we must focus on "the parcel as a whole." We have consistently rejected such an approach to the "denominator" question. Thus, the District Court erred when it disaggregated petitioners' property into temporal segments corresponding to the regulations at issue and then analyzed whether petitioners were deprived of all economically viable use during each period. The starting point for the court's analysis should have been to ask whether there was a total taking of the entire parcel; if not, then *Penn Central* was the proper framework.

An interest in real property is defined by the metes and bounds that describe its geographic dimensions and the term of years that describes the temporal aspect of the owner's interest. See Restatement of Property §§ 7-9 (1936). Both dimensions must be considered if the interest is to be viewed in its entirety. Hence, a permanent deprivation of the owner's use of the entire area is a taking of "the parcel as a whole," whereas a temporary restriction that merely causes a diminution in value is not. Logically, a fee simple estate cannot be rendered valueless by a temporary prohibition on economic use, because the property will recover value as soon as the prohibition is lifted.

Neither *Lucas,* nor *First English,* nor any of our other regulatory takings cases compels us to accept petitioners' categorical submission. In fact, these cases make clear that the categorical rule in *Lucas* was carved out for the "extraordinary case" in which a regulation permanently deprives property of all value; the default rule remains that, in the regulatory taking context, we require a more fact specific inquiry. Nevertheless, we will consider whether the interest in protecting individual property owners from bearing public burdens "which, in all fairness and justice, should be borne by the public as a whole," justifies creating a new rule for these circumstances.

V

[T]he ultimate constitutional question is whether the concepts of "fairness and justice" that underlie the Takings Clause will be better served by [a] categorical rule or by a *Penn Central* inquiry into all of the relevant circumstances in particular cases. From that perspective, the extreme categorical rule that any deprivation of all economic use, no matter how brief, constitutes a compensable taking surely cannot be sustained. Petitioners' broad submission would apply to numerous "normal delays in obtaining building permits, changes in zoning ordinances, variances, and the like," as well as to orders temporarily prohibiting access to crime scenes, businesses that violate health codes, fire-damaged buildings, or other areas that we cannot now foresee. Such a rule would undoubtedly require changes in numerous practices that have long been considered permissible exercises of the police power. As Justice Holmes warned in *Mahon,* "[g]overnment hardly could go on if to some extent values incident to property could not be diminished without paying for every such change in the general law." A rule that required compensation for every delay in the use of property would render routine government processes prohibitively expensive or encourage hasty decisionmaking. Such an important change in the law should be the product of legislative rulemaking rather than adjudication.

More importantly, for reasons set out at some length by Justice O'Connor in her concurring opinion in Palazzolo v. Rhode Island (2001), we are persuaded that the better approach to claims that a regulation has effected a temporary taking "requires careful examination and weighing of all the relevant circumstances." Our polestar remains the principles set forth in *Penn Central* itself and our other cases that govern partial regulatory takings. Under these cases, interference with investment-backed expectations is one of a number of factors that a court must examine.

[W]e have eschewed "any 'set formula' for determining when 'justice and fairness' require that economic injuries caused by public action be compensated by the government, rather than remain disproportionately concentrated on a few persons." The outcome instead "depends largely 'upon the particular circumstances [in that] case.' "

In rejecting petitioners' per se rule, we do not hold that the temporary nature of a land-use restriction precludes finding that it effects a taking; we simply recognize that it should not be given exclusive significance one way or the other. A narrower rule that excluded the normal delays associated with processing permits, or that covered only delays of more than a year, would certainly have a less severe impact on prevailing practices, but it would still impose serious financial constraints on the planning process. Unlike the "extraordinary circumstance" in which the government deprives a property owner of all economic use, moratoria like Ordinance 81-5 and Resolution 83-21 are used widely among land-use planners to preserve the status quo while formulating a more permanent development strategy. In fact, the consensus in the planning community appears to be that moratoria, or "interim development controls" as they are often called, are an essential tool of successful development. Yet even the weak version of petitioners' categorical rule would treat these interim measures as takings regardless of the good faith of the planners, the reasonable expectations of the landowners, or the actual impact of the moratorium on property values.

The interest in facilitating informed decisionmaking by regulatory agencies counsels against adopting a per se rule that would impose such severe costs on their deliberations. Otherwise, the financial constraints of compensating property owners during a moratorium may force officials to rush through the planning process or to abandon the practice altogether. To the extent that communities are forced to abandon using moratoria, landowners will have incentives to develop their property quickly before a comprehensive plan can be enacted, thereby fostering inefficient and ill-conceived growth.

We would create a perverse system of incentives were we to hold that landowners must wait for a taking claim to ripen so that planners can make well-reasoned decisions while, at the same time, holding that those planners must compensate landowners for the delay. Indeed, the interest in protecting the decisional process is even stronger when an agency is developing a regional plan than when it is considering a permit for a single parcel. In the proceedings involving the Lake Tahoe Basin, for example, the moratoria enabled TRPA to obtain the benefit of comments and criticisms from interested parties, such as the petitioners, during its deliberations. Since a categorical rule tied to the length of deliberations would likely create added pressure on decisionmakers to reach a quick resolution of land-use questions, it would only serve to disadvantage those landowners and interest groups who are not as organized or familiar with the planning process. Moreover, with a temporary ban on development there is a lesser risk that individual landowners will be "singled out" to bear a special burden that should be shared by the public as a whole. At least with a moratorium there is a clear "reciprocity of advantage," because it protects the interests of all affected landowners against immediate construction that might be inconsistent with the provisions of the plan that is ultimately adopted. "While each of us is burdened somewhat by such restrictions, we, in turn, benefit greatly from the restrictions that are placed on others." In fact, there is reason to believe property values often will continue to increase despite a moratorium. Such an increase makes sense in this context because property values throughout the Basin can be expected to reflect the added assurance that Lake Tahoe will remain in its pristine state. Since in some cases a 1-year moratorium may not impose a burden at all, we should not adopt a rule that assumes moratoria always force individuals to bear a special burden that should be shared by the public as a whole.

It may well be true that any moratorium that lasts for more than one year should be viewed with special skepticism. But given the fact that the District Court found that the 32 months required by TRPA to formulate the 1984 Regional Plan was not unreasonable, we could not possibly conclude that every delay of over one year is constitutionally unacceptable. Formulating a general rule of this kind is a suitable task for state legislatures. In our view, the duration of the restriction is one of the important factors that a court must consider in the appraisal of a regulatory takings claim, but with respect to that factor as with respect to other factors, the "temptation to adopt what amount to per se rules in either direction must be resisted." There may be moratoria that last longer than one year which interfere with reasonable investment-backed expectations, but as the District Court's opinion illustrates, petitioners' proposed rule is simply "too blunt an instrument," for identifying those cases. We conclude, therefore, that the interest in "fairness and justice" will be best served by relying on the familiar *Penn Central* approach when deciding cases like this, rather than by attempting to craft a new categorical rule.

Chief Justice REHNQUIST, with whom Justice SCALIA and Justice THOMAS join, dissenting.

For over half a decade petitioners were prohibited from building homes, or any other structures, on their land. Because the Takings Clause requires the government to pay compensation when it deprives owners of all economically viable use of their land, see Lucas v. South Carolina Coastal Council (1992), and because a ban on all development lasting almost six years does not resemble any traditional land-use planning device, I dissent.

I

"A court cannot determine whether a regulation has gone 'too far' unless it knows how far the regulation goes." In failing to undertake this inquiry, the Court ignores much of the impact of respondent's conduct on petitioners. Instead, it relies on the flawed determination of the Court of Appeals that the relevant time period lasted only from August 1981 until April 1984. During that period, Ordinance 81-5 and Regulation 83-21 prohibited development pending the adoption of a new regional land-use plan. The adoption of the 1984 Regional

Plan (hereinafter Plan or 1984 Plan) did not, however, change anything from the petitioners' standpoint. After the adoption of the 1984 Plan, petitioners still could make no use of their land. Because respondent caused petitioners' inability to use their land from 1981 through 1987, that is the appropriate period of time from which to consider their takings claim.

II

I now turn to determining whether a ban on all economic development lasting almost six years is a taking. *Lucas* reaffirmed our "frequently expressed" view that "when the owner of real property has been called upon to sacrifice all economically beneficial uses in the name of the common good, that is, to leave his property economically idle, he has suffered a taking." The District Court in this case held that the ordinances and resolutions in effect between August 24, 1981, and April 25, 1984, "did in fact deny the plaintiffs all economically viable use of their land." The Court of Appeals did not overturn this finding. And the 1984 injunction, issued because the environmental thresholds issued by respondent did not permit the development of single-family residences, forced petitioners to leave their land economically idle for at least another three years. The Court does not dispute that petitioners were forced to leave their land economically idle during this period. But the Court refuses to apply *Lucas* on the ground that the deprivation was "temporary."

Neither the Takings Clause nor our case law supports such a distinction. For one thing, a distinction between "temporary" and "permanent" prohibitions is tenuous. The "temporary" prohibition in this case that the Court finds is not a taking lasted almost six years. The "permanent" prohibition that the Court held to be a taking in *Lucas* lasted less than two years. Under the Court's decision today, the takings question turns entirely on the initial label given a regulation, a label that is often without much meaning. There is every incentive for government to simply label any prohibition on development "temporary," or to fix a set number of years. As in this case, this initial designation does not preclude the government from repeatedly extending the "temporary" prohibition into a long-term ban on all development. The Court now holds that such a designation by the government is conclusive even though in fact the moratorium greatly exceeds the time initially specified. Apparently, the Court would not view even a 10-year moratorium as a taking under *Lucas* because the moratorium is not "permanent."

More fundamentally, even if a practical distinction between temporary and permanent deprivations were plausible, to treat the two differently in terms of takings law would be at odds with the justification for the *Lucas* rule. The *Lucas* rule is derived from the fact that a "total deprivation of use is, from the landowner's point of view, the equivalent of a physical appropriation." The regulation in *Lucas* was the "practical equivalence" of a long-term physical appropriation, i.e., a condemnation, so the Fifth Amendment required compensation.

Lucas is implicated when the government deprives a landowner of "all economically beneficial or productive use of land." The District Court found, and the Court agrees, that the moratorium "temporarily" deprived petitioners of "'all economically viable use of their land.'" Because the rationale for the *Lucas* rule applies just as strongly in this case, the "temporary" denial of all viable use of land for six years is a taking.

III

The Court worries that applying *Lucas* here compels finding that an array of traditional, short-term, land-use planning devices are takings. But since the beginning of our regulatory takings jurisprudence, we have recognized that property rights "are enjoyed under an implied limitation." Thus, in *Lucas*, after holding that the regulation prohibiting all economically beneficial use of the coastal land came within our categorical takings rule, we nonetheless inquired into whether such a result "inhere[d] in the title itself, in the restrictions that background principles of the State's law of property and nuisance already place upon land ownership." Because the regulation at issue in *Lucas* purported to be permanent, or at least long term, we concluded that the only implied limitation of state property law that could achieve a similar long-term deprivation of all economic use would be something "achieved in the courts—by adjacent landowners (or other uniquely affected persons) under the State's law of private nuisance, or by the State under its complementary power to abate nuisances that affect the public generally, or otherwise."

When a regulation merely delays a final land use decision, we have recognized that there are other background principles of state property law that prevent the delay from being deemed a taking. We thus noted in *First English* that our discussion of temporary takings did not apply "in the case of normal delays in obtaining building permits, changes in zoning ordinances, variances, and the like." Thus, the short-term delays attendant to zoning and permit regimes are a longstanding feature of state property law and part of a landowner's reasonable investment-backed expectations.

But a moratorium prohibiting all economic use for a period of six years is not one of the longstanding, implied limitations of state property law. Moratoria are "interim controls on the use of land that seek to maintain the status quo with respect to land development in an area by either 'freezing' existing land uses or by allowing the issuance of building permits for only certain land uses that would not be inconsistent with a contemplated zoning plan or zoning change."

But this case does not require us to decide as a categorical matter whether moratoria prohibiting all economic use are an implied limitation of state property law, because the duration of this "moratorium" far exceeds that of ordinary moratoria. As the Court recognizes, state statutes authorizing the issuance of moratoria often limit the moratoria's duration. California, where much of the land at issue in this case is located, provides that a moratorium "shall be of no further force and effect 45 days from its date of adoption," and caps extension of the moratorium so that the total duration cannot exceed two years. Another State limits moratoria to 120 days, with the possibility of a single 6-month extension. Ore. Rev. Stat. Ann. § 197.520(4) (1997). Others limit moratoria to six months without any possibility of an extension. See Colo. Rev. Stat. § 30-28-121 (2001); N.J. Stat. Ann. § 40:55D-90(b) (1991). Indeed, it has long been understood that moratoria on development exceeding these short time periods are not a legitimate planning device.

Because the prohibition on development of nearly six years in this case cannot be said to resemble any "implied limitation" of state property law, it is a taking that requires compensation.

Lake Tahoe is a national treasure and I do not doubt that respondent's efforts at preventing further degradation of the lake were made in good faith in furtherance of the public interest. But, as is the case with most governmental action that furthers the public interest, the Constitution requires that the costs and burdens be borne by the public at large, not by a few targeted citizens. Justice Holmes' admonition of 80 years ago again rings true: "We are in danger of forgetting that a strong public desire to improve the public condition is not enough to warrant achieving the desire by a shorter cut than the constitutional way of paying for the change."

Justice THOMAS, with whom Justice SCALIA joins, dissenting.

I join the Chief Justice's dissent. I write separately to address the majority's conclusion that the temporary moratorium at issue here was not a taking because it was not a "taking of 'the parcel as a whole.'" While this questionable rule has been applied to various alleged regulatory takings, it was, in my view, rejected in the context of temporal deprivations of property by First English Evangelical Lutheran Church of Glendale v. County of Los Angeles (1987), which held that temporary and permanent takings "are not different in kind" when a landowner is deprived of all beneficial use of his land. I had thought that *First English* put to rest the notion that the "relevant denominator" is land's infinite life. Consequently, a regulation effecting a total deprivation of the use of a so-called "temporal slice" of property is compensable under the Takings Clause unless background principles of state property law prevent it from being deemed a taking; "total deprivation of use is, from the landowner's point of view, the equivalent of a physical appropriation."

A taking is exactly what occurred in this case. No one seriously doubts that the land use regulations at issue rendered petitioners' land unsusceptible of any economically beneficial use. This was true at the inception of the moratorium, and it remains true today. These individuals and families were deprived of the opportunity to build single-family homes as permanent, retirement, or vacation residences on land upon which such construction was authorized when purchased. The Court assures them that "a temporary prohibition on economic use" cannot be a taking because "logically . . . the property will recover value as soon as the prohibition is lifted." But the "logical" assurance that a "temporary restriction . . . merely causes a diminution in value," is cold comfort to the property owners in this case or any other. After all, "[i]n the long run we are all dead." John Maynard Keynes, Monetary Reform 88 (1924).

I would hold that regulations prohibiting all productive uses of property are subject to *Lucas'* per se rule, regardless of whether the property so burdened retains theoretical useful life and value if, and when, the "temporary" moratorium is lifted. To my mind, such potential future value bears on the amount of compensation due and has nothing to do with the question whether there was a taking in the first place. It is regrettable that the Court has charted a markedly different path today.

Chapter 7

Equal Protection

C. Classifications Based on Race and National Origin

*DRAWING ELECTION DISTRICTS TO INCREASE MINORITY
REPRESENTATION (casebook, p. 639)*

As the casebook indicates, in a series of cases during the 1990s, the Supreme
Court held that the government may use race as a "predominant factor" in
drawing election district lines to benefit racial minorities only if it meets strict
scrutiny. In Hunt v. Cromartie, below, the Supreme Court reversed a three-judge
federal district court's holding that race was the predominant factor in drawing
district lines for a congressional seat in North Carolina.

Justice Breyer's majority opinion drew a distinction between race being used
for political reasons (such as to create a majority Democratic district) as opposed
to for affirmative action reasons (to increase the likelihood of electing minority
representatives). In reading the case, remember that there will be redistricting all
over the country as a result of the 2000 census and many challenges to these
new districts. In considering the decision, it is important to think about how a
federal district court judge can apply the distinction drawn by the Court. Notice
also that the Supreme Court overturns the district court's fact-finding as clearly
erroneous; this is something that is relatively uncommon. A key difference
between the majority and the dissent in this case concerns the proper application
of this standard for appellate review.

HUNT v. CROMARTIE
121 S. Ct. 1452 (2001)

Justice BREYER delivered the opinion of the Court.

In this appeal, we review a three-judge District Court's determination that
North Carolina's legislature used race as the "predominant factor" in drawing its
12th Congressional District's 1997 boundaries. The court's findings, in our
view, are clearly erroneous. We therefore reverse its conclusion that the State
violated the Equal Protection Clause.

I

This "racial districting" litigation is before us for the fourth time. Our first two holdings addressed North Carolina's former Congressional District 12, one of two North Carolina congressional districts drawn in 1992 that contained a majority of African-American voters. See Shaw v. Reno (1993) (Shaw I); Shaw v. Hunt (1996) (Shaw II).

A

In *Shaw I*, the Court considered whether plaintiffs' factual allegation—that the legislature had drawn the former district's boundaries for race-based reasons—if true, could underlie a legal holding that the legislature had violated the Equal Protection Clause. The Court held that it could. It wrote that a violation may exist where the legislature's boundary drawing, though "race neutral on its face," nonetheless can be understood only as an effort to "separate voters into different districts on the basis of race," and where the "separation lacks sufficient justification."

In *Shaw II*, the Court reversed a subsequent three-judge District Court's holding that the boundary-drawing law in question did not violate the Constitution. This Court found that the district's "unconventional," snakelike shape, the way in which its boundaries split towns and counties, its predominately African-American racial make-up, and its history, together demonstrated a deliberate effort to create a "majority-black" district in which race "could not be compromised," not simply a district designed to "protec[t] Democratic incumbents." And the Court concluded that the legislature's use of racial criteria was not justified.

B

Our third holding focused on a new District 12, the boundaries of which the legislature had redrawn in 1997. Hunt v. Cromartie (1999). A three-judge District Court, with one judge dissenting, had granted summary judgment in favor of those challenging the district's boundaries. The court found that the legislature again had "used criteria . . . that are facially race driven," in violation of the Equal Protection Clause. It based this conclusion upon "uncontroverted material facts" showing that the boundaries created an unusually shaped district, split counties and cities, and in particular placed almost all heavily Democratic-registered, predominantly African-American voting precincts, inside the district while locating some heavily Democratic-registered, predominantly white precincts, outside the district. This latter circumstance, said the court, showed that the legislature was trying to maximize new District 12's African-American voting strength, not the district's Democratic voting strength.

This Court reversed. We agreed with the District Court that the new district's shape, the way in which it split towns and counties, and its heavily African-

American voting population all helped the plaintiffs' case. But neither that evidence by itself, nor when coupled with the evidence of Democratic registration, was sufficient to show, on summary judgment, the unconstitutional race-based objective that plaintiffs claimed. That is because there was a genuine issue of material fact as to whether the evidence also was consistent with a constitutional political objective, namely, the creation of a safe Democratic seat.

C

On remand, the parties undertook additional discovery. The three-judge District Court held a three-day trial. And the court again held (over a dissent) that the legislature had unconstitutionally drawn District 12's new 1997 boundaries. It found that the legislature had tried "(1) [to] cur[e] the [previous district's] constitutional defects" while also "(2) drawing the plan to maintain the existing partisan balance in the State's congressional delegation." It added that to "achieve the second goal," the legislature "drew the new plan (1) to avoid placing two incumbents in the same district and (2) to preserve the partisan core of the existing districts." The court concluded that the "plan as enacted largely reflects these directives." But the court also found "as a matter of fact that the General Assembly . . . used criteria . . . that are facially race driven" without any compelling justification for doing so.

The court based its latter, constitutionally critical, conclusion in part upon the district's snakelike shape, the way in which it split cities and towns, and its heavily African-American (47%) voting population—all matters that this Court had considered when it found summary judgment inappropriate. The court also based this conclusion upon a specific finding—absent when we previously considered this litigation—that the legislature had drawn the boundaries in order "to collect precincts with high racial identification rather than political identification."

II

The issue in this case is evidentiary. We must determine whether there is adequate support for the District Court's key findings, particularly the ultimate finding that the legislature's motive was predominantly racial, not political. In making this determination, we are aware that, under *Shaw I* and later cases, the burden of proof on the plaintiffs (who attack the district) is a "demanding one." The Court has specified that those who claim that a legislature has improperly used race as a criterion, in order, for example, to create a majority-minority district, must show at a minimum that the "legislature subordinated traditional race-neutral districting principles . . . to racial considerations." Miller v. Johnson (1995). Race must not simply have been "a motivation for the drawing of a majority minority district," but "the 'predominant factor' motivating the legislature's districting decision." Plaintiffs must show that a facially neutral law "is unexplainable on grounds other than race."

The Court also has made clear that the underlying districting decision is one that ordinarily falls within a legislature's sphere of competence. Hence, the legislature "must have discretion to exercise the political judgment necessary to balance competing interests," and courts must "exercise extraordinary caution in adjudicating claims that a State has drawn district lines on the basis of race," especially appropriate in this case, where the State has articulated a legitimate political explanation for its districting decision, and the voting population is one in which race and political affiliation are highly correlated.

We also are aware that we review the District Court's findings only for "clear error." In applying this standard, we, like any reviewing court, will not reverse a lower court's finding of fact simply because we "would have decided the case differently." Rather, a reviewing court must ask whether "on the entire evidence," it is "left with the definite and firm conviction that a mistake has been committed."

Where an intermediate court reviews, and affirms, a trial court's factual findings, this Court will not "lightly overturn" the concurrent findings of the two lower courts. But in this instance there is no intermediate court, and we are the only court of review. Moreover, the trial here at issue was not lengthy and the key evidence consisted primarily of documents and expert testimony. Credibility evaluations played a minor role. Accordingly, we find that an extensive review of the District Court's findings, for clear error, is warranted. That review leaves us "with the definite and firm conviction," that the District Court's key findings are mistaken.

III

The critical District Court determination—the matter for which we remanded this litigation—consists of the finding that race rather than politics pre-dominantly explains District 12's 1997 boundaries. That determination rests upon three findings (the district's shape, its splitting of towns and counties, and its high African-American voting population) that we previously found in-sufficient to support summary judgment. Given the undisputed evidence that racial identification is highly correlated with political affiliation in North Carolina, these facts in and of themselves cannot, as a matter of law, support the District Court's judgment. The District Court rested, however, upon new sub-sidiary findings to conclude that District 12's lines are the product of no "mer[e] correlat[ion]," but are instead a result of the predominance of race in the legis-lature's line-drawing process.

In considering each subsidiary finding, we have given weight to the fact that the District Court was familiar with this litigation, heard the testimony of each witness, and considered all the evidence with care. Nonetheless, we cannot accept the District Court's findings as adequate for reasons which we shall spell out in detail and which we can summarize as follows:

First, the primary evidence upon which the District Court relied for its "race, not politics," conclusion is evidence of voting registration, not voting behavior;

and that is precisely the kind of evidence that we said was inadequate the last time this case was before us. Second, the additional evidence to which appellees' expert, Dr. Weber, pointed, and the statements made by Senator Cooper and Gerry Cohen, simply do not provide significant additional support for the District Court's conclusion. Third, the District Court, while not accepting the contrary conclusion of appellants' expert, Dr. Peterson, did not (and as far as the record reveals, could not) reject much of the significant supporting factual information he provided. Fourth, in any event, appellees themselves have provided us with charts summarizing evidence of voting behavior and those charts tend to refute the court's "race not politics" conclusion.

IV

We concede the record contains a modicum of evidence offering support for the District Court's conclusion. That evidence includes the Cohen e-mail, Senator Cooper's reference to "racial balance," and to a minor degree, some aspects of Dr. Weber's testimony. The evidence taken together, however, does not show that racial considerations predominated in the drawing of District 12's boundaries. That is because race in this case correlates closely with political behavior. The basic question is whether the legislature drew District 12's boundaries because of race rather than because of political behavior (coupled with traditional, nonracial districting considerations). It is not, as the dissent contends, whether a legislature may defend its districting decisions based on a "stereotype" about African-American voting behavior. And given the fact that the party attacking the legislature's decision bears the burden of proving that racial considerations are "dominant and controlling," given the "demanding" nature of that burden of proof, and given the sensitivity, the "extraordinary caution," that district courts must show to avoid treading upon legislative prerogatives, the attacking party has not successfully shown that race, rather than politics, predominantly accounts for the result. The record leaves us with the "definite and firm conviction," that the District Court erred in finding to the contrary. And we do not believe that providing appellees a further opportunity to make their "precinct swapping" arguments in the District Court could change this result.

We can put the matter more generally as follows: In a case such as this one where majority-minority districts (or the approximate equivalent) are at issue and where racial identification correlates highly with political affiliation, the party attacking the legislatively drawn boundaries must show at the least that the legislature could have achieved its legitimate political objectives in alternative ways that are comparably consistent with traditional districting principles. That party must also show that those districting alternatives would have brought about significantly greater racial balance. Appellees failed to make any such showing here. We conclude that the District Court's contrary findings are clearly erroneous.

Justice THOMAS, with whom the Chief Justice, Justice SCALIA, and Justice KENNEDY join, dissenting.

The issue for the District Court was whether racial considerations were predominant in the design of North Carolina's Congressional District 12. The issue for this Court is simply whether the District Court's factual finding—that racial considerations did predominate—was clearly erroneous. Because I do not believe the court below committed clear error, I respectfully dissent.

I

The District Court's conclusion that race was the predominant factor motivating the North Carolina Legislature is a factual finding. We are not permitted to reverse the court's finding "simply because [we are] convinced that [we] would have decided the case differently." "Where there are two permissible views of the evidence, the factfinder's choice between them cannot be clearly erroneous." We should upset the District Court's finding only if we are "'left with the definite and firm conviction that a mistake has been committed.'"

The Court does cite cases that address the correct standard of review, and does couch its conclusion in "clearly erroneous" terms. But these incantations of the correct standard are empty gestures, contradicted by the Court's conclusion that it must engage in "extensive review." In several ways, the Court ignores its role as a reviewing court and engages in its own factfinding enterprise. First, the Court suggests that there is some significance to the absence of an intermediate court in this action. This cannot be a legitimate consideration. If it were legitimate, we would have mentioned it in prior redistricting cases. After all, in *Miller* and *Shaw*, we also did not have the benefit of intermediate appellate review. Moreover, the implication of the Court's argument is that intermediate courts, because they are the first reviewers of the factfinder's conclusions, should engage in a level of review more rigorous than clear error review. This suggestion is not supported by law. Second, the Court appears to discount clear error review here because the trial was "not lengthy." Even if considerations such as the length of the trial were relevant in deciding how to review factual findings, an assumption about which I have my doubts, these considerations would not counsel against deference in this action. The trial was not "just a few hours" long, it lasted for three days in which the court heard the testimony of 12 witnesses. And quite apart from the total trial time, the District Court sifted through hundreds of pages of deposition testimony and expert analysis, including statistical analysis. It also should not be forgotten that one member of the panel has reviewed the iterations of District 12 since 1992. If one were to calibrate clear error review according to the trier of fact's familiarity with the case, there is simply no question that the court here gained a working knowledge of the facts of this litigation in myriad ways over a period far longer than three days.

Third, the Court downplays deference to the District Court's finding by highlighting that the key evidence was expert testimony requiring no traditional credibility determinations. As a factual matter, the Court overlooks the District Court's express assessment of the legislative redistricting leader's credibility. Although we have recognized that particular weight should be given to a trial court's credibility determinations, we have never held that factual findings based on documentary evidence and expert testimony justify "extensive review." On the contrary, we explained in *Anderson* that "[t]he rationale for deference . . . is not limited to the superiority of the trial judge's position to make determinations of credibility."

Finally, perhaps the best evidence that the Court has emptied clear error review of meaningful content in the redistricting context (and the strongest testament to the fact that the District Court was dealing with a complex fact pattern) is the Court's foray into the minutiae of the record. I do not doubt this Court's ability to sift through volumes of facts or to argue its interpretation of those facts persuasively. But I do doubt the wisdom, efficiency, increased accuracy, and legitimacy of an extensive review that is any more searching than clear error review.

II

Reviewing for clear error, I cannot say that the District Court's view of the evidence was impermissible. First, the court relied on objective measures of compactness, which show that District 12 is the most geographically scattered district in North Carolina, to support its conclusion that the district's design was not dictated by traditional districting concerns. Although this evidence was available when we held that summary judgment was inappropriate, we certainly did not hold that it was irrelevant in determining whether racial gerrymandering occurred. On the contrary, we determined that there was a triable issue of fact. Moreover, although we acknowledged "that a district's unusual shape can give rise to an inference of political motivation," we "doubt[ed] that a bizarre shape equally supports a political inference and a racial one." As we explained, "[s]ome districts . . . are 'so highly irregular that [they] rationally cannot be understood as anything other than an effort to segregat[e] . . . voters' on the basis of race."

Second, the court relied on the expert opinion of Dr. Weber, who interpreted statistical data to conclude that there were Democratic precincts with low black populations excluded from District 12, which would have created a more compact district had they been included.

Third, the court credited Dr. Weber's testimony that the districting decisions could not be explained by political motives.

Finally, the court found that other evidence demonstrated that race was foremost on the legislative agenda: an e-mail from the drafter of the 1992 and

1997 plans to senators in charge of legislative redistricting, the computer capability to draw the district by race, and statements made by Senator Cooper that the legislature was going to be able to avoid *Shaw*'s majority-minority trigger by ending just short of the majority. The e-mail, in combination with the indirect evidence, is evidence ample enough to support the District Court's finding for purposes of clear error review. The drafter of the redistricting plans reported in the bluntest of terms: "I have moved Greensboro Black community into the 12th [District], and now need to take . . . 60,000 out of the 12th [District]." Certainly the District Court was entitled to believe that the drafter was targeting voters and shifting district boundaries purely on the basis of race. The Court tries to belittle the import of this evidence by noting that the e-mail does not discuss why blacks were being targeted. However, the District Court was assigned the task of determining whether, not why, race predominated. As I see it, this inquiry is sufficient to answer the constitutional question because racial gerrymandering offends the Constitution whether the motivation is malicious or benign. It is not a defense that the legislature merely may have drawn the district based on the stereotype that blacks are reliable Democratic voters.

If I were the District Court, I might have reached the same conclusion that the Court does, that "[t]he evidence taken together . . . does not show that racial considerations predominated in the drawing of District 12's boundaries." But I am not the trier of fact, and it is not my role to weigh evidence in the first instance. The only question that this Court should decide is whether the District Court's finding of racial predominance was clearly erroneous. In light of the direct evidence of racial motive and the inferences that may be drawn from the circumstantial evidence, I am satisfied that the District Court's finding was permissible, even if not compelled by the record.

D. Gender Classifications

3. Gender Classifications Benefiting Women (casebook, p. 658)

The casebook, in discussing gender classifications benefiting women, focuses on two areas: gender classifications benefiting women based on role stereotypes (p. 658); and gender classifications benefiting women as a remedy (p. 669). In Nguyen v. Immigration and Naturalization Service, below, the Court allows a third type of gender classification: gender classifications benefiting women because of biological differences between men and women. The Court allows a difference in I.N.S. rules favoring mothers over fathers because of the greater certainty as to the identity of the mother as compared to the father and the greater opportunity that mothers have in establishing a relationship with their children.

Notice in reading the decision some of the key differences between the majority and the dissent: The majority articulates the test as intermediate scrutiny, whereas the dissent emphasizes that there also must be an "exceedingly persuasive justification" for the gender classification; the dissent emphasizes that only "actual" legislative purposes are sufficient, whereas the majority does not; and the majority and the dissent differ as to whether the law is based on stereotypes or biological differences between men and women.

NGUYEN v. IMMIGRATION AND NATURALIZATION SERVICE
121 S. Ct. 2053 (2001)

Justice KENNEDY delivered the opinion of the Court.

Title 8 U.S.C. § 1409 governs the acquisition of United States citizenship by persons born to one United States citizen parent and one noncitizen parent when the parents are unmarried and the child is born outside of the United States or its possessions. The statute imposes different requirements for the child's acquisition of citizenship depending upon whether the citizen parent is the mother or the father. The question before us is whether the statutory distinction is consistent with the equal protection guarantee embedded in the Due Process Clause of the Fifth Amendment.

I

Petitioner Tuan Ahn Nguyen was born in Saigon, Vietnam, on September 11, 1969, to copetitioner Joseph Boulais and a Vietnamese citizen. Boulais and Nguyen's mother were not married. Boulais always has been a citizen of the United States, and he was in Vietnam under the employ of a corporation. After he and Nguyen's mother ended their relationship, Nguyen lived for a time with the family of Boulais' new Vietnamese girlfriend. In June 1975, Nguyen, then almost six years of age, came to the United States. He became a lawful permanent resident and was raised in Texas by Boulais.

In 1992, when Nguyen was 22, he pleaded guilty in a Texas state court to two counts of sexual assault on a child. He was sentenced to eight years in prison on each count. Three years later, the United States Immigration and Naturalization Service (INS) initiated deportation proceedings against Nguyen as an alien who had been convicted of two crimes involving moral turpitude, as well as an aggravated felony. Though later he would change his position and argue he was a United States citizen, Nguyen testified at his deportation hearing that he was a citizen of Vietnam. The Immigration Judge found him deportable.

Nguyen appealed to the Board of Immigration of Appeals and, in 1998, while the matter was pending, his father obtained an order of parentage from a state court, based on DNA testing. By this time, Nguyen was 28 years old. The Board dismissed Nguyen's appeal, rejecting his claim to United States citizenship because he had failed to establish compliance with 8 U.S.C. § 1409(a), which sets forth the requirements for one who was born out of wedlock and abroad to a citizen father and a noncitizen mother.

Nguyen and Boulais appealed to the Court of Appeals for the Fifth Circuit, arguing that § 1409 violates equal protection by providing different rules for attainment of citizenship by children born abroad and out of wedlock depending upon whether the one parent with American citizenship is the mother or the father. The court rejected the constitutional challenge.

We hold that § 1409(a) is consistent with the constitutional guarantee of equal protection.

II

The general requirement for acquisition of citizenship by a child born outside the United States and its outlying possessions and to parents who are married, one of whom is a citizen and the other of whom is an alien, is set forth in 8 U.S.C. § 1401(g). The statute provides that the child is also a citizen if, before the birth, the citizen parent had been physically present in the United States for a total of five years, at least two of which were after the parent turned 14 years of age.

As to an individual born under the same circumstances, save that the parents are unwed, § 1409(a) sets forth the following requirements where the father is the citizen parent and the mother is an alien:

> (1) a blood relationship between the person and the father is established by clear and convincing evidence,
> (2) the father had the nationality of the United States at the time of the person's birth,
> (3) the father (unless deceased) has agreed in writing to provide financial support for the person until the person reaches the age of 18 years, and
> (4) while the person is under the age of 18 years—
>> (A) the person is legitimated under the law of the person's residence or domicile,
>> (B) the father acknowledges paternity of the person in writing under oath, or
>> (C) the paternity of the person is established by adjudication of a competent court.

When the citizen parent of the child born abroad and out of wedlock is the child's mother, the requirements for the transmittal of citizenship are described in § 1409(c):

> (c) Notwithstanding the provision of subsection (a) of this section, a person born, after December 23, 1952, outside the United States and out of wedlock

shall be held to have acquired at birth the nationality status of his mother, if the mother had the nationality of the United States at the time of such person's birth, and if the mother had previously been physically present in the United States or one of its outlying possessions for a continuous period of one year.

Section 1409(a) thus imposes a set of requirements on the children of citizen fathers born abroad and out of wedlock to a noncitizen mother that are not imposed under like circumstances when the citizen parent is the mother.

III

For a gender-based classification to withstand equal protection scrutiny, it must be established "'at least that the [challenged] classification serves important governmental objectives and that the discriminatory means employed are substantially related to the achievement of those objectives." United States v. Virginia (1996). For reasons to follow, we conclude § 1409 satisfies this standard. Given that determination, we need not decide whether some lesser degree of scrutiny pertains because the statute implicates Congress' immigration and naturalization power.

Before considering the important governmental interests advanced by the statute, two observations concerning the operation of the provision are in order. First, a citizen mother expecting a child and living abroad has the right to re-enter the United States so the child can be born here and be a 14th Amendment citizen. From one perspective, then, the statute simply ensures equivalence between two expectant mothers who are citizens abroad if one chooses to reenter for the child's birth and the other chooses not to return, or does not have the means to do so. This equivalence is not a factor if the single citizen parent living abroad is the father. For, unlike the unmarried mother, the unmarried father as a general rule cannot control where the child will be born.

Second, although § 1409(a)(4) requires certain conduct to occur before the child of a citizen father, born out of wedlock and abroad, reaches 18 years of age, it imposes no limitations on when an individual who qualifies under the statute can claim citizenship. The statutory treatment of citizenship is identical in this respect whether the citizen parent is the mother or the father. A person born to a citizen parent of either gender may assert citizenship, assuming compliance with statutory preconditions, regardless of his or her age. And while the conditions necessary for a citizen mother to transmit citizenship under § 1409(c) exist at birth, citizen fathers and/or their children have 18 years to satisfy the requirements of § 1409(a)(4).

The statutory distinction relevant in this case, then, is that § 1409(a)(4) requires one of three affirmative steps to be taken if the citizen parent is the father, but not if the citizen parent is the mother: legitimation; a declaration of paternity under oath by the father; or a court order of paternity. Congress' decision to impose requirements on unmarried fathers that differ from those on unmarried mothers is based on the significant difference between their respective relationships to the potential citizen at the time of birth. Specifically, the imposition of the requirement for a paternal relationship, but not a maternal one, is justified by two important governmental objectives. We discuss each in turn.

A

The first governmental interest to be served is the importance of assuring that a biological parent-child relationship exists. In the case of the mother, the relation is verifiable from the birth itself. The mother's status is documented in most instances by the birth certificate or hospital records and the witnesses who attest to her having given birth.

In the case of the father, the uncontestable fact is that he need not be present at the birth. If he is present, furthermore, that circumstance is not incontrovertible proof of fatherhood. Fathers and mothers are not similarly situated with regard to the proof of biological parenthood. The imposition of a different set of rules for making that legal determination with respect to fathers and mothers is neither surprising nor troublesome from a constitutional perspective. Section 1409(a)(4)'s provision of three options for a father seeking to establish paternity—legitimation, paternity oath, and court order of paternity—is designed to ensure an acceptable documentation of paternity.

Petitioners argue that the requirement of § 1409(a)(1), that a father provide clear and convincing evidence of parentage, is sufficient to achieve the end of establishing paternity, given the sophistication of modern DNA tests. Section 1409(a)(1) does not actually mandate a DNA test, however. The Constitution, moreover, does not require that Congress elect one particular mechanism from among many possible methods of establishing paternity, even if that mechanism arguably might be the most scientifically advanced method. With respect to DNA testing, the expense, reliability, and availability of such testing in various parts of the world may have been of particular concern to Congress. The requirement of § 1409(a)(4) represents a reasonable conclusion by the legislature that the satisfaction of one of several alternatives will suffice to establish the blood link between father and child required as a predicate to the child's acquisition of citizenship. Given the proof of motherhood that is inherent in birth itself, it is unremarkable that Congress did not require the same affirmative steps of mothers.

B

The second important governmental interest furthered in a substantial manner by § 1409(a)(4) is the determination to ensure that the child and the citizen parent have some demonstrated opportunity or potential to develop not just a relationship that is recognized, as a formal matter, by the law, but one that consists of the real, everyday ties that provide a connection between child and citizen parent and, in turn, the United States. In the case of a citizen mother and a child born overseas, the opportunity for a meaningful relationship between citizen parent and child inheres in the very event of birth, an event so often critical to our constitutional and statutory understandings of citizenship. The mother knows that the child is in being and is hers and has an initial point of contact with him. There is at least an opportunity for mother and child to develop a real, meaningful relationship.

The same opportunity does not result from the event of birth, as a matter of biological inevitability, in the case of the unwed father. Given the 9-month interval between conception and birth, it is not always certain that a father will know that a child was conceived, nor is it always clear that even the mother will be sure of the father's identity. This fact takes on particular significance in the case of a child born overseas and out of wedlock. One concern in this context has always been with young people, men for the most part, who are on duty with the Armed Forces in foreign countries.

When we turn to the conditions which prevail today, we find that the passage of time has produced additional and even more substantial grounds to justify the statutory distinction. The ease of travel and the willingness of Americans to visit foreign countries have resulted in numbers of trips abroad that must be of real concern when we contemplate the prospect of accepting petitioners' argument, which would mandate, contrary to Congress' wishes, citizenship by male parentage subject to no condition save the father's previous length of residence in this country. In 1999 alone, Americans made almost 25 million trips abroad, excluding trips to Canada and Mexico. Visits to Canada and Mexico add to this figure almost 34 million additional visits. And the average American overseas traveler spent 15.1 nights out of the United States in 1999.

Principles of equal protection do not require Congress to ignore this reality. To the contrary, these facts demonstrate the critical importance of the Government's interest in ensuring some opportunity for a tie between citizen father and foreign born child which is a reasonable substitute for the opportunity manifest between mother and child at the time of birth. Indeed, especially in light of the number of Americans who take short sojourns abroad, the prospect that a father might not even know of the conception is a realistic possibility. Even if a father knows of the fact of conception, moreover, it does not follow that he will be present at the birth of the child. Thus, unlike the case of the mother, there is no assurance that the father and his biological child will ever meet. Without an initial point of contact with the child by a father who knows the child is his own, there is no opportunity for father and child to begin a relationship. Section 1409 takes the unremarkable step of ensuring that such an opportunity, inherent in the event of birth as to the mother-child relationship, exists between father and child before citizenship is conferred upon the latter.

The importance of the governmental interest at issue here is too profound to be satisfied merely by conducting a DNA test. The fact of paternity can be established even without the father's knowledge, not to say his presence. Paternity can be established by taking DNA samples even from a few strands of hair, years after the birth. Yet scientific proof of biological paternity does nothing, by itself, to ensure contact between father and child during the child's minority.

Congress is well within its authority in refusing, absent proof of at least the opportunity for the development of a relationship between citizen parent and child, to commit this country to embracing a child as a citizen entitled as of birth to the full protection of the United States, to the absolute right to enter its borders, and to full participation in the political process. If citizenship is to be conferred by the unwitting means petitioners urge, so that its acquisition abroad bears little relation to the realities of the child's own ties and allegiances, it is for Congress, not this Court, to make that determination. Congress has not taken that path but has instead chosen, by means of § 1409, to ensure in the case of father and child the opportunity for a relationship to develop, an opportunity which the event of birth itself provides for the mother and child. It should be unobjectionable for Congress to require some evidence of a minimal opportunity for the development of a relationship with the child in terms the male can fulfill.

Petitioners and their amici argue in addition that, rather than fulfilling an important governmental interest, § 1409 merely embodies a gender-based stereotype. Although the above discussion should illustrate that, contrary to petitioners' assertions, § 1409 addresses an undeniable difference in the circumstance of the parents at the time a child is born, it should be noted, furthermore, that the difference does not result from some stereotype, defined as a frame of mind resulting from irrational or uncritical analysis. There is nothing irrational or improper in the recognition that at the moment of birth—a critical event in the statutory scheme and in the whole tradition of citizenship law—the mother's knowledge of the child and the fact of parenthood have been established in a way not guaranteed in the case of the unwed father. This is not a stereotype.

To fail to acknowledge even our most basic biological differences—such as the fact that a mother must be present at birth but the father need not be—risks making the guarantee of equal protection superficial, and so disserving it. Mechanistic classification of all our differences as stereotypes would operate to obscure those misconceptions and prejudices that are real. The distinction embodied in the statutory scheme here at issue is not marked by misconception and prejudice, nor does it show disrespect for either class. The difference between men and women in relation to the birth process is a real one, and the principle of equal protection does not forbid Congress to address the problem at hand in a manner specific to each gender.

Justice O'CONNOR, with whom Justice SOUTER, Justice GINSBURG, and Justice BREYER join, dissenting.

In a long line of cases spanning nearly three decades, this Court has applied heightened scrutiny to legislative classifications based on sex. The Court today confronts another statute that classifies individuals on the basis of their sex. While the Court invokes heightened scrutiny, the manner in which it explains and applies this standard is a stranger to our precedents. Because the Immigration and Naturalization Service (INS) has not shown an exceedingly persuasive justification for the sex-based classification embodied in 8 U.S.C. § 1409(a)(4) —i.e., because it has failed to establish at least that the classification substantially relates to the achievement of important governmental objectives— I would reverse the judgment of the Court of Appeals.

I

Sex-based statutes, even when accurately reflecting the way most men or women behave, deny individuals opportunity. Such generalizations must be viewed not in isolation, but in the context of our Nation's "long and unfortunate history of sex discrimination." Sex-based generalizations both reflect and reinforce "fixed notions concerning the roles and abilities of males and females."

For these reasons, a party who seeks to defend a statute that classifies individuals on the basis of sex "must carry the burden of showing an 'exceedingly persuasive justification' for the classification." The defender of the classification meets this burden "only by showing at least that the classification serves 'important governmental objectives and that the discriminatory means employed' are 'substantially related to the achievement of those objectives.'"

Heightened scrutiny does not countenance justifications that "rely on overbroad generalizations about the different talents, capacities, or preferences of males and females." Rational basis review, by contrast, is much more tolerant of the use of broad generalizations about different classes of individuals, so long as the classification is not arbitrary or irrational. Moreover, overbroad sex-based generalizations are impermissible even when they enjoy empirical support.

The most important difference between heightened scrutiny and rational basis review, of course, is the required fit between the means employed and the ends served. Under heightened scrutiny, the discriminatory means must be "substantially related" to an actual and important governmental interest. Under rational basis scrutiny, the means need only be "rationally related" to a conceivable and legitimate state end. The fact that other means are better suited to the achievement of governmental ends therefore is of no moment under rational basis review. But because we require a much tighter fit between means and ends under heightened scrutiny, the availability of sex-neutral alternatives to a sex-based classification is often highly probative of the validity of the classification.

II

The Court recites the governing substantive standard for heightened scrutiny of sex-based classifications, but departs from the guidance of our precedents concerning such classifications in several ways.

For example, the majority hypothesizes about the interests served by the statute and fails adequately to inquire into the actual purposes of § 1409(a)(4).

The Court also does not always explain adequately the importance of the interests that it claims to be served by the provision. The majority also fails carefully to consider whether the sex-based classification is being used impermissibly "as a proxy for other, more germane bases of classification," and instead casually dismisses the relevance of available sex-neutral alternatives. And, contrary to the majority's conclusion, the fit between the means and ends of § 1409(a)(4) is far too attenuated for the provision to survive heightened scrutiny. In all, the majority opinion represents far less than the rigorous application of heightened scrutiny that our precedents require.

A

According to the Court, "[t]he first governmental interest to be served is the importance of assuring that a biological parent-child relationship exists." The majority does not elaborate on the importance of this interest, which presumably lies in preventing fraudulent conveyances of citizenship. Nor does the majority demonstrate that this is one of the actual purposes of § 1409(a)(4). Assuming that Congress actually had this purpose in mind in enacting parts of § 1409(a)(4), the INS does not appear to rely on this interest in its effort to sustain § 1409(a)(4)'s sex-based classification. In light of the reviewing court's duty to "determine whether the proffered justification is 'exceedingly persuasive,'" this disparity between the majority's defense of the statute and the INS' proffered justifications is striking, to say the least.

The gravest defect in the Court's reliance on this interest, however, is the insufficiency of the fit between § 1409(a)(4)'s discriminatory means and the asserted end. Section 1409(c) imposes no particular burden of proof on mothers wishing to convey citizenship to their children. By contrast, § 1409(a)(1), which petitioners do not challenge before this Court, requires that "a blood relationship between the person and the father [be] established by clear and convincing evidence." The virtual certainty of a biological link that modern DNA testing affords reinforces the sufficiency of § 1409(a)(1).

If rational basis scrutiny were appropriate in this case, then the claim that "[t]he Constitution . . . does not require that Congress elect one particular mechanism from among many possible methods of establishing paternity," would have much greater force. But fidelity to the Constitution's pledge of equal protection demands more when a facially sex-based classification is at issue. This is not because we sit in judgment of the wisdom of laws in one instance but not the other, but rather because of the potential for "injury . . . to personal dignity" that inheres in or accompanies so many sex-based classifications.

B

The Court states that "[t]he second important governmental interest furthered in a substantial manner by § 1409(a)(4) is the determination to ensure that the child and the citizen parent have some demonstrated opportunity or potential to develop not just a relationship that is recognized, as a formal matter, by the law, but one that consists of the real, everyday ties that provide a connection between child and citizen parent and, in turn, the United States." The Court again fails to demonstrate that this was Congress' actual purpose in enacting § 1409(a)(4). The majority's focus on "some demonstrated opportunity or potential to develop . . . real, everyday ties," in fact appears to be the type of hypothesized rationale that is insufficient under heightened scrutiny.

Assuming, as the majority does, that Congress was actually concerned about ensuring a "demonstrated opportunity" for a relationship, it is questionable whether such an opportunity qualifies as an "important" governmental interest apart from the existence of an actual relationship. By focusing on "opportunity" rather than reality, the majority presumably improves the chances of a sufficient means-end fit. But in doing so, it dilutes significantly the weight of the interest. It is difficult to see how, in this citizenship-conferral context, anyone profits from a "demonstrated opportunity" for a relationship in the absence of the fruition of an actual tie. Children who have an "opportunity" for such a tie with a parent, of course, may never develop an actual relationship with that parent. If a child grows up in a foreign country without any postbirth contact with the citizen parent, then the child's never-realized "opportunity" for a relationship with the citizen seems singularly irrelevant to the appropriateness of granting citizenship to that child. Likewise, where there is an actual relationship, it is the actual relationship that does all the work in rendering appropriate a grant of citizenship, regardless of when and how the opportunity for that relationship arose.

Under the present law, the statute on its face accords different treatment to a mother who is by nature present at birth and a father who is by choice present at birth even though those two individuals are similarly situated with respect to the "opportunity" for a relationship. The mother can transmit her citizenship at birth, but the father cannot do so in the absence of at least one other affirmative act. The different statutory treatment is solely on account of the sex of the similarly situated individuals. This type of treatment is patently inconsistent with the promise of equal protection of the laws.

Indeed, the idea that a mother's presence at birth supplies adequate assurance of an opportunity to develop a relationship while a father's presence at birth does not would appear to rest only on an overbroad sex-based generalization. A mother may not have an opportunity for a relationship if the child is removed from his or her mother on account of alleged abuse or neglect, or if the child and mother are separated by tragedy, such as disaster or war, of the sort apparently present in this case. There is no reason, other than stereotype, to say that fathers who are present at birth lack an opportunity for a relationship on similar terms. The "[p]hysical differences between men and women," therefore do not justify § 1409(a)(4)'s discrimination.

No one should mistake the majority's analysis for a careful application of this Court's equal protection jurisprudence concerning sex-based classifications.

Today's decision instead represents a deviation from a line of cases in which we have vigilantly applied heightened scrutiny to such classifications to determine whether a constitutional violation has occurred. I trust that the depth and vitality of these precedents will ensure that today's error remains an aberration. I respectfully dissent.

Chapter 8

Fundamental Rights Under Due Process and Equal Protection

I. The Right to Vote

4. Counting "Uncounted" Votes in a Presidential Election: Bush v. Gore (new, following casebook p. 832)

On December 12, 2000, for the first time in American history, the Supreme Court essentially decided who would be the next President of the United States. Without a doubt, this is one of the most important Supreme Court decisions in history.

The presentation begins with a summary of the events leading up to the Supreme Court's ruling, followed by the decision, and finally I suggest some of the issues to be considered in appraising the case.

The Events Leading Up to Bush v. Gore

The presidential election of Tuesday, November 7, 2000, was one of the closest in American history. By early Wednesday morning, it was clear that the Democratic candidate, Vice President Al Gore, won the national popular vote, but the outcome of the electoral vote was uncertain. The presidency turned on Florida and its 25 electoral votes. Early on election night, the television networks called Gore the winner in Florida, only to retract their prediction later in the evening. In the early hours of Wednesday, November 8, the networks declared Bush the winner of Florida and the presidency, only to recant that a short time later and to conclude that the outcome in Florida, and thus of the national election, was too close to call.

On November 8, the Florida Division of Elections reported that Bush had received 2,909,135 votes, and Gore had received 2,907,351 votes. Florida law provides for a recount of votes if the election is decided by less than one-half of a percent of the votes cast.[1] Because the difference in votes between the two candidates was less than one-half of a percent, Gore immediately asked for a machine recount of the tally of votes in four counties: Volusia, Palm Beach, Broward, and Miami-Dade counties. On November 9, Secretary of State Katherine Harris declined to extend the statutory deadline for county vote totals beyond November 14. By this point, the machine recount had narrowed Bush's lead to a mere 327 votes.

Upon learning of the close margin between him and Bush, Gore petitioned and received permission to have a hand recount in the four counties in question. On Saturday, November 11, Bush sued in federal district court to block the manual recount, but this request was denied.

However, Secretary of State Harris emphasized that she would enforce the November 14 deadline and that she would not accept late recounts from counties in Florida. She said that the Florida election statute required counties to report their votes within one week of the election, unless one of the statutory exceptions was met. These included "proof of fraud that affects the outcome of the election," "substantial noncompliance with statutory election procedures, and a reasonable doubt exists as to whether the certified results expressed the will of the voters," or where compliance with the deadline is "prevented as a result of an act of God, or extenuating circumstances beyond their control."

The four counties submitted their responses and requested acceptance of late completion of totals; each one was denied by Harris. A suit was brought against Harris in Florida district court to compel her to accept the time for the reporting of the results. On Friday, November 17, the Florida state trial court ruled in favor of Harris. On Monday, November 20, the Florida Supreme Court held a nationally televised hearing. On Tuesday night, November 21, the Florida Supreme Court unanimously reversed the trial court and ordered that the Secretary of State accept hand recounts from the four counties if they were completed by Sunday, November 26, at 5:00 p.m., or Monday morning, if the Secretary of State was not open for business on Sunday afternoon.

The Florida Supreme Court ruled that Florida's Secretary of State abused her discretion in refusing to extend the deadline for certifying elections so as to provide the needed time for the recounts. The Court said that it was confronted with a conflict between two statutes. One statute, Fla. Stat. § 102.111, provides that local election canvassing boards must provide their results "by 5:00 of the seventh day following an election." This law was amended in 1989, by

---

1. The Florida statute, § 102.141(4), provides:

(4) If the returns for any office reflect that a candidate was defeated or eliminated by one-half of a percent or less of the votes cast for such office . . . the board responsible for certifying the results of the vote on such race or measure shall order a recount of the votes cast with respect to such office or measure.

§ 102.112, which provides that election results may be ignored and board members shall be fined if these deadlines are not met.

However, another statute, Fla. Stat. § 102.166(4)(a), specifically allows any candidate to request a manual recount. This provision states: "[A]ny candidate whose name appeared on the ballot . . . or any political party whose candidates' name appeared on the ballot may file a written request with the county canvassing board for a manual recount." The law provides that the written request may be made prior to the time the Board certifies the returns or within 72 hours after the election, whichever occurs later.

The Florida Supreme Court expressly noted that these statutes "conflict." The court relied on "traditional rules of statutory construction"—such as that specific laws prevail over general ones and the more recently enacted law takes precedence over the older one—and concluded that Harris erred in denying the extension of time for the counting.

The Florida Supreme Court also said that "a statutory provision will not be construed in such a way that renders meaningless or absurd any other statutory provision." In order to effectuate the law allowing recounts, the court concluded that there must be time for doing so. The court said that the Secretary of State's refusal to accept hand recounts was wrong because it completely negated the statute that expressly provided for this.

On Friday, November 24, the day after Thanksgiving, the Supreme Court granted certiorari in this case, and scheduled oral argument for the following Friday, December 1. In an unprecedented order, the Court permitted the broadcasting of the oral argument immediately after it was finished. A few days later, in Bush v. Palm Beach County Canvassing Bd., 121 S. Ct. 471 (2000), the Supreme Court remanded the case back to the Florida Supreme Court for clarification of its earlier decision. The United States Supreme Court, in a per curiam opinion, said that it was unclear whether the Florida court's decision was based on its interpretation of the Florida Constitution or Florida statutes. The former apparently would be an impermissible basis for decision, while the latter would be acceptable, based on the United States Supreme Court's interpretation of federal election laws. On Monday, December 11—the same day the Supreme Court held oral argument in Bush v. Gore—the Florida Supreme Court issued a decision saying that its decision was based on interpreting Florida's statutes, not its constitution.

Meanwhile, on Sunday, November 26, some counties asked for additional time to complete their counting. For example, Palm Beach County asked for two additional hours beyond the Sunday 5:00 p.m. deadline set by the Florida Supreme Court, particularly because the state Supreme Court expressly had allowed the Secretary of State to wait until Monday morning before receiving the recount totals. The Secretary of State refused all requests for extensions. On Sunday night, November 26, the Florida Elections Canvassing Commission certified the election results: Bush was determined to be the winner of Florida by 537 votes and thus the winner of Florida's 25 electoral votes.

On Monday, November 27, Gore filed suit in Florida under the Florida law providing for "contests" of election results.[2] This provision, § 102.168(3)(c), provides that "[r]eceipt of a number of illegal votes or rejection of a number of legal votes sufficient to change or place in doubt the result of the election" shall be grounds for a contest. The statute authorizes a court, if it finds that there are successful grounds for a contest, to "provide any relief appropriate under such circumstances." Fla. Stat. § 102.168(8).

On Saturday and Sunday, December 2 and 3, a Florida state trial court held a hearing as to whether Gore had met the statutory requirements for a successful contest. On Monday, December 4, the Florida trial court ruled against Gore on the grounds that Gore failed to prove a "reasonable probability" that the election would have turned out differently if not for problems counting ballots.

The Florida Supreme Court granted review and scheduled oral arguments for Thursday, December 7. On Friday afternoon, December 8, the Florida Supreme Court, by a 4-3 decision, reversed the trial court. The Florida Supreme Court ruled that the trial court had used the wrong standard in insisting that Gore demonstrate a "reasonable probability" that the election would have been decided differently. The Florida Supreme Court said that the statute requires only a showing of "[r]eceipt of a number of illegal votes or rejection of a number of legal votes sufficient to change or place in doubt the result of the election."

The Florida Supreme Court ordered "the Supervisor of Elections and the Canvassing Boards, as well as the necessary public officials, in all counties that have not conducted a manual recount or tabulation of the undervotes . . . to do so forthwith, said tabulation to take place in the individual counties where the ballots are located." The Florida Supreme Court also determined that Palm Beach County and Miami-Dade County, in their earlier manual recounts, had identified a net gain of 215 and 168 legal votes for Vice President Gore, and that these should be included in the vote total even though they were reported after the deadline of Sunday, November 26.

Just hours after the Florida Supreme Court's decision, on Friday night, December 8, a Florida trial court judge ordered that the counting of the uncounted votes commence the next morning and that it be completed by Sunday afternoon, December 10, at 2:00 p.m. The judge said that he would resolve any disputes.

---

2. It should be noted that other lawsuits, unrelated to the specific issues in Bush v. Gore, were going on simultaneously. For example, voters in Palm Beach County brought a lawsuit seeking a new election there based on the so-called butterfly ballot, which they claimed violated Florida law and caused several thousand votes intended for Gore to be mistakenly cast for Pat Buchanan. The Florida trial court concluded that it lacked the constitutional authority to order a new election and the Florida Supreme Court denied review. Also, there were lawsuits in two counties claiming that election officials had illegally filled in missing information on requests for absentee ballots. Both Florida trial court judges held that this was not a basis for refusing to count the absentee ballots because the actions of the election officials did not in any way taint the ballots themselves.

On Saturday morning, counting commenced as ordered. At the same time, Bush asked the United States Supreme Court to stay the counting and grant certiorari in the case. In the early afternoon on Saturday, the Supreme Court, in a 5-4 ruling, stayed the counting of the votes in Florida. Justice Stevens dissented on the grounds that there was not an irreparable injury, which is a requirement for such a stay. Justice Scalia wrote a short opinion, not joined by any other Justice, in which he said that the requirements for a stay were met. He said that Bush had shown a likelihood of prevailing on the merits and also irreparable injury. Justice Scalia said that there were two such harms: first, there would be a cloud over the legitimacy of a Bush presidency if the counting showed Gore ahead, but the counting was disallowed by the Supreme Court; and second, handling of the ballots would lead to their degradation and prevent a more accurate counting later if that were ordered by the Court.

On Monday, December 11, the Supreme Court held oral arguments. Again, they were broadcast immediately after their completion. On Tuesday night, December 12, at approximately 10:00 p.m., eastern time, the Court released its opinion in Bush v. Gore.

The Decision

BUSH v. GORE
121 S. Ct. 525 (2000)

PER CURIAM.

I

On December 8, 2000, the Supreme Court of Florida ordered that the Circuit Court of Leon County tabulate by hand 9,000 ballots in Miami-Dade County. It also ordered the inclusion in the certified vote totals of 215 votes identified in Palm Beach County and 168 votes identified in Miami-Dade County for Vice President Albert Gore, Jr., and Senator Joseph Lieberman, Democratic Candidates for President and Vice President. The Supreme Court noted that petitioner, Governor George W. Bush, asserted that the net gain for Vice President Gore in Palm Beach County was 176 votes, and directed the Circuit Court to resolve that dispute on remand.

The court further held that relief would require manual recounts in all Florida counties where so-called undervotes had not been subject to manual tabulation. The court ordered all manual recounts to begin at once. Governor Bush and Richard Cheney, Republican Candidates for the Presidency and Vice Presidency, filed an emergency application for a stay of this mandate. On December 9, we granted the application, treated the application as a petition for a writ of certiorari, and granted certiorari.

On November 8, 2000, the day following the Presidential election, the Florida Division of Elections reported that petitioner, Governor Bush, had received 2,909,135 votes, and respondent, Vice President Gore, had received 2,907,351 votes, a margin of 1,784 for Governor Bush. Because Governor Bush's margin of victory was less than "one-half of a percent . . . of the votes cast," an automatic machine recount was conducted under § 102.141(4) of the election code, the results of which showed Governor Bush still winning the race but by a diminished margin. Vice President Gore then sought manual recounts in Volusia, Palm Beach, Broward, and Miami-Dade Counties, pursuant to Florida's election protest provisions. Fla. Stat. § 102.166 (2000). A dispute arose concerning the deadline for local county canvassing boards to submit their returns to the Secretary of State (Secretary). The Secretary declined to waive the November 14 deadline imposed by statute. The Florida Supreme Court, however, set the deadline at November 26. We granted certiorari and vacated the Florida Supreme Court's decision, finding considerable uncertainty as to the grounds on which it was based. Bush v. Palm Beach County Canvassing Bd. (2000) (per curiam). On December 11, the Florida Supreme Court issued a decision on remand reinstating that date.

On November 26, the Florida Elections Canvassing Commission certified the results of the election and declared Governor Bush the winner of Florida's 25 electoral votes. On November 27, Vice President Gore, pursuant to Florida's contest provisions, filed a complaint in Leon County Circuit Court contesting the certification. He sought relief pursuant to § 102.168(3)(c), which provides that "[r]eceipt of a number of illegal votes or rejection of a number of legal votes sufficient to change or place in doubt the result of the election" shall be grounds for a contest. The Circuit Court denied relief, stating that Vice President Gore failed to meet his burden of proof. He appealed to the First District Court of Appeal, which certified the matter to the Florida Supreme Court.

Accepting jurisdiction, the Florida Supreme Court affirmed in part and reversed in part. The court held that the Circuit Court had been correct to reject Vice President Gore's challenge to the results certified in Nassau County and his challenge to the Palm Beach County Canvassing Board's determination that 3,300 ballots cast in that county were not, in the statutory phrase, "legal votes."

The Supreme Court held that Vice President Gore had satisfied his burden of proof under § 102.168(3)(c) with respect to his challenge to Miami-Dade County's failure to tabulate, by manual count, 9,000 ballots on which the machines had failed to detect a vote for President ("undervotes"). Noting the closeness of the election, the Court explained that "[o]n this record, there can be no question that there are legal votes within the 9,000 uncounted votes sufficient to place the results of this election in doubt." A "legal vote," as determined by the Supreme Court, is "one in which there is a 'clear indication of the intent of the voter.'" The court therefore ordered a hand recount of the 9,000 ballots in Miami-Dade County. Observing that the contest provisions vest broad discretion in the circuit judge to "provide any relief appropriate under such circumstances,"

Fla. Stat. § 102.168(8) (2000), the Supreme Court further held that the Circuit Court could order "the Supervisor of Elections and the Canvassing Boards, as well as the necessary public officials, in all counties that have not conducted a manual recount or tabulation of the undervotes ... to do so forthwith, said tabulation to take place in the individual counties where the ballots are located."

The Supreme Court also determined that both Palm Beach County and Miami-Dade County, in their earlier manual recounts, had identified a net gain of 215 and 168 legal votes for Vice President Gore. Rejecting the Circuit Court's conclusion that Palm Beach County lacked the authority to include the 215 net votes submitted past the November 26 deadline, the Supreme Court explained that the deadline was not intended to exclude votes identified after that date through ongoing manual recounts. As to Miami-Dade County, the Court concluded that although the 168 votes identified were the result of a partial recount, they were "legal votes [that] could change the outcome of the election." The Supreme Court therefore directed the Circuit Court to include those totals in the certified results, subject to resolution of the actual vote total from the Miami-Dade partial recount.

The petition presents the following questions: whether the Florida Supreme Court established new standards for resolving Presidential election contests, thereby violating Art. II, § 1, cl. 2, of the United States Constitution and failing to comply with 3 U.S.C. § 5, and whether the use of standardless manual recounts violates the Equal Protection and Due Process Clauses. With respect to the equal protection question, we find a violation of the Equal Protection Clause.

II

A

The closeness of this election, and the multitude of legal challenges which have followed in its wake, have brought into sharp focus a common, if heretofore unnoticed, phenomenon. Nationwide statistics reveal that an estimated 2% of ballots cast do not register a vote for President for whatever reason, including deliberately choosing no candidate at all or some voter error, such as voting for two candidates or insufficiently marking a ballot. See Ho, More Than 2M Ballots Uncounted, AP Online (Nov. 28, 2000); Kelley, Balloting Problems Not Rare But Only In A Very Close Election Do Mistakes And Mismarking Make A Difference, Omaha World-Herald (Nov. 15, 2000). In certifying election results, the votes eligible for inclusion in the certification are the votes meeting the properly established legal requirements.

This case has shown that punch card balloting machines can produce an unfortunate number of ballots which are not punched in a clean, complete way by the voter. After the current counting, it is likely legislative bodies nationwide will examine ways to improve the mechanisms and machinery for voting.

B

The individual citizen has no federal constitutional right to vote for electors for the President of the United States unless and until the state legislature chooses a statewide election as the means to implement its power to appoint members of the Electoral College. U.S. Const., Art. II, § 1. This is the source for the statement in McPherson v. Blacker (1892), that the State legislature's power to select the manner for appointing electors is plenary; it may, if it so chooses, select the electors itself, which indeed was the manner used by State legislatures in several States for many years after the Framing of our Constitution. History has now favored the voter, and in each of the several States the citizens themselves vote for Presidential electors. When the state legislature vests the right to vote for President in its people, the right to vote as the legislature has prescribed is fundamental; and one source of its fundamental nature lies in the equal weight accorded to each vote and the equal dignity owed to each voter.

The right to vote is protected in more than the initial allocation of the franchise. Equal protection applies as well to the manner of its exercise. Having once granted the right to vote on equal terms, the State may not, by later arbitrary and disparate treatment, value one person's vote over that of another. See, e.g., Harper v. Virginia Bd. of Elections (1966) ("[O]nce the franchise is granted to the electorate, lines may not be drawn which are inconsistent with the Equal Protection Clause of the Fourteenth Amendment"). It must be remembered that "the right of suffrage can be denied by a debasement or dilution of the weight of a citizen's vote just as effectively as by wholly prohibiting the free exercise of the franchise." Reynolds v. Sims (1964).

There is no difference between the two sides of the present controversy on these basic propositions. Respondents say that the very purpose of vindicating the right to vote justifies the recount procedures now at issue. The question before us, however, is whether the recount procedures the Florida Supreme Court has adopted are consistent with its obligation to avoid arbitrary and disparate treatment of the members of its electorate.

Much of the controversy seems to revolve around ballot cards designed to be perforated by a stylus but which, either through error or deliberate omission, have not been perforated with sufficient precision for a machine to count them. In some cases a piece of the card—a chad—is hanging, say by two corners. In other cases there is no separation at all, just an indentation.

The Florida Supreme Court has ordered that the intent of the voter be discerned from such ballots. For purposes of resolving the equal protection challenge, it is not necessary to decide whether the Florida Supreme Court had the authority under the legislative scheme for resolving election disputes to define what a legal vote is and to mandate a manual recount implementing that definition. The recount mechanisms implemented in response to the decisions of the Florida Supreme Court do not satisfy the minimum requirement for non-arbitrary treatment of voters necessary to secure the fundamental right. Florida's basic command for the count of legally cast votes is to consider the "intent of the voter." This is unobjectionable as an abstract proposition and a starting principle. The problem inheres in the absence of specific standards to ensure its equal application. The formulation of uniform rules to determine intent based on these recurring circumstances is practicable and, we conclude, necessary.

The law does not refrain from searching for the intent of the actor in a multitude of circumstances; and in some cases the general command to ascertain intent is not susceptible to much further refinement. In this instance, however, the question is not whether to believe a witness but how to interpret the marks or holes or scratches on an inanimate object, a piece of cardboard or paper which, it is said, might not have registered as a vote during the machine count. The factfinder confronts a thing, not a person. The search for intent can be confined by specific rules designed to ensure uniform treatment.

The want of those rules here has led to unequal evaluation of ballots in various respects. As seems to have been acknowledged at oral argument, the standards for accepting or rejecting contested ballots might vary not only from county to county but indeed within a single county from one recount team to another.

The record provides some examples. A monitor in Miami-Dade County testified at trial that he observed that three members of the county canvassing board applied different standards in defining a legal vote. And testimony at trial also revealed that at least one county changed its evaluative standards during the counting process. Palm Beach County, for example, began the process with a 1990 guideline which precluded counting completely attached chads, switched to a rule that considered a vote to be legal if any light could be seen through a chad, changed back to the 1990 rule, and then abandoned any pretense of a per se rule, only to have a court order that the county consider dimpled chads legal. This is not a process with sufficient guarantees of equal treatment.

An early case in our one person, one vote jurisprudence arose when a State accorded arbitrary and disparate treatment to voters in its different counties. Gray v. Sanders (1963). The Court found a constitutional violation. We relied on these principles in the context of the Presidential selection process in Moore v. Ogilvie (1969), where we invalidated a county-based procedure that diluted the influence of citizens in larger counties in the nominating process. There we observed that "[t]he idea that one group can be granted greater voting strength than another is hostile to the one man, one vote basis of our representative government."

The State Supreme Court ratified this uneven treatment. It mandated that the recount totals from two counties, Miami-Dade and Palm Beach, be included in the certified total. The court also appeared to hold sub silentio that the recount totals from Broward County, which were not completed until after the original November 14 certification by the Secretary of State, were to be considered part of the new certified vote totals even though the county certification was not contested by Vice President Gore. Yet each of the counties used varying standards to determine what was a legal vote. Broward County used a more forgiving standard than Palm Beach County, and uncovered almost three times as many new votes, a result markedly disproportionate to the difference in population between the counties.

In addition, the recounts in these three counties were not limited to so-called undervotes but extended to all of the ballots. The distinction has real consequences. A manual recount of all ballots identifies not only those ballots which show no vote but also those which contain more than one, the so-called overvotes. Neither category will be counted by the machine. This is not a trivial concern. At oral argument, respondents estimated there are as many as 110,000 overvotes statewide. As a result, the citizen whose ballot was not read by a machine because he failed to vote for a candidate in a way readable by a machine may still have his vote counted in a manual recount; on the other hand, the citizen who marks two candidates in a way discernable by the machine will not have the same opportunity to have his vote count, even if a manual examination of the ballot would reveal the requisite indicia of intent. Furthermore, the citizen who marks two candidates, only one of which is discernable by the machine, will have his vote counted even though it should have been read as an invalid ballot. The State Supreme Court's inclusion of vote counts based on these variant standards exemplifies concerns with the remedial processes that were under way.

That brings the analysis to yet a further equal protection problem. The votes certified by the court included a partial total from one county, Miami-Dade. The Florida Supreme Court's decision thus gives no assurance that the recounts included in a final certification must be complete. This accommodation no doubt results from the truncated contest period established by the Florida Supreme Court, at respondents' own urging. The press of time does not diminish the constitutional concern. A desire for speed is not a general excuse for ignoring equal protection guarantees.

In addition to these difficulties the actual process by which the votes were to be counted under the Florida Supreme Court's decision raises further concerns. That order did not specify who would recount the ballots. The county canvassing boards were forced to pull together ad hoc teams comprised of judges from various Circuits who had no previous training in handling and interpreting ballots. Furthermore, while others were permitted to observe, they were prohibited from objecting during the recount.

The recount process, in its features here described, is inconsistent with the minimum procedures necessary to protect the fundamental right of each voter in the special instance of a statewide recount under the authority of a single state judicial officer. Our consideration is limited to the present circumstances, for the problem of equal protection in election processes generally presents many complexities.

The question before the Court is not whether local entities, in the exercise of their expertise, may develop different systems for implementing elections. Instead, we are presented with a situation where a state court with the power to assure uniformity has ordered a statewide recount with minimal procedural safeguards. When a court orders a statewide remedy, there must be at least some assurance that the rudimentary requirements of equal treatment and fundamental fairness are satisfied.

Given the Court's assessment that the recount process underway was probably being conducted in an unconstitutional manner, the Court stayed the order directing the recount so it could hear this case and render an expedited decision. The contest provision, as it was mandated by the State Supreme Court, is not well calculated to sustain the confidence that all citizens must have in the outcome of elections. The State has not shown that its procedures include the necessary safeguards. The problem, for instance, of the estimated 110,000 overvotes has not been addressed.

Upon due consideration of the difficulties identified to this point, it is obvious that the recount cannot be conducted in compliance with the requirements of equal protection and due process without substantial additional work. It would require not only the adoption (after opportunity for argument) of adequate state-wide standards for determining what is a legal vote, and practicable procedures to implement them, but also orderly judicial review of any disputed matters that might arise. In addition, the Secretary of State has advised that the recount of only a portion of the ballots requires that the vote tabulation equipment be used to screen out undervotes, a function for which the machines were not designed. If a recount of overvotes were also required, perhaps even a second screening would be necessary. Use of the equipment for this purpose, and any new software developed for it, would have to be evaluated for accuracy by the Secretary of State, as required by [Florida law].

The Supreme Court of Florida has said that the legislature intended the State's electors to "participat[e] fully in the federal electoral process," as provided in 3 U.S.C. § 5. That statute, in turn, requires that any controversy or contest that is designed to lead to a conclusive selection of electors be completed by December 12. That date is upon us, and there is no recount procedure in place under the State Supreme Court's order that comports with minimal constitutional standards. Because it is evident that any recount seeking to meet the December 12 date will be unconstitutional for the reasons we have discussed, we reverse the judgment of the Supreme Court of Florida ordering a recount to proceed.

Seven Justices of the Court agree that there are constitutional problems with the recount ordered by the Florida Supreme Court that demand a remedy. The only disagreement is as to the remedy. Because the Florida Supreme Court has said that the Florida Legislature intended to obtain the safe-harbor benefits of 3 U.S.C. § 5, Justice BREYER's proposed remedy—remanding to the Florida Supreme Court for its ordering of a constitutionally proper contest until December 18—contemplates action in violation of the Florida election code, and hence could not be part of an "appropriate" order authorized by Fla. Stat. § 102.168(8) (2000). . . .

None are more conscious of the vital limits on judicial authority than are the members of this Court, and none stand more in admiration of the Constitution's design to leave the selection of the President to the people, through their legislatures, and to the political sphere. When contending parties invoke the process of the courts, however, it becomes our unsought responsibility to resolve the federal and constitutional issues the judicial system has been forced to confront.

The judgment of the Supreme Court of Florida is reversed, and the case is remanded for further proceedings not inconsistent with this opinion.

Chief Justice REHNQUIST, with whom Justice SCALIA and Justice THOMAS join, concurring.

We join the per curiam opinion. We write separately because we believe there are additional grounds that require us to reverse the Florida Supreme Court's decision.

I

We deal here not with an ordinary election, but with an election for the President of the United States. In Burroughs v. United States (1934), we said: "While presidential electors are not officers or agents of the federal government, they exercise federal functions under, and discharge duties in virtue of authority conferred by, the Constitution of the United States. The President is vested with the executive power of the nation. The importance of his election and the vital character of its relationship to and effect upon the welfare and safety of the whole people cannot be too strongly stated."

In most cases, comity and respect for federalism compel us to defer to the decisions of state courts on issues of state law. That practice reflects our understanding that the decisions of state courts are definitive pronouncements of the will of the States as sovereigns. Of course, in ordinary cases, the distribution of powers among the branches of a State's government raises no questions of federal constitutional law, subject to the requirement that the government be republican in character. But there are a few exceptional cases in which the Constitution imposes a duty or confers a power on a particular branch of a State's government. This is one of them. Article II, § 1, cl. 2, provides that "[e]ach State shall appoint, in such Manner as the Legislature thereof may direct," electors for President and Vice President. Thus, the text of the election law itself, and not just its interpretation by the courts of the States, takes on independent significance.

3 U.S.C. § 5 informs our application of Art. II, § 1, cl. 2, to the Florida statutory scheme, which, as the Florida Supreme Court acknowledged, took that statute into account. Section 5 provides that the State's selection of electors "shall be conclusive, and shall govern in the counting of the electoral votes" if the electors are chosen under laws enacted prior to election day, and if the

selection process is completed six days prior to the meeting of the electoral college. As we noted in Bush v. Palm Beach County Canvassing Bd. (2000), "Since § 5 contains a principle of federal law that would assure finality of the State's determination if made pursuant to a state law in effect before the election, a legislative wish to take advantage of the 'safe harbor' would counsel against any construction of the Election Code that Congress might deem to be a change in the law."

If we are to respect the legislature's Article II powers, therefore, we must ensure that postelection state-court actions do not frustrate the legislative desire to attain the "safe harbor" provided by § 5. In Florida, the legislature has chosen to hold statewide elections to appoint the State's 25 electors. Importantly, the legislature has delegated the authority to run the elections and to oversee election disputes to the Secretary of State, and to state circuit courts. Isolated sections of the code may well admit of more than one interpretation, but the general coherence of the legislative scheme may not be altered by judicial interpretation so as to wholly change the statutorily provided apportionment of responsibility among these various bodies. In any election but a Presidential election, the Florida Supreme Court can give as little or as much deference to Florida's executives as it chooses, so far as Article II is concerned, and this Court will have no cause to question the court's actions. But, with respect to a Presidential election, the court must be both mindful of the legislature's role under Article II in choosing the manner of appointing electors and deferential to those bodies expressly empowered by the legislature to carry out its constitutional mandate.

In order to determine whether a state court has infringed upon the legislature's authority, we necessarily must examine the law of the State as it existed prior to the action of the court. Though we generally defer to state courts on the interpretation of state law, there are of course areas in which the Constitution requires this Court to undertake an independent, if still deferential, analysis of state law.

This inquiry does not imply a disrespect for state courts but rather a respect for the constitutionally prescribed role of state legislatures. To attach definitive weight to the pronouncement of a state court, when the very question at issue is whether the court has actually departed from the statutory meaning, would be to abdicate our responsibility to enforce the explicit requirements of Article II.

II

Acting pursuant to its constitutional grant of authority, the Florida Legislature has created a detailed, if not perfectly crafted, statutory scheme that provides for appointment of Presidential electors by direct election.

In its latest opinion, however, the court empties certification of [election results as prescribed by Florida law of] virtually all legal consequence during the contest, and in doing so departs from the provisions enacted by the Florida Legislature. The court determined that canvassing boards' decisions regarding whether to recount ballots past the certification deadline are to be reviewed de novo, although the election code clearly vests discretion whether to recount in the boards, and sets strict deadlines subject to the Secretary's rejection of late tallies and monetary fines for tardiness. Moreover, the Florida court held that all late vote tallies arriving during the contest period should be automatically included in the certification regardless of the certification deadline, thus virtually eliminating both the deadline and the Secretary's discretion to disregard recounts that violate it.

Moreover, the court's interpretation of "legal vote," and hence its decision to order a contest-period recount, plainly departed from the legislative scheme. Florida statutory law cannot reasonably be thought to require the counting of improperly marked ballots. Each Florida precinct before election day provides instructions on how properly to cast a vote; each polling place on election day contains a working model of the voting machine it uses; and each voting booth contains a sample ballot. In precincts using punch-card ballots, voters are instructed to punch out the ballot cleanly:

AFTER VOTING, CHECK YOUR BALLOT CARD TO BE SURE YOUR VOTING SELECTIONS ARE CLEARLY AND CLEANLY PUNCHED AND THERE ARE NO CHIPS LEFT HANGING ON THE BACK OF THE CARD.

No reasonable person would call it "an error in the vote tabulation," Fla. Stat. § 102.166(5), or a "rejection of legal votes," Fla. Stat. § 102.168(3)(c), when electronic or electromechanical equipment performs precisely in the manner designed, and fails to count those ballots that are not marked in the manner that these voting instructions explicitly and prominently specify. The scheme that the Florida Supreme Court's opinion attributes to the legislature is one in which machines are required to be "capable of correctly counting votes," but which nonetheless regularly produces elections in which legal votes are predictably not tabulated, so that in close elections manual recounts are regularly required. This is of course absurd. The Secretary of State, who is authorized by law to issue binding interpretations of the election code, rejected this peculiar reading of the statutes. The Florida Supreme Court, although it must defer to the Secretary's interpretations, see Krivanek v. Take Back Tampa Political Committee (Fla. 1993), rejected her reasonable interpretation and embraced the peculiar one.

But as we indicated in our remand of the earlier case, in a Presidential election the clearly expressed intent of the legislature must prevail. And there is no basis for reading the Florida statutes as requiring the counting of improperly marked ballots, as an examination of the Florida Supreme Court's textual analysis shows. For the court to step away from this established practice, prescribed by the Secretary of State, the state official charged by the legislature with "responsibility to . . . [o]btain and maintain uniformity in the application, operation, and interpretation of the election laws," § 97.012(1), was to depart from the legislative scheme.

III

The scope and nature of the remedy ordered by the Florida Supreme Court jeopardizes the "legislative wish" to take advantage of the safe harbor provided by 3 U.S.C. § 5. December 12, 2000, is the last date for a final determination of the Florida electors that will satisfy § 5. Yet in the late afternoon of December 8th—four days before this deadline—the Supreme Court of Florida ordered recounts of tens of thousands of so-called "undervotes" spread through 64 of the State's 67 counties. This was done in a search for elusive—perhaps delusive— certainty as to the exact count of 6 million votes. But no one claims that these ballots have not previously been tabulated; they were initially read by voting machines at the time of the election, and thereafter reread by virtue of Florida's automatic recount provision. No one claims there was any fraud in the election. The Supreme Court of Florida ordered this additional recount under the provision of the election code giving the circuit judge the authority to provide relief that is "appropriate under such circumstances."

Surely when the Florida Legislature empowered the courts of the State to grant "appropriate" relief, it must have meant relief that would have become final by the cut-off date of 3 U.S.C. § 5. In light of the inevitable legal chall- enges and ensuing appeals to the Supreme Court of Florida and petitions for certiorari to this Court, the entire recounting process could not possibly be completed by that date.

Given all these factors, and in light of the legislative intent identified by the Florida Supreme Court to bring Florida within the "safe harbor" provision of 3 U.S.C. § 5, the remedy prescribed by the Supreme Court of Florida cannot be deemed an "appropriate" one as of December 8. It significantly departed from the statutory framework in place on November 7, and authorized open-ended further proceedings which could not be completed by December 12, thereby preventing a final determination by that date. For these reasons, in addition to those given in the per curiam, we would reverse.

Justice STEVENS, with whom Justice GINSBURG and Justice BREYER join, dissenting.

The Constitution assigns to the States the primary responsibility for determining the manner of selecting the Presidential electors. When questions arise about the meaning of state laws, including election laws, it is our settled practice to accept the opinions of the highest courts of the States as providing the final answers. On rare occasions, however, either federal statutes or the Federal Constitution may require federal judicial intervention in state elections. This is not such an occasion.

The federal questions that ultimately emerged in this case are not substantial. Article II provides that "[e]ach State shall appoint, in such Manner as the Legislature thereof may direct, a Number of Electors." It does not create state legislatures out of whole cloth, but rather takes them as they come—as creatures born of, and constrained by, their state constitutions. The legislative power in

Florida is subject to judicial review pursuant to Article V of the Florida Constitution, and nothing in Article II of the Federal Constitution frees the state legislature from the constraints in the state constitution that created it. Moreover, the Florida Legislature's own decision to employ a unitary code for all elections indicates that it intended the Florida Supreme Court to play the same role in Presidential elections that it has historically played in resolving electoral disputes. The Florida Supreme Court's exercise of appellate jurisdiction therefore was wholly consistent with, and indeed contemplated by, the grant of authority in Article II.

It hardly needs stating that Congress, pursuant to 3 U.S.C. § 5, did not impose any affirmative duties upon the States that their governmental branches could "violate." Rather, § 5 provides a safe harbor for States to select electors in contested elections "by judicial or other methods" established by laws prior to the election day. Section 5, like Article II, assumes the involvement of the state judiciary in interpreting state election laws and resolving election disputes under those laws. Neither § 5 nor Article II grants federal judges any special authority to substitute their views for those of the state judiciary on matters of state law.

Nor are petitioners correct in asserting that the failure of the Florida Supreme Court to specify in detail the precise manner in which the "intent of the voter" is to be determined rises to the level of a constitutional violation. We found such a violation when individual votes within the same State were weighted unequally, see, e.g., Reynolds v. Sims (1964), but we have never before called into question the substantive standard by which a State determines that a vote has been legally cast. And there is no reason to think that the guidance provided to the factfinders, specifically the various canvassing boards, by the "intent of the voter" standard is any less sufficient—or will lead to results any less uniform—than, for example, the "beyond a reasonable doubt" standard employed everyday by ordinary citizens in courtrooms across this country.

Admittedly, the use of differing substandards for determining voter intent in different counties employing similar voting systems may raise serious concerns. Those concerns are alleviated—if not eliminated—by the fact that a single impartial magistrate will ultimately adjudicate all objections arising from the recount process. Of course, as a general matter, "[t]he interpretation of constitutional principles must not be too literal. We must remember that the machinery of government would not work if it were not allowed a little play in its joints." Bain Peanut Co. of Tex. v. Pinson (1931) (Holmes, J.). If it were otherwise, Florida's decision to leave to each county the determination of what balloting system to employ—despite enormous differences in accuracy—might run afoul of equal protection. So, too, might the similar decisions of the vast majority of state legislatures to delegate to local authorities certain decisions with respect to voting systems and ballot design.[3]

---

3. The percentage of nonvotes in this election in counties using a punch-card system was 3.92%; in contrast, the rate of error under the more modern optical-scan systems was only 1.43%. Put in other terms, for every 10,000 votes cast, punch-card systems result in 250 more nonvotes than

Even assuming that aspects of the remedial scheme might ultimately be found to violate the Equal Protection Clause, I could not subscribe to the majority's disposition of the case. As the majority explicitly holds, once a state legislature determines to select electors through a popular vote, the right to have one's vote counted is of constitutional stature. As the majority further acknowledges, Florida law holds that all ballots that reveal the intent of the voter constitute valid votes. Recognizing these principles, the majority nonetheless orders the termination of the contest proceeding before all such votes have been tabulated. Under their own reasoning, the appropriate course of action would be to remand to allow more specific procedures for implementing the legislature's uniform general standard to be established.

In the interest of finality, however, the majority effectively orders the disenfranchisement of an unknown number of voters whose ballots reveal their intent—and are therefore legal votes under state law—but were for some reason rejected by ballot-counting machines. It does so on the basis of the deadlines set forth in Title 3 of the United States Code. But, as I have already noted, those provisions merely provide rules of decision for Congress to follow when selecting among conflicting slates of electors. They do not prohibit a State from counting what the majority concedes to be legal votes until a bona fide winner is determined. Indeed, in 1960, Hawaii appointed two slates of electors and Congress chose to count the one appointed on January 4, 1961, well after the Title 3 deadlines. Thus, nothing prevents the majority, even if it properly found an equal protection violation, from ordering relief appropriate to remedy that violation without depriving Florida voters of their right to have their votes counted. As the majority notes, "[a] desire for speed is not a general excuse for ignoring equal protection guarantees."

Finally, neither in this case, nor in its earlier opinion in Palm Beach County Canvassing Bd. v. Harris, did the Florida Supreme Court make any substantive change in Florida electoral law. Its decisions were rooted in long-established precedent and were consistent with the relevant statutory provisions, taken as a whole. It did what courts do—it decided the case before it in light of the legislature's intent to leave no legally cast vote uncounted. In so doing, it relied on the sufficiency of the general "intent of the voter" standard articulated by the state legislature, coupled with a procedure for ultimate review by an impartial judge, to resolve the concern about disparate evaluations of contested ballots. If we assume—as I do—that the members of that court and the judges who would have carried out its mandate are impartial, its decision does not even raise a colorable federal question.

What must underlie petitioners' entire federal assault on the Florida election procedures is an unstated lack of confidence in the impartiality and capacity of the state judges who would make the critical decisions if the vote count were to

---

optical-scan systems. A total of 3,718,305 votes were cast under punch-card systems, and 2,353,811 votes were cast under optical-scan systems. [Footnote by Justice Stevens.]

proceed. Otherwise, their position is wholly without merit. The endorsement of that position by the majority of this Court can only lend credence to the most cynical appraisal of the work of judges throughout the land. It is confidence in the men and women who administer the judicial system that is the true backbone of the rule of law. Time will one day heal the wound to that confidence that will be inflicted by today's decision. One thing, however, is certain. Although we may never know with complete certainty the identity of the winner of this year's Presidential election, the identity of the loser is perfectly clear. It is the Nation's confidence in the judge as an impartial guardian of the rule of law. I respectfully dissent.

Justice SOUTER, with whom Justice BREYER joins and with whom Justice STEVENS and Justice GINSBURG join with regard to all but Part C, dissenting.

The Court should not have reviewed either Bush v. Palm Beach County Canvassing Bd., or this case, and should not have stopped Florida's attempt to recount all undervote ballots, by issuing a stay of the Florida Supreme Court's orders during the period of this review. If this Court had allowed the State to follow the course indicated by the opinions of its own Supreme Court, it is entirely possible that there would ultimately have been no issue requiring our review, and political tension could have worked itself out in the Congress following the procedure provided in 3 U.S.C. § 15. The case being before us, however, its resolution by the majority is another erroneous decision.

As will be clear, I am in substantial agreement with the dissenting opinions of Justice Stevens, Justice Ginsburg, and Justice Breyer. I write separately only to say how straightforward the issues before us really are. There are three issues: whether the State Supreme Court's interpretation of the statute providing for a contest of the state election results somehow violates 3 U.S.C. § 5; whether that court's construction of the state statutory provisions governing contests impermissibly changes a state law from what the State's legislature has provided, in violation of Article II, § 1, cl. 2, of the national Constitution; and whether the manner of interpreting markings on disputed ballots failing to cause machines to register votes for President (the undervote ballots) violates the equal protection or due process guaranteed by the Fourteenth Amendment. None of these issues is difficult to describe or to resolve.

A

The 3 U.S.C. § 5 issue is not serious. That provision sets certain conditions for treating a State's certification of Presidential electors as conclusive in the event that a dispute over recognizing those electors must be resolved in the Congress under 3 U.S.C. § 15. Conclusiveness requires selection under a legal scheme in place before the election, with results determined at least six days before the date set for casting electoral votes. But no State is required to conform to § 5 if it cannot do that (for whatever reason); the sanction for failing to satisfy the conditions of § 5 is simply loss of what has been called its "safe harbor." And even that determination is to be made, if made anywhere, in the Congress.

B

The second matter here goes to the State Supreme Court's interpretation of certain terms in the state statute governing election "contests." The issue is whether the judgment of the State Supreme Court has displaced the state legislature's provisions for election contests: is the law as declared by the court different from the provisions made by the legislature, to which the national Constitution commits responsibility for determining how each State's Presidential electors are chosen? Bush does not, of course, claim that any judicial act interpreting a statute of uncertain meaning is enough to displace the legislative provision and violate Article II; statutes require interpretation, which does not without more affect the legislative character of a statute within the meaning of the Constitution. What Bush does argue, as I understand the contention, is that the interpretation of § 102.168 was so unreasonable as to transcend the accepted bounds of statutory interpretation, to the point of being a nonjudicial act and producing new law untethered to the legislative act in question.

The starting point for evaluating the claim that the Florida Supreme Court's interpretation effectively re-wrote § 102.168 must be the language of the provision on which Gore relies to show his right to raise this contest: that the previously certified result in Bush's favor was produced by "rejection of a number of legal votes sufficient to change or place in doubt the result of the election." Fla. Stat. § 102.168(3)(c) (2000). None of the state court's interpretations is unreasonable to the point of displacing the legislative enactment quoted.

1. The statute does not define a "legal vote," the rejection of which may affect the election. The State Supreme Court was therefore required to define it, and in doing that the court looked to another election statute, § 101.5614(5), dealing with damaged or defective ballots, which contains a provision that no vote shall be disregarded "if there is a clear indication of the intent of the voter as determined by a canvassing board." The court read that objective of looking to the voter's intent as indicating that the legislature probably meant "legal vote" to mean a vote recorded on a ballot indicating what the voter intended. It is perfectly true that the majority might have chosen a different reading. But even so, there is no constitutional violation in following the majority view; Article II is unconcerned with mere disagreements about interpretive merits.

2. The Florida court next interpreted "rejection" to determine what act in the counting process may be attacked in a contest. Again, the statute does not define the term. The court majority read the word to mean simply a failure to count. That reading is certainly within the bounds of common sense, given the objective to give effect to a voter's intent if that can be determined. A different reading, of course, is possible. The majority might have concluded that "rejec-

tion" should refer to machine malfunction, or that a ballot should not be treated as "reject[ed]" in the absence of wrongdoing by election officials, lest contests be so easy to claim that every election will end up in one. There is, however, nothing nonjudicial in the Florida majority's more hospitable reading.

3. The same is true about the court majority's understanding of the phrase "votes sufficient to change or place in doubt" the result of the election in Florida. The court held that if the uncounted ballots were so numerous that it was reasonably possible that they contained enough "legal" votes to swing the election, this contest would be authorized by the statute. While the majority might have thought (as the trial judge did) that a probability, not a possibility, should be necessary to justify a contest, that reading is not required by the statute's text, which says nothing about probability. Whatever people of good will and good sense may argue about the merits of the Florida court's reading, there is no warrant for saying that it transcends the limits of reasonable statutory interpretation to the point of supplanting the statute enacted by the "legislature" within the meaning of Article II.

In sum, the interpretations by the Florida court raise no substantial question under Article II. That court engaged in permissible construction in determining that Gore had instituted a contest authorized by the state statute, and it proceeded to direct the trial judge to deal with that contest in the exercise of the discretionary powers generously conferred by Fla. Stat. § 102.168(8) (2000), to "fashion such orders as he or she deems necessary to ensure that each allegation in the complaint is investigated, examined, or checked, to prevent or correct any alleged wrong, and to provide any relief appropriate under such circumstances."

C

It is only on the third issue before us that there is a meritorious argument for relief, as this Court's Per Curiam opinion recognizes. It is an issue that might well have been dealt with adequately by the Florida courts if the state proceedings had not been interrupted, and if not disposed of at the state level it could have been considered by the Congress in any electoral vote dispute. But because the course of state proceedings has been interrupted, time is short, and the issue is before us, I think it sensible for the Court to address it.

Petitioners have raised an equal protection claim in the charge that unjustifiably disparate standards are applied in different electoral jurisdictions to otherwise identical facts. It is true that the Equal Protection Clause does not forbid the use of a variety of voting mechanisms within a jurisdiction, even though different mechanisms will have different levels of effectiveness in recording voters' intentions; local variety can be justified by concerns about cost, the potential value of innovation, and so on. But evidence in the record here suggests that a different order of disparity obtains under rules for determining a voter's intent that have been applied (and could continue to be applied) to identical types of ballots used in identical brands of machines and exhibiting identical physical characteristics (such as "hanging" or "dimpled" chads). I can conceive of no legitimate state interest served by these differing treatments of the expressions of voters' fundamental rights. The differences appear wholly arbitrary.

In deciding what to do about this, we should take account of the fact that electoral votes are due to be cast in six days. I would therefore remand the case to the courts of Florida with instructions to establish uniform standards for evaluating the several types of ballots that have prompted differing treatments, to be applied within and among counties when passing on such identical ballots in any further recounting (or successive recounting) that the courts might order.

Unlike the majority, I see no warrant for this Court to assume that Florida could not possibly comply with this requirement before the date set for the meeting of electors, December 18. To recount these manually would be a tall order, but before this Court stayed the effort to do that the courts of Florida were ready to do their best to get that job done. There is no justification for denying the State the opportunity to try to count all disputed ballots now. I respectfully dissent.

Justice GINSBURG, with whom Justice STEVENS joins, and with whom Justice SOUTER and Justice BREYER join as to Part I, dissenting.

I

The Chief Justice acknowledges that provisions of Florida's Election Code "may well admit of more than one interpretation." But instead of respecting the state high court's province to say what the State's Election Code means, the Chief Justice maintains that Florida's Supreme Court has veered so far from the ordinary practice of judicial review that what it did cannot properly be called judging. My colleagues have offered a reasonable construction of Florida's law. Their construction coincides with the view of one of Florida's seven Supreme Court justices. I might join the Chief Justice were it my commission to interpret Florida law. But disagreement with the Florida court's interpretation of its own State's law does not warrant the conclusion that the justices of that court have legislated. There is no cause here to believe that the members of Florida's high court have done less than "their mortal best to discharge their oath of office," and no cause to upset their reasoned interpretation of Florida law.

No doubt there are cases in which the proper application of federal law may hinge on interpretations of state law. Unavoidably, this Court must sometimes examine state law in order to protect federal rights. But we have dealt with such cases ever mindful of the full measure of respect we owe to interpretations of state law by a State's highest court.

In deferring to state courts on matters of state law, we appropriately recognize that this Court acts as an "'outside[r]' lacking the common exposure to local law·

which comes from sitting in the jurisdiction." That recognition has sometimes prompted us to resolve doubts about the meaning of state law by certifying issues to a State's highest court, even when federal rights are at stake. Notwithstanding our authority to decide issues of state law underlying federal claims, we have used the certification devise to afford state high courts an opportunity to inform us on matters of their own State's law because such restraint "helps build a cooperative judicial federalism." I would have thought the "cautious approach" we counsel when federal courts address matters of state law, and our commitment to "build[ing] cooperative judicial federalism," demanded greater restraint.

Rarely has this Court rejected outright an interpretation of state law by a state high court. As Justice Breyer convincingly explains, this case involves nothing close to the kind of recalcitrance by a state high court that warrants extraordinary action by this Court. The Florida Supreme Court concluded that counting every legal vote was the overriding concern of the Florida Legislature when it enacted the State's Election Code. The court surely should not be bracketed with state high courts of the Jim Crow South.

The Chief Justice says that Article II, by providing that state legislatures shall direct the manner of appointing electors, authorizes federal superintendence over the relationship between state courts and state legislatures, and licenses a departure from the usual deference we give to state court interpretations of state law. The Framers of our Constitution, however, understood that in a republican government, the judiciary would construe the legislature's enactments. By holding that Article II requires our revision of a state court's construction of state laws in order to protect one organ of the State from another, the Chief Justice contradicts the basic principle that a State may organize itself as it sees fit. Article II does not call for the scrutiny undertaken by this Court.

The extraordinary setting of this case has obscured the ordinary principle that dictates its proper resolution: Federal courts defer to state high courts' interpretations of their state's own law. This principle reflects the core of federalism, on which all agree. The Chief Justice's solicitude for the Florida Legislature comes at the expense of the more fundamental solicitude we owe to the legislature's sovereign. Were the other members of this Court as mindful as they generally are of our system of dual sovereignty, they would affirm the judgment of the Florida Supreme Court.

II

I agree with Justice Stevens that petitioners have not presented a substantial equal protection claim. Ideally, perfection would be the appropriate standard for judging the recount. But we live in an imperfect world, one in which thousands of votes have not been counted. I cannot agree that the recount adopted by the Florida court, flawed as it may be, would yield a result any less fair or precise than the certification that preceded that recount.

Even if there were an equal protection violation, I would agree with Justice Stevens, Justice Souter, and Justice Breyer that the Court's concern about "the December 12 deadline," is misplaced. Time is short in part because of the Court's entry of a stay on December 9, several hours after an able circuit judge in Leon County had begun to superintend the recount process. More fundamentally, the Court's reluctance to let the recount go forward—despite its suggestion that "[t]he search for intent can be confined by specific rules designed to ensure uniform treatment,"—ultimately turns on its own judgment about the practical realities of implementing a recount, not the judgment of those much closer to the process.

Equally important, as Justice Breyer explains, the December 12 "deadline" for bringing Florida's electoral votes into 3 U.S.C. § 5's safe harbor lacks the significance the Court assigns it. Were that date to pass, Florida would still be entitled to deliver electoral votes Congress must count unless both Houses find that the votes "ha[d] not been . . . regularly given." 3 U.S.C. § 15. The statute identifies other significant dates. See, e.g., § 7 (specifying December 18 as the date electors "shall meet and give their votes"); § 12 (specifying "the fourth Wednesday in December"—this year, December 27—as the date on which Congress, if it has not received a State's electoral votes, shall request the state secretary of state to send a certified return immediately). But none of these dates has ultimate significance in light of Congress' detailed provisions for determining, on "the sixth day of January," the validity of electoral votes.

The Court assumes that time will not permit "orderly judicial review of any disputed matters that might arise." But no one has doubted the good faith and diligence with which Florida election officials, attorneys for all sides of this controversy, and the courts of law have performed their duties. Notably, the Florida Supreme Court has produced two substantial opinions within 29 hours of oral argument. In sum, the Court's conclusion that a constitutionally adequate recount is impractical is a prophecy the Court's own judgment will not allow to be tested. Such an untested prophecy should not decide the Presidency of the United States. I dissent.

Justice BREYER, with whom Justice STEVENS and Justice GINSBURG join except as to Part I-A-1, and with whom Justice SOUTER joins as to Part I, dissenting.

The Court was wrong to take this case. It was wrong to grant a stay. It should now vacate that stay and permit the Florida Supreme Court to decide whether the recount should resume.

I

The political implications of this case for the country are momentous. But the federal legal questions presented, with one exception, are insubstantial.

A

1

The majority raises three Equal Protection problems with the Florida Supreme Court's recount order: first, the failure to include overvotes in the manual recount; second, the fact that all ballots, rather than simply the undervotes, were recounted in some, but not all, counties; and third, the absence of a uniform, specific standard to guide the recounts. As far as the first issue is concerned, petitioners presented no evidence, to this Court or to any Florida court, that a manual recount of overvotes would identify additional legal votes. The same is true of the second, and, in addition, the majority's reasoning would seem to invalidate any state provision for a manual recount of individual counties in a statewide election.

The majority's third concern does implicate principles of fundamental fairness. The majority concludes that the Equal Protection Clause requires that a manual recount be governed not only by the uniform general standard of the "clear intent of the voter," but also by uniform subsidiary standards (for example, a uniform determination whether indented, but not perforated, "undervotes" should count). The opinion points out that the Florida Supreme Court ordered the inclusion of Broward County's undercounted "legal votes" even though those votes included ballots that were not perforated but simply "dimpled," while newly recounted ballots from other counties will likely include only votes determined to be "legal" on the basis of a stricter standard. In light of our previous remand, the Florida Supreme Court may have been reluctant to adopt a more specific standard than that provided for by the legislature for fear of exceeding its authority under Article II. However, since the use of different standards could favor one or the other of the candidates, since time was, and is, too short to permit the lower courts to iron out significant differences through ordinary judicial review, and since the relevant distinction was embodied in the order of the State's highest court, I agree that, in these very special circumstances, basic principles of fairness may well have counseled the adoption of a uniform standard to address the problem. In light of the majority's disposition, I need not decide whether, or the extent to which, as a remedial matter, the Constitution would place limits upon the content of the uniform standard.

2

Nonetheless, there is no justification for the majority's remedy, which is simply to reverse the lower court and halt the recount entirely. An appropriate remedy would be, instead, to remand this case with instructions that, even at this late date, would permit the Florida Supreme Court to require recounting all undercounted votes in Florida, including those from Broward, Volusia, Palm Beach, and Miami-Dade Counties, whether or not previously recounted prior to the end of the protest period, and to do so in accordance with a single-uniform substandard.

The majority justifies stopping the recount entirely on the ground that there is no more time. In particular, the majority relies on the lack of time for the Secretary to review and approve equipment needed to separate undervotes. But the majority reaches this conclusion in the absence of any record evidence that the recount could not have been completed in the time allowed by the Florida Supreme Court. The majority finds facts outside of the record on matters that state courts are in a far better position to address. Of course, it is too late for any such recount to take place by December 12, the date by which election disputes must be decided if a State is to take advantage of the safe harbor provisions of 3 U.S.C. § 5. Whether there is time to conduct a recount prior to December 18, when the electors are scheduled to meet, is a matter for the state courts to determine. And whether, under Florida law, Florida could or could not take further action is obviously a matter for Florida courts, not this Court, to decide.

By halting the manual recount, and thus ensuring that the uncounted legal votes will not be counted under any standard, this Court crafts a remedy out of proportion to the asserted harm. And that remedy harms the very fairness interests the Court is attempting to protect. The manual recount would itself redress a problem of unequal treatment of ballots. As Justice STEVENS points out, the ballots of voters in counties that use punch-card systems are more likely to be disqualified than those in counties using optical-scanning systems. According to recent news reports, variations in the undervote rate are even more pronounced. See Fessenden, No-Vote Rates Higher in Punch Card Count, N.Y. Times, Dec. 1, 2000, p. A29 (reporting that 0.3% of ballots cast in 30 Florida counties using optical-scanning systems registered no Presidential vote, in comparison to 1.53% in the 15 counties using Votomatic punch card ballots). Thus, in a system that allows counties to use different types of voting systems, voters already arrive at the polls with an unequal chance that their votes will be counted. I do not see how the fact that this results from counties' selection of different voting machines rather than a court order makes the outcome any more fair. Nor do I understand why the Florida Supreme Court's recount order, which helps to redress this inequity, must be entirely prohibited based on a deficiency that could easily be remedied.

B

The remainder of petitioners' claims, which are the focus of the Chief Justice's concurrence, raise no significant federal questions. I cannot agree that the Chief Justice's unusual review of state law in this case is justified by reference either to Art. II, § 1, or to 3 U.S.C. § 5. Moreover, even were such review proper, the conclusion that the Florida Supreme Court's decision contravenes federal law is untenable.

While conceding that, in most cases, "comity and respect for federalism compel us to defer to the decisions of state courts on issues of state law," the concurrence relies on some combination of Art. II, § 1, and 3 U.S.C. § 5 to justify the majority's conclusion that this case is one of the few in which we may lay that fundamental principle aside. The concurrence's logic turns the presumption that legislatures would wish to take advantage of § 5's "safe harbor" provision into a mandate that trumps other statutory provisions and overrides the intent that the legislature did express.

But, in any event, the concurrence, having conducted its review, now reaches the wrong conclusion. It says that "the Florida Supreme Court's interpretation of the Florida election laws impermissibly distorted them beyond what a fair reading required, in violation of Article II." But what precisely is the distortion? Apparently, it has three elements. First, the Florida court, in its earlier opinion, changed the election certification date from November 14 to November 26. Second, the Florida court ordered a manual recount of "undercounted" ballots that could not have been fully completed by the December 12 "safe harbor" deadline. Third, the Florida court, in the opinion now under review, failed to give adequate deference to the determinations of canvassing boards and the Secretary.

To characterize the first element as a "distortion," however, requires the concurrence to second-guess the way in which the state court resolved a plain conflict in the language of different statutes. In any event, that issue no longer has any practical importance and cannot justify the reversal of the different Florida court decision before us now.

To characterize the second element as a "distortion" requires the concurrence to overlook the fact that the inability of the Florida courts to conduct the recount on time is, in significant part, a problem of the Court's own making. The Florida Supreme Court thought that the recount could be completed on time, and, within hours, the Florida Circuit Court was moving in an orderly fashion to meet the deadline. This Court improvidently entered a stay. As a result, we will never know whether the recount could have been completed.

Nor can one characterize the third element as "impermissibl[e] distort[ing]" once one understands that there are two sides to the opinion's argument that the Florida Supreme Court "virtually eliminated the Secretary's discretion." The Florida statute in question was amended in 1999 to provide that the "grounds for contesting an election" include the "rejection of a number of legal votes sufficient to . . . place in doubt the result of the election." And the parties have argued about the proper meaning of the statute's term "legal vote." Nor can one say that the Court's ultimate determination is so unreasonable as to amount to a constitutionally "impermissible distort[ion]" of Florida law. The Florida Supreme Court, applying this definition, decided, on the basis of the record, that respondents had shown that the ballots undercounted by the voting machines contained enough "legal votes" to place "the results" of the election "in doubt." Since only a few hundred votes separated the candidates, and since the "undercounted" ballots numbered tens of thousands, it is difficult to see how anyone could find this conclusion unreasonable—however strict the standard used to measure the voter's "clear intent." Nor did this conclusion "strip" canvassing boards of their discretion. The boards retain their traditional discretionary authority during the protest period.

II

Despite the reminder that this case involves "an election for the President of the United States," no preeminent legal concern, or practical concern related to legal questions, required this Court to hear this case, let alone to issue a stay that stopped Florida's recount process in its tracks. With one exception, petitioners' claims do not ask us to vindicate a constitutional provision designed to protect a basic human right. See, e.g., Brown v. Board of Education (1954). Petitioners invoke fundamental fairness, namely, the need for procedural fairness, including finality. But with the one "equal protection" exception, they rely upon law that focuses, not upon that basic need, but upon the constitutional allocation of power.

Respondents invoke a competing fundamental consideration—the need to determine the voter's true intent. But they look to state law, not to federal constitutional law, to protect that interest. Neither side claims electoral fraud, dishonesty, or the like. And the more fundamental equal protection claim might have been left to the state court to resolve if and when it was discovered to have mattered. It could still be resolved through a remand conditioned upon issuance of a uniform standard; it does not require reversing the Florida Supreme Court.

Of course, the selection of the President is of fundamental national importance. But that importance is political, not legal. And this Court should resist the temptation unnecessarily to resolve tangential legal disputes, where doing so threatens to determine the outcome of the election.

The Constitution and federal statutes themselves make clear that restraint is appropriate. They set forth a road map of how to resolve disputes about electors, even after an election as close as this one. That road map foresees resolution of electoral disputes by state courts. But it nowhere provides for involvement by the United States Supreme Court.

To the contrary, the Twelfth Amendment commits to Congress the authority and responsibility to count electoral votes. A federal statute, the Electoral Count Act, enacted after the close 1876 Hayes-Tilden Presidential election, specifies that, after States have tried to resolve disputes (through "judicial" or other means), Congress is the body primarily authorized to resolve remaining disputes. The legislative history of the Act makes clear its intent to commit the power to resolve such disputes to Congress, rather than the courts.

Moreover, Congress was fully aware of the danger that would arise should it ask judges, unarmed with appropriate legal standards, to resolve a hotly contested Presidential election contest. Just after the 1876 Presidential election, Florida, South Carolina, and Louisiana each sent two slates of electors to Washington. Without these States, Tilden, the Democrat, had 184 electoral votes, one short of the number required to win the Presidency. With those States, Hayes, his Republican opponent, would have had 185. In order to choose between the two slates of electors, Congress decided to appoint an electoral commission composed of five Senators, five Representatives, and five Supreme Court Justices. Initially the Commission was to be evenly divided between Republicans and Democrats, with Justice David Davis, an Independent, to possess the decisive vote. However, when at the last minute the Illinois Legislature elected Justice Davis to the United States Senate, the final position on the Commission was filled by Supreme Court Justice Joseph P. Bradley.

The Commission divided along partisan lines, and the responsibility to cast the deciding vote fell to Justice Bradley. He decided to accept the votes by the Republican electors, and thereby awarded the Presidency to Hayes. Justice Bradley immediately became the subject of vociferous attacks. Bradley was accused of accepting bribes, of being captured by railroad interests, and of an eleventh-hour change in position after a night in which his house "was surrounded by the carriages" of Republican partisans and railroad officials.

For present purposes, the relevance of this history lies in the fact that the participation in the work of the electoral commission by five Justices, including Justice Bradley, did not lend that process legitimacy. Nor did it assure the public that the process had worked fairly, guided by the law. Rather, it simply embroiled Members of the Court in partisan conflict, thereby undermining respect for the judicial process. And the Congress that later enacted the Electoral Count Act knew it. This history may help to explain why I think it not only legally wrong, but also most unfortunate, for the Court simply to have terminated the Florida recount. Those who caution judicial restraint in resolving political disputes have described the quintessential case for that restraint as a case marked, among other things, by the "strangeness of the issue," its "intractability to principled resolution," its "sheer momentousness, . . . which tends to unbalance judicial judgment," and "the inner vulnerability, the self-doubt of an institution which is electorally irresponsible and has no earth to draw strength from." Alexander Bickel, The Least Dangerous Branch (1962). Those characteristics mark this case.

At the same time, as I have said, the Court is not acting to vindicate a fundamental constitutional principle, such as the need to protect a basic human liberty. No other strong reason to act is present. Congressional statutes tend to obviate the need. And, above all, in this highly politicized matter, the appearance of a split decision runs the risk of undermining the public's confidence in the Court itself. That confidence is a public treasure. It has been built slowly over many years, some of which were marked by a Civil War and the tragedy of segregation. It is a vitally necessary ingredient of any successful effort to protect basic liberty and, indeed, the rule of law itself. We run no risk of returning to the days when a President (responding to this Court's efforts to protect the Cherokee Indians) might have said, "John Marshall has made his decision; now let him enforce it!" But we do risk a self-inflicted wound—a wound that may harm not just the Court, but the Nation.

I fear that in order to bring this agonizingly long election process to a definitive conclusion, we have not adequately attended to that necessary "check upon our own exercise of power," "our own sense of self-restraint." United States v. Butler (1936) (Stone, J., dissenting). Justice Brandeis once said of the Court, "The most important thing we do is not doing." What it does today, the Court should have left undone. I would repair the damage done as best we now can, by permitting the Florida recount to continue under uniform standards. I respectfully dissent.

Issues to Consider Concerning Bush v. Gore

There are many issues to consider regarding Bush v. Gore. First, was the case justiciable? Gore did not raise justiciability issues in his briefs or at oral argument. Yet, justiciability is jurisdictional; the Court must raise it on its own. The question is whether Bush had standing to raise the equal protection claims of the Florida voters. Also, was the case ripe for review at the time it was decided by the United States Supreme Court? Should the Court have found that the matter was a political question and left it to Congress to ultimately resolve?

Second, was the Court correct in finding a denial of equal protection? Seven of the Justices expressed concern over a denial of equal protection from counting votes without uniform standards. However, it is notable that Justices Souter and Breyer, who shared this concern with the majority, did not file opinions "concurring in part and dissenting in part," but rather just dissented. How, exactly, was equal protection denied? Also, there will be the issue of whether the Court has created a new principle of equality in voting that will be the basis for future successful challenges to variations within a state in election practices. Several such suits already have been filed.

Third, was the Court justified in ending the counting in Florida? The Court, in its per curiam opinion, said that the Florida Supreme Court had indicated that it wanted to follow the December 12 deadline set by the federal "safe harbor" statute. Since it was December 12, the Supreme Court ordered an end to the counting. But because it was an issue of Florida state law, should the Supreme Court have remanded the case for the Florida Supreme Court to decide the content of Florida law under the unprecedented circumstances?

On December 13, 2000, the day after Bush v. Gore was decided, Al Gore conceded the election to George W. Bush. Rightly or wrongly, for the first time in history, the Supreme Court decided a presidential election.

Chapter 9

First Amendment: Freedom of Expression

B. Free Speech Methodology

1. The Distinction Between Content-Based and Content-Neutral Laws

a. The Importance of the Distinction (casebook, p. 904)

In Republican Party of Minnesota v. White, below, the Supreme Court considered a particularly difficult issue: Are restrictions on the speech of candidates for judicial office, precluding statements on disputed political and legal issues, an impermissible content-based restriction on political speech? Or is this one of the rare situations where a content-based restriction is permissible as meeting strict scrutiny based on the government's interest in preserving the judicial independence and the appearance of judicial impartiality? The Court, in a 5-4 decision, declared the Minnesota regulation unconstitutional.

REPUBLICAN PARTY OF MINNESOTA v. WHITE
122 S. Ct. 2528 (2002)

Justice SCALIA delivered the opinion of the Court.

The question presented in this case is whether the First Amendment permits the Minnesota Supreme Court to prohibit candidates for judicial election in that State from announcing their views on disputed legal and political issues.

I

Since Minnesota's admission to the Union in 1858, the State's Constitution has provided for the selection of all state judges by popular election. Since 1912, those elections have been nonpartisan. Since 1974, they have been subject to a legal restriction which states that a "candidate for a judicial office, including an incumbent judge," shall not "announce his or her views on disputed legal or political issues." Minn. Code of Judicial Conduct, Canon 5(A)(3)(d)(i) (2000). This prohibition, promulgated by the Minnesota Supreme Court and based on Canon 7(B) of the 1972 American Bar Association (ABA) Model Code of Judicial Conduct, is known as the "announce clause." Incumbent judges who violate it are subject to discipline, including removal, censure, civil penalties, and suspension without pay. Lawyers who run for judicial office also must comply with the announce clause. Those who violate it are subject to, inter alia, disbarment, suspension, and probation. Rule 8.4(a); Minn. Rules on Lawyers Professional Responsibility 8-14, 15(a) (2002).

In 1996, one of the petitioners, Gregory Wersal, ran for associate justice of the Minnesota Supreme Court. In the course of the campaign, he distributed literature criticizing several Minnesota Supreme Court decisions on issues such as crime, welfare, and abortion. A complaint against Wersal challenging, among other things, the propriety of this literature was filed with the Office of Lawyers Professional Responsibility, the agency which, under the direction of the Minnesota Lawyers Professional Responsibility Board, investigates and prosecutes ethical violations of lawyer candidates for judicial office. The Lawyers Board dismissed the complaint; with regard to the charges that his campaign materials violated the announce clause, it expressed doubt whether the clause could constitutionally be enforced. Nonetheless, fearing that further ethical complaints would jeopardize his ability to practice law, Wersal withdrew from the election. In 1998, Wersal ran again for the same office. Early in that race, he sought an advisory opinion from the Lawyers Board with regard to whether it planned to enforce the announce clause. The Lawyers Board responded equivocally, stating that, although it had significant doubts about the constitutionality of the provision, it was unable to answer his question because he had not submitted a list of the announcements he wished to make. Shortly thereafter, Wersal filed this lawsuit in Federal District Court against respondents, seeking a declaration that the announce clause violates the First Amendment and an injunction against its enforcement.

II

Before considering the constitutionality of the announce clause, we must be clear about its meaning. Its text says that a candidate for judicial office shall not "announce his or her views on disputed legal or political issues." Minn. Code of Judicial Conduct, Canon 5(A)(3)(d)(i) (2002). We know that "announc[ing] . . . views" on an issue covers much more than promising to decide an issue a particular way. The prohibition extends to the candidate's mere statement of his current position, even if he does not bind himself to maintain that position after election. All the parties agree this is the case, because the Minnesota Code contains a so-called "pledges or promises" clause, which separately prohibits judicial candidates from making "pledges or promises of conduct in office other than the faithful and impartial performance of the duties of the office,"—a prohibition that is not challenged here and on which we express no view.

In light of the constitutional concerns, the District Court construed the clause to reach only disputed issues that are likely to come before the candidate if he is elected judge. The Eighth Circuit accepted this limiting interpretation by the District Court, and in addition construed the clause to allow general discussions of case law and judicial philosophy. The Supreme Court of Minnesota adopted these interpretations as well when it ordered enforcement of the announce clause in accordance with the Eighth Circuit's opinion.

It seems to us, however, that—like the text of the announce clause itself—these limitations upon the text of the announce clause are not all that they appear to be. First, respondents acknowledged at oral argument that statements critical of past judicial decisions are not permissible if the candidate also states that he is against stare decisis. Thus, candidates must choose between stating their views critical of past decisions and stating their views in opposition to stare decisis. Or, to look at it more concretely, they may state their view that prior decisions were erroneous only if they do not assert that they, if elected, have any power to eliminate erroneous decisions.

Second, limiting the scope of the clause to issues likely to come before a court is not much of a limitation at all. One would hardly expect the "disputed legal or political issues" raised in the course of a state judicial election to include such matters as whether the Federal Government should end the embargo of Cuba. Quite obviously, they will be those legal or political disputes that are the proper (or by past decisions have been made the improper) business of the state courts. And within that relevant category, "[t]here is almost no legal or political issue that is unlikely to come before a judge of an American court, state or federal, of general jurisdiction."

Third, construing the clause to allow "general" discussions of case law and judicial philosophy turns out to be of little help in an election campaign. At oral argument, respondents gave, as an example of this exception, that a candidate is free to assert that he is a "'strict constructionist.'" But that, like most other philosophical generalities, has little meaningful content for the electorate unless it is exemplified by application to a particular issue of construction likely to come before a court—for example, whether a particular statute runs afoul of any provision of the Constitution. Respondents conceded that the announce clause would prohibit the candidate from exemplifying his philosophy in this fashion. Without such application to real-life issues, all candidates can claim to be "strict constructionists" with equal (and unhelpful) plausibility.

In any event, it is clear that the announce clause prohibits a judicial candidate from stating his views on any specific nonfanciful legal question within the province of the court for which he is running, except in the context of discussing past decisions—and in the latter context as well, if he expresses the view that he is not bound by stare decisis.

Respondents contend that this still leaves plenty of topics for discussion on the campaign trail. These include a candidate's "character," "education," "work habits," and "how [he] would handle administrative duties if elected." Indeed, the Judicial Board has printed a list of preapproved questions which judicial candidates are allowed to answer. These include how the candidate feels about cameras in the courtroom, how he would go about reducing the caseload, how the costs of judicial administration can be reduced, and how he proposes to ensure that minorities and women are treated more fairly by the court system. Whether this list of preapproved subjects, and other topics not prohibited by the announce clause, adequately fulfill the First Amendment's guarantee of freedom of speech is the question to which we now turn.

III

As the Court of Appeals recognized, the announce clause both prohibits speech on the basis of its content and burdens a category of speech that is "at the core of our First Amendment freedoms"—speech about the qualifications of candidates for public office. The Court of Appeals concluded that the proper test to be applied to determine the constitutionality of such a restriction is what our cases have called strict scrutiny. The parties do not dispute that this is correct. Under the strict-scrutiny test, respondents have the burden to prove that the announce clause is (1) narrowly tailored, to serve (2) a compelling state interest. In order for respondents to show that the announce clause is narrowly tailored, they must demonstrate that it does not "unnecessarily circumscrib[e] protected expression." Brown v. Hartlage (1982).

The Court of Appeals concluded that respondents had established two interests as sufficiently compelling to justify the announce clause: preserving the impartiality of the state judiciary and preserving the appearance of the impartiality of the state judiciary. Respondents reassert these two interests before us, arguing that the first is compelling because it protects the due process rights of litigants, and that the second is compelling because it preserves public confidence in the judiciary. Respondents are rather vague, however, about what they mean by "impartiality." Indeed, although the term is used throughout the Eighth Circuit's opinion, the briefs, the Minnesota Code of Judicial Conduct, and the ABA Codes of Judicial Conduct, none of these sources bothers to define it. Clarity on this point is essential before we can decide whether impartiality is indeed a compelling state interest, and, if so, whether the announce clause is narrowly tailored to achieve it.

A

One meaning of "impartiality" in the judicial context—and of course its root meaning—is the lack of bias for or against either party to the proceeding. Impartiality in this sense assures equal application of the law. That is, it guarantees a party that the judge who hears his case will apply the law to him in the same way he applies it to any other party. This is the traditional sense in which the term is used. It is also the sense in which it is used in the cases cited by respondents and amici for the proposition that an impartial judge is essential to due process.

We think it plain that the announce clause is not narrowly tailored to serve impartiality (or the appearance of impartiality) in this sense. Indeed, the clause is barely tailored to serve that interest at all, inasmuch as it does not restrict speech for or against particular parties, but rather speech for or against particular issues. To be sure, when a case arises that turns on a legal issue on which the judge (as a candidate) had taken a particular stand, the party taking the opposite stand is likely to lose. But not because of any bias against that party, or favoritism toward the other party. Any party taking that position is just as likely to lose. The judge is applying the law (as he sees it) evenhandedly.

B

It is perhaps possible to use the term "impartiality" in the judicial context (though this is certainly not a common usage) to mean lack of preconception in favor of or against a particular legal view. This sort of impartiality would be concerned, not with guaranteeing litigants equal application of the law, but rather with guaranteeing them an equal chance to persuade the court on the legal points in their case. Impartiality in this sense may well be an interest served by the announce clause, but it is not a compelling state interest, as strict scrutiny requires. A judge's lack of predisposition regarding the relevant legal issues in a case has never been thought a necessary component of equal justice, and with good reason. For one thing, it is virtually impossible to find a judge who does not have preconceptions about the law. As then-Justice Rehnquist observed of our own Court: "Since most Justices come to this bench no earlier than their middle years, it would be unusual if they had not by that time formulated at least some tentative notions that would influence them in their interpretation of the sweeping clauses of the Constitution and their interaction with one another. It would be not merely unusual, but extraordinary, if they had not at least given opinions as to constitutional issues in their previous legal careers." Laird v. Tatum (1972). Indeed, even if it were possible to select judges who did not have preconceived views on legal issues, it would hardly be desirable to do so. "Proof that a Justice's mind at the time he joined the Court was a complete tabula rasa in the area of constitutional adjudication would be evidence of lack of qualification, not lack of bias." The Minnesota Constitution positively forbids the selection to courts of general jurisdiction of judges who are impartial in the sense of having no views on the law. Minn. Const., Art. VI, § 5 ("Judges of the supreme court, the court of appeals and the district court shall be learned in the law"). And since avoiding judicial preconceptions on legal issues is neither possible nor desirable, pretending otherwise by attempting to preserve the "appearance" of that type of impartiality can hardly be a compelling state interest either.

C

A third possible meaning of "impartiality" (again not a common one) might be described as openmindedness. This quality in a judge demands, not that he have no preconceptions on legal issues, but that he be willing to consider views that oppose his preconceptions, and remain open to persuasion, when the issues arise in a pending case. This sort of impartiality seeks to guarantee each litigant, not an equal chance to win the legal points in the case, but at least some chance of doing so. It may well be that impartiality in this sense, and the appearance of it, are desirable in the judiciary, but we need not pursue that inquiry, since we do not believe the Minnesota Supreme Court adopted the announce clause for that purpose.

Respondents argue that the announce clause serves the interest in openmindedness, or at least in the appearance of openmindedness, because it relieves a judge from pressure to rule a certain way in order to maintain consistency with statements the judge has previously made. The problem is, however, that statements in election campaigns are such an infinitesimal portion of the public commitments to legal positions that judges (or judges-to-be) undertake, that this object of the prohibition is implausible. Before they arrive on the bench (whether by election or otherwise) judges have often committed themselves on legal issues that they must later rule upon.

More common still is a judge's confronting a legal issue on which he has expressed an opinion while on the bench. Most frequently, of course, that prior expression will have occurred in ruling on an earlier case. But judges often state their views on disputed legal issues outside the context of adjudication—in classes that they conduct, and in books and speeches. Like the ABA Codes of Judicial Conduct, the Minnesota Code not only permits but encourages this. See Minn. Code of Judicial Conduct, Canon 4(B) (2002) ("A judge may write, lecture, teach, speak and participate in other extra-judicial activities concerning the law . . ."); Minn. Code of Judicial Conduct, Canon 4(B), Comment (2002) ("To the extent that time permits, a judge is encouraged to do so . . . "). That is quite incompatible with the notion that the need for openmindedness (or for the appearance of openmindedness) lies behind the prohibition at issue here.

The short of the matter is this: In Minnesota, a candidate for judicial office may not say "I think it is constitutional for the legislature to prohibit same-sex marriages." He may say the very same thing, however, up until the very day before he declares himself a candidate, and may say it repeatedly (until litigation is pending) after he is elected. As a means of pursuing the objective of openmindedness that respondents now articulate, the announce clause is so woefully underinclusive as to render belief in that purpose a challenge to the credulous.

Justice Stevens asserts that statements made in an election campaign pose a special threat to openmindedness because the candidate, when elected judge, will have a particular reluctance to contradict them. That might be plausible, perhaps, with regard to campaign promises. A candidate who says "If elected, I will vote to uphold the legislature's power to prohibit same-sex marriages" will positively be breaking his word if he does not do so (although one would be naive not to recognize that campaign promises are—by long democratic tradition—the least binding form of human commitment). But, as noted earlier, the Minnesota Supreme Court has adopted a separate prohibition on campaign "pledges or promises," which is not challenged here. The proposition that judges feel significantly greater compulsion, or appear to feel significantly greater compulsion, to maintain consistency with nonpromissory statements made during a judicial campaign than with such statements made before or after the campaign is not self-evidently true. It seems to us quite likely, in fact, that in many cases the opposite is true. We doubt, for example, that a mere statement of position enunciated during the pendency of an election will be regarded by a judge as more binding—or as more likely to subject him to popular disfavor if reconsidered—than a carefully considered holding that the judge set forth in an earlier opinion denying some individual's claim to justice. In any event, it suffices to say that respondents have not carried the burden imposed by our strict-scrutiny test to establish this proposition (that campaign statements are uniquely destructive of openmindedness) on which the validity of the announce clause rests. We do not agree with Justice Stevens' broad assertion that "to the extent that [statements on legal issues] seek to enhance the popularity of the candidate by indicating how he would rule in specific cases if elected, they evidence a lack of fitness for office." Of course all statements on real-world legal issues "indicate" how the speaker would rule "in specific cases." And if making such statements (of honestly held views) with the hope of enhancing one's chances with the electorate displayed a lack of fitness for office, so would similarly motivated honest statements of judicial candidates made with the hope of enhancing their chances of confirmation by the Senate, or indeed of appointment by the President. Since such statements are made, we think, in every confirmation hearing, Justice Stevens must contemplate a federal bench filled with the unfit.

Moreover, the notion that the special context of electioneering justifies an abridgment of the right to speak out on disputed issues sets our First Amendment jurisprudence on its head. "[D]ebate on the qualifications of candidates" is "at the core of our electoral process and of the First Amendment freedoms," not at the edges. "The role that elected officials play in our society makes it all the more imperative that they be allowed freely to express themselves on matters of current public importance." Wood v. Georgia (1962). "It is simply not the function of government to select which issues are worth discussing or debating in the course of a political campaign." We have never allowed the government to prohibit candidates from communicating relevant information to voters during an election.

Justice Ginsburg would do so—and much of her dissent confirms rather than refutes our conclusion that the purpose behind the announce clause is not openmindedness in the judiciary, but the undermining of judicial elections. She contends that the announce clause must be constitutional because due process would be denied if an elected judge sat in a case involving an issue on which he had previously announced his view. She reaches this conclusion because, she says, such a judge would have a "direct, personal, substantial, and pecuniary interest" in ruling consistently with his previously announced view, in order to reduce the risk that he will be "voted off the bench and thereby lose [his] salary and emoluments." But elected judges—regardless of whether they have announced any views beforehand—always face the pressure of an electorate who might disagree with their rulings and therefore vote them off the bench. Surely the judge who frees Timothy McVeigh places his job much more at risk than the judge who (horror of horrors!) reconsiders his previously announced view on a disputed legal issue. So if, as Justice Ginsburg claims, it violates due process for a judge to sit in a case in which ruling one way rather than another increases his prospects for reelection, then—quite simply—the practice of electing judges is itself a violation of due process. It is not difficult to understand how one with these views would approve the election-nullifying effect of the announce clause. They are not, however, the views reflected in the Due Process Clause of the Fourteenth Amendment, which has coexisted with the election of judges ever since it was adopted.

IV

To sustain the announce clause, the Eighth Circuit relied heavily on the fact that a pervasive practice of prohibiting judicial candidates from discussing disputed legal and political issues developed during the last half of the 20th century. It is true that a "universal and long-established" tradition of prohibiting certain conduct creates "a strong presumption" that the prohibition is constitutional.

The practice of prohibiting speech by judicial candidates on disputed issues, however, is neither long nor universal. At the time of the founding, only Vermont (before it became a State) selected any of its judges by election. Starting with Georgia in 1812, States began to provide for judicial election, a development rapidly accelerated by Jacksonian democracy. By the time of the Civil War, the great majority of States elected their judges. We know of no restrictions upon statements that could be made by judicial candidates (including judges) throughout the 19th and the first quarter of the 20th century. Indeed, judicial elections were generally partisan during this period, the movement toward nonpartisan judicial elections not even beginning until the 1870's. Thus, not only were judicial candidates (including judges) discussing disputed legal and political issues on the campaign trail, but they were touting party affiliations and angling for party nominations all the while.

The first code regulating judicial conduct was adopted by the ABA in 1924. It contained a provision akin to the announce clause: "A candidate for judicial position . . . should not announce in advance his conclusions of law on disputed issues to secure class support. . . ." ABA Canon of Judicial Ethics 30 (1924). The States were slow to adopt the canons, however. "By the end of World War

II, the canons . . . were binding by the bar associations or supreme courts of only eleven states." Even today, although a majority of States have adopted either the announce clause or its 1990 ABA successor, adoption is not unanimous. Of the 31 States that select some or all of their appellate and general-jurisdiction judges by election, 4 have adopted no candidate-speech restriction comparable to the announce clause, and 1 prohibits only the discussion of "pending litigation." This practice, relatively new to judicial elections and still not universally adopted, does not compare well with the traditions deemed worthy of our attention in prior cases.

There is an obvious tension between the article of Minnesota's popularly approved Constitution which provides that judges shall be elected, and the Minnesota Supreme Court's announce clause which places most subjects of interest to the voters off limits.

The Minnesota Supreme Court's canon of judicial conduct prohibiting candidates for judicial election from announcing their views on disputed legal and political issues violates the First Amendment. Accordingly, we reverse the grant of summary judgment to respondents and remand the case for proceedings consistent with this opinion.

Justice O'CONNOR, concurring.

I join the opinion of the Court but write separately to express my concerns about judicial elections generally. Respondents claim that "[t]he Announce Clause is necessary . . . to protect the State's compelling governmental interes[t] in an actual and perceived . . . impartial judiciary." I am concerned that, even aside from what judicial candidates may say while campaigning, the very practice of electing judges undermines this interest.

We of course want judges to be impartial, in the sense of being free from any personal stake in the outcome of the cases to which they are assigned. But if judges are subject to regular elections they are likely to feel that they have at least some personal stake in the outcome of every publicized case. Elected judges cannot help being aware that if the public is not satisfied with the outcome of a particular case, it could hurt their reelection prospects. See Eule, Crocodiles in the Bathtub: State Courts, Voter Initiatives and the Threat of Electoral Reprisal, 65 U. Colo. L. Rev. 733, 739 (1994) (quoting former California Supreme Court Justice Otto Kaus' statement that ignoring the political consequences of visible decisions is " 'like ignoring a crocodile in your bathtub'"); Bright & Keenan, Judges and the Politics of Death: Deciding Between the Bill of Rights and the Next Election in Capital Cases, 75 B.U. L. Rev. 759, 793-794 (1995) (citing statistics indicating that judges who face elections are far more likely to override jury sentences of life without parole and impose the death penalty than are judges who do not run for election). Even if judges were able to suppress their awareness of the potential electoral consequences of their decisions and refrain from acting on it, the public's confidence in the judiciary could be undermined simply by the possibility that judges would be unable to do so.

Moreover, contested elections generally entail campaigning. And campaigning for a judicial post today can require substantial funds. Unless the pool of judicial candidates is limited to those wealthy enough to independently fund their campaigns, a limitation unrelated to judicial skill, the cost of campaigning requires judicial candidates to engage in fundraising. Yet relying on campaign donations may leave judges feeling indebted to certain parties or interest groups. See Thomas, National L.J., Mar. 16, 1998, p. A8, col. 1 (reporting that a study by the public interest group Texans for Public Justice found that 40 percent of the $9,200,000 in contributions of $100 or more raised by seven of Texas' nine Supreme Court justices for their 1994 and 1996 elections "came from parties and lawyers with cases before the court or contributors closely linked to these parties"). Even if judges were able to refrain from favoring donors, the mere possibility that judges' decisions may be motivated by the desire to repay campaign contributors is likely to undermine the public's confidence in the judiciary.

Minnesota has chosen to select its judges through contested popular elections instead of through an appointment system or a combined appointment and retention election system along the lines of the Missouri Plan. In doing so the State has voluntarily taken on the risks to judicial bias described above. As a result, the State's claim that it needs to significantly restrict judges' speech in order to protect judicial impartiality is particularly troubling. If the State has a problem with judicial impartiality, it is largely one the State brought upon itself by continuing the practice of popularly electing judges.

Justice KENNEDY, concurring.

I agree with the Court that Minnesota's prohibition on judicial candidates' announcing their legal views is an unconstitutional abridgment of the freedom of speech. There is authority for the Court to apply strict scrutiny analysis to resolve some First Amendment cases, and the Court explains in clear and forceful terms why the Minnesota regulatory scheme fails that test. So I join its opinion.

I adhere to my view, however, that content-based speech restrictions that do not fall within any traditional exception should be invalidated without inquiry into narrow tailoring or compelling government interests. The speech at issue here does not come within any of the exceptions to the First Amendment recognized by the Court. "Here, a law is directed to speech alone where the speech in question is not obscene, not defamatory, not words tantamount to an act otherwise criminal, not an impairment of some other constitutional right, not an incitement to lawless action, and not calculated or likely to bring about imminent harm the State has the substantive power to prevent. No further inquiry is necessary to reject the State's argument that the statute should be upheld."

The political speech of candidates is at the heart of the First Amendment, and direct restrictions on the content of candidate speech are simply beyond the power of government to impose. Here, Minnesota has sought to justify its speech restriction as one necessary to maintain the integrity of its judiciary.

Nothing in the Court's opinion should be read to cast doubt on the vital importance of this state interest. Courts, in our system, elaborate principles of law in the course of resolving disputes. The power and the prerogative of a court to perform this function rest, in the end, upon the respect accorded to its judgments. The citizen's respect for judgments depends in turn upon the issuing court's absolute probity. Judicial integrity is, in consequence, a state interest of the highest order.

Minnesota may choose to have an elected judiciary. It may strive to define those characteristics that exemplify judicial excellence. It may enshrine its definitions in a code of judicial conduct. It may adopt recusal standards more rigorous than due process requires, and censure judges who violate these standards. What Minnesota may not do, however, is censor what the people hear as they undertake to decide for themselves which candidate is most likely to be an exemplary judicial officer. Deciding the relevance of candidate speech is the right of the voters, not the State. See Brown v. Hartlage (1982). The law in question here contradicts the principle that unabridged speech is the foundation of political freedom.

If Minnesota believes that certain sorts of candidate speech disclose flaws in the candidate's credentials, democracy and free speech are their own correctives. The legal profession, the legal academy, the press, voluntary groups, political and civic leaders, and all interested citizens can use their own First Amendment freedoms to protest statements inconsistent with standards of judicial neutrality and judicial excellence. Indeed, if democracy is to fulfill its promise, they must do so. They must reach voters who are uninterested or uninformed or blinded by partisanship, and they must urge upon the voters a higher and better understanding of the judicial function and a stronger commitment to preserving its finest traditions. Free elections and free speech are a powerful combination: Together they may advance our understanding of the rule of law and further a commitment to its precepts.

These considerations serve but to reinforce the conclusion that Minnesota's regulatory scheme is flawed. By abridging speech based on its content, Minnesota impeaches its own system of free and open elections.

Justice STEVENS, with whom Justice SOUTER, Justice GINSBURG, and Justice BREYER join, dissenting.

The limits of the Court's holding are evident: Even if the Minnesota Lawyers Professional Responsibility Board (Board) may not sanction a judicial candidate for announcing his views on issues likely to come before him, it may surely advise the electorate that such announcements demonstrate the speaker's unfitness for judicial office. If the solution to harmful speech must be more speech, so be it. The Court's reasoning, however, will unfortunately endure beyond the next election cycle. By obscuring the fundamental distinction between campaigns for the judiciary and the political branches, and by failing to recognize the difference between statements made in articles or opinions and those made on the campaign trail, the Court defies any sensible notion of the judicial office and the importance of impartiality in that context.

The Court's disposition rests on two seriously flawed premises—an inaccurate appraisal of the importance of judicial independence and impartiality, and an assumption that judicial candidates should have the same freedom "'to express themselves on matters of current public importance'" as do all other elected officials. Elected judges, no less than appointed judges, occupy an office of trust that is fundamentally different from that occupied by policymaking officials. Although the fact that they must stand for election makes their job more difficult than that of the tenured judge, that fact does not lessen their duty to respect essential attributes of the judicial office that have been embedded in Anglo-American law for centuries.

There is a critical difference between the work of the judge and the work of other public officials. In a democracy, issues of policy are properly decided by majority vote; it is the business of legislators and executives to be popular. But in litigation, issues of law or fact should not be determined by popular vote; it is the business of judges to be indifferent to unpopularity.

Consistent with that fundamental attribute of the office, countless judges in countless cases routinely make rulings that are unpopular and surely disliked by at least 50 percent of the litigants who appear before them. It is equally common for them to enforce rules that they think unwise, or that are contrary to their personal predilections. For this reason, opinions that a lawyer may have expressed before becoming a judge, or a judicial candidate, do not disqualify anyone for judicial service because every good judge is fully aware of the distinction between the law and a personal point of view. It is equally clear, however, that such expressions after a lawyer has been nominated to judicial office shed little, if any, light on his capacity for judicial service. Indeed, to the extent that such statements seek to enhance the popularity of the candidate by indicating how he would rule in specific cases if elected, they evidence a lack of fitness for the office.

Of course, any judge who faces reelection may believe that he retains his office only so long as his decisions are popular. Nevertheless, the elected judge, like the lifetime appointee, does not serve a constituency while holding that office. He has a duty to uphold the law and to follow the dictates of the Constitution. If he is not a judge on the highest court in the State, he has an obligation to follow the precedent of that court, not his personal views or public opinion polls. He may make common law, but judged on the merits of individual cases, not as a mandate from the voters.

But we do know that a judicial candidate, who announces his views in the context of a campaign, is effectively telling the electorate: "Vote for me because I believe X, and I will judge cases accordingly." Once elected, he may feel free to disregard his campaign statements, but that does not change the fact that the judge announced his position on an issue likely to come before him as a reason to vote for him. Minnesota has a compelling interest in sanctioning such statements. A candidate for judicial office who goes beyond the expression of "general observation about the law . . . in order to obtain favorable consideration" of his candidacy, demonstrates either a lack of impartiality or a lack of understanding of the importance of maintaining public confidence in the impartiality of the judiciary. It is only by failing to recognize the distinction, between statements made during a campaign or confirmation hearing and those made before announcing one's candidacy, that the Court is able to conclude: "[S]ince avoiding judicial preconceptions on legal issues is neither possible nor desirable, pretending otherwise by attempting to preserve the 'appearance' of that type of impartiality can hardly be a compelling state interest either."

Even when "impartiality" is defined in its narrowest sense to embrace only "the lack of bias for or against either party to the proceeding," the announce clause serves that interest. Expressions that stress a candidate's unbroken record of affirming convictions for rape, for example, imply a bias in favor of a particular litigant (the prosecutor) and against a class of litigants (defendants in rape cases). Contrary to the Court's reasoning in its first attempt to define impartiality, an interpretation of the announce clause that prohibits such statements serves the State's interest in maintaining both the appearance of this form of impartiality and its actuality.

The Court boldly asserts that respondents have failed to carry their burden of demonstrating "that campaign statements are uniquely destructive of open-mindedness." But the very purpose of most statements prohibited by the announce clause is to convey the message that the candidate's mind is not open on a particular issue. The lawyer who writes an article advocating harsher penalties for polluters surely does not commit to that position to the same degree as the candidate who says "vote for me because I believe all polluters deserve harsher penalties." At the very least, such statements obscure the appearance of open-mindedness. More importantly, like the reasoning in the Court's opinion, they create the false impression that the standards for the election of political candidates apply equally to candidates for judicial office.

The Court seems to have forgotten its prior evaluation of the importance of maintaining public confidence in the "disinterestedness" of the judiciary. Commenting on the danger that participation by judges in a political assignment might erode that public confidence, we wrote: "While the problem of individual bias is usually cured through recusal, no such mechanism can overcome the appearance of institutional partiality that may arise from judiciary involvement in the making of policy. The legitimacy of the Judicial Branch ultimately depends on its reputation for impartiality and nonpartisanship. That reputation may not be borrowed by the political Branches to cloak their work in the neutral colors of judicial action." Conversely, the judicial reputation for impartiality and openmindedness is compromised by electioneering that emphasizes the candidate's personal predilections rather than his qualifications for judicial office.

The disposition of this case on the flawed premise that the criteria for the election to judicial office should mirror the rules applicable to political elections is profoundly misguided. I therefore respectfully dissent.

Justice GINSBURG, with whom Justice STEVENS, Justice SOUTER, and Justice BREYER join, dissenting.

Whether state or federal, elected or appointed, judges perform a function fundamentally different from that of the people's elected representatives. Legislative and executive officials act on behalf of the voters who placed them in office; "judge[s] represen[t] the Law." Unlike their counterparts in the political branches, judges are expected to refrain from catering to particular constituencies or committing themselves on controversial issues in advance of adversarial presentation. Their mission is to decide "individual cases and controversies" on individual records, neutrally applying legal principles, and, when necessary, "stand[ing] up to what is generally supreme in a democracy: the popular will." A judiciary capable of performing this function, owing fidelity to no person or party, is a "longstanding Anglo-American tradition," an essential bulwark of constitutional government, a constant guardian of the rule of law. The guarantee of an independent, impartial judiciary enables society to "withdraw certain subjects from the vicissitudes of political controversy, to place them beyond the reach of majorities and officials and to establish them as legal principles to be applied by the courts." West Virginia Bd. of Ed. v. Barnette (1943). "Without this, all the reservations of particular rights or privileges would amount to nothing." The Federalist No. 78, p. 466 (C. Rossiter ed. 1961).

The ability of the judiciary to discharge its unique role rests to a large degree on the manner in which judges are selected. The Framers of the Federal Constitution sought to advance the judicial function through the structural protections of Article III, which provide for the selection of judges by the President on the advice and consent of the Senate, generally for lifetime terms. Through its own Constitution, Minnesota, in common with most other States, has decided to allow its citizens to choose judges directly in periodic elections. But Minnesota has not thereby opted to install a corps of political actors on the bench; rather, it has endeavored to preserve the integrity of its judiciary by other means. Recognizing that the influence of political parties is incompatible with the judge's role, for example, Minnesota has designated all judicial elections nonpartisan. And it has adopted a provision, here called the Announce Clause, designed to prevent candidates for judicial office from "publicly making known how they would decide issues likely to come before them as judges."

The question this case presents is whether the First Amendment stops Minnesota from furthering its interest in judicial integrity through this precisely targeted speech restriction.

I

The speech restriction must fail, in the Court's view, because an electoral process is at stake; if Minnesota opts to elect its judges, the Court asserts, the State may not rein in what candidates may say.

I do not agree with this unilocular, "an election is an election," approach. Instead, I would differentiate elections for political offices, in which the First Amendment holds full sway, from elections designed to select those whose office it is to administer justice without respect to persons. Minnesota's choice to elect its judges, I am persuaded, does not preclude the State from installing an election process geared to the judicial office.

Legislative and executive officials serve in representative capacities. They are agents of the people; their primary function is to advance the interests of their constituencies. Candidates for political offices, in keeping with their representative role, must be left free to inform the electorate of their positions on specific issues. Armed with such information, the individual voter will be equipped to cast her ballot intelligently, to vote for the candidate committed to positions the voter approves. Campaign statements committing the candidate to take sides on contentious issues are therefore not only appropriate in political elections, they are "at the core of our electoral process," for they "enhance the accountability of government officials to the people whom they represent."

Judges, however, are not political actors. They do not sit as representatives of particular persons, communities, or parties; they serve no faction or constituency. "[I]t is the business of judges to be indifferent to popularity." They must strive to do what is legally right, all the more so when the result is not the one "the home crowd" wants. Even when they develop common law or give concrete meaning to constitutional text, judges act only in the context of individual cases, the outcome of which cannot depend on the will of the public.

Thus, the rationale underlying unconstrained speech in elections for political office—that representative government depends on the public's ability to choose agents who will act at its behest—does not carry over to campaigns for the bench. As to persons aiming to occupy the seat of judgment, the Court's unrelenting reliance on decisions involving contests for legislative and executive posts is manifestly out of place. In view of the magisterial role judges must fill in a system of justice, a role that removes them from the partisan fray, States may limit judicial campaign speech by measures impermissible in elections for political office.[1]

---

1. The author of the Court's opinion declined on precisely these grounds to tell the Senate whether he would overrule a particular case:

> Let us assume that I have people arguing before me to do it or not to do it. I think it is quite a thing to be arguing to somebody who you know has made a representation in the course of his confirmation hearings, and that is, by way of condition to his being confirmed, that he will do this or do that. I think I would be in a very bad position to adjudicate the case without being accused of having a less than impartial view of the matter. 13 R. Mersky & J. Jacobstein, The Supreme Court of the United States: Hearings and Reports on Successful and Unsuccessful Nominations of Supreme Court Justices by the Senate Judiciary Committee, 1916-1986, 131 (1989) (hearings before the Senate Judiciary Committee on the nomination of then-Judge Scalia). [Footnote by Justice Ginsburg.]

II

Proper resolution of this case requires correction of the Court's distorted construction of the provision before us for review. According to the Court, the Announce Clause "prohibits a judicial candidate from stating his views on any specific nonfanciful legal question within the province of the court for which he is running, except in the context of discussing past decisions—and in the latter context as well, if he expresses the view that he is not bound by stare decisis." In two key respects, that construction misrepresents the meaning of the Announce Clause as interpreted by the Eighth Circuit and embraced by the Minnesota Supreme Court, which has the final word on this matter.

First and most important, the Court ignores a crucial limiting construction placed on the Announce Clause by the courts below. The provision does not bar a candidate from generally "stating [her] views" on legal questions; it prevents her from "publicly making known how [she] would decide" disputed issues. That limitation places beyond the scope of the Announce Clause a wide range of comments that may be highly informative to voters. Consistent with the Eighth Circuit's construction, such comments may include, for example, statements of historical fact ("As a prosecutor, I obtained 15 drunk driving convictions"); qualified statements ("Judges should use sparingly their discretion to grant lenient sentences to drunk drivers"); and statements framed at a sufficient level of generality ("Drunk drivers are a threat to the safety of every driver"). What remains within the Announce Clause is the category of statements that essentially commit the candidate to a position on a specific issue, such as "I think all drunk drivers should receive the maximum sentence permitted by law."

Second, the Court misportrays the scope of the Clause as applied to a candidate's discussion of past decisions. The Court concludes that "statements critical of past judicial decisions are not permissible if the candidate also states that he is against stare decisis." That conclusion, however, draws no force from the meaning attributed to the Announce Clause by the Eighth Circuit. In line with the Minnesota Board on Judicial Standards, the Court of Appeals stated without qualification that the Clause "does not prohibit candidates from discussing appellate court decisions."

The Announce Clause is thus more tightly bounded, and campaigns conducted under that provision more robust, than the Court acknowledges.

Judicial candidates in Minnesota may not only convey general information about themselves, they may also describe their conception of the role of a judge and their views on a wide range of subjects of interest to the voters. Further, they may discuss, criticize, or defend past decisions of interest to voters. What candidates may not do—simply or with sophistication—is remove themselves from the constraints characteristic of the judicial office and declare how they would decide an issue, without regard to the particular context in which it is presented, sans briefs, oral argument, and, as to an appellate bench, the benefit of one's colleagues' analyses. Properly construed, the Announce Clause prohibits only a discrete subcategory of the statements the Court's misinterpretation encompasses.

This Court has recognized in the past, as Justice O'Connor does today, a "fundamental tension between the ideal character of the judicial office and the real world of electoral politics." We have no warrant to resolve that tension, however, by forcing States to choose one pole or the other. Judges are not politicians, and the First Amendment does not require that they be treated as politicians simply because they are chosen by popular vote. Nor does the First Amendment command States who wish to promote the integrity of their judges in fact and appearance to abandon systems of judicial selection that the people, in the exercise of their sovereign prerogatives, have devised.

For more than three-quarters of a century, States like Minnesota have endeavored, through experiment tested by experience, to balance the constitutional interests in judicial integrity and free expression within the unique setting of an elected judiciary.The Announce Clause, borne of this long effort, "comes to this Court bearing a weighty title of respect." I would uphold it as an essential component in Minnesota's accommodation of the complex and competing concerns in this sensitive area.

3. Prior Restraints

c. *Licensing as a Prior Restraint*

In the October 2001 Term, the Supreme Court had the occasion to consider the constitutionality of two permit systems. In Thomas v. Chicago Park District, below, the Court upheld a licensing system as a condition for use of a city park. But in Watchtower Bible and Tract Society of New York v. Village of Stratton, the Court declared unconstitutional a city's ordinance requiring a permit for canvassing or soliciting in a neighborhood. Each case is presented below. In reading these cases, it is important to focus on how these permit systems are different and why one is constitutional, while the other is not.

THOMAS AND WINDY CITY HEMP DEVELOPMENT
BOARD v. CHICAGO PARK DISTRICT
122 S. Ct. 775 (2002)

Justice SCALIA delivered the opinion of the Court.

This case presents the question whether a municipal park ordinance requiring individuals to obtain a permit before conducting large-scale events must, consistent with the First Amendment, contain the procedural safeguards described in Freedman v. Maryland (1965).

I

Respondent, the Chicago Park District (Park District), is responsible for operating public parks and other public property in Chicago. [T]he Park District adopted an ordinance that requires a person to obtain a permit in order to "conduct a public assembly, parade, picnic, or other event involving more than fifty individuals," or engage in an activity such as "creat[ing] or emit[ting] any Amplified Sound." The ordinance provides that "[a]pplications for permits shall be processed in order of receipt," and the Park District must decide whether to grant or deny an application within 14 days unless, by written notice to the applicant, it extends the period an additional 14 days. Applications can be denied on any of 13 specified grounds. If the Park District denies an application, it must clearly set forth in writing the grounds for denial and, where feasible, must propose measures to cure defects in the application. When the basis for denial is prior receipt of a competing application for the same time and place, the Park District must suggest alternative times or places. An unsuccessful applicant has seven days to file a written appeal to the General Superintendent of the Park District, who must act on the appeal within seven days. If the General Superintendent affirms a permit denial, the applicant may seek judicial review in state court by common-law certiorari.

Petitioners have applied to the Park District on several occasions for permits to hold rallies advocating the legalization of marijuana. The Park District has granted some permits and denied others. Not satisfied, petitioners filed an action pursuant to 42 U.S.C. § 1983 in the United States District Court for the Northern District of Illinois, alleging that the Park District's ordinance is unconstitutional on its face.

II

The First Amendment's guarantee of "the freedom of speech, or of the press" prohibits a wide assortment of government restraints upon expression, but the core abuse against which it was directed was the scheme of licensing laws implemented by the monarch and Parliament to contain the "evils" of the printing press in 16th- and 17-century England. The Printing Act of 1662 had "prescribed what could be printed, who could print, and who could sell." It punished the publication of any book or pamphlet without a license and required that all works be submitted for approval to a government official, who wielded broad authority to suppress works that he found to be " 'heretical, seditious, schismatical, or offensive.' " The English licensing system expired at the end of the 17th century, but the memory of its abuses was still vivid enough in colonial times that Blackstone warned against the "restrictive power" of such a "licenser"—an administrative official who enjoyed unconfined authority to pass judgment on the content of speech.

In Freedman v. Maryland (1965), we confronted a state law that enacted a strikingly similar system of prior restraint for motion pictures. It required that every motion picture film be submitted to a Board of Censors before the film was shown anywhere in the State. The Board enjoyed authority to reject films that it considered "'obscene'" or that "'tend[ed], in the judgment of the Board, to debase or corrupt morals or incite to crimes,'" characteristics defined by the statute in broad terms. The statute punished the exhibition of a film not submitted to the Board for advance approval, even where the film would have received a license had it been properly submitted. It was no defense that the content of the film was protected by the First Amendment.

We recognized in *Freedman* that a scheme conditioning expression on a licensing body's prior approval of content "presents peculiar dangers to con-stitutionally protected speech." "[T]he censor's business is to censor," and a licensing body likely will overestimate the dangers of controversial speech when determining, without regard to the film's actual effect on an audience, whether speech is likely "'to incite'" or to "'corrupt [the] morals.'" In response to these grave "dangers of a censorship system," we held that a film licensing process must contain certain procedural safeguards in order to avoid constituting an invalid prior restraint: "(1) any restraint prior to judicial review can be imposed only for a specified brief period during which the status quo must be maintained; (2) expeditious judicial review of that decision must be available; and (3) the censor must bear the burden of going to court to suppress the speech and must bear the burden of proof once in court."

Petitioners contend that the Park District, like the Board of Censors in *Freedman,* must initiate litigation every time it denies a permit and that the or-dinance must specify a deadline for judicial review of a challenge to a permit de-nial. We reject those contentions. *Freedman* is inapposite because the licensing scheme at issue here is not subject-matter censorship but content-neutral time, place, and manner regulation of the use of a public forum. The Park District's ordinance does not authorize a licensor to pass judgment on the content of speech: None of the grounds for denying a permit has anything to do with what a speaker might say. Indeed, the ordinance (unlike the classic censorship scheme) is not even directed to communicative activity as such, but rather to all activity conducted in a public park. The picnicker and soccer-player, no less than the political activist or parade marshal, must apply for a permit if the 50-person limit is to be exceeded. And the object of the permit system (as plainly indicated by the permissible grounds for permit denial) is not to exclude communication of a particular content, but to coordinate multiple uses of limited space, to assure preservation of the park facilities, to prevent uses that are dangerous, unlawful, or impermissible under the Park District's rules, and to assure financial accountability for damage caused by the event. As the Court of Appeals well put it: "[T]o allow unregulated access to all comers could easily reduce rather than enlarge the park's utility as a forum for speech."

We have never required that a content-neutral permit scheme regulating speech in a public forum adhere to the procedural requirements set forth in *Freedman.* "A licensing standard which gives an official authority to censor the content of a speech differs toto coelo from one limited by its terms, or by non-discriminatory practice, to considerations of public safety and the like." Niemotko v. Maryland (1951) (Frankfurter, J., concurring in result). "[T]he [permit] required is not the kind of prepublication license deemed a denial of liberty since the time of John Milton but a ministerial, police routine for adjusting the rights of citizens so that the opportunity for effective freedom of speech may be preserved." Poulos v. New Hampshire (1953). Regulations of the use of a public forum that ensure the safety and convenience of the people are not "inconsistent with civil liberties but . . . [are] one of the means of safeguarding the good order upon which [civil liberties] ultimately depend." Such a traditional exercise of authority does not raise the censorship concerns that prompted us to impose the extraordinary procedural safeguards on the film licensing process in *Freedman*.

III

Of course even content-neutral time, place, and manner restrictions can be applied in such a manner as to stifle free expression. Where the licensing official enjoys unduly broad discretion in determining whether to grant or deny a permit, there is a risk that he will favor or disfavor speech based on its content. We have thus required that a time, place, and manner regulation contain adequate standards to guide the official's decision and render it subject to effective judicial review. Petitioners contend that the Park District's ordinance fails this test.

We think not. As we have described, the Park District may deny a permit only for one or more of the reasons set forth in the ordinance. See n. 1, supra. It may deny, for example, when the application is incomplete or contains a material falsehood or misrepresentation; when the applicant has damaged Park District property on prior occasions and has not paid for the damage; when a permit has been granted to an earlier applicant for the same time and place; when the intended use would present an unreasonable danger to the health or safety of park users or Park District employees; or when the applicant has violated the terms of a prior permit. Moreover, the Park District must process applications within 28 days, and must clearly explain its reasons for any denial. These grounds are reasonably specific and objective, and do not leave the decision "to the whim of the administrator." They provide "'narrowly drawn, reasonable and definite standards'" to guide the licensor's determination. And they are enforceable on review—first by appeal to the General Superintendent of the Park District, and then by writ of common-law certiorari in the Illinois courts.

Petitioners contend that the criteria set forth in the ordinance are insufficiently precise because they are described as grounds on which the Park District "may" deny a permit, rather than grounds on which it must do so. This, they contend, allows the Park District to waive the permit requirements for some favored speakers, while insisting upon them for others. That is certainly not the intent of the ordinance, which the Park District has reasonably interpreted to permit overlooking only those inadequacies that, under the circumstances, do no harm to the policies furthered by the application requirements. Granting waivers to favored speakers (or, more precisely, denying them to disfavored speakers) would of course be unconstitutional, but we think that this abuse must be dealt with if and when a pattern of unlawful favoritism appears, rather than by insisting upon a degree of rigidity that is found in few legal arrangements. On petitioners' theory, every obscenity law, or every law placing limits upon political expenditures, contains a constitutional flaw, since it merely permits, but does not require, prosecution. The prophylaxis achieved by insisting upon a rigid, no-waiver application of the ordinance requirements would be far outweighed, we think, by the accompanying senseless prohibition of speech (and of other activity in the park) by organizations that fail to meet the technical requirements of the ordinance but for one reason or another pose no risk of the evils that those requirements are designed to avoid. On balance, we think the permissive nature of the ordinance furthers, rather than constricts, free speech.

WATCHTOWER BIBLE AND TRACT SOCIETY OF NEW YORK, INC. v. VILLAGE OF STRATTON
122 S. Ct. ___ (2002)

Justice STEVENS delivered the opinion of the Court.

Petitioners contend that a village ordinance making it a misdemeanor to engage in door-to-door advocacy without first registering with the mayor and receiving a permit violates the First Amendment. Through this facial challenge, we consider the door-to-door canvassing regulation not only as it applies to religious proselytizing, but also to anonymous political speech and the distribution of handbills.

I

Petitioner Watchtower Bible and Tract Society of New York, Inc., coordinates the preaching activities of Jehovah's Witnesses throughout the United States and publishes Bibles and religious periodicals that are widely distributed. Petitioner Wellsville, Ohio, Congregation of Jehovah's Witnesses, Inc., supervises the activities of approximately 59 members in a part of Ohio that includes the Village of Stratton (Village). Petitioners offer religious literature without cost to anyone interested in reading it. They allege that they do not solicit contributions or orders for the sale of merchandise or services, but they do accept donations.

Petitioners brought this action against the Village and its mayor in the United States District Court for the Southern District of Ohio, seeking an injunction against the enforcement of several sections of Ordinance No. 1998-5 regulating uninvited peddling and solicitation on private property in the Village. Petitioners' complaint alleged that the ordinance violated several constitutional rights, including the free exercise of religion, free speech, and the freedom of the press.

Section 116.01 prohibits "canvassers" and others from "going in and upon" private residential property for the purpose of promoting any "cause" without first having obtained a permit pursuant to § 116.03. That section provides that any canvasser who intends to go on private property to promote a cause, must obtain a "Solicitation Permit" from the office of the mayor; there is no charge for the permit, and apparently one is issued routinely after an applicant fills out a fairly detailed "Solicitor's Registration Form." The canvasser is then authorized to go upon premises that he listed on the registration form, but he must carry the permit upon his person and exhibit it whenever requested to do so by a police officer or by a resident. The ordinance sets forth grounds for the denial or revocation of a permit, but the record before us does not show that any application has been denied or that any permit has been revoked. Petitioners did not apply for a permit.

A section of the ordinance that petitioners do not challenge establishes a procedure by which a resident may prohibit solicitation even by holders of permits. If the resident files a "No Solicitation Registration Form" with the mayor, and also posts a "No Solicitation" sign on his property, no uninvited canvassers may enter his property, unless they are specifically authorized to do so in the "No Solicitation Registration Form" itself. Only 32 of the Village's 278 residents filed such forms.

II

For over 50 years, the Court has invalidated restrictions on door-to-door canvassing and pamphleteering. It is more than historical accident that most of these cases involved First Amendment challenges brought by Jehovah's Witnesses, because door-to-door canvassing is mandated by their religion. Moreover, because they lack significant financial resources, the ability of the Witnesses to proselytize is seriously diminished by regulations that burden their efforts to canvass door-to-door.

Although our past cases involving Jehovah's Witnesses, most of which were decided shortly before and during World War II, do not directly control the question we confront today, they provide both a historical and analytical backdrop for consideration of petitioners' First Amendment claim that the breadth of the Village's ordinance offends the First Amendment. From these decisions, several themes emerge that guide our consideration of the ordinance at issue here.

First, the cases emphasize the value of the speech involved. For example, in Murdock v. Pennsylvania, the Court noted that "hand distribution of religious tracts is an age-old form of missionary evangelism—as old as the history of printing presses. It has been a potent force in various religious movements down through the years. . . . This form of religious activity occupies the same high estate under the First Amendment as do worship in the churches and preaching from the pulpits. It has the same claim to protection as the more orthodox and conventional exercises of religion. It also has the same claim as the others to the guarantees of freedom of speech and freedom of the press." In addition, the cases discuss extensively the historical importance of door-to-door canvassing and pamphleteering as vehicles for the dissemination of ideas.

Despite the emphasis on the important role that door-to-door canvassing and pamphleteering has played in our constitutional tradition of free and open discussion, these early cases also recognized the interests a town may have in some form of regulation, particularly when the solicitation of money is involved. Despite recognition of these interests as legitimate, our precedent is clear that there must be a balance between these interests and the effect of the regulations on First Amendment rights. We "must 'be astute to examine the effect of the challenged legislation' and must 'weigh the circumstances and . . . appraise the substantiality of the reasons advanced in support of the regulation.'"

Finally, the cases demonstrate that efforts of the Jehovah's Witnesses to resist speech regulation have not been a struggle for their rights alone. In *Martin,* after cataloging the many groups that rely extensively upon this method of communication, the Court summarized that "[d]oor to door distribution of circulars is essential to the poorly financed causes of little people."

III

The Village argues that three interests are served by its ordinance: the prevention of fraud, the prevention of crime, and the protection of residents' privacy. We have no difficulty concluding, in light of our precedent, that these are important interests that the Village may seek to safeguard through some form of regulation of solicitation activity. We must also look, however, to the amount of speech covered by the ordinance and whether there is an appropriate balance between the affected speech and the governmental interests that the ordinance purports to serve.

The text of the Village's ordinance prohibits "canvassers" from going on private property for the purpose of explaining or promoting any "cause," unless they receive a permit and the residents visited have not opted for a "no solicitation" sign. Had this provision been construed to apply only to commercial activities and the solicitation of funds, arguably the ordinance would have been tailored to the Village's interest in protecting the privacy of its residents and preventing fraud. Yet, even though the Village has explained that the ordinance was adopted to serve those interests, it has never contended that it should be so narrowly interpreted. To the contrary, the Village's administration of its ordinance unquestionably demonstrates that the provisions apply to a significant number of noncommercial "canvassers" promoting a wide variety of "causes."

Indeed, on the "No Solicitation Forms" provided to the residents, the canvassers include "Camp Fire Girls," "Jehovah's Witnesses," "Political Candidates," "Trick or Treaters during Halloween Season," and "Persons Affiliated with Stratton Church." The ordinance unquestionably applies, not only to religious causes, but to political activity as well. It would seem to extend to "residents casually soliciting the votes of neighbors," or ringing doorbells to enlist support for employing a more efficient garbage collector.

The mere fact that the ordinance covers so much speech raises constitutional concerns. It is offensive—not only to the values protected by the First Amendment, but to the very notion of a free society—that in the context of everyday public discourse a citizen must first inform the government of her desire to speak to her neighbors and then obtain a permit to do so. Even if the issuance of permits by the mayor's office is a ministerial task that is performed promptly and at no cost to the applicant, a law requiring a permit to engage in such speech constitutes a dramatic departure from our national heritage and constitutional tradition.

Three obvious examples illustrate the pernicious effect of such a permit requirement. First, as our cases involving distribution of unsigned handbills demonstrate, there are a significant number of persons who support causes anonymously. "The decision to favor anonymity may be motivated by fear of economic or official retaliation, by concern about social ostracism, or merely by a desire to preserve as much of one's privacy as possible." McIntyre v. Ohio Elections Comm'n (1995). The requirement that a canvasser must be identified in a permit application filed in the mayor's office and available for public inspection necessarily results in a surrender of that anonymity.

Second, requiring a permit as a prior condition on the exercise of the right to speak imposes an objective burden on some speech of citizens holding religious or patriotic views. As our World War II-era cases dramatically demonstrate, there are a significant number of persons whose religious scruples will prevent them from applying for such a license. There are no doubt other patriotic citizens, who have such firm convictions about their constitutional right to engage in uninhibited debate in the context of door-to-door advocacy, that they would prefer silence to speech licensed by a petty official.

Third, there is a significant amount of spontaneous speech that is effectively banned by the ordinance. A person who made a decision on a holiday or a weekend to take an active part in a political campaign could not begin to pass out handbills until after he or she obtained the required permit. Even a spontaneous decision to go across the street and urge a neighbor to vote against the mayor could not lawfully be implemented without first obtaining the mayor's permission.

The breadth and unprecedented nature of this regulation does not alone render the ordinance invalid. Also central to our conclusion that the ordinance does not pass First Amendment scrutiny is that it is not tailored to the Village's stated interests. Even if the interest in preventing fraud could adequately support the ordinance insofar as it applies to commercial transactions and the solicitation of funds, that interest provides no support for its application to petitioners, to political campaigns, or to enlisting support for unpopular causes. The Village, however, argues that the ordinance is nonetheless valid because it serves the two additional interests of protecting the privacy of the resident and the prevention of crime.

With respect to the former, it seems clear that § 107 of the ordinance, which provides for the posting of "No Solicitation" signs and which is not challenged in this case, coupled with the resident's unquestioned right to refuse to engage in conversation with unwelcome visitors, provides ample protection for the unwilling listener. The annoyance caused by an uninvited knock on the front door is the same whether or not the visitor is armed with a permit.

With respect to the latter, it seems unlikely that the absence of a permit would preclude criminals from knocking on doors and engaging in conversations not covered by the ordinance. They might, for example, ask for directions or permission to use the telephone, or pose as surveyers or census takers. Or they might register under a false name with impunity because the ordinance contains no provision for verifying an applicant's identity or organizational credentials. Moreover, the Village did not assert an interest in crime prevention below, and there is an absence of any evidence of a special crime problem related to door-to-door solicitation in the record before us.

The rhetoric used in the World War II-era opinions that repeatedly saved petitioners' coreligionists from petty prosecutions reflected the Court's evaluation of the First Amendment freedoms that are implicated in this case. The value judgment that then motivated a united democratic people fighting to defend those very freedoms from totalitarian attack is unchanged. It motivates our decision today.

Justice BREYER, with whom Justice SOUTER and Justice GINSBURG join, concurring.

While joining the Court's opinion, I write separately to note that the dissent's "crime prevention" justification for this ordinance is not a strong one. For one thing, there is no indication that the legislative body that passed the ordinance considered this justification. In the intermediate scrutiny context, the Court ordinarily does not supply reasons the legislative body has not given.

But it is not just that. It is also intuitively implausible to think that Stratton's ordinance serves any governmental interest in preventing such crimes. As the Court notes, several categories of potential criminals will remain entirely untouched by the ordinance. And as to those who might be affected by it, "[w]e have never accepted mere conjecture as adequate to carry a First Amendment burden."

Because Stratton did not rely on the crime prevention justification, because Stratton has not now "present[ed] more than anecdote and supposition," and because the relationship between the interest and the ordinance is doubtful, I am unwilling to assume that these conjectured benefits outweigh the cost of abridging the speech covered by the ordinance.

Justice SCALIA, with whom Justice THOMAS joins, concurring in the judgment.

I concur in the judgment, for many but not all of the reasons set forth in the opinion for the Court. I do not agree, for example, that one of the causes of the invalidity of Stratton's ordinance is that some people have a religious objection to applying for a permit, and others (posited by the Court) "have such firm convictions about their constitutional right to engage in uninhibited debate in the context of door-to-door advocacy, that they would prefer silence to speech licensed by a petty official."

If a licensing requirement is otherwise lawful, it is in my view not invalidated by the fact that some people will choose, for religious reasons, to forgo speech rather than observe it. That would convert an invalid free-exercise claim, see Employment Div., Dept. of Human Resources of Ore. v. Smith (1990), into a valid free-speech claim—and a more destructive one at that. Whereas the free-exercise claim, if acknowledged, would merely exempt Jehovah's Witnesses from the licensing requirement, the free-speech claim exempts everybody, thanks to Jehovah's Witnesses.

As for the Court's fairy-tale category of "patriotic citizens," who would rather be silenced than licensed in a manner that the Constitution (but for their "patriotic" objection) would permit: If our free-speech jurisprudence is to be determined by the predicted behavior of such crackpots, we are in a sorry state indeed.

Chief Justice REHNQUIST, dissenting.

Stratton is a village of 278 people located along the Ohio River where the borders of Ohio, West Virginia, and Pennsylvania converge. It is strung out along a multilane highway connecting it with the cities of East Liverpool to the north and Steubenville and Weirton, West Virginia, to the south. One may doubt how much legal help a village of this size has available in drafting an ordinance such as the present one, but even if it had availed itself of a battery of constitutional lawyers, they would have been of little use in the town's effort. For the Court today ignores the cases on which those lawyers would have relied, and comes up with newly fashioned doctrine. This doctrine contravenes well-established precedent, renders local governments largely impotent to address the very real safety threat that canvassers pose, and may actually result in less of the door-to-door communication that it seeks to protect.

More than half a century ago we recognized that canvassers, "whether selling pots or distributing leaflets, may lessen the peaceful enjoyment of a home," and that "burglars frequently pose as canvassers, either in order that they may have a pretense to discover whether a house is empty and hence ripe for burglary, or for the purpose of spying out the premises in order that they may return later."

Martin v. City of Struthers (1943). These problems continue to be associated with door-to-door canvassing, as are even graver ones.

A recent double murder in Hanover, New Hampshire, a town of approximately 7,500 that would appear tranquil to most Americans but would probably seem like a bustling town of Dartmouth College students to Stratton residents, illustrates these dangers. Two teenagers murdered a married couple of Dartmouth College professors, Half and Susanne Zantop, in the Zantop's home. Investigators have concluded, based on the confession of one of the teenagers, that the teenagers went door-to-door intent on stealing access numbers to bank debit cards and then killing their owners. See Dartmouth Professors Called Random Targets, Washington Post, Feb. 20, 2002, p. A2. Their modus operandi was to tell residents that they were conducting an environmental survey for school. They canvassed a few homes where no one answered. At another, the resident did not allow them in to conduct the "survey." They were allowed into the Zantop home. After conducting the phony environmental survey, they stabbed the Zantops to death.

In order to reduce these very grave risks associated with canvassing, the 278 "'little people,'" of Stratton, who, unlike petitioners, do not have a team of attorneys at their ready disposal, enacted the ordinance at issue here. The residents did not prohibit door-to-door communication, they simply required that canvassers obtain a permit before going door-to-door. And the village does not have the discretion to reject an applicant who completes the application.

The town had little reason to suspect that the negligible burden of having to obtain a permit runs afoul of the First Amendment. For over 60 years, we have categorically stated that a permit requirement for door-to-door canvassers, which gives no discretion to the issuing authority, is constitutional. The Court today, however, abruptly changes course and invalidates the ordinance.

The Stratton ordinance does not prohibit door-to-door canvassing; it merely requires that canvassers fill out a form and receive a permit. The mayor does not exercise any discretion in deciding who receives a permit; approval of the permit is automatic upon proper completion of the form. And petitioners do not contend in this Court that the ordinance is vague.

Just as troubling as the Court's ignoring over 60 years of precedent is the difficulty of discerning from the Court's opinion what exactly it is about the Stratton ordinance that renders it unconstitutional. It is not clear what test the Court is applying, or under which part of that indeterminate test the ordinance fails. We are instead told that the "breadth of speech affected" and "the nature of the regulation" render the permit requirement unconstitutional. Under a straightforward application of the applicable First Amendment framework, however, the ordinance easily passes muster.

There is no support in our case law for applying anything more stringent than intermediate scrutiny to the ordinance. The ordinance is content neutral and does not bar anyone from going door-to-door in Stratton. It merely regulates the manner in which one must canvass: A canvasser must first obtain a permit. It is, or perhaps I should say was, settled that the "government may impose reasonable restrictions on the time, place, or manner of protected speech, provided the restrictions 'are justified without reference to the content of the regulated speech, that they are narrowly tailored to serve a significant governmental interest, and that they leave open ample alternative channels for communication of the information.'"

The Court suggests that Stratton's regulation of speech warrants greater scrutiny. But it would be puzzling if regulations of speech taking place on another citizen's private property warranted greater scrutiny than regulations of speech taking place in public forums. Common sense and our precedent say just the opposite. In *Hynes*, the Court explained: "'Of all the methods of spreading unpopular ideas, [house-to-house canvassing] seems the least entitled to extensive protection. The possibilities of persuasion are slight compared with the certainties of annoyance. Great as is the value of exposing citizens to novel views, home is one place where a man ought to be able to shut himself up in his own ideas if he desires.'"

The Stratton regulation is aimed at three significant governmental interests: the prevention of fraud, the prevention of crime, and the protection of privacy. The Court concedes that "in light of our precedent, . . . these are important interests that [Stratton] may seek to safeguard through some form of regulation of solicitation activity." Although initially recognizing the important interest in preventing crime, the Court later indicates that the "absence of any evidence of a special crime problem related to door-to-door solicitation in the record before us" lessens this interest. But the village is entitled to rely on our assertion in *Martin* that door-to-door canvassing poses a risk of crime, and the experience of other jurisdictions with crime stemming from door-to-door canvassing.

The next question is whether the ordinance serves the important interests of protecting privacy and preventing fraud and crime. With respect to the interest in protecting privacy, the Court concludes that "[t]he annoyance caused by an uninvited knock on the front door is the same whether or not the visitor is armed with a permit." True, but that misses the key point: the permit requirement results in fewer uninvited knocks. Those who have complied with the permit requirement are less likely to visit residences with no trespassing signs, as it is much easier for the authorities to track them down.

The Court also fails to grasp how the permit requirement serves Stratton's interest in preventing crime. We have approved of permit requirements for those engaging in protected First Amendment activity because of a common-sense recognition that their existence both deters and helps detect wrongdoing. And while some people, intent on committing burglaries or violent crimes, are not likely to be deterred by the prospect of a misdemeanor for violating the permit ordinance, the ordinance's effectiveness does not depend on criminals registering.

The ordinance prevents and detects serious crime by making it a crime not to register. Take the Hanover double murder discussed earlier. The murderers did not achieve their objective until they visited their fifth home over a period of seven months. If Hanover had a permit requirement, the teens may have been stopped before they achieved their objective. One of the residents they visited may have informed the police that there were two canvassers who lacked a permit. Such neighborly vigilance, though perhaps foreign to those residing in modern day cities, is not uncommon in small towns. Or the police on their own may have discovered that two canvassers were violating the ordinance. Apprehension for violating the permit requirement may well have frustrated the teenagers' objectives; it certainly would have assisted in solving the murders had the teenagers gone ahead with their plan.

Of course, the Stratton ordinance does not guarantee that no canvasser will ever commit a burglary or violent crime. The Court seems to think this dooms the ordinance, erecting an insurmountable hurdle that a law must provide a fool-proof method of preventing crime. In order to survive intermediate scrutiny, however, a law need not solve the crime problem, it need only further the interest in preventing crime. Some deterrence of serious criminal activity is more than enough to survive intermediate scrutiny.

The final requirement of intermediate scrutiny is that a regulation leave open ample alternatives for expression. Undoubtedly, ample alternatives exist here. Most obviously, canvassers are free to go door-to-door after filling out the permit application. And those without permits may communicate on public sidewalks, on street corners, through the mail, or through the telephone.

Ironically, however, today's decision may result in less of the door-to-door communication that the Court extols. As the Court recognizes, any homeowner may place a "No Solicitation" sign on his or her property, and it is a crime to violate that sign. In light of today's decision depriving Stratton residents of the degree of accountability and safety that the permit requirement provides, more and more residents may decide to place these signs in their yards and cut off door-to-door communication altogether.

4.   What Is an Infringement of Freedom of Speech?

UNCONSTITUTIONAL CONDITIONS (casebook, p. 961)

In Legal Services Corporation v. Velazquez, the Supreme Court declared unconstitutional a provision in a federal statute that prevented recipients of federal Legal Services Corporation funding from challenging the validity of welfare laws. In reading the case, focus especially on how the Court distinguishes earlier decisions, such as Rust v. Sullivan (casebook, p. 963), and whether the distinction is persuasive. Also, consider whether other restrictions on recipients of Legal Services Corporation funding, such as prohibitions on bringing class action suits or challenging laws regulating abortions, are constitutional in light of *Velazquez*.

LEGAL SERVICES CORPORATION v. VELAZQUEZ
121 S. Ct. 1043 (2001)

Justice KENNEDY delivered the opinion of the Court.

In 1974, Congress enacted the Legal Services Corporation Act. The Act establishes the Legal Services Corporation (LSC) as a District of Columbia nonprofit corporation. LSC's mission is to distribute funds appropriated by Congress to eligible local grantee organizations "for the purpose of providing financial support for legal assistance in noncriminal proceedings or matters to persons financially unable to afford legal assistance."

LSC grantees consist of hundreds of local organizations governed, in the typical case, by local boards of directors. In many instances the grantees are funded by a combination of LSC funds and other public or private sources. The grantee organizations hire and supervise lawyers to provide free legal assistance to indigent clients. Each year LSC appropriates funds to grantees or recipients that hire and supervise lawyers for various professional activities, including representation of indigent clients seeking welfare benefits.

This suit requires us to decide whether one of the conditions imposed by Congress on the use of LSC funds violates the First Amendment rights of LSC grantees and their clients. For purposes of our decision, the restriction, to be quoted in further detail, prohibits legal representation funded by recipients of LSC moneys if the representation involves an effort to amend or otherwise challenge existing welfare law. As interpreted by the LSC and by the Government, the restriction prevents an attorney from arguing to a court that a state statute conflicts with a federal statute or that either a state or federal statute by its terms or in its application is violative of the United States Constitution.

I

From the inception of the LSC, Congress has placed restrictions on its use of funds. For instance, the LSC Act prohibits recipients from making available LSC funds, program personnel, or equipment to any political party, to any political campaign, or for use in "advocating or opposing any ballot measures." The Act further proscribes use of funds in most criminal proceedings and in litigation involving nontherapeutic abortions, secondary school desegregation, military desertion, or violations of the Selective Service statute. Fund recipients are barred from bringing class-action suits unless express approval is obtained from LSC.

The relevant portion of § 504(a)(16) prohibits funding of any organization "that initiates legal representation or participates in any other way, in litigation, lobbying, or rulemaking, involving an effort to reform a Federal or State welfare system, except that this paragraph shall not be construed to preclude a recipient from representing an individual eligible client who is seeking specific relief from a welfare agency if such relief does not involve an effort to amend or otherwise challenge existing law in effect on the date of the initiation of the representation."

The prohibitions apply to all of the activities of an LSC grantee, including those paid for by non-LSC funds. We are concerned with the statutory provision which excludes LSC representation in cases which "involve an effort to amend or otherwise challenge existing law in effect on the date of the initiation of the representation."

In 1997, LSC adopted final regulations clarifying § 504(a)(16). LSC interpreted the statutory provision to allow indigent clients to challenge welfare agency determinations of benefit ineligibility under interpretations of existing law. For example, an LSC grantee could represent a welfare claimant who argued that an agency made an erroneous factual determination or that an agency misread or misapplied a term contained in an existing welfare statute. According to LSC, a grantee in that position could argue as well that an agency policy violated existing law. Under LSC's interpretation, however, grantees could not accept representations designed to change welfare laws, much less argue against the constitutionality or statutory validity of those laws. Even in cases where constitutional or statutory challenges became apparent after representation was well under way, LSC advised that its attorneys must withdraw.

II

The United States and LSC rely on Rust v. Sullivan (1991), as support for the LSC program restrictions. In *Rust*, Congress established program clinics to provide subsidies for doctors to advise patients on a variety of family planning topics. Congress did not consider abortion to be within its family planning objectives, however, and it forbade doctors employed by the program from discussing abortion with their patients. Recipients of funds under Title X of the Public Health Service Act, challenged the Act's restriction that provided that none of the Title X funds appropriated for family planning services could "be used in programs where abortion is a method of family planning." The recipients argued that the regulations constituted impermissible viewpoint discrimination favoring an antiabortion position over a proabortion approach in the sphere of family planning. They asserted as well that Congress had imposed an unconstitutional condition on recipients of federal funds by requiring them to relinquish their right to engage in abortion advocacy and counseling in exchange for the subsidy.

We upheld the law, reasoning that Congress had not discriminated against viewpoints on abortion, but had "merely chosen to fund one activity to the exclusion of the other." The restrictions were considered necessary "to ensure that the limits of the federal program [were] observed." Title X did not single out a particular idea for suppression because it was dangerous or disfavored; rather, Congress prohibited Title X doctors from counseling that was outside the scope of the project.

The Court in *Rust* did not place explicit reliance on the rationale that the counseling activities of the doctors under Title X amounted to governmental speech; when interpreting the holding in later cases, however, we have explained *Rust* on this understanding. We have said that viewpoint-based funding decisions can be sustained in instances in which the government is itself the speaker, see Board of Regents of Univ. of Wis. System v. Southworth (2000), or instances, like *Rust*, in which the government "used private speakers to transmit information pertaining to its own program." Rosenberger v. Rector and Visitors of Univ. of Va. (1995). As we said in *Rosenberger*, "[w]hen the government disburses public funds to private entities to convey a governmental message, it may take legitimate and appropriate steps to ensure that its message is neither garbled nor distorted by the grantee." The latitude which may exist for restrictions on speech where the government's own message is being delivered flows in part from our observation that, "[w]hen the government speaks, for instance to promote its own policies or to advance a particular idea, it is, in the end, accountable to the electorate and the political process for its advocacy. If the citizenry objects, newly elected officials later could espouse some different or contrary position."

Neither the latitude for government speech nor its rationale applies to subsidies for private speech in every instance, however. As we have pointed out, "[i]t does not follow . . . that viewpoint-based restrictions are proper when the [government] does not itself speak or subsidize transmittal of a message it favors but instead expends funds to encourage a diversity of views from private speakers."

Although the LSC program differs from the program at issue in *Rosenberger* in that its purpose is not to "encourage a diversity of views," the salient point is that, like the program in *Rosenberger*, the LSC program was designed to facilitate private speech, not to promote a governmental message. Congress funded LSC grantees to provide attorneys to represent the interests of indigent clients. In the specific context of § 504(a)(16) suits for benefits, an LSC-funded attorney speaks on the behalf of the client in a claim against the government for welfare benefits. The lawyer is not the government's speaker. The attorney defending the decision to deny benefits will deliver the government's message in the litigation. The LSC lawyer, however, speaks on the behalf of his or her private, indigent client.

The Government has designed this program to use the legal profession and the established Judiciary of the States and the Federal Government to accomplish its end of assisting welfare claimants in determination or receipt of their benefits. The advice from the attorney to the client and the advocacy by the attorney to the courts cannot be classified as governmental speech even under a generous understanding of the concept. In this vital respect this suit is distinguishable from *Rust*.

The private nature of the speech involved here, and the extent of LSC's regulation of private expression, are indicated further by the circumstance that the Government seeks to use an existing medium of expression and to control it, in a class of cases, in ways which distort its usual functioning. Where the government uses or attempts to regulate a particular medium, we have been informed by its accepted usage in determining whether a particular restriction on speech is necessary for the program's purposes and limitations.

When the government creates a limited forum for speech, certain restrictions may be necessary to define the limits and purposes of the program. The same is true when the government establishes a subsidy for specified ends. As this suit involves a subsidy, limited forum cases such as *Perry*, *Lamb's Chapel* and *Rosenberger* may not be controlling in a strict sense, yet they do provide some instruction. Here the program presumes that private, nongovernmental speech is necessary, and a substantial restriction is placed upon that speech. At oral argument and in its briefs the LSC advised us that lawyers funded in the Government program may not undertake representation in suits for benefits if they must advise clients respecting the questionable validity of a statute which defines benefit eligibility and the payment structure. The limitation forecloses advice or legal assistance to question the validity of statutes under the Constitution of the United States. It extends further, it must be noted, so that state statutes inconsistent with federal law under the Supremacy Clause may be neither challenged nor questioned.

By providing subsidies to LSC, the Government seeks to facilitate suits for benefits by using the State and Federal courts and the independent bar on which those courts depend for the proper performance of their duties and responsibilities. Restricting LSC attorneys in advising their clients and in presenting arguments and analyses to the courts distorts the legal system by altering the traditional role of the attorneys in much the same way broadcast systems or student publication networks were changed in the limited forum cases we have cited. Just as government in those cases could not elect to use a broadcasting network or a college publication structure in a regime which prohibits speech necessary to the proper functioning of those systems, it may not design a subsidy to effect this serious and fundamental restriction on advocacy of attorneys and the functioning of the judiciary.

LSC has advised us, furthermore, that upon determining a question of statutory validity is present in any anticipated or pending case or controversy, the LSC-funded attorney must cease the representation at once. This is true whether the validity issue becomes apparent during initial attorney-client consultations or in the midst of litigation proceedings.

Interpretation of the law and the Constitution is the primary mission of the judiciary when it acts within the sphere of its authority to resolve a case or controversy. Marbury v. Madison (1803). An informed, independent judiciary presumes an informed, independent bar. Under § 504(a)(16), however, cases would be presented by LSC attorneys who could not advise the courts of serious questions of statutory validity. The disability is inconsistent with the proposition that attorneys should present all the reasonable and well-grounded arguments necessary for proper resolution of the case. By seeking to prohibit the analysis of certain legal issues and to truncate presentation to the courts, the enactment under review prohibits speech and expression upon which courts must depend for the proper exercise of the judicial power. Congress cannot wrest the law from the Constitution which is its source.

The restriction imposed by the statute here threatens severe impairment of the judicial function. Section 504(a)(16) sifts out cases presenting constitutional challenges in order to insulate the Government's laws from judicial inquiry. If the restriction on speech and legal advice were to stand, the result would be two tiers of cases. In cases where LSC counsel were attorneys of record, there would be lingering doubt whether the truncated representation had resulted in complete analysis of the case, full advice to the client, and proper presentation to the court. The courts and the public would come to question the adequacy and fairness of professional representations when the attorney, either consciously to comply with this statute or unconsciously to continue the representation despite the statute, avoided all reference to questions of statutory validity and constitutional authority. A scheme so inconsistent with accepted separation-of-powers principles is an insufficient basis to sustain or uphold the restriction on speech.

It is no answer to say the restriction on speech is harmless because, under LSC's interpretation of the Act, its attorneys can withdraw. This misses the point. The statute is an attempt to draw lines around the LSC program to exclude from litigation those arguments and theories Congress finds unacceptable but which by their nature are within the province of the courts to consider.

The restriction on speech is even more problematic because in cases where the attorney withdraws from a representation, the client is unlikely to find other counsel. The explicit premise for providing LSC attorneys is the necessity to make available representation "to persons financially unable to afford legal assistance." There often will be no alternative source for the client to receive vital information respecting constitutional and statutory rights bearing upon claimed benefits. Thus, with respect to the litigation services Congress has funded, there is no alternative channel for expression of the advocacy Congress seeks to restrict. This is in stark contrast to *Rust*. There, a patient could receive the approved Title X family planning counseling funded by the Government and later could consult an affiliate or independent organization to receive abortion counseling. Unlike indigent clients who seek LSC representation, the patient in *Rust* was not required to forfeit the Government-funded advice when she also received abortion counseling through alternative channels. Because LSC attorneys must withdraw whenever a question of a welfare statute's validity arises, an individual could not obtain joint representation so that the constitutional challenge would be presented by a non-LSC attorney, and other, permitted, arguments advanced by LSC counsel.

Congress was not required to fund an LSC attorney to represent indigent clients; and when it did so, it was not required to fund the whole range of legal representations or relationships. The LSC and the United States, however, in effect ask us to permit Congress to define the scope of the litigation it funds to exclude certain vital theories and ideas. The attempted restriction is designed to insulate the Government's interpretation of the Constitution from judicial challenge. The Constitution does not permit the Government to confine litigants and their attorneys in this manner. We must be vigilant when Congress imposes rules and conditions which in effect insulate its own laws from legitimate judicial challenge. Where private speech is involved, even Congress' antecedent funding decision cannot be aimed at the suppression of ideas thought inimical to the Government's own interest. For the reasons we have set forth, the funding condition is invalid.

Justice SCALIA, with whom the Chief Justice, Justice O'CONNOR, and Justice THOMAS join, dissenting.

Section 504(a)(16) of the Omnibus Consolidated Rescissions and Appropriations Act of 1996 (Appropriations Act) defines the scope of a federal spending program. It does not directly regulate speech, and it neither establishes a public forum nor discriminates on the basis of viewpoint. The Court agrees with all this, yet applies a novel and unsupportable interpretation of our public-forum precedents to declare § 504(a)(16) facially unconstitutional. This holding not only has no foundation in our jurisprudence; it is flatly contradicted by a recent decision that is on all fours with the present case.

The LSC Act is a federal subsidy program, not a federal regulatory program, and "[t]here is a basic difference between [the two]." Maher v. Roe (1977). Regulations directly restrict speech; subsidies do not. Subsidies, it is true, may indirectly abridge speech, but only if the funding scheme is "'manipulated' to have a 'coercive effect'" on those who do not hold the subsidized position. National Endowment for Arts v. Finley (1998). Proving unconstitutional coercion is difficult enough when the spending program has universal coverage and excludes only certain speech—such as a tax exemption scheme excluding lobbying expenses. The Court has found such programs unconstitutional only when the exclusion was "aimed at the suppression of dangerous ideas." Speiser v. Randall (1958). Proving the requisite coercion is harder still when a spending program is not universal but limited, providing benefits to a restricted number of recipients, see Rust v. Sullivan (1991). The Court has found such selective spending unconstitutionally coercive only once, when the government created a public forum with the spending program but then discriminated in distributing funding within the forum on the basis of viewpoint. See Rosenberger v. Rector and Visitors of Univ. of Va. (1995). When the limited spending program does not create a public forum, proving coercion is virtually impossible, because simply denying a subsidy "does not 'coerce' belief," and because the criterion of unconstitutionality is whether denial of the subsidy threatens "to drive certain ideas or viewpoints from the marketplace." Absent such a threat, "the Government may allocate . . . funding according to criteria that would be impermissible were direct regulation of speech or a criminal penalty at stake."

In Rust v. Sullivan, the Court applied these principles to a statutory scheme that is in all relevant respects indistinguishable from § 504(a)(16). The statute in *Rust* authorized grants for the provision of family planning services, but provided that "[n]one of the funds . . . shall be used in programs where abortion is a method of family planning." Valid regulations implementing the statute required funding recipients to refer pregnant clients "for appropriate prenatal . . . services by furnishing a list of available providers that promote the welfare of mother and unborn child," but forbade them to refer a pregnant woman specifically to an abortion provider, even upon request. We rejected a First Amendment free-speech challenge to the funding scheme, explaining that "[t]he Government can, without violating the Constitution, selectively fund a program to encourage certain activities it believes to be in the public interest, without at the same time funding an alternative program which seeks to deal with the problem another way." This was not, we said, the type of "discriminat[ion] on the basis of viewpoint" that triggers strict scrutiny, because the "'decision not to subsidize the exercise of a fundamental right does not infringe the right.'"

The same is true here. The LSC Act, like the scheme in *Rust*, does not create a public forum. Far from encouraging a diversity of views, it has always, as the Court accurately states, "placed restrictions on its use of funds." Nor does § 504(a)(16) discriminate on the basis of viewpoint, since it funds neither challenges to nor defenses of existing welfare law. The provision simply declines to subsidize a certain class of litigation, and under *Rust* that decision "does not infringe the right" to bring such litigation. The Court's repeated claims that § 504(a)(16) "restricts" and "prohibits" speech, and "insulates" laws from judicial review, are simply baseless. No litigant who, in the absence of LSC funding, would bring a suit challenging existing welfare law is deterred from doing so by § 504(a)(16). *Rust* thus controls these cases and compels the conclusion that § 504(a)(16) is constitutional.

The Court contends that *Rust* is different because the program at issue subsidized government speech, while the LSC funds private speech. This is so unpersuasive it hardly needs response. If the private doctors' confidential advice to their patients at issue in *Rust* constituted "government speech," it is hard to imagine what subsidized speech would not be government speech. Moreover, the majority's contention that the subsidized speech in these cases is not government speech because the lawyers have a professional obligation to represent the interests of their clients founders on the reality that the doctors in *Rust* had a professional obligation to serve the interests of their patients, which at the time of *Rust* we had held to be highly relevant to the permissible scope of federal regulation. Even respondents agree that "the true speaker in *Rust* was not the government, but a doctor."

The Court further asserts that these cases are different from *Rust* because the welfare funding restriction "seeks to use an existing medium of expression and to control it . . . in ways which distort its usual functioning." This is wrong on both the facts and the law. It is wrong on the law because there is utterly no precedent for the novel and facially implausible proposition that the First Amendment has anything to do with government funding that—though it does not actually abridge anyone's speech—"distorts an existing medium of expression." None of the three cases cited by the Court mentions such an odd principle.

The Court's "nondistortion" principle is also wrong on the facts, since there is no basis for believing that § 504(a)(16), by causing "cases [to] be presented by LSC attorneys who [can]not advise the courts of serious questions of statutory validity," will distort the operation of the courts. It may well be that the bar of § 504(a)(16) will cause LSC-funded attorneys to decline or to withdraw from cases that involve statutory validity. But that means at most that fewer statutory challenges to welfare laws will be presented to the courts because of the unavailability of free legal services for that purpose. So what? The same result would ensue from excluding LSC-funded lawyers from welfare litigation entirely. It is not the mandated, nondistortable function of the courts to inquire into all "serious questions of statutory validity" in all cases. Courts must consider only those questions of statutory validity that are presented by litigants, and if the Government chooses not to subsidize the presentation of some such questions, that in no way "distorts" the courts' role.

Finally, the Court is troubled "because in cases where the attorney withdraws from a representation, the client is unlikely to find other counsel." That is surely irrelevant, since it leaves the welfare recipient in no worse condition than he would have been in had the LSC program never been enacted. Respondents properly concede that even if welfare claimants cannot obtain a lawyer anywhere else, the Government is not required to provide one. It is hard to see how providing free legal services to some welfare claimants (those whose claims do not challenge the applicable statutes) while not providing it to others is beyond the range of legitimate legislative choice. *Rust* rejected a similar argument.

This has been a very long discussion to make a point that is embarrassingly simple: The LSC subsidy neither prevents anyone from speaking nor coerces anyone to change speech, and is indistinguishable in all relevant respects from the subsidy upheld in Rust v. Sullivan. There is no legitimate basis for declaring § 504(a)(16) facially unconstitutional.

C. Types of Unprotected and Less Protected Speech

3. Sexually Oriented Speech

b. Child Pornography (casebook, p. 1022)

In Ashcroft v. Free Speech Coalition, below, the Court considered whether the government may ban non-obscene child pornography that does not use children in its production. The Court declared this unconstitutional, emphasizing that the government's interest in banning child pornography is in protecting children; if no children are used in the production of the material, the government does not have an adequate interest to justify prohibiting the material.

ASHCROFT v. THE FREE SPEECH COALITION
122 S. Ct. 1389 (2002)

Justice KENNEDY delivered the opinion of the Court.

We consider in this case whether the Child Pornography Prevention Act of 1996 (CPPA), abridges the freedom of speech. The CPPA extends the federal prohibition against child pornography to sexually explicit images that appear to depict minors but were produced without using any real children. The statute prohibits, in specific circumstances, possessing or distributing these images, which may be created by using adults who look like minors or by using computer imaging. The new technology, according to Congress, makes it possible to create realistic images of children who do not exist.

By prohibiting child pornography that does not depict an actual child, the statute goes beyond New York v. Ferber (1982), which distinguished child pornography from other sexually explicit speech because of the State's interest in protecting the children exploited by the production process. As a general rule, pornography can be banned only if obscene, but under *Ferber,* pornography showing minors can be proscribed whether or not the images are obscene under the definition set forth in Miller v. California (1973). *Ferber* recognized that "[t]he *Miller* standard, like all general definitions of what may be banned as obscene, does not reflect the State's particular and more compelling interest in prosecuting those who promote the sexual exploitation of children."

The CPPA, however, is not directed at speech that is obscene; Congress has proscribed those materials through a separate statute. 18 U.S.C. §§ 1460-1466. Like the law in *Ferber,* the CPPA seeks to reach beyond obscenity, and it makes no attempt to conform to the *Miller* standard. For instance, the statute would reach visual depictions, such as movies, even if they have redeeming social value.

The principal question to be resolved, then, is whether the CPPA is constitutional where it proscribes a significant universe of speech that is neither obscene under *Miller* nor child pornography under *Ferber.*

I

Before 1996, Congress defined child pornography as the type of depictions at issue in *Ferber,* images made using actual minors. The CPPA retains that prohibition and adds three other prohibited categories of speech, of which the first, § 2256(8)(B), and the third, § 2256(8)(D), are at issue in this case. Section

2256(8)(B) prohibits "any visual depiction, including any photograph, film, video, picture, or computer or computer-generated image or picture" that "is, or appears to be, of a minor engaging in sexually explicit conduct." The prohibition on "any visual depiction" does not depend at all on how the image is produced. The section captures a range of depictions, sometimes called "virtual child pornography," which include computer-generated images, as well as images produced by more traditional means. For instance, the literal terms of the statute embrace a Renaissance painting depicting a scene from classical mythology, a "picture" that "appears to be, of a minor engaging in sexually explicit conduct." The statute also prohibits Hollywood movies, filmed without any child actors, if a jury believes an actor "appears to be" a minor engaging in "actual or simulated . . . sexual intercourse."

These images do not involve, let alone harm, any children in the production process; but Congress decided the materials threaten children in other, less direct, ways. Pedophiles might use the materials to encourage children to participate in sexual activity. "[A] child who is reluctant to engage in sexual activity with an adult, or to pose for sexually explicit photographs, can sometimes be convinced by viewing depictions of other children 'having fun' participating in such activity." Furthermore, pedophiles might "whet their own sexual appetites" with the pornographic images, "thereby increasing the creation and distribution of child pornography and the sexual abuse and exploitation of actual children." Under these rationales, harm flows from the content of the images, not from the means of their production. In addition, Congress identified another problem created by computer-generated images: Their existence can make it harder to prosecute pornographers who do use real minors. As imaging technology improves, Congress found, it becomes more difficult to prove that a particular picture was produced using actual children. To ensure that defendants possessing child pornography using real minors cannot evade prosecution, Congress extended the ban to virtual child pornography.

Section 2256(8)(C) prohibits a more common and lower tech means of creating virtual images, known as computer morphing. Rather than creating original images, pornographers can alter innocent pictures of real children so that the children appear to be engaged in sexual activity. Although morphed images may fall within the definition of virtual child pornography, they implicate the interests of real children and are in that sense closer to the images in *Ferber*. Respondents do not challenge this provision, and we do not consider it.

Respondents do challenge § 2256(8)(D). Like the text of the "appears to be" provision, the sweep of this provision is quite broad. Section 2256(8)(D) defines child pornography to include any sexually explicit image that was "advertised, promoted, presented, described, or distributed in such a manner that conveys the impression" it depicts "a minor engaging in sexually explicit conduct." The statute is not so limited in its reach, however, as it punishes even those possessors who took no part in pandering. Once a work has been described as child pornography, the taint remains on the speech in the hands of subsequent possessors, making possession unlawful even though the content otherwise would not be objectionable.

I

[A] law imposing criminal penalties on protected speech is a stark example of speech suppression. The CPPA's penalties are indeed severe. A first offender may be imprisoned for 15 years. § 2252A(b)(1). A repeat offender faces a prison sentence of not less than 5 years and not more than 30 years in prison. While even minor punishments can chill protected speech, see Wooley v. Maynard (1977), this case provides a textbook example of why we permit facial challenges to statutes that burden expression. With these severe penalties in force, few legitimate movie producers or book publishers, or few other speakers in any capacity, would risk distributing images in or near the uncertain reach of this law. The Constitution gives significant protection from overbroad laws that chill speech within the First Amendment's vast and privileged sphere. Under this principle, the CPPA is unconstitutional on its face if it prohibits a substantial amount of protected expression.

The sexual abuse of a child is a most serious crime and an act repugnant to the moral instincts of a decent people. In its legislative findings, Congress recognized that there are subcultures of persons who harbor illicit desires for children and commit criminal acts to gratify the impulses. Congress also found that surrounding the serious offenders are those who flirt with these impulses and trade pictures and written accounts of sexual activity with young children.

Congress may pass valid laws to protect children from abuse, and it has. The prospect of crime, however, by itself does not justify laws suppressing protected speech. As a general principle, the First Amendment bars the government from dictating what we see or read or speak or hear. As we have noted, the CPPA is much more than a supplement to the existing federal prohibition on obscenity. Under Miller v. California, the Government must prove that the work, taken as a whole, appeals to the prurient interest, is patently offensive in light of community standards, and lacks serious literary, artistic, political, or scientific value. The CPPA, however, extends to images that appear to depict a minor engaging in sexually explicit activity without regard to the *Miller* requirements.

The materials need not appeal to the prurient interest. Any depiction of sexually explicit activity, no matter how it is presented, is proscribed. The CPPA applies to a picture in a psychology manual, as well as a movie depicting the horrors of sexual abuse. It is not necessary, moreover, that the image be patently offensive. Pictures of what appear to be 17-year-olds engaging in sexually explicit activity do not in every case contravene community standards.

The CPPA prohibits speech despite its serious literary, artistic, political, or scientific value. The statute proscribes the visual depiction of an idea—that of teenagers engaging in sexual activity—that is a fact of modern society and has been a theme in art and literature throughout the ages. Under the CPPA, images are prohibited so long as the persons appear to be under 18 years of age. This is higher than the legal age for marriage in many States, as well as the age at which persons may consent to sexual relations. See § 2243(a) (age of consent in the federal maritime and territorial jurisdiction is 16); U.S. National Survey of State Laws 384-388 (R. Leiter ed., 3d ed. 1999) (48 States permit 16-year-olds to marry with parental consent); W. Eskridge & N. Hunter, Sexuality, Gender, and the Law 1021-1022 (1997) (in 39 States and the District of Columbia, the age of consent is 16 or younger).

Both themes—teenage sexual activity and the sexual abuse of children— have inspired countless literary works. William Shakespeare created the most famous pair of teenage lovers, one of whom is just 13 years of age. See Romeo and Juliet, act I, sc. 2, l. 9 ("She hath not seen the change of fourteen years"). In the drama, Shakespeare portrays the relationship as something splendid and innocent, but not juvenile. The work has inspired no less than 40 motion pictures, some of which suggest that the teenagers consummated their relationship. Shakespeare may not have written sexually explicit scenes for the Elizabethan audience, but were modern directors to adopt a less conventional approach, that fact alone would not compel the conclusion that the work was obscene.

Contemporary movies pursue similar themes. Last year's Academy Awards featured the movie, Traffic, which was nominated for Best Picture. The film portrays a teenager, identified as a 16-year-old, who becomes addicted to drugs. The viewer sees the degradation of her addiction, which in the end leads her to a filthy room to trade sex for drugs. The year before, American Beauty won the Academy Award for Best Picture. In the course of the movie, a teenage girl engages in sexual relations with her teenage boyfriend, and another yields herself to the gratification of a middle-aged man. The film also contains a scene where, although the movie audience understands the act is not taking place, one character believes he is watching a teenage boy performing a sexual act on an older man.

Our society, like other cultures, has empathy and enduring fascination with the lives and destinies of the young. Art and literature express the vital interest we all have in the formative years we ourselves once knew, when wounds can be so grievous, disappointment so profound, and mistaken choices so tragic, but when moral acts and self-fulfillment are still in reach. Whether or not the films we mention violate the CPPA, they explore themes within the wide sweep of the statute's prohibitions. If these films, or hundreds of others of lesser note that explore those subjects, contain a single graphic depiction of sexual activity within the statutory definition, the possessor of the film would be subject to severe punishment without inquiry into the work's redeeming value. This is inconsistent with an essential First Amendment rule: The artistic merit of a work does not depend on the presence of a single explicit scene.

Under *Miller*, the First Amendment requires that redeeming value be judged by considering the work as a whole. Where the scene is part of the narrative, the work itself does not for this reason become obscene, even though the scene in isolation might be offensive. For this reason, and the others we have noted, the CPPA cannot be read to prohibit obscenity, because it lacks the required link between its prohibitions and the affront to community standards prohibited by the definition of obscenity.

The Government seeks to address this deficiency by arguing that speech prohibited by the CPPA is virtually indistinguishable from child pornography, which may be banned without regard to whether it depicts works of value. Where the images are themselves the product of child sexual abuse, *Ferber* recognized that the State had an interest in stamping it out without regard to any judgment about its content. The production of the work, not its content, was the target of the statute. The fact that a work contained serious literary, artistic, or other value did not excuse the harm it caused to its child participants. It was simply "unrealistic to equate a community's toleration for sexually oriented materials with the permissible scope of legislation aimed at protecting children from sexual exploitation."

In contrast to the speech in Ferber, speech that itself is the record of sexual abuse, the CPPA prohibits speech that records no crime and creates no victims by its production. Virtual child pornography is not "intrinsically related" to the sexual abuse of children, as were the materials in *Ferber*. While the Government asserts that the images can lead to actual instances of child abuse, the causal link is contingent and indirect. The harm does not necessarily follow from the speech, but depends upon some unquantified potential for subsequent criminal acts.

The Government says these indirect harms are sufficient because, as *Ferber* acknowledged, child pornography rarely can be valuable speech. This argument, however, suffers from two flaws. First, *Ferber*'s judgment about child pornography was based upon how it was made, not on what it communicated. The second flaw in the Government's position is that *Ferber* did not hold that child pornography is by definition without value. On the contrary, the Court recognized some works in this category might have significant value, but relied on virtual images—the very images prohibited by the CPPA—as an alternative and permissible means of expression: "[I]f it were necessary for literary or artistic value, a person over the statutory age who perhaps looked younger could be utilized. Simulation outside of the prohibition of the statute could provide another alternative." *Ferber*, then, not only referred to the distinction between actual and virtual child pornography, it relied on it as a reason supporting its holding. *Ferber* provides no support for a statute that eliminates the distinction and makes the alternative mode criminal as well.

III

The CPPA, for reasons we have explored, is inconsistent with *Miller* and finds no support in *Ferber*. The Government seeks to justify its prohibitions in other ways. It argues that the CPPA is necessary because pedophiles may use virtual child pornography to seduce children. There are many things innocent in themselves, however, such as cartoons, video games, and candy, that might be used for immoral purposes, yet we would not expect those to be prohibited because they can be misused. The Government, of course, may punish adults who provide unsuitable materials to children, and it may enforce criminal penalties for unlawful solicitation. The precedents establish, however, that speech within the rights of adults to hear may not be silenced completely in an attempt to shield children from it.

Here, the Government wants to keep speech from children not to protect them from its content but to protect them from those who would commit other crimes. The principle, however, remains the same: The Government cannot ban speech fit for adults simply because it may fall into the hands of children. The evil in question depends upon the actor's unlawful conduct, conduct defined as criminal quite apart from any link to the speech in question. This establishes that the speech ban is not narrowly drawn. The objective is to prohibit illegal conduct, but this restriction goes well beyond that interest by restricting the speech available to law-abiding adults.

The Government submits further that virtual child pornography whets the appetites of pedophiles and encourages them to engage in illegal conduct. This rationale cannot sustain the provision in question. The mere tendency of speech to encourage unlawful acts is not a sufficient reason for banning it. The government "cannot constitutionally premise legislation on the desirability of controlling a person's private thoughts." First Amendment freedoms are most in danger when the government seeks to control thought or to justify its laws for that impermissible end. The right to think is the beginning of freedom, and speech must be protected from the government because speech is the beginning of thought.

The Government has shown no more than a remote connection between speech that might encourage thoughts or impulses and any resulting child abuse. Without a significantly stronger, more direct connection, the Government may not prohibit speech on the ground that it may encourage pedophiles to engage in illegal conduct.

The Government next argues that its objective of eliminating the market for pornography produced using real children necessitates a prohibition on virtual images as well. Virtual images, the Government contends, are indistinguishable from real ones; they are part of the same market and are often exchanged. In this way, it is said, virtual images promote the trafficking in works produced through the exploitation of real children. The hypothesis is somewhat implausible. If virtual images were identical to illegal child pornography, the illegal images would be driven from the market by the indistinguishable substitutes. Few pornographers would risk prosecution by abusing real children if fictional, computerized images would suffice. In the case of the material covered by *Ferber*, the creation of the speech is itself the crime of child abuse; the prohibition deters the crime by removing the profit motive.

Finally, the Government says that the possibility of producing images by using computer imaging makes it very difficult for it to prosecute those who produce pornography by using real children. Experts, we are told, may have difficulty in saying whether the pictures were made by using real children or by using computer imaging. The necessary solution, the argument runs, is to prohibit both kinds of images. The argument, in essence, is that protected speech may be banned as a means to ban unprotected speech. This analysis turns the First Amendment upside down.

The Government may not suppress lawful speech as the means to suppress unlawful speech. Protected speech does not become unprotected merely because it resembles the latter. The Constitution requires the reverse. "[T]he possible harm to society in permitting some unprotected speech to go unpunished is outweighed by the possibility that protected speech of others may be muted. . . . " Broadrick v. Oklahoma. The overbreadth doctrine prohibits the Government from banning unprotected speech if a substantial amount of protected speech is prohibited or chilled in the process.

In sum, § 2256(8)(B) covers materials beyond the categories recognized in *Ferber* and *Miller,* and the reasons the Government offers in support of limiting the freedom of speech have no justification in our precedents or in the law of the First Amendment. The provision abridges the freedom to engage in a substantial amount of lawful speech. For this reason, it is overbroad and unconstitutional.

Justice THOMAS, concurring in the judgment.

In my view, the Government's most persuasive asserted interest in support of the Child Pornography Prevention Act of 1996 (CPPA), is the prosecution rationale—that persons who possess and disseminate pornographic images of real children may escape conviction by claiming that the images are computer-generated, thereby raising a reasonable doubt as to their guilt. At this time, however, the Government asserts only that defendants raise such defenses, not that they have done so successfully. In fact, the Government points to no case in which a defendant has been acquitted based on a "computer-generated images" defense. While this speculative interest cannot support the broad reach of the CPPA, technology may evolve to the point where it becomes impossible to enforce actual child pornography laws because the Government cannot prove that certain pornographic images are of real children. In the event this occurs, the Government should not be foreclosed from enacting a regulation of virtual child pornography that contains an appropriate affirmative defense or some other narrowly drawn restriction.

Justice O'CONNOR, with whom the Chief Justice and Justice SCALIA join as to Part II, concurring in the judgment in part and dissenting in part.

The Child Pornography Prevention Act of 1996 (CPPA) proscribes the "knowin[g]" reproduction, distribution, sale, reception, or possession of images that fall under the statute's definition of child pornography. In my view, however, respondents fail to present sufficient evidence to demonstrate that the ban on virtual-child pornography is overbroad. Because invalidation due to overbreadth is such "strong medicine," I would strike down the prohibition of pornography that "appears to be" of minors only insofar as it is applied to the class of youthful-adult pornography.

Respondents assert that the CPPA's prohibitions of youthful-adult pornography, virtual-child pornography, and material that "conveys the impression" that it contains actual-child pornography are overbroad, that the prohibitions are content-based regulations not narrowly tailored to serve a compelling Government interest, and that the prohibitions are unconstitutionally vague.

I disagree with the Court, however, that the CPPA's prohibition of virtual-child pornography is overbroad. Before I reach that issue, there are two preliminary questions: whether the ban on virtual-child pornography fails strict scrutiny and whether that ban is unconstitutionally vague. I would answer both in the negative.

The Court has long recognized that the Government has a compelling interest in protecting our Nation's children. This interest is promoted by efforts directed against sexual offenders and actual-child pornography. These efforts, in turn, are supported by the CPPA's ban on virtual-child pornography. Such images whet the appetites of child molesters, who may use the images to seduce young children. Of even more serious concern is the prospect that defendants indicted for the production, distribution, or possession of actual-child pornography may evade liability by claiming that the images attributed to them are in fact computer-generated. Respondents may be correct that no defendant has successfully employed this tactic. But, given the rapid pace of advances in computer-graphics technology, the Government's concern is reasonable.

Respondents argue that, even if the Government has a compelling interest to justify banning virtual-child pornography, the "appears to be . . . of a minor" language is not narrowly tailored to serve that interest. They assert that the CPPA would capture even cartoon-sketches or statues of children that were sexually suggestive. Such images surely could not be used, for instance, to seduce children. I agree. A better interpretation of "appears to be . . . of" is "virtually indistinguishable from"—an interpretation that would not cover the examples respondents provide. Not only does the text of the statute comfortably bear this narrowing interpretation, the interpretation comports with the language that Congress repeatedly used in its findings of fact.

Reading the statute only to bar images that are virtually indistinguishable from actual children would not only assure that the ban on virtual-child pornography is narrowly tailored, but would also assuage any fears that the "appears to be . . . of a minor" language is vague. The narrow reading greatly limits any risks from "discriminatory enforcement." Respondents maintain that the "virtually indistinguishable from" language is also vague because it begs the question: from whose perspective? This problem is exaggerated. This Court has never required "mathematical certainty" or "meticulous specificity" from the language of a statute.

The Court concludes that the CPPA's ban on virtual-child pornography is overbroad. The basis for this holding is unclear. Although a content-based regulation may serve a compelling state interest, and be as narrowly tailored as possible while substantially serving that interest, the regulation may unintentionally ensnare speech that has serious literary, artistic, political, or scientific value or that does not threaten the harms sought to be combated by the Government. If so, litigants may challenge the regulation on its face as overbroad, but in doing so they bear the heavy burden of demonstrating that the regulation forbids a substantial amount of valuable or harmless speech. Respondents have not made such a demonstration. Respondents provide no examples of films or other materials that are wholly computer-generated and contain images that "appea[r] to be . . . of minors" engaging in indecent conduct, but that have serious value or do not facilitate child abuse. Their overbreadth challenge therefore fails.

Although in my view the CPPA's ban on youthful-adult pornography appears to violate the First Amendment, the ban on virtual-child pornography does not. Heeding this caution, I would strike the "appears to be" provision only insofar as it is applied to the subset of cases involving youthful-adult pornography.

In sum, I would strike down the CPPA's ban on material that "conveys the impression" that it contains actual-child pornography, but uphold the ban on pornographic depictions that "appea[r] to be" of minors so long as it is not applied to youthful-adult pornography.

Chief Justice REHNQUIST, with whom Justice SCALIA joins in part, dissenting.

I agree with Part II of Justice O'Connor's opinion concurring in the judgment in part and dissenting in part. Congress has a compelling interest in ensuring the ability to enforce prohibitions of actual child pornography, and we should defer to its findings that rapidly advancing technology soon will make it all but impossible to do so.

I also agree with Justice O'Connor that serious First Amendment concerns would arise were the Government ever to prosecute someone for simple distribution or possession of a film with literary or artistic value, such as "Traffic" or "American Beauty." I write separately, however, because the Child Pornography Prevention Act of 1996 (CPPA) need not be construed to reach such materials.

We normally do not strike down a statute on First Amendment grounds "when a limiting instruction has been or could be placed on the challenged statute."

Indeed, we should be loath to construe a statute as banning film portrayals of Shakespearian tragedies, without some indication—from text or legislative history—that such a result was intended. In fact, Congress explicitly instructed that such a reading of the CPPA would be wholly unwarranted.

This narrow reading of "sexually explicit conduct" not only accords with the text of the CPPA and the intentions of Congress; it is exactly how the phrase was understood prior to the broadening gloss the Court gives it today. Indeed, had "sexually explicit conduct" been thought to reach the sort of material the Court says it does, then films such as "Traffic" and "American Beauty" would not have been made the way they were. "Traffic" won its Academy Award in 2001. "American Beauty" won its Academy Award in 2000. But the CPPA has been on the books, and has been enforced, since 1996. The chill felt by the Court, has apparently never been felt by those who actually make movies.

To the extent the CPPA prohibits possession or distribution of materials that "convey the impression" of a child engaged in sexually explicit conduct, that prohibition can and should be limited to reach "the sordid business of pandering" which lies outside the bounds of First Amendment protection. Ginzburg v. United States (1966).

The First Amendment may protect the video shop owner or film distributor who promotes material as "entertaining" or "acclaimed" regardless of whether the material contains depictions of youthful looking adult actors engaged in nonobscene but sexually suggestive conduct. The First Amendment does not, however, protect the panderer. Thus, materials promoted as conveying the impression that they depict actual minors engaged in sexually explicit conduct do not escape regulation merely because they might warrant First Amendment protection if promoted in a different manner. I would construe "conveys the impression" as limited to the panderer, which makes the statute entirely consistent with *Ginzburg* and other cases.

c. *Protected, but Low Value Sexual Speech*

i. Zoning Ordinances (casebook, p. 1025)

In City of Los Angeles v. Alameda Books, Inc., the Supreme Court considered what evidence is necessary to justify a local zoning ordinance regulating the locale of adult entertainment businesses. Specifically, the Court upheld, though without a majority opinion, a city ordinance that prevented two adult businesses from being located in the same building structure.

CITY OF LOS ANGELES v. ALAMEDA BOOKS, INC.
122 S. Ct. 1728 (2002)

Justice O'CONNOR announced the judgment of the Court and delivered an opinion, in which the Chief Justice, Justice SCALIA, and Justice THOMAS join.

Los Angeles Municipal Code § 12.70(C) (1983), as amended, prohibits "the establishment or maintenance of more than one adult entertainment business in the same building, structure or portion thereof." Respondents, two adult establishments that each operated an adult bookstore and an adult video arcade in the same building, filed a suit alleging that § 12.70(C) violates the First Amendment and seeking declaratory and injunctive relief. The District Court granted summary judgment to respondents, finding that the city of Los Angeles' prohibition was a content-based regulation of speech that failed strict scrutiny. The Court of Appeals for the Ninth Circuit affirmed, but on different grounds. It held that, even if § 12.70(C) were a content-neutral regulation, the city failed to demonstrate that the prohibition was designed to serve a substantial government interest. Specifically, the Court of Appeals found that the city failed to present evidence upon which it could reasonably rely to demonstrate a link between multiple-use adult establishments and negative secondary effects. Therefore, the Court of Appeals held the Los Angeles prohibition on such establishments invalid under Renton v. Playtime Theatres, Inc. (1986), and its precedents interpreting that case. We reverse and remand. The city of Los Angeles may reasonably rely on a study it conducted some years before enacting the present version of § 12.70(C) to demonstrate that its ban on multiple-use adult establishments serves its interest in reducing crime.

I

In 1977, the city of Los Angeles conducted a comprehensive study of adult establishments and concluded that concentrations of adult businesses are associated with higher rates of prostitution, robbery, assaults, and thefts in surrounding communities. Accordingly, the city enacted an ordinance prohibiting the establishment, substantial enlargement, or transfer of ownership of an adult arcade, bookstore, cabaret, motel, theater, or massage parlor or a place for sexual encounters within 1,000 feet of another such enterprise or within 500 feet of any religious institution, school, or public park.

There is evidence that the intent of the city council when enacting this prohibition was not only to disperse distinct adult establishments housed in separate buildings, but also to disperse distinct adult businesses operated under common ownership and housed in a single structure. Subsequent to enactment, the city realized that this method of calculating distances created a loophole permitting the concentration of multiple adult enterprises in a single structure.

Concerned that allowing an adult-oriented department store to replace a strip of adult establishments could defeat the goal of the original ordinance, the city council amended § 12.70(C) by adding a prohibition on "the establishment or maintenance of more than one adult entertainment business in the same building, structure or portion thereof." The amended ordinance defines an "Adult Entertainment Business" as an adult arcade, bookstore, cabaret, motel, theater, or massage parlor or a place for sexual encounters, and notes that each of these enterprises "shall constitute a separate adult entertainment business even if operated in conjunction with another adult entertainment business at the same establishment."

Respondents, Alameda Books, Inc., and Highland Books, Inc., are two adult establishments operating in Los Angeles. Neither is located within 1,000 feet of another adult establishment or 500 feet of any religious institution, public park, or school. Each establishment occupies less than 3,000 square feet. Both respondents rent and sell sexually oriented products, including videocassettes. Additionally, both provide booths where patrons can view videocassettes for a fee. Although respondents are located in different buildings, each operates its retail sales and rental operations in the same commercial space in which its video booths are located. There are no physical distinctions between the different operations within each establishment and each establishment has only one entrance.

II

In Renton v. Playtime Theatres, Inc., this Court considered the validity of a municipal ordinance that prohibited any adult movie theater from locating within 1,000 feet of any residential zone, family dwelling, church, park, or school. Our analysis of the ordinance proceeded in three steps. First, we found that the ordinance did not ban adult theaters altogether, but merely required that they be distanced from certain sensitive locations. The ordinance was properly analyzed, therefore, as a time, place, and manner regulation. We next considered whether the ordinance was content neutral or content based. If the regulation were content based, it would be considered presumptively invalid and subject to strict scrutiny. We held, however, that the *Renton* ordinance was aimed not at the content of the films shown at adult theaters, but rather at the secondary effects of such theaters on the surrounding community, namely at crime rates, property values, and the quality of the city's neighborhoods. Therefore, the ordinance was deemed content neutral. Finally, given this finding, we stated that the ordinance would be upheld so long as the city of Renton showed that its ordinance was designed to serve a substantial government interest and that reasonable alternative avenues of communication remained available. We concluded that Renton had met this burden, and we upheld its ordinance.

The Court of Appeals applied the same analysis to evaluate the Los Angeles ordinance challenged in this case. First, the Court of Appeals found that the Los Angeles ordinance was not a complete ban on adult entertainment establishments, but rather a sort of adult zoning regulation, which *Renton* considered a time, place, and manner regulation. The Court of Appeals turned to the second step of the *Renton* analysis, but did not draw any conclusions about whether the Los Angeles ordinance was content based. It explained that, even if the Los Angeles ordinance were content neutral, the city had failed to demonstrate, as required by the third step of the *Renton* analysis, that its prohibition on multiple-use adult establishments was designed to serve its substantial interest in reducing crime. The Court of Appeals noted that the primary evidence relied upon by Los Angeles to demonstrate a link between combination adult businesses and harmful secondary effects was the 1977 study conducted by the city's planning department. The Court of Appeals found, however, that the city could not rely on that study because it did not "'suppor[t] a reasonable belief that [the] com-

bination [of] businesses . . . produced harmful secondary effects of the type
asserted.'"

The central component of the 1977 study is a report on city crime patterns
provided by the Los Angeles Police Department. That report indicated that,
during the period from 1965 to 1975, certain crime rates grew much faster in
Hollywood, which had the largest concentration of adult establishments in the
city, than in the city of Los Angeles as a whole. For example, robberies increased 3 times faster and prostitution 15 times faster in Hollywood than
citywide.

The Court of Appeals misunderstood the implications of the 1977 study.
While the study reveals that areas with high concentrations of adult establishments are associated with high crime rates, areas with high concentrations of
adult establishments are also areas with high concentrations of adult operations,
albeit each in separate establishments. It was therefore consistent with the
findings of the 1977 study, and thus reasonable, for Los Angeles to suppose that
a concentration of adult establishments is correlated with high crime rates
because a concentration of operations in one locale draws, for example, a greater
concentration of adult consumers to the neighborhood, and a high density of
such consumers either attracts or generates criminal activity. The assumption
behind this theory is that having a number of adult operations in one single adult
establishment draws the same dense foot traffic as having a number of distinct
adult establishments in close proximity, much as minimalls and department
stores similarly attract the crowds of consumers. Under this view, it is rational
for the city to infer that reducing the concentration of adult operations in a
neighborhood, whether within separate establishments or in one large establishment, will reduce crime rates.

Neither the Court of Appeals, nor respondents, nor the dissent provides any
reason to question the city's theory. In particular, they do not offer a competing
theory, let alone data, that explains why the elevated crime rates in neighborhoods with a concentration of adult establishments can be attributed entirely
to the presence of permanent walls between, and separate entrances to, each
individual adult operation. While the city certainly bears the burden of providing
evidence that supports a link between concentrations of adult operations and
asserted secondary effects, it does not bear the burden of providing evidence that
rules out every theory for the link between concentrations of adult establishments that is inconsistent with its own.

The error that the Court of Appeals made is that it required the city to prove
that its theory about a concentration of adult operations attracting crowds of customers, much like a minimall or department store does, is a necessary consequence of the 1977 study. For example, the Court of Appeals refused to allow
the city to draw the inference that "the expansion of an adult bookstore to include an adult arcade would increase" business activity and "produce the
harmful secondary effects identified in the Study." It reasoned that such an
inference would justify limits on the inventory of an adult bookstore, not a ban

on the combination of an adult bookstore and an adult arcade. The Court of Appeals simply replaced the city's theory—that having many different operations in close proximity attracts crowds—with its own—that the size of an operation attracts crowds. If the Court of Appeals' theory is correct, then inventory limits make more sense. If the city's theory is correct, then a prohibition on the combination of businesses makes more sense. Both theories are consistent with the data in the 1977 study. The Court of Appeals' analysis, however, implicitly requires the city to prove that its theory is the only one that can plausibly explain the data because only in this manner can the city refute the Court of Appeals' logic.

Respondents make the same logical error as the Court of Appeals when they suggest that the city's prohibition on multiuse establishments will raise crime rates in certain neighborhoods because it will force certain adult businesses to relocate to areas without any other adult businesses. Respondents' claim assumes that the 1977 study proves that all adult businesses, whether or not they are located near other adult businesses, generate crime. This is a plausible reading of the results from the 1977 study, but respondents do not demonstrate that it is a compelled reading. Nor do they provide evidence that refutes the city's interpretation of the study, under which the city's prohibition should on balance reduce crime. If this Court were nevertheless to accept respondents' speculation, it would effectively require that the city provide evidence that not only supports the claim that its ordinance serves an important government interest, but also does not provide support for any other approach to serve that interest.

In *Renton,* we specifically refused to set such a high bar for municipalities that want to address merely the secondary effects of protected speech. We held that a municipality may rely on any evidence that is "reasonably believed to be relevant" for demonstrating a connection between speech and a substantial, independent government interest. This is not to say that a municipality can get away with shoddy data or reasoning. The municipality's evidence must fairly support the municipality's rationale for its ordinance. If plaintiffs fail to cast direct doubt on this rationale, either by demonstrating that the municipality's evidence does not support its rationale or by furnishing evidence that disputes the municipality's factual findings, the municipality meets the standard set forth in *Renton.* If plaintiffs succeed in casting doubt on a municipality's rationale in either manner, the burden shifts back to the municipality to supplement the record with evidence renewing support for a theory that justifies its ordinance. This case is at a very early stage in this process. It arrives on a summary judgment motion by respondents defended only by complaints that the 1977 study fails to prove that the city's justification for its ordinance is necessarily correct. Therefore, we conclude that the city, at this stage of the litigation, has complied with the evidentiary requirement in *Renton.*

Our deference to the evidence presented by the city of Los Angeles is the product of a careful balance between competing interests. One the one hand, we have an "obligation to exercise independent judgment when First Amendment rights are implicated." On the other hand, we must acknowledge that the Los Angeles City Council is in a better position than the Judiciary to gather and evaluate data on local problems. We are also guided by the fact that *Renton* requires that municipal ordinances receive only intermediate scrutiny if they are content neutral. There is less reason to be concerned that municipalities will use these ordinances to discriminate against unpopular speech.

Justice SCALIA, concurring.

I join the plurality opinion because I think it represents a correct application of our jurisprudence concerning regulation of the "secondary effects" of pornographic speech. As I have said elsewhere, however, in a case such as this our First Amendment traditions make "secondary effects" analysis quite unnecessary. The Constitution does not prevent those communities that wish to do so from regulating, or indeed entirely suppressing, the business of pandering sex.

Justice KENNEDY, concurring in the judgment.

Speech can produce tangible consequences. It can change minds. It can prompt actions. These primary effects signify the power and the necessity of free speech. Speech can also cause secondary effects, however, unrelated to the impact of the speech on its audience. A newspaper factory may cause pollution, and a billboard may obstruct a view. These secondary consequences are not always immune from regulation by zoning laws even though they are produced by speech.

Municipal governments know that high concentrations of adult businesses can damage the value and the integrity of a neighborhood. The damage is measurable; it is all too real. The law does not require a city to ignore these consequences if it uses its zoning power in a reasonable way to ameliorate them without suppressing speech. A city's "interest in attempting to preserve the quality of urban life is one that must be accorded high respect." Young v. American Mini Theatres, Inc. (1976).

The question in this case is whether Los Angeles can seek to reduce these tangible, adverse consequences by separating adult speech businesses from one another—even two businesses that have always been under the same roof. In my view our precedents may allow the city to impose its regulation in the exercise of the zoning authority. The city is not, at least, to be foreclosed by summary judgment, so I concur in the judgment.

This separate statement seems to me necessary, however, for two reasons. First, Renton v. Playtime Theatres, Inc. described a similar ordinance as "content neutral," and I agree with the dissent that the designation is imprecise. Second, in my view, the plurality's application of *Renton* might constitute a subtle expansion, with which I do not concur.

I

In *Renton,* the Court determined that while the material inside adult bookstores and movie theaters is speech, the consequent sordidness outside is not. The challenge is to correct the latter while leaving the former, as far as possible, untouched. If a city can decrease the crime and blight associated with certain speech by the traditional exercise of its zoning power, and at the same time leave the quantity and accessibility of the speech substantially undiminished, there is no First Amendment objection. This is so even if the measure identifies the problem outside by reference to the speech inside—that is, even if the measure is in that sense content based.

On the other hand, a city may not regulate the secondary effects of speech by suppressing the speech itself. A city may not, for example, impose a content-based fee or tax. This is true even if the government purports to justify the fee by reference to secondary effects. Though the inference may be inexorable that a city could reduce secondary effects by reducing speech, this is not a permissible strategy. The purpose and effect of a zoning ordinance must be to reduce secondary effects and not to reduce speech.

A zoning measure can be consistent with the First Amendment if it is likely to cause a significant decrease in secondary effects and a trivial decrease in the quantity of speech. It is well documented that multiple adult businesses in close proximity may change the character of a neighborhood for the worse. Those same businesses spread across the city may not have the same deleterious effects. At least in theory, a dispersal ordinance causes these businesses to separate rather than to close, so negative externalities are diminished but speech is not.

The calculus is a familiar one to city planners, for many enterprises other than adult businesses also cause undesirable externalities. Factories, for example, may cause pollution, so a city may seek to reduce the cost of that externality by restricting factories to areas far from residential neighborhoods. With careful urban planning a city in this way may reduce the costs of pollution for communities, while at the same time allowing the productive work of the factories to continue. The challenge is to protect the activity inside while controlling side effects outside.

Such an ordinance might, like a speech restriction, be "content based." It might, for example, single out slaughterhouses for specific zoning treatment, restricting them to a particularly remote part of town. Without knowing more, however, one would hardly presume that because the ordinance is specific to that business, the city seeks to discriminate against it or help a favored group. One would presume, rather, that the ordinance targets not the business but its particular noxious side effects. The business might well be the city's most valued enterprise; nevertheless, because of the pollution it causes, it may warrant special zoning treatment. This sort of singling out is not impermissible content discrimination; it is sensible urban planning.

True, the First Amendment protects speech and not slaughterhouses. But in both contexts, the inference of impermissible discrimination is not strong. An equally strong inference is that the ordinance is targeted not at the activity, but at its side effects. If a zoning ordinance is directed to the secondary effects of adult speech, the ordinance does not necessarily constitute impermissible content discrimination. A zoning law need not be blind to the secondary effects of adult speech, so long as the purpose of the law is not to suppress it.

The ordinance at issue in this case is not limited to expressive activities. It also extends, for example, to massage parlors, which the city has found to cause similar secondary effects. This ordinance, moreover, is just one part of an elaborate web of land-use regulations in Los Angeles, all of which are intended to promote the social value of the land as a whole without suppressing some activities or favoring others. All this further suggests that the ordinance is more in the nature of a typical land-use restriction and less in the nature of a law suppressing speech.

For these reasons, the ordinance is not so suspect that we must employ the usual rigorous analysis that content-based laws demand in other instances. The ordinance may be a covert attack on speech, but we should not presume it to be so. In the language of our First Amendment doctrine it calls for intermediate and not strict scrutiny, as we held in *Renton.*

II

In *Renton,* the Court began by noting that a zoning ordinance is a time, place, or manner restriction. The Court then proceeded to consider the question whether the ordinance was "content based." The ordinance "by its terms [was] designed to prevent crime, protect the city's retail trade, maintain property values, and generally protec[t] and preserv[e] the quality of [the city's] neighborhoods, commercial districts, and the quality of urban life, not to suppress the expression of unpopular views."

On this premise, the Court designated the restriction "content neutral." The Court appeared to recognize, however, that the designation was something of a fiction, which, perhaps, is why it kept the phrase in quotes. After all, whether a statute is content neutral or content based is something that can be determined on the face of it; if the statute describes speech by content then it is content based. And the ordinance in *Renton* "treat[ed] theaters that specialize in adult films differently from other kinds of theaters." The fiction that this sort of ordinance is content neutral—or "content neutral"—is perhaps more confusing than helpful, as Justice Souter demonstrates. It is also not a fiction that has commanded our consistent adherence. These ordinances are content based and we should call them so.

Nevertheless, for the reasons discussed above, the central holding of *Renton* is sound: A zoning restriction that is designed to decrease secondary effects and not speech should be subject to intermediate rather than strict scrutiny. Generally, the government has no power to restrict speech based on content, but there are exceptions to the rule. And zoning regulations do not automatically raise the specter of impermissible content discrimination, even if they are content based, because they have a prima facie legitimate purpose: to limit the negative externalities of land use. As a matter of common experience, these sorts of ordinances are more like a zoning restriction on slaughterhouses and less like a tax on unpopular newspapers. The zoning context provides a built-in legitimate rationale, which rebuts the usual presumption that content-based restrictions are unconstitutional. For this reason, we apply intermediate rather than strict scrutiny.

III

The narrow question presented in this case is whether the ordinance at issue is invalid "because the city did not study the negative effects of such combinations of adult businesses, but rather relied on judicially approved statutory precedent from other jurisdictions." This question is actually two questions. First, what proposition does a city need to advance in order to sustain a secondary-effects ordinance? Second, how much evidence is required to support the proposition? The plurality skips to the second question and gives the correct answer; but in my view more attention must be given to the first.

At the outset, we must identify the claim a city must make in order to justify a content-based zoning ordinance. As discussed above, a city must advance some basis to show that its regulation has the purpose and effect of suppressing secondary effects, while leaving the quantity and accessibility of speech substantially intact. The ordinance may identify the speech based on content, but only as a shorthand for identifying the secondary effects outside. A city may not assert that it will reduce secondary effects by reducing speech in the same proportion. The rationale of the ordinance must be that it will suppress secondary effects—and not by suppressing speech.

The plurality's statement of the proposition to be supported is somewhat different. It suggests that Los Angeles could reason as follows: (1) "a concentration of operations in one locale draws . . . a greater concentration of adult consumers to the neighborhood, and a high density of such consumers either attracts or generates criminal activity"; (2) "having a number of adult operations in one single adult establishment draws the same dense foot traffic as having a number of distinct adult establishments in close proximity"; (3) "reducing the concentration of adult operations in a neighborhood, whether within separate establishments or in one large establishment, will reduce crime rates."

These propositions all seem reasonable, and the inferences required to get from one to the next are sensible. Nevertheless, this syllogism fails to capture an important part of the inquiry. The plurality's analysis does not address how speech will fare under the city's ordinance. As discussed, the necessary rationale for applying intermediate scrutiny is the promise that zoning ordinances like this one may reduce the costs of secondary effects without substantially reducing speech. For this reason, it does not suffice to say that inconvenience will reduce demand and fewer patrons will lead to fewer secondary effects. This reasoning would as easily justify a content-based tax: Increased prices will reduce demand, and fewer customers will mean fewer secondary effects. But a content-based tax may not be justified in this manner. It is no trick to reduce secondary effects by reducing speech or its audience; but a city may not attack secondary effects indirectly by attacking speech.

The analysis requires a few more steps. If two adult businesses are under the same roof, an ordinance requiring them to separate will have one of two results: One business will either move elsewhere or close. The city's premise cannot be the latter. It is true that cutting adult speech in half would probably reduce secondary effects proportionately. But again, a promised proportional reduction does not suffice. Content-based taxes could achieve that, yet these are impermissible.

The premise, therefore, must be that businesses—even those that have always been under one roof—will for the most part disperse rather than shut down. True, this premise has its own conundrum. The claim, therefore, must be that this ordinance will cause two businesses to split rather than one to close, that the quantity of speech will be substantially undiminished, and that total secondary effects will be significantly reduced. This must be the rationale of a dispersal statute.

Only after identifying the proposition to be proved can we ask the second part of the question presented: is there sufficient evidence to support the proposition? As to this, we have consistently held that a city must have latitude to experiment, at least at the outset, and that very little evidence is required. As a general matter, courts should not be in the business of second-guessing fact-bound empirical assessments of city planners. The Los Angeles City Council knows the streets of Los Angeles better than we do. It is entitled to rely on that knowledge; and if its inferences appear reasonable, we should not say there is no basis for its conclusion.

In this case the proposition to be shown is supported by a single study and common experience. The city's study shows a correlation between the concentration of adult establishments and crime. Two or more adult businesses in close proximity seem to attract a critical mass of unsavory characters and the crime rate may increase as a result. The city, therefore, sought to disperse these businesses. This original ordinance is not challenged here, and we may assume that it is constitutional.

If we assume that the study supports the original ordinance, then most of the necessary analysis follows. We may posit that two adult stores next door to each other attract 100 patrons per day. The two businesses split apart might attract 49 patrons each. (Two patrons, perhaps, will be discouraged by the inconvenience of the separation—a relatively small cost to speech.) On the other hand, the reduction in secondary effects might be dramatic, because secondary effects may require a critical mass. Depending on the economics of vice, 100 potential customers/victims might attract a coterie of thieves, prostitutes, and other ne'er-do-wells; yet 49 might attract none at all. If so, a dispersal ordinance would cause a great reduction in secondary effects at very small cost to speech. Indeed, the very absence of secondary effects might increase the audience for the speech;

perhaps for every two people who are discouraged by the inconvenience of two-stop shopping, another two are encouraged by hospitable surroundings. In that case, secondary effects might be eliminated at no cost to speech whatsoever, and both the city and the speaker will have their interests well served.

Only one small step remains to justify the ordinance at issue in this case. The city may next infer—from its study and from its own experience—that two adult businesses under the same roof are no better than two next door. The city could reach the reasonable conclusion that knocking down the wall between two adult businesses does not ameliorate any undesirable secondary effects of their proximity to one another. If the city's first ordinance was justified, therefore, then the second is too. Dispersing two adult businesses under one roof is reasonably likely to cause a substantial reduction in secondary effects while reducing speech very little.

IV

These propositions are well established in common experience and in zoning policies that we have already examined, and for these reasons this ordinance is not invalid on its face. If these assumptions can be proved unsound at trial, then the ordinance might not withstand intermediate scrutiny. The ordinance does, however, survive the summary judgment motion that the Court of Appeals ordered granted in this case.

Justice SOUTER, with whom Justice STEVENS and Justice GINSBURG join, and with whom Justice BREYER joins as to Part II, dissenting.

In 1977, the city of Los Angeles studied sections of the city with high and low concentrations of adult business establishments catering to the market for the erotic. The city found no certain correlation between the location of those establishments and depressed property values, but it did find some correlation between areas of higher concentrations of such business and higher crime rates. On that basis, Los Angeles followed the examples of other cities in adopting a zoning ordinance requiring dispersion of adult establishments. The city subsequently amended its ordinance to forbid clusters of such businesses at one address, as in a mall. The city has, in turn, taken a third step to apply this amendment to prohibit even a single proprietor from doing business in a traditional way that combines an adult bookstore, selling books, magazines, and videos, with an adult arcade, consisting of open viewing booths, where potential purchasers of videos can view them for a fee.

From a policy of dispersing adult establishments, the city has thus moved to a policy of dividing them in two. The justification claimed for this application of the new policy remains, however, the 1977 survey, as supplemented by the authority of one decided case on regulating adult arcades in another State. The case authority is not on point, and the 1977 survey provides no support for the breakup policy. Its evidentiary insufficiency bears emphasis and is the principal reason that I respectfully dissent from the Court's judgment today.

I

This ordinance stands or falls on the results of what our cases speak of as intermediate scrutiny, generally contrasted with the demanding standard applied under the First Amendment to a content-based regulation of expression. The variants of middle-tier tests cover a grab-bag of restrictive statutes, with a corresponding variety of justifications. While spoken of as content neutral, these regulations are not uniformly distinct from the content-based regulations calling for scrutiny that is strict, and zoning of businesses based on their sales of expressive adult material receives mid-level scrutiny, even though it raises a risk of content-based restriction. It is worth being clear, then, on how close to a content basis adult business zoning can get, and why the application of a middle-tier standard to zoning regulation of adult bookstores calls for particular care.

Although this type of land-use restriction has even been called a variety of time, place, or manner regulation, equating a secondary-effects zoning regulation with a mere regulation of time, place, or manner jumps over an important difference between them. A restriction on loudspeakers has no obvious relationship to the substance of what is broadcast, while a zoning regulation of businesses in adult expression just as obviously does. And while it may be true that an adult business is burdened only because of its secondary effects, it is clearly burdened only if its expressive products have adult content. Thus, the Court has recognized that this kind of regulation, though called content neutral, occupies a kind of limbo between full-blown, content-based restrictions and regulations that apply without any reference to the substance of what is said.

It would in fact make sense to give this kind of zoning regulation a First Amendment label of its own, and if we called it content correlated, we would not only describe it for what it is, but keep alert to a risk of content-based regulation that it poses. The risk lies in the fact that when a law applies selectively only to speech of particular content, the more precisely the content is identified, the greater is the opportunity for government censorship. Adult speech refers not merely to sexually explicit content, but to speech reflecting a favorable view of being explicit about sex and a favorable view of the practices it depicts; a restriction on adult content is thus also a restriction turning on a particular viewpoint, of which the government may disapprove.

This risk of viewpoint discrimination is subject to a relatively simple safeguard, however. If combating secondary effects of property devaluation and crime is truly the reason for the regulation, it is possible to show by empirical evidence that the effects exist, that they are caused by the expressive activity subject to the zoning, and that the zoning can be expected either to ameliorate them or to enhance the capacity of the government to combat them (say, by concentrating them in one area), without suppressing the expressive activity itself. This capacity of zoning regulation to address the practical problems without eliminating the speech is, after all, the only possible excuse for speaking of secondary-effects zoning as akin to time, place, or manner regulations.

In examining claims that there are causal relationships between adult businesses and an increase in secondary effects (distinct from disagreement), and between zoning and the mitigation of the effects, stress needs to be placed on the empirical character of the demonstration available.

Equal stress should be placed on the point that requiring empirical justification of claims about property value or crime is not demanding anything Herculean. Increased crime, like prostitution and muggings, and declining property values in areas surrounding adult businesses, are all readily observable, often to the untrained eye and certainly to the police officer and urban planner. These harms can be shown by police reports, crime statistics, and studies of market value, all of which are within a municipality's capacity or available from the distilled experiences of comparable communities.

And precisely because this sort of evidence is readily available, reviewing courts need to be wary when the government appeals, not to evidence, but to an uncritical common sense in an effort to justify such a zoning restriction. It is not that common sense is always illegitimate in First Amendment demonstration. The need for independent proof varies with the point that has to be established, and zoning can be supported by common experience when there is no reason to question it. We have appealed to common sense in analogous cases, even if we have disagreed about how far it took us.

But we must be careful about substituting common assumptions for evidence, when the evidence is as readily available as public statistics and municipal property valuations, lest we find out when the evidence is gathered that the assumptions are highly debatable. The record in this very case makes the point. It has become a commonplace, based on our own cases, that concentrating adult establishments drives down the value of neighboring property used for other purposes. In fact, however, the city found that general assumption unjustified by its 1977 study.

The lesson is that the lesser scrutiny applied to content-correlated zoning restrictions is no excuse for a government's failure to provide a factual demonstration for claims it makes about secondary effects; on the contrary, this is what demands the demonstration. In this case, however, the government has not shown that bookstores containing viewing booths, isolated from other adult establishments, increase crime or produce other negative secondary effects in surrounding neighborhoods, and we are thus left without substantial justification for viewing the city's First Amendment restriction as content correlated but not simply content based. By the same token, the city has failed to show any causal relationship between the breakup policy and elimination or regulation of secondary effects.

II

Our cases on the subject have referred to studies, undertaken with varying degrees of formality, showing the geographical correlations between the presence or concentration of adult business establishments and enhanced crime rates or depressed property values. Although we have held that intermediate scrutiny of secondary-effects legislation does not demand a fresh evidentiary study of its factual basis if the published results of investigations elsewhere are "reasonably" thought to be applicable in a different municipal setting, the city here took responsibility to make its own enquiry. As already mentioned, the study was inconclusive as to any correlation between adult business and lower property values, and it reported no association between higher crime rates and any isolated adult establishments. But it did find a geographical correlation of higher concentrations of adult establishments with higher crime rates, and with this study in hand, Los Angeles enacted its 1978 ordinance requiring dispersion of adult stores and theaters. This original position of the ordinance is not challenged today, and I will assume its justification on the theory accepted in *Young,* that eliminating concentrations of adult establishments will spread out the documented secondary effects and render them more manageable that way.

The application of the 1983 amendment now before us is, however, a different matter. My concern is not with the assumption behind the amendment itself, that a conglomeration of adult businesses under one roof, as in a minimall or adult department store, will produce undesirable secondary effects comparable to what a cluster of separate adult establishments brings about. That may or may not be so. The assumption that is clearly unsupported, however, goes to the city's supposed interest in applying the amendment to the book and video stores in question, and in applying it to break them up. The city, of course, claims no interest in the proliferation of adult establishments, the ostensible consequence of splitting the sales and viewing activities so as to produce two stores where once there was one. Nor does the city assert any interest in limiting the sale of adult expressive material as such, or reducing the number of adult video booths in the city, for that would be clear content-based regulation, and the city was careful in its 1977 report to disclaim any such intent.

Rather, the city apparently assumes that a bookstore selling videos and providing viewing booths produces secondary effects of crime, and more crime than would result from having a single store without booths in one part of town and a video arcade in another. But the city neither says this in so many words nor proffers any evidence to support even the simple proposition that an otherwise lawfully located adult bookstore combined with video booths will produce any criminal effects. The Los Angeles study treats such combined stores as one, and draws no general conclusion that individual stores spread apart from other adult establishments (as under the basic Los Angeles ordinance) are associated with any degree of criminal activity above the general norm; nor has the city called the Court's attention to any other empirical study, or even anecdotal police evidence, that supports the city's assumption. In fact, if the Los Angeles study sheds any light whatever on the city's position, it is the light of skepticism, for we may fairly suspect that the study said nothing about the secondary effects of freestanding stores because no effects were observed. The reasonable supposition, then, is that splitting some of them up will have no consequence for secondary effects whatever. The inescapable point is that the city does not even claim that the 1977 study provides any support for its assumption.

If we take the city's breakup policy at its face, enforcing it will mean that in every case two establishments will operate instead of the traditional one. Since the city presumably does not wish merely to multiply adult establishments, it makes sense to ask what offsetting gain the city may obtain from its new break-up policy. The answer may lie in the fact that two establishments in place of one will entail two business overheads in place of one: two monthly rents, two electricity bills, two payrolls. Every month business will be more expensive than it used to be, perhaps even twice as much. That sounds like a good strategy for driving out expressive adult businesses. It sounds, in other words, like a policy of content-based regulation. I respectfully dissent.

e.   Profanity and "Indecent" Speech

iii.   The Internet (casebook, p. 1044)

After Reno v. ACLU (casebook, p. 1044) declared unconstitutional the Communications Decency Act of 1996, Congress enacted the Child On-Line Protection Act to regulate the availability to minors of sexual material on the Internet. In Ashcroft v. ACLU, below, the Court did not resolve the constitutionality of this law. The Court simply decided that the standard "contemporary community standards" is not unduly vague. One important issue discussed in the opinions, but not resolved, is how "community standards" are to be determined for a national medium such as the Internet.

ASHCROFT v. AMERICAN CIVIL LIBERTIES UNION
122 S. Ct. 1700 (2002)

Justice THOMAS announced the judgment of the Court and delivered the opinion of the Court with respect to Parts I, II, and IV, an opinion with respect to Parts III-A, III-C, and III-D, in which the Chief Justice and Justice SCALIA join, and an opinion with respect to Part III-B, in which the Chief Justice, Justice O'CONNOR, and Justice SCALIA join.

This case presents the narrow question whether the Child Online Protection Act's (COPA or Act) use of "community standards" to identify "material that is harmful to minors" violates the First Amendment. We hold that this aspect of COPA does not render the statute facially unconstitutional.

I

"The Internet . . . offer[s] a forum for a true diversity of political discourse, unique opportunities for cultural development, and myriad avenues for intellectual activity." While "surfing" the World Wide Web, the primary method of remote information retrieval on the Internet today, individuals can access material about topics ranging from aardvarks to Zoroastrianism. One can use the Web to read thousands of newspapers published around the globe, purchase tickets for a matinee at the neighborhood movie theater, or follow the progress of any Major League Baseball team on a pitch-by-pitch basis. The Web also contains a wide array of sexually explicit material, including hardcore pornography. In 1998, for instance, there were approximately 28,000 adult sites promoting pornography on the Web. Because "[n]avigating the Web is relatively straightforward," and access to the Internet is widely available in homes, schools, and libraries across the country, children may discover this pornographic material either by deliberately accessing pornographic Web sites or by stumbling upon them.

Congress first attempted to protect children from exposure to pornographic material on the Internet by enacting the Communications Decency Act of 1996 (CDA). The CDA prohibited the knowing transmission over the Internet of obscene or indecent messages to any recipient under 18 years of age. It also forbade any individual from knowingly sending over or displaying on the Internet certain "patently offensive" material in a manner available to persons under 18 years of age. [I]n Reno v. American Civil Liberties Union, we held that the CDA's regulation of indecent transmissions, and the display of patently offensive material, ran afoul of the First Amendment. We concluded that "the CDA lack[ed] the precision that the First Amendment requires when a statute regulates the content of speech" because, "[i]n order to deny minors access to potentially harmful speech, the CDA effectively suppress[ed] a large amount of speech that adults ha[d] a constitutional right to receive and to address to one another."

Apparently responding to our objections to the breadth of the CDA's coverage, Congress limited the scope of COPA's coverage in at least three ways. First, while the CDA applied to communications over the Internet as a whole, including, for example, e-mail messages, COPA applies only to material displayed on the World Wide Web. Second, unlike the CDA, COPA covers only communications made "for commercial purposes." And third, while the CDA prohibited "indecent" and "patently offensive" communications, COPA restricts only the narrower category of "material that is harmful to minors."

Drawing on the three-part test for obscenity set forth in Miller v. California (1973), COPA defines "material that is harmful to minors" as "any communication, picture, image, graphic image file, article, recording, writing, or other matter of any kind that is obscene or that —

> (A) the average person, applying contemporary community standards, would find, taking the material as a whole and with respect to minors, is designed to appeal to, or is designed to pander to, the prurient interest;
> (B) depicts, describes, or represents, in a manner patently offensive with respect to minors, an actual or simulated sexual act or sexual contact, an

actual or simulated normal or perverted sexual act, or a lewd exhibition of the genitals or post-pubescent female breast; and

(C) taken as a whole, lacks serious literary, artistic, political, or scientific value for minors."

Like the CDA, COPA also provides affirmative defenses to those subject to prosecution under the statute. An individual may qualify for a defense if he, "in good faith, has restricted access by minors to material that is harmful to minors —(A) by requiring the use of a credit card, debit account, adult access code, or adult personal identification number; (B) by accepting a digital certificate that verifies age; or (C) by any other reasonable measures that are feasible under available technology." Persons violating COPA are subject to both civil and criminal sanctions. A civil penalty of up to $50,000 may be imposed for each violation of the statute. Criminal penalties consist of up to six months in prison and/or a maximum fine of $50,000. An additional fine of $50,000 may be imposed for any intentional violation of the statute. § 231(a).

One month before COPA was scheduled to go into effect, respondents filed a lawsuit challenging the constitutionality of the statute in the United States District Court for the Eastern District of Pennsylvania. The District Court granted respondents' motion for a preliminary injunction, barring the Government from enforcing the Act until the merits of respondents' claims could be adjudicated. Focusing on respondents' claim that COPA abridged the free speech rights of adults, the District Court concluded that respondents had established a likelihood of success on the merits. The District Court reasoned that because COPA constitutes content-based regulation of sexual expression protected by the First Amendment, the statute, under this Court's precedents, was "presumptively invalid" and "subject to strict scrutiny." The District Court then held that respondents were likely to establish at trial that COPA could not withstand such scrutiny because, among other reasons, it was not apparent that COPA was the least restrictive means of preventing minors from accessing "harmful to minors" material.

The Attorney General of the United States appealed the District Court's ruling. The United States Court of Appeals for the Third Circuit affirmed. Rather than reviewing the District Court's "holding that COPA was not likely to succeed in surviving strict scrutiny analysis," the Court of Appeals based its decision entirely on a ground that was not relied upon below and that was "virtually ignored by the parties and the amicus in their respective briefs." The Court of Appeals concluded that COPA's use of "contemporary community standards" to identify material that is harmful to minors rendered the statute substantially overbroad. Because "Web publishers are without any means to limit access to their sites based on the geographic location of particular Internet users," the Court of Appeals reasoned that COPA would require "any material that might be deemed harmful by the most puritan of communities in any state" to be placed behind an age or credit card verification system. Hypothesizing that this step would require Web publishers to shield "vast amounts of material," the Court of Appeals was "persuaded that this aspect of COPA, without reference to its other provisions, must lead inexorably to a holding of a likelihood of unconstitutionality of the entire COPA statute."

II

Obscene speech, for example, has long been held to fall outside the purview of the First Amendment. See, e.g., Roth v. United States (1957). But this Court struggled in the past to define obscenity in a manner that did not impose an impermissible burden on protected speech. Ending over a decade of turmoil, this Court in Miller [v. California (1973)] set forth the governing three-part test for assessing whether material is obscene and thus unprotected by the First Amendment: "(a) [W]hether 'the average person, applying contemporary community standards' would find that the work, taken as a whole, appeals to the prurient interest; (b) whether the work depicts or describes, in a patently offensive way, sexual conduct specifically defined by the applicable state law; and (c) whether the work, taken as a whole, lacks serious literary, artistic, political, or scientific value."

Miller adopted the use of "community standards" from Roth, which repudiated an earlier approach for assessing objectionable material. Beginning in the 19th century, English courts and some American courts allowed material to be evaluated from the perspective of particularly sensitive persons. See, e.g., Queen v. Hicklin [1868]. But in Roth, this Court held that this sensitive person standard was "unconstitutionally restrictive of the freedoms of speech and press" and approved a standard requiring that material be judged from the perspective of "the average person, applying contemporary community standards." The Court preserved the use of community standards in formulating the Miller test, explaining that they furnish a valuable First Amendment safeguard: "[T]he primary concern . . . is to be certain that . . . [material] will be judged by its impact on an average person, rather than a particularly susceptible or sensitive person—or indeed a totally insensitive one."

III

The Court of Appeals, however, concluded that this Court's prior community standards jurisprudence "has no applicability to the Internet and the Web" because "Web publishers are currently without the ability to control the geographic scope of the recipients of their communications." We therefore must decide whether this technological limitation renders COPA's reliance on community standards constitutionally infirm.

A

In addressing this question, the parties first dispute the nature of the community standards that jurors will be instructed to apply when assessing, in prosecutions under COPA, whether works appeal to the prurient interest of minors and are patently offensive with respect to minors. Respondents contend that jurors will evaluate material using "local community standards," while petitioner maintains that jurors will not consider the community standards of any particular geographic area, but rather will be "instructed to consider the standards of the adult community as a whole, without geographic specification."

In the context of this case, which involves a facial challenge to a statute that has never been enforced, we do not think it prudent to engage in speculation as to whether certain hypothetical jury instructions would or would not be consistent with COPA, and deciding this case does not require us to do so. It is sufficient to note that community standards need not be defined by reference to a precise geographic area. Absent geographic specification, a juror applying community standards will inevitably draw upon personal "knowledge of the community or vicinage from which he comes."

B

Because juries would apply different standards across the country, and Web publishers currently lack the ability to limit access to their sites on a geographic basis, the Court of Appeals feared that COPA's "community standards" component would effectively force all speakers on the Web to abide by the "most puritan" community's standards. And such a requirement, the Court of Appeals concluded, "imposes an overreaching burden and restriction on constitutionally protected speech."

In evaluating the constitutionality of the CDA, this Court expressed a similar concern over that statute's use of community standards to identify patently offensive material on the Internet. The CDA's use of community standards to identify patently offensive material, however, was particularly problematic in light of that statute's unprecedented breadth and vagueness. The statute covered communications depicting or describing "sexual or excretory activities or organs" that were "patently offensive as measured by contemporary community standards"—a standard somewhat similar to the second prong of *Miller*'s three-prong test. But the CDA did not include any limiting terms resembling *Miller*'s additional two prongs. It neither contained any requirement that restricted material appeal to the prurient interest nor excluded from the scope of its coverage works with serious literary, artistic, political, or scientific value. The tremendous breadth of the CDA magnified the impact caused by differences in community standards across the country, restricting Web publishers from openly displaying a significant amount of material that would have constituted protected speech in some communities across the country but run afoul of community standards in others.

COPA, by contrast, does not appear to suffer from the same flaw because it applies to significantly less material than did the CDA and defines the harmful-to-minors material restricted by the statute in a manner parallel to the *Miller* definition of obscenity. To fall within the scope of COPA, works must not only "depic[t], describ[e], or represen[t], in a manner patently offensive with respect to minors," particular sexual acts or parts of the anatomy, they must also be designed to appeal to the prurient interest of minors and "taken as a whole, lac[k] serious literary, artistic, political, or scientific value for minors."

These additional two restrictions substantially limit the amount of material covered by the statute. Material appeals to the prurient interest, for instance, only if it is in some sense erotic. Of even more significance, however, is COPA's exclusion of material with serious value for minors. [T]he relevant question is "whether a reasonable person would find . . . value in the material, taken as a whole." Thus, the serious value requirement "allows appellate courts to impose some limitations and regularity on the definition by setting, as a matter of law, a national floor for socially redeeming value."

C

When the scope of an obscenity statute's coverage is sufficiently narrowed by a "serious value" prong and a "prurient interest" prong, we have held that requiring a speaker disseminating material to a national audience to observe varying community standards does not violate the First Amendment.

While Justice Kennedy and Justice Stevens question the applicability of this Court's community standards jurisprudence to the Internet, we do not believe that the medium's "unique characteristics" justify adopting a different approach. If a publisher chooses to send its material into a particular community, this Court's jurisprudence teaches that it is the publisher's responsibility to abide by that community's standards. The publisher's burden does not change simply because it decides to distribute its material to every community in the Nation. Nor does it change because the publisher may wish to speak only to those in a "community where avant garde culture is the norm," but nonetheless utilizes a medium that transmits its speech from coast to coast. If a publisher wishes for its material to be judged only by the standards of particular communities, then it need only take the simple step of utilizing a medium that enables it to target the release of its material into those communities.

D

Respondents argue that COPA is "unconstitutionally overbroad" because it will require Web publishers to shield some material behind age verification screens that could be displayed openly in many communities across the Nation if Web speakers were able to limit access to their sites on a geographic basis. "[T]o prevail in a facial challenge," however, "it is not enough for a plaintiff to show 'some' overbreadth." Rather, "the overbreadth of a statute must not only be real, but substantial as well." Broadrick v. Oklahoma (1973). At this stage of the litigation, respondents have failed to satisfy this burden, at least solely as a result of COPA's reliance on community standards. Because Congress has narrowed the range of content restricted by COPA in a manner analogous to *Miller*'s definition of obscenity, we conclude, that any variance caused by the statute's reliance on community standards is not substantial enough to violate the First Amendment.

IV

The scope of our decision today is quite limited. We hold only that COPA's reliance on community standards to identify "material that is harmful to minors" does not by itself render the statute substantially overbroad for purposes of the First Amendment. We do not express any view as to whether COPA suffers from substantial overbreadth for other reasons, whether the statute is unconstitutionally vague, or whether the District Court correctly concluded that the statute likely will not survive strict scrutiny analysis once adjudication of the case is completed below. While respondents urge us to resolve these questions at this time, prudence dictates allowing the Court of Appeals to first examine these difficult issues.

Petitioner does not ask us to vacate the preliminary injunction entered by the District Court, and in any event, we could not do so without addressing matters yet to be considered by the Court of Appeals. As a result, the Government remains enjoined from enforcing COPA absent further action by the Court of Appeals or the District Court.

Justice O'CONNOR, concurring in part and concurring in the judgment.

I agree with the plurality that even if obscenity on the Internet is defined in terms of local community standards, respondents have not shown that the Child Online Protection Act (COPA) is overbroad solely on the basis of the variation in the standards of different communities. Like Justice Breyer, however, I write separately to express my views on the constitutionality and desirability of adopting a national standard for obscenity for regulation of the Internet.

The plurality's opinion argues that, even under local community standards, the variation between the most and least restrictive communities is not so great with respect to the narrow category of speech covered by COPA as to, alone, render the statute substantially overbroad. I agree, given respondents' failure to provide examples of materials that lack literary, artistic, political, and scientific value for minors, which would nonetheless result in variation among communities judging the other elements of the test. Respondents' examples of material for which community standards would vary include such things as the appropriateness of sex education and the desirability of adoption by same-sex couples. Material addressing the latter topic, however, seems highly unlikely to be seen to appeal to the prurient interest in any community, and educational material like the former must, on any objective inquiry, have scientific value for minors.

But respondents' failure to prove substantial overbreadth on a facial challenge in this case still leaves open the possibility that the use of local community standards will cause problems for regulation of obscenity on the Internet, for adults as well as children, in future cases. In an as-applied challenge, for instance, individual litigants may still dispute that the standards of a community more restrictive than theirs should apply to them. And in future facial challenges to regulation of obscenity on the Internet, litigants may make a more convincing case for substantial overbreadth. Where adult speech is concerned, for instance, there may in fact be a greater degree of disagreement about what is patently offensive or appeals to the prurient interest.

Our precedents do not forbid adoption of a national standard. Local community-based standards originated with Miller v. California (1973). In that case, we approved jury instructions that based the relevant "community standards" on those of the State of California rather than on the Nation as a whole. But we said nothing about the constitutionality of jury instructions that would contemplate a national standard—i.e., requiring that the people who live in all of these places hold themselves to what the nationwide community of adults would find was patently offensive and appealed to the prurient interest.

To be sure, the Court in *Miller* also stated that a national standard might be "unascertainable," and "[un]realistic." But where speech on the Internet is concerned, I do not share that skepticism. It is true that our Nation is diverse, but many local communities encompass a similar diversity. For instance, in *Miller* itself, the jury was instructed to consider the standards of the entire State of California, a large (today, it has a population of greater than 33 million people) and diverse State that includes both Berkeley and Bakersfield. If the *Miller* Court believed generalizations about the standards of the people of California were possible, and that jurors would be capable of assessing them, it is difficult to believe that similar generalizations are not also possible for the Nation as a whole. Moreover, the existence of the Internet, and its facilitation of national dialogue, has itself made jurors more aware of the views of adults in other parts of the United States. Although jurors asked to evaluate the obscenity of speech based on a national standard will inevitably base their assessments to some extent on their experience of their local communities, I agree with Justice Breyer that the lesser degree of variation that would result is inherent in the jury system and does not necessarily pose a First Amendment problem. In my view, a national standard is not only constitutionally permissible, but also reasonable.

Justice BREYER, concurring in part and concurring in the judgment.

I write separately because I believe that Congress intended the statutory word "community" to refer to the Nation's adult community taken as a whole, not to geographically separate local areas. The statutory language does not explicitly describe the specific "community" to which it refers. It says only that the "average person, applying contemporary community standards" must find that the "material as a whole and with respect to minors, is designed to appeal to, or is designed to pander to, the prurient interest. . . . "

In the statute's legislative history, however, Congress made clear that it did not intend this ambiguous statutory phrase to refer to separate standards that might differ significantly among different communities. The relevant House of Representatives Report says: "The Committee recognizes that the applicability of community standards in the context of the Web is controversial, but understands it as an 'adult' standard, rather than a 'geographic' standard, and one that is reasonably constant among adults in America with respect to what is suitable for minors."

This statement, reflecting what apparently was a uniform view within Congress, makes clear that the standard, and the relevant community, is national and adult. At the same time, this view of the statute avoids the need to examine the serious First Amendment problem that would otherwise exist. To read the statute as adopting the community standards of every locality in the United States would provide the most puritan of communities with a heckler's Internet veto affecting the rest of the Nation. The technical difficulties associated with efforts to confine Internet material to particular geographic areas make the problem particularly serious. A nationally uniform adult-based standard—which Congress, in its Committee Report, said that it intended—significantly alleviates any special need for First Amendment protection. Of course some regional variation may remain, but any such variations are inherent in a system that draws jurors from a local geographic area and they are not, from the perspective of the First Amendment, problematic.

Justice KENNEDY, with whom Justice SOUTER and Justice GINSBURG join, concurring in the judgment.

If a law restricts substantially more speech than is justified, it may be subject to a facial challenge. There is a very real likelihood that the Child Online Protection Act (COPA or Act) is overbroad and cannot survive such a challenge. Indeed, content-based regulations like this one are presumptively invalid abridgements of the freedom of speech. Yet COPA is a major federal statute, enacted in the wake of our previous determination that its predecessor violated the First Amendment. Congress and the President were aware of our decision, and we should assume that in seeking to comply with it they have given careful consideration to the constitutionality of the new enactment. For these reasons, even if this facial challenge appears to have considerable merit, the Judiciary must proceed with caution and identify overbreadth with care before invalidating the Act.

In this case, the District Court issued a preliminary injunction against enforcement of COPA, finding it too broad across several dimensions. The Court of Appeals affirmed, but on a different ground. To observe only that community standards vary across the country is to ignore the antecedent question: community standards as to what? Whether the national variation in community standards produces overbreadth requiring invalidation of COPA, depends on the breadth of COPA's coverage and on what community standards are being invoked. Only by identifying the universe of speech burdened by COPA is it possible to discern whether national variation in community standards renders the speech restriction overbroad. In short, the ground on which the Court of Appeals relied cannot be separated from those that it overlooked.

The statute, for instance, applies only to "communication for commercial purposes." The Court of Appeals, however, did not consider the amount of commercial communication, the number of commercial speakers, or the character of commercial speech covered by the Act. Likewise, the statute's definition of "harmful to minors" requires material to be judged "as a whole." The notion of judging work as a whole is familiar in other media, but more difficult to define on the World Wide Web. It is unclear whether what is to be judged as a whole is a single image on a Web page, a whole Web page, an entire multipage Web site, or an interlocking set of Web sites. Some examination of the group of covered speakers and the categories of covered speech is necessary in order to comprehend the extent of the alleged overbreadth.

The Court of Appeals found that COPA in effect subjects every Internet speaker to the standards of the most puritanical community in the United States. This concern is a real one, but it alone cannot suffice to invalidate COPA without careful examination of the speech and the speakers within the ambit of the Act. For this reason, I join the judgment of the Court vacating the opinion of the Court of Appeals and remanding for consideration of the statute as a whole. Unlike Justice Thomas, however, I would not assume that the Act is narrow enough to render the national variation in community standards unproblematic. Indeed, if the District Court correctly construed the statute across its other dimensions, then the variation in community standards might well justify enjoining enforcement of the Act. I would leave that question to the Court of Appeals in the first instance.

Justice STEVENS, dissenting.

Appeals to prurient interests are commonplace on the Internet, as in older media. Many of those appeals lack serious value for minors as well as adults. Some are offensive to certain viewers but welcomed by others. For decades, our cases have recognized that the standards for judging their acceptability vary from viewer to viewer and from community to community. Those cases developed the requirement that communications should be protected if they do not violate contemporary community standards. In its original form, the community standard provided a shield for communications that are offensive only to the least tolerant members of society. Thus, the Court "has emphasized on more than one occasion that a principal concern in requiring that a judgment be made on the basis of 'contemporary community standards' is to assure that the material is judged neither on the basis of each juror's personal opinion, nor by its effect on a particularly sensitive or insensitive person or group." In the context of the Internet, however, community standards become a sword, rather than a shield. If a prurient appeal is offensive in a puritan village, it may be a crime to post it on the World Wide Web.

The Child Online Protection Act (COPA) restricts access by adults as well as children to materials that are "harmful to minors." COPA is a substantial improvement over its predecessor, the Communications Decency Act of 1996 (CDA), which we held unconstitutional five years ago in Reno v. American Civil Liberties Union (1997) (ACLU I). Congress has thoughtfully addressed several of the First Amendment problems that we identified in that case. Nevertheless, COPA preserves the use of contemporary community standards to define which materials are harmful to minors. As we explained in *ACLU I,* "the 'community standards' criterion as applied to the Internet means that any communication available to a nationwide audience will be judged by the standards of the Community most likely to be offended by the message."

We have recognized that the State has a compelling interest in protecting minors from harmful speech, and on one occasion we upheld a restriction on indecent speech that was made available to the general public, because it could be accessed by minors, FCC v. Pacifica Foundation (1978). On the other hand, we have repeatedly rejected the position that the free speech rights of adults can be limited to what is acceptable for children.

COPA not only restricts speech that is made available to the general public, it also covers a medium in which speech cannot be segregated to avoid communities where it is likely to be considered harmful to minors. The Internet presents a unique forum for communication because information, once posted, is accessible everywhere on the network at once. The speaker cannot control access based on the location of the listener, nor can it choose the pathways through which its speech is transmitted. By approving the use of community standards in this context, Justice Thomas endorses a construction of COPA that has "the intolerable consequence of denying some sections of the country access to material, there deemed acceptable, which in others might be considered offensive to prevailing community standards of decency."

Justice Thomas points to several other provisions in COPA to argue that any overbreadth will be rendered insubstantial by the rest of the statute. These provisions afford little reassurance, however, as they only marginally limit the sweep of the statute. It is true that, in addition to COPA's "appeals to the prurient interest of minors" prong, the material must be "patently offensive with respect to minors" and it must lack "serious literary, artistic, political, or scientific value for minors." Nonetheless, the "patently offensive" prong is judged according to contemporary community standards as well. Whatever disparity exists between various communities' assessment of the content that appeals to the prurient interest of minors will surely be matched by their differing opinions as to whether descriptions of sexual acts or depictions of nudity are patently offensive with respect to minors. Nor does the requirement that the material be "in some sense erotic," substantially narrow the category of images covered. Arguably every depiction of nudity—partial or full—is in some sense erotic with respect to minors.

Petitioner's argument that the "serious value" prong minimizes the statute's overbreadth is also unpersuasive. Although we have recognized that the serious value determination in obscenity cases should be based on an objective, reasonable person standard, Pope v. Illinois (1987), this criterion is inadequate to cure COPA's overbreadth because COPA adds an important qualifying phrase to the standard Miller v. California (1973) formulation of the serious value prong. The question for the jury is not whether a reasonable person would conclude that the materials have serious value; instead, the jury must determine whether the materials have serious value for minors. Congress reasonably concluded that a substantial number of works, which have serious value for adults, do not have serious value for minors. Thus, even though the serious value prong limits the total amount of speech covered by the statute, it remains true that there is a significant amount of protected speech within the category of materials that have no serious value for minors. That speech is effectively prohibited whenever the least tolerant communities find it harmful to minors. While the objective nature of the inquiry may eliminate any worry that the serious value determination will be made by the least tolerant community, it does not change the fact that, within the subset of images deemed to have no serious value for minors, the decision whether minors and adults throughout the country will have access to that speech will still be made by the most restrictive community.

In the context of most other media, using community standards to differentiate between permissible and impermissible speech has two virtues. As mentioned above, community standards originally served as a shield to protect speakers from the least tolerant members of society. By aggregating values at the community level, the *Miller* test eliminated the outliers at both ends of the spectrum and provided some predictability as to what constitutes obscene speech. But community standards also serve as a shield to protect audience members, by allowing people to self-sort based on their preferences. Those who abhor and those who tolerate sexually explicit speech can seek out like-minded people and settle in communities that share their views on what is acceptable for themselves and their children. This sorting mechanism, however, does not exist in cyberspace; the audience cannot self-segregate. As a result, in the context of the Internet this shield also becomes a sword, because the community that wishes to live without certain material not only rids itself, but the entire Internet of the offending speech.

In sum, I would affirm the judgment of the Court of Appeals and therefore respectfully dissent.

4. Commercial Speech

c. *The Test for Evaluating Regulation of Commercial Speech (casebook, p. 1063)*

g. *Regulating Commercial Speech to Achieve Other Goals (casebook, p. 1072)*

In Lorillard Tobacco Co. v. Riley, the Supreme Court considered the constitutionality of Massachusetts' regulations of tobacco advertising. The most significant aspects of the regulations prevented advertising of tobacco products within 1,000 feet of a school or playground and required that places selling tobacco products place ads for these items at least five feet off the ground to avoid being at eye-level for children. The Supreme Court declared these regulations of cigarette advertising to be preempted by federal law. This aspect of the decision, and the dissent concerning it, is presented in Chapter 4. The federal law, however, only concerns cigarettes and not cigars or smokeless tobacco. Therefore, the Court considered whether the restrictions on advertising of these products violated the First Amendment.

The case seems particularly important in reaffirming that *Central Hudson's* four-part test is used in evaluating government regulation of commercial speech. The decision also is significant in limiting the ability of the government to regulate advertising so as to discourage harmful behavior.

LORILLARD TOBACCO CO. v. RILEY

121 S. Ct. 2404 (June 28, 2001)

O'CONNOR, J., delivered the opinion of the Court, Part I of which was unanimous; Parts III-A, III-C, and III-D of which were joined by REHNQUIST, C.J., and SCALIA, KENNEDY, SOUTER, and THOMAS, JJ.; Part III-B-1 of which was joined by REHNQUIST, C.J., and STEVENS, SOUTER, GINSBURG, and BREYER, JJ.; and Parts III-B-2 of which was joined by REHNQUIST, C.J., and SCALIA, KENNEDY, and THOMAS, JJ.

In January 1999, the Attorney General of Massachusetts promulgated comprehensive regulations governing the advertising and sale of cigarettes, smokeless tobacco, and cigars.

The cigar regulations that are still at issue provide:

> (1) Retail Sales Practices.   Except as otherwise provided, it shall be an unfair or deceptive act or practice for any person who sells or distributes cigars or little cigars directly to consumers within Massachusetts to engage in any of the following practices:

(a) sampling of cigars or little cigars or promotional give-aways of cigars or little cigars.

(2) Retail Outlet Sales Practices.   Except as otherwise provided, it shall be an unfair or deceptive act or practice for any person who sells or distributes cigars or little cigars through a retail outlet located within Massachusetts to engage in any of the following retail outlet sales practices:

(c) Using self-service displays of cigars or little cigars;

(d) Failing to place cigars and little cigars out of the reach of all consumers, and in a location accessible only to outlet personnel.

(5) Advertising Restrictions.   Except as [otherwise provided], it shall be an unfair or deceptive act or practice for any manufacturer, distributor or retailer to engage in any of the following practices:

(a) Outdoor advertising of cigars or little cigars, including advertising in enclosed stadiums and advertising from within a retail establishment that is directed toward or visible from the outside of the establishment, in any location within a 1,000 foot radius of any public playground, playground area in a public park, elementary school or secondary school;

(b) Point-of-sale advertising of cigars or little cigars any portion of which is placed lower than five feet from the floor of any retail establishment which is located within a one thousand foot radius of any public playground, playground area in a public park, elementary school or secondary school, and which is not an adult-only retail establishment.

The term "advertisement" is defined as:

any oral, written, graphic, or pictorial statement or representation, made by, or on behalf of, any person who manufactures, packages, imports for sale, distributes or sells within Massachusetts [tobacco products], the purpose or effect of which is to promote the use or sale of the product. Advertisement includes, without limitation, any picture, logo, symbol, motto, selling message, graphic display, visual image, recognizable color or pattern of colors, or any other indicia of product identification identical or similar to, or identifiable with, those used for any brand of [tobacco product]. This includes, without limitation, utilitarian items and permanent or semi-permanent fixtures with such indicia of product identification such as lighting fixtures, awnings, display cases, clocks and door mats, but does not include utilitarian items with a volume of 200 cubic inches or less.

[Similar regulations were adopted for smokeless tobacco products.]

[In Part II of the opinion, the Court declared the restriction of cigarette advertising to be preempted by federal law. This part of the opinion is presented in Chapter 4.]

III

By its terms, the FCLAA's pre-emption provision only applies to cigarettes. Accordingly, we must evaluate the smokeless tobacco and cigar petitioners' First Amendment challenges to the State's outdoor and point-of-sale advertising regulations.

A

For over 25 years, the Court has recognized that commercial speech does not fall outside the purview of the First Amendment. Instead, the Court has afforded commercial speech a measure of First Amendment protection "'commensurate'" with its position in relation to other constitutionally guaranteed expression. In recognition of the "distinction between speech proposing a commercial transaction, which occurs in an area traditionally subject to government regulation, and other varieties of speech," we developed a framework for analyzing regulations of commercial speech that is "substantially similar" to the test for time, place, and manner restrictions. The analysis contains four elements:

> At the outset, we must determine whether the expression is protected by the First Amendment. For commercial speech to come within that provision, it at least must concern lawful activity and not be misleading. Next, we ask whether the asserted governmental interest is substantial. If both inquiries yield positive answers, we must determine whether the regulation directly advances the governmental interest asserted, and whether it is not more extensive than is necessary to serve that interest. Central Hudson Gas & Electric Corp. v. Public Service Commission of New York (1980).

Petitioners urge us to reject the *Central Hudson* analysis and apply strict scrutiny. They are not the first litigants to do so. Admittedly, several Members of the Court have expressed doubts about the *Central Hudson* analysis and whether it should apply in particular cases. But we see "no need to break new ground. *Central Hudson*, as applied in our more recent commercial speech cases, provides an adequate basis for decision."

Only the last two steps of *Central Hudson*'s four-part analysis are at issue here. The Attorney General has assumed for purposes of summary judgment that petitioners' speech is entitled to First Amendment protection. With respect to the second step, none of the petitioners contests the importance of the State's interest in preventing the use of tobacco products by minors.

The third step of *Central Hudson* concerns the relationship between the harm that underlies the State's interest and the means identified by the State to advance that interest. It requires that "the speech restriction directly and materially advanc[e] the asserted governmental interest. 'This burden is not satisfied by mere speculation or conjecture; rather, a governmental body seeking to sustain a restriction on commercial speech must demonstrate that the harms it recites are real and that its restriction will in fact alleviate them to a material degree.'"

We do not, however, require that "empirical data come . . . accompanied by a surfeit of background information. . . . [W]e have permitted litigants to justify speech restrictions by reference to studies and anecdotes pertaining to different locales altogether, or even, in a case applying strict scrutiny, to justify restrictions based solely on history, consensus, and 'simple common sense.'" Florida Bar v. Went For It, Inc. (1995).

The last step of the *Central Hudson* analysis "complements" the third step, "asking whether the speech restriction is not more extensive than necessary to serve the interests that support it." We have made it clear that "the least restrictive means" is not the standard; instead, the case law requires a reasonable "'fit between the legislature's ends and the means chosen to accomplish those ends, . . . a means narrowly tailored to achieve the desired objective.'" Focusing on the third and fourth steps of the *Central Hudson* analysis, we first address the outdoor advertising and point-of-sale advertising regulations for smokeless tobacco and cigars. We then address the sales practices regulations for all tobacco products.

B

The outdoor advertising regulations prohibit smokeless tobacco or cigar advertising within a 1,000-foot radius of a school or playground. The District Court and Court of Appeals concluded that the Attorney General had identified a real problem with underage use of tobacco products, that limiting youth exposure to advertising would combat that problem, and that the regulations burdened no more speech than necessary to accomplish the State's goal. The smokeless tobacco and cigar petitioners take issue with all of these conclusions.

1

The smokeless tobacco and cigar petitioners contend that the Attorney General's regulations do not satisfy *Central Hudson*'s third step. They maintain that although the Attorney General may have identified a problem with underage cigarette smoking, he has not identified an equally severe problem with respect to underage use of smokeless tobacco or cigars. The smokeless tobacco petitioner emphasizes the "lack of parity" between cigarettes and smokeless tobacco. The cigar petitioners catalogue a list of differences between cigars and other tobacco products, including the characteristics of the products and marketing strategies. The petitioners finally contend that the Attorney General cannot prove that advertising has a causal link to tobacco use such that limiting advertising will materially alleviate any problem of underage use of their products.

In previous cases, we have acknowledged the theory that product advertising stimulates demand for products, while suppressed advertising may have the opposite effect. The Attorney General cites numerous studies to support this theory in the case of tobacco products. The Attorney General relies in part on evidence gathered by the Food and Drug Administration (FDA) in its attempt to regulate the advertising of cigarettes and smokeless tobacco. The FDA made specific findings with respect to smokeless tobacco. The FDA concluded that "[t]he recent and very large increase in the use of smokeless tobacco products by young people and the addictive nature of these products has persuaded the agency that these products must be included in any regulatory approach that is designed to help prevent future generations of young people from becoming addicted to nicotine-containing tobacco products." Researchers tracked a dramatic shift in patterns of smokeless tobacco use from older to younger users over the past 30 years. Another study documented the targeting of youth through smokeless tobacco sales and advertising techniques.

The Attorney General presents different evidence with respect to cigars. There was no data on underage cigar use prior to 1996 because the behavior was considered "uncommon enough not to be worthy of examination." More recently, however, data on youth cigar use has emerged. The National Cancer Institute concluded in its 1998 Monograph that the rate of cigar use by minors is increasing and that, in some States, the cigar use rates are higher than the smokeless tobacco use rates for minors. Studies have also demonstrated a link between advertising and demand for cigars. After Congress recognized the power of images in advertising and banned cigarette advertising in electronic media, television advertising of small cigars "increased dramatically in 1972 and 1973," "filled the void left by cigarette advertisers," and "sales . . . soared."

Our review of the record reveals that the Attorney General has provided ample documentation of the problem with underage use of smokeless tobacco and cigars. In addition, we disagree with petitioners' claim that there is no evidence that preventing targeted campaigns and limiting youth exposure to advertising will decrease underage use of smokeless tobacco and cigars. On this record and in the posture of summary judgment, we are unable to conclude that the Attorney General's decision to regulate advertising of smokeless tobacco and cigars in an effort to combat the use of tobacco products by minors was based on mere "speculation [and] conjecture."

2

Whatever the strength of the Attorney General's evidence to justify the outdoor advertising regulations, however, we conclude that the regulations do not satisfy the fourth step of the *Central Hudson* analysis. The final step of the *Central Hudson* analysis, the "critical inquiry in this case," requires a reasonable fit between the means and ends of the regulatory scheme. The Attorney General's regulations do not meet this standard. The broad sweep of the regulations indicates that the Attorney General did not "carefully calculat[e] the costs and benefits associated with the burden on speech imposed" by the regulations.

The outdoor advertising regulations prohibit any smokeless tobacco or cigar advertising within 1,000 feet of schools or playgrounds. In the District Court, petitioners maintained that this prohibition would prevent advertising in 87% to 91% of Boston, Worcester, and Springfield, Massachusetts. The 87% to 91% figure appears to include not only the effect of the regulations, but also the limitations imposed by other generally applicable zoning restrictions. The Attorney General disputed petitioners' figures but "concede[d] that the reach of the regulations is substantial." Thus, the Court of Appeals concluded that the regulations prohibit advertising in a substantial portion of the major metropolitan areas of Massachusetts.

The substantial geographical reach of the Attorney General's outdoor advertising regulations is compounded by other factors. "Outdoor" advertising includes not only advertising located outside an establishment, but also advertising inside a store if that advertising is visible from outside the store. The regulations restrict advertisements of any size and the term advertisement also includes oral statements.

In some geographical areas, these regulations would constitute nearly a complete ban on the communication of truthful information about smokeless tobacco and cigars to adult consumers. The breadth and scope of the regulations, and the process by which the Attorney General adopted the regulations, do not demonstrate a careful calculation of the speech interests involved.

First, the Attorney General did not seem to consider the impact of the 1,000-foot restriction on commercial speech in major metropolitan areas. The Attorney General apparently selected the 1,000-foot distance based on the FDA's decision to impose an identical 1,000-foot restriction when it attempted to regulate cigarette and smokeless tobacco advertising. But the FDA's 1,000-foot regulation was not an adequate basis for the Attorney General to tailor the Massachusetts regulations. The degree to which speech is suppressed—or alternative avenues for speech remain available—under a particular regulatory scheme tends to be case specific. And a case specific analysis makes sense, for although a State or locality may have common interests and concerns about underage smoking and the effects of tobacco advertisements, the impact of a restriction on speech will undoubtedly vary from place to place. The FDA's regulations would have had widely disparate effects nationwide. Even in Massachusetts, the effect of the Attorney General's speech regulations will vary based on whether a locale is rural, suburban, or urban. The uniformly broad sweep of the geographical limitation demonstrates a lack of tailoring.

In addition, the range of communications restricted seems unduly broad. For instance, it is not clear from the regulatory scheme why a ban on oral communications is necessary to further the State's interest. Apparently that restriction means that a retailer is unable to answer inquiries about its tobacco products if that communication occurs outdoors. Similarly, a ban on all signs of any size seems ill suited to target the problem of highly visible billboards, as opposed to smaller signs. To the extent that studies have identified particular advertising and promotion practices that appeal to youth, tailoring would involve targeting those practices while permitting others. As crafted, the regulations make no distinction among practices on this basis.

The State's interest in preventing underage tobacco use is substantial, and even compelling, but it is no less true that the sale and use of tobacco products by adults is a legal activity. We must consider that tobacco retailers and manufacturers have an interest in conveying truthful information about their products to adults, and adults have a corresponding interest in receiving truthful information about tobacco products. In a case involving indecent speech on the Internet we explained that "the governmental interest in protecting children from harmful materials . . . does not justify an unnecessarily broad suppression of speech addressed to adults." Reno v. American Civil Liberties Union (1997).

In some instances, Massachusetts' outdoor advertising regulations would impose particularly onerous burdens on speech. For example, we disagree with the Court of Appeals' conclusion that because cigar manufacturers and retailers conduct a limited amount of advertising in comparison to other tobacco products, "the relative lack of cigar advertising also means that the burden imposed on cigar advertisers is correspondingly small." If some retailers have relatively small advertising budgets, and use few avenues of communication, then the Attorney General's outdoor advertising regulations potentially place a greater, not lesser, burden on those retailers' speech. Furthermore, to the extent that cigar products and cigar advertising differ from that of other tobacco products, that difference should inform the inquiry into what speech restrictions are necessary.

In addition, a retailer in Massachusetts may have no means of communicating to passersby on the street that it sells tobacco products because alternative forms of advertisement, like newspapers, do not allow that retailer to propose an instant transaction in the way that onsite advertising does. The ban on any indoor advertising that is visible from the outside also presents problems in establishments like convenience stores, which have unique security concerns that counsel in favor of full visibility of the store from the outside. It is these sorts of considerations that the Attorney General failed to incorporate into the regulatory scheme.

We conclude that the Attorney General has failed to show that the outdoor advertising regulations for smokeless tobacco and cigars are not more extensive than necessary to advance the State's substantial interest in preventing underage tobacco use.

C

Massachusetts has also restricted indoor, point-of-sale advertising for smokeless tobacco and cigars. Advertising cannot be "placed lower than five feet from the floor of any retail establishment which is located within a one thousand foot radius of" any school or playground. We conclude that the point-of-sale advertising regulations fail both the third and fourth steps of the *Central Hudson* analysis. A regulation cannot be sustained if it " 'provides only ineffective or remote support for the government's purpose,' " or if there is "little chance" that the restriction will advance the State's goal. As outlined above, the State's goal is to prevent minors from using tobacco products and to curb demand for that activity by limiting youth exposure to advertising. The 5 foot rule does not seem to advance that goal. Not all children are less than 5 feet tall, and those who are certainly have the ability to look up and take in their surroundings.

Massachusetts may wish to target tobacco advertisements and displays that entice children, much like floor-level candy displays in a convenience store, but the blanket height restriction does not constitute a reasonable fit with that goal. The Court of Appeals recognized that the efficacy of the regulation was questionable, but decided that "[i]n any event, the burden on speech imposed by the provision is very limited." There is no de minimis exception for a speech restriction that lacks sufficient tailoring or justification. We conclude that the restriction on the height of indoor advertising is invalid under *Central Hudson*'s third and fourth prongs.

D

The Attorney General also promulgated a number of regulations that restrict sales practices by cigarette, smokeless tobacco, and cigar manufacturers and retailers. Among other restrictions, the regulations bar the use of self-service displays and require that tobacco products be placed out of the reach of all consumers in a location accessible only to salespersons. The cigarette petitioners do not challenge the sales practices regulations on pre-emption grounds. As we read the regulations, they basically require tobacco retailers to place tobacco products behind counters and require customers to have contact with a salesperson before they are able to handle a tobacco product.

The cigarette and smokeless tobacco petitioners contend that "the same First Amendment principles that require invalidation of the outdoor and indoor advertising restrictions require invalidation of the display regulations at issue in this case."

We reject these contentions. Assuming that petitioners have a cognizable speech interest in a particular means of displaying their products, these regulations withstand First Amendment scrutiny. Massachusetts' sales practices provisions regulate conduct that may have a communicative component, but Massachusetts seeks to regulate the placement of tobacco products for reasons unrelated to the communication of ideas. We conclude that the State has demonstrated a substantial interest in preventing access to tobacco products by minors and has adopted an appropriately narrow means of advancing that interest. Unattended displays of tobacco products present an opportunity for access without the proper age verification required by law. Thus, the State prohibits self-service and other displays that would allow an individual to obtain tobacco products without direct contact with a salesperson. It is clear that the regulations leave open ample channels of communication. The regulations do not significantly impede adult access to tobacco products. Moreover, retailers have other means of exercising any cognizable speech interest in the presentation of their products. We presume that vendors may place empty tobacco packaging on open display, and display actual tobacco products so long as that display is only accessible to sales personnel. As for cigars, there is no indication in the regulations that a customer is unable to examine a cigar prior to purchase, so long as that examination takes place through a salesperson.

We conclude that the sales practices regulations withstand First Amendment scrutiny. The means chosen by the State are narrowly tailored to prevent access to tobacco products by minors, are unrelated to expression, and leave open alternative avenues for vendors to convey information about products and for would-be customers to inspect products before purchase.

Justice KENNEDY, with whom Justice SCALIA joins, concurring in part and concurring in the judgment.

The obvious overbreadth of the outdoor advertising restrictions suffices to invalidate them under the fourth part of the test in Central Hudson Gas & Elec. Corp. v. Public Serv. Comm'n of N.Y. (1980). As a result, in my view, there is no need to consider whether the restrictions satisfy the third part of the test, a proposition about which there is considerable doubt. Neither are we required to consider whether *Central Hudson* should be retained in the face of the substantial objections that can be made to it. My continuing concerns that the test gives insufficient protection to truthful, nonmisleading commercial speech require me to refrain from expressing agreement with the Court's application of the third part of *Central Hudson*.

Justice THOMAS, concurring in part and concurring in the judgment.

I join the opinion of the Court, [but] I continue to believe that when the government seeks to restrict truthful speech in order to suppress the ideas it conveys, strict scrutiny is appropriate, whether or not the speech in question may be characterized as "commercial." I would subject all of the advertising restrictions to strict scrutiny and would hold that they violate the First Amendment.

I have observed previously that there is no "philosophical or historical basis for asserting that 'commercial' speech is of 'lower value' than 'noncommercial' speech." Indeed, I doubt whether it is even possible to draw a coherent distinction between commercial and noncommercial speech. It should be clear that if these regulations targeted anything other than advertising for commercial products—if, for example, they were directed at billboards promoting political candidates—all would agree that the restrictions should be subjected to strict scrutiny. In my view, an asserted government interest in keeping people ignorant by suppressing expression "is per se illegitimate and can no more justify regulation of 'commercial' speech than it can justify regulation of 'noncommercial' speech." That is essentially the interest asserted here, and, adhering to the views I expressed in *44 Liquormart*, I would subject the Massachusetts regulations to strict scrutiny.

Even if one accepts the premise that commercial speech generally is entitled to a lower level of constitutional protection than are other forms of speech, it does not follow that the regulations here deserve anything less than strict scrutiny. Although we have recognized several categories of speech that normally receive reduced First Amendment protection, or no First Amendment protection at all, we have never held that the government may regulate speech within those categories in any way that it wishes. Rather, we have said "that these areas of speech can, consistently with the First Amendment, be regulated because of their constitutionally proscribable content." R.A.V. v. St. Paul (1992). Even when speech falls into a category of reduced constitutional protection, the government may not engage in content discrimination for reasons unrelated to those characteristics of the speech that place it within the category. For example, a city may ban obscenity (because obscenity is an unprotected category), but it may not ban "only those legally obscene works that contain criticism of the city government."

Whatever power the State may have to regulate commercial speech, it may not use that power to limit the content of commercial speech, as it has done here, "for reasons unrelated to the preservation of a fair bargaining process." Such content-discriminatory regulation—like all other content-based regulation of speech—must be subjected to strict scrutiny.

Under strict scrutiny, the advertising ban may be saved only if it is narrowly tailored to promote a compelling government interest. If that interest could be served by an alternative that is less restrictive of speech, then the State must use that alternative instead. Applying this standard, the regulations here must fail.

Underlying many of the arguments of respondents and their amici is the idea that tobacco is in some sense sui generis—that it is so special, so unlike any other object of regulation, that application of normal First Amendment principles should be suspended. Smoking poses serious health risks, and advertising may induce children (who lack the judgment to make an intelligent decision about whether to smoke) to begin smoking, which can lead to addiction. The State's assessment of the urgency of the problem posed by tobacco is a policy judgment, and it is not this Court's place to second-guess it. Nevertheless, it seems appropriate to point out that to uphold the Massachusetts tobacco regulations would be to accept a line of reasoning that would permit restrictions on advertising for a host of other products.

Tobacco use is, we are told, "the single leading cause of preventable death in the United States." The second largest contributor to mortality rates in the United States is obesity. It is associated with increased incidence of diabetes, hypertension, and coronary artery disease, and it represents a public health problem that is rapidly growing worse. Although the growth of obesity over the last few decades has had many causes, a significant factor has been the increased availability of large quantities of high-calorie, high-fat foods. Such foods, of course, have been aggressively marketed and promoted by fast food companies.

Respondents say that tobacco companies are covertly targeting children in their advertising. Fast food companies do so openly. Moreover, there is considerable evidence that they have been successful in changing children's eating behavior. The effect of advertising on children's eating habits is significant for two reasons. First, childhood obesity is a serious health problem in its own right. Second, eating preferences formed in childhood tend to persist in adulthood. So even though fast food is not addictive in the same way tobacco is, children's exposure to fast food advertising can have deleterious consequences that are difficult to reverse.

To take another example, the third largest cause of preventable deaths in the United States is alcohol. Alcohol use is associated with tens of thousands of deaths each year from cancers and digestive diseases. And the victims of alcohol use are not limited to those who drink alcohol. In 1996, over 17,000 people were killed, and over 321,000 people were injured, in alcohol-related car accidents. Each year, alcohol is involved in several million violent crimes, including almost 200,000 sexual assaults.

Although every State prohibits the sale of alcohol to those under age 21, much alcohol advertising is viewed by children. Not surprisingly, there is considerable evidence that exposure to alcohol advertising is associated with under-age drinking. Like underage tobacco use, underage drinking has effects that cannot be undone later in life. Those who begin drinking early are much more likely to become dependent on alcohol. Indeed, the probability of lifetime alcohol dependence decreases approximately 14 percent with each additional year of age at which alcohol is first used. And obviously the effects of underage drinking are irreversible for the nearly 1,700 Americans killed each year by teenage drunk drivers.

Respondents have identified no principle of law or logic that would preclude the imposition of restrictions on fast food and alcohol advertising similar to those they seek to impose on tobacco advertising. In effect, they seek a "vice" exception to the First Amendment. No such exception exists. If it did, it would have almost no limit, for "any product that poses some threat to public health or public morals might reasonably be characterized by a state legislature as relating to 'vice activity.'" That is why "a 'vice' label that is unaccompanied by a corresponding prohibition against the commercial behavior at issue fails to provide a principled justification for the regulation of commercial speech about that activity."

No legislature has ever sought to restrict speech about an activity it regarded as harmless and inoffensive. Calls for limits on expression always are made when the specter of some threatened harm is looming. The identity of the harm may vary. People will be inspired by totalitarian dogmas and subvert the Republic. They will be inflamed by racial demagoguery and embrace hatred and bigotry. Or they will be enticed by cigarette advertisements and choose to smoke, risking disease. It is therefore no answer for the State to say that the makers of cigarettes are doing harm: perhaps they are. But in that respect they are no different from the purveyors of other harmful products, or the advocates of harmful ideas. When the State seeks to silence them, they are all entitled to the protection of the First Amendment.

Justice STEVENS, concurring in part and dissenting in part, joined by Justices GINSBURG and BREYER.

I would, however, reach different dispositions as to the 1,000-foot rule and the height restrictions for indoor advertising, and my evaluation of the sales practice restrictions differs from the Court's.

THE 1,000-FOOT RULE

I am in complete accord with the Court's analysis of the importance of the interests served by the advertising restrictions. As the Court lucidly explains, few interests are more "compelling," than ensuring that minors do not become addicted to a dangerous drug before they are able to make a mature and informed decision as to the health risks associated with that substance. Unlike other products sold for human consumption, tobacco products are addictive and ultimately lethal for many long-term users. When that interest is combined with the State's concomitant concern for the effective enforcement of its laws regarding the sale of tobacco to minors, it becomes clear that Massachusetts' regulations serve interests of the highest order and are, therefore, immune from any ends-based challenge, whatever level of scrutiny one chooses to employ.

Nevertheless, noble ends do not save a speech-restricting statute whose means are poorly tailored. Such statutes may be invalid for two different reasons. First, the means chosen may be insufficiently related to the ends they purportedly serve. Alternatively, the statute may be so broadly drawn that, while effectively achieving its ends, it unduly restricts communications that are unrelated to its policy aims. The second difficulty is most frequently encountered when government adopts measures for the protection of children that impose substantial restrictions on the ability of adults to communicate with one another.

To my mind, the 1,000-foot rule does not present a tailoring problem of the first type. For reasons cogently explained in our prior opinions and in the opinion of the Court, we may fairly assume that advertising stimulates consumption and, therefore, that regulations limiting advertising will facilitate efforts to stem consumption.

However, I share the majority's concern as to whether the 1,000-foot rule unduly restricts the ability of cigarette manufacturers to convey lawful information to adult consumers. This, of course, is a question of line-drawing. While a ban on all communications about a given subject would be the most effective way to prevent children from exposure to such material, the state cannot by fiat reduce the level of discourse to that which is "fit for children."

Finding the appropriate balance is no easy matter. Though many factors plausibly enter the equation when calculating whether a child-directed location restriction goes too far in regulating adult speech, one crucial question is whether the regulatory scheme leaves available sufficient "alternative avenues of communication." Because I do not think the record contains sufficient information to enable us to answer that question, I would vacate the award of summary judgment upholding the 1,000-foot rule and remand for trial on that issue.

THOMPSON v. WESTERN STATES MEDICAL CENTER, 122 S. Ct. 1497 (2002). The Supreme Court declared unconstitutional a provision of federal law that prohibited advertisement of "compounded drugs." These are combinations of drugs made by pharmacists that have not been specifically approved by the Food and Drug Administration. In an opinion by Justice O'Connor, the Court reiterated that the *Central Hudson* (casebook, p. 1063) test is used for commercial speech. Justice O'Connor said that the test for "determining whether a particular commercial speech regulation is constitutionally permissible. Under that test we ask as a threshold matter whether the commercial speech concerns unlawful activity or is misleading. If so, then the speech is not protected by the First Amendment. If the speech concerns lawful activity and is not misleading, however, we next ask 'whether the asserted governmental interest is substantial.' If it is, then we 'determine whether the regulation directly advances the governmental interest asserted,' and, finally, 'whether it is not more extensive than is necessary to serve that interest.' Each of these latter three inquiries must be answered in the affirmative for the regulation to be found constitutional."

The Court declared the prohibition on advertising unconstitutional. The Court said that the government failed to prove that the ban on advertising will undermine the federal interest in having new drugs approved by the FDA. Moreover, as to the argument that advertising will encourage increased use of these drugs, the Court said:

The dissent describes another governmental interest—an interest in prohibiting the sale of compounded drugs to "patients who may not clearly need them," and argues that "Congress could . . . conclude that the advertising restrictions 'directly advance'" that interest. Nowhere in its briefs, however, does the Government argue that this interest motivated the advertising ban. Although, for the reasons given by the dissent, Congress conceivably could have enacted the advertising ban to advance this interest, we have generally only sustained statutes on the basis of hypothesized justifications when reviewing statutes merely to determine whether they are rational. The *Central Hudson* test is significantly stricter than the rational basis test, however, requiring the Government not only to identify specifically "a substantial interest to be achieved by [the] restrictio[n] on commercial speech," but also to prove that the regulation "directly advances" that interest and is "not more extensive than is necessary to serve that interest." The Government has not met any of these requirements with regard to the interest the dissent describes.

Even if the Government had argued that the FDAMA's speech-related restrictions were motivated by a fear that advertising compounded drugs would put people who do not need such drugs at risk by causing them to convince their doctors to prescribe the drugs anyway, that fear would fail to justify the restrictions. Aside from the fact that this concern rests on the questionable assumption that doctors would prescribe unnecessary medications (an assumption the dissent is willing to make based on one magazine article and one survey, neither of which was relied upon by the Government), this concern amounts to a fear that people would make bad decisions if given truthful information about compounded drugs. We have previously rejected the notion that the Government has an interest in preventing the dissemination of truthful commercial information in order to prevent members of the public from making bad decisions with the information.

5. Reputation, Privacy, Publicity and the First Amendment: Torts and the First Amendment

c. Public Disclosure of Private Facts (casebook, p. 1097)

As the casebook indicates (pp. 1097-1102), the Supreme Court has held that the government cannot impose liability for the truthful reporting of information lawfully obtained from government records. In Bartnicki v. Vopper, the Court considered privacy in relation to the First Amendment in another context. A radio station broadcast a tape of a conversation that had been illegally intercepted and recorded. The issue was whether the First Amendment precluded liability under federal and state law against the radio station and its employees for broadcasting the tape.

BARTNICKI v. VOPPER
121 S. Ct. 1753 (2001)

Justice STEVENS delivered the opinion of the Court.

These cases raise an important question concerning what degree of protection, if any, the First Amendment provides to speech that discloses the contents of an illegally intercepted communication. That question is both novel and narrow. Despite the fact that federal law has prohibited such disclosures since 1934, this is the first time that we have confronted such an issue.

The suit at hand involves the repeated intentional disclosure of an illegally intercepted cellular telephone conversation about a public issue. The persons who made the disclosures did not participate in the interception, but they did know—or at least had reason to know—that the interception was unlawful. Accordingly, these cases present a conflict between interests of the highest order— on the one hand, the interest in the full and free dissemination of information concerning public issues, and, on the other hand, the interest in individual privacy and, more specifically, in fostering private speech. The Framers of the First Amendment surely did not foresee the advances in science that produced the conversation, the interception, or the conflict that gave rise to this action.

I

During 1992 and most of 1993, the Pennsylvania State Education Association, a union representing the teachers at the Wyoming Valley West High School, engaged in collective-bargaining negotiations with the school board. Petitioner Kane, then the president of the local union, testified that the negotiations were "'contentious'" and received "a lot of media attention." In May 1993, petitioner Bartnicki, who was acting as the union's "chief negotiator," used the cellular phone in her car to call Kane and engage in a lengthy conversation about the status of the negotiations. An unidentified person intercepted and recorded that call.

In their conversation, Kane and Bartnicki discussed the timing of a proposed strike, difficulties created by public comment on the negotiations, and the need for a dramatic response to the board's intransigence. At one point, Kane said: "'If they're not gonna move for three percent, we're gonna have to go to their, their homes . . . To blow off their front porches, we'll have to do some work on some of those guys. (PAUSES). Really, uh, really and truthfully because this is, you know, this is bad news. (UNDECIPHERABLE).'"

In the early fall of 1993, the parties accepted a non-binding arbitration proposal that was generally favorable to the teachers. In connection with news reports about the settlement, respondent Vopper, a radio commentator who had been critical of the union in the past, played a tape of the intercepted conversation on his public affairs talk show. Another station also broadcast the tape, and local newspapers published its contents. After filing suit against Vopper and other representatives of the media, Bartnicki and Kane (hereinafter petitioners) learned through discovery that Vopper had obtained the tape from Jack Yocum, the head of a local taxpayers' organization that had opposed the union's demands throughout the negotiations. Yocum, who was added as a defendant, testified that he had found the tape in his mailbox shortly after the interception and recognized the voices of Bartnicki and Kane. Yocum played the tape for some members of the school board, and later delivered the tape itself to Vopper.

II

In their amended complaint, petitioners alleged that their telephone conversation had been surreptitiously intercepted by an unknown person using an electronic device, that Yocum had obtained a tape of that conversation, and that he intentionally disclosed it to Vopper, as well as other individuals and media representatives. Thereafter, Vopper and other members of the media repeatedly published the contents of that conversation. The amended complaint alleged that each of the defendants "knew or had reason to know" that the recording of the private telephone conversation had been obtained by means of an illegal interception. Relying on both federal and Pennsylvania statutory provisions, petitioners sought actual damages, statutory damages, punitive damages, and attorney's fees and costs.

III

As we pointed out in Berger v. New York (1967), sophisticated (and not so sophisticated) methods of eavesdropping on oral conversations and intercepting telephone calls have been practiced for decades, primarily by law enforcement authorities. In *Berger*, we held that New York's broadly written statute authorizing the police to conduct wiretaps violated the Fourth Amendment. Largely in response to that decision, and to our holding in Katz v. United States (1967), that the attachment of a listening and recording device to the outside of a telephone booth constituted a search, Congress undertook to draft comprehensive legislation both authorizing the use of evidence obtained by electronic surveillance on specified conditions, and prohibiting its use otherwise. The ultimate result of those efforts was Title III of the Omnibus Crime Control and Safe Streets Act of 1968. One of the stated purposes of that title was "to protect effectively the privacy of wire and oral communications." In addition to authorizing and regulating electronic surveillance for law enforcement purposes, Title III also regulated private conduct. One part of those regulations defined five offenses punishable by a fine of not more than $10,000, by imprisonment for not more than five years, or by both. Subsection (a) applied to any person who "willfully intercepts . . . any wire or oral communication." Subsection (b) applied to the intentional use of devices designed to intercept oral conversations; subsection (d) applied to the use of the contents of illegally intercepted wire or oral communications; and subsection (e) prohibited the unauthorized disclosure of the contents of interceptions that were authorized for law enforcement purposes. Subsection (c), the original version of the provision most directly at issue in this case, applied to any person who "willfully discloses, or endeavors to disclose, to any other person the contents of any wire or oral communication, knowing or having reason to know that the information was obtained through the interception of a wire or oral communication in violation of this subsection." The oral communications protected by the Act were only those "uttered by a person exhibiting an expectation that such communication is not subject to interception under circumstances justifying such expectation."

As enacted in 1968, Title III did not apply to the monitoring of radio transmissions. In the Electronic Communications Privacy Act of 1986, however, Congress enlarged the coverage of Title III to prohibit the interception of "electronic" as well as oral and wire communications. By reason of that amendment, as well as a 1994 amendment which applied to cordless telephone communications, Title III now applies to the interception of conversations over both cellular and cordless phones.

IV

The constitutional question before us concerns the validity of the statutes as applied to the specific facts of this case. Because of the procedural posture of the case, it is appropriate to make certain important assumptions about those facts.

We accept petitioners' submission that the interception was intentional, and therefore unlawful, and that, at a minimum, respondents "had reason to know" that it was unlawful. Accordingly, the disclosure of the contents of the intercepted conversation by Yocum to school board members and to representatives of the media, as well as the subsequent disclosures by the media defendants to the public, violated the federal and state statutes. Under the provisions of the federal statute, as well as its Pennsylvania analog, petitioners are thus entitled to recover damages from each of the respondents. The only question is whether the application of these statutes in such circumstances violates the First Amendment.

In answering that question, we accept respondents' submission on three factual matters that serve to distinguish most of the cases that have arisen under [the statute]. First, respondents played no part in the illegal interception. Rather, they found out about the interception only after it occurred, and in fact never learned the identity of the person or persons who made the interception. Second, their access to the information on the tapes was obtained lawfully, even though the information itself was intercepted unlawfully by someone else. Third, the subject matter of the conversation was a matter of public concern. If the statements about the labor negotiations had been made in a public arena—during a bargaining session, for example—they would have been newsworthy. This would also be true if a third party had inadvertently overheard Bartnicki making the same statements to Kane when the two thought they were alone.

V

We agree with petitioners that [the federal statute], as well as its Pennsylvania analog, is in fact a content-neutral law of general applicability. In determining whether a regulation is content based or content neutral, we look to the purpose behind the regulation; typically, "[g]overnment regulation of expressive activity is content neutral so long as it is 'justified without reference to the content of the regulated speech.'" Ward v. Rock Against Racism (1989).

In this case, the basic purpose of the statute at issue is to "protec[t] the privacy of wire[, electronic,] and oral communications." The statute does not distinguish based on the content of the intercepted conversations, nor is it justified by reference to the content of those conversations. Rather, the communications at issue are singled out by virtue of the fact that they were illegally intercepted—by virtue of the source, rather than the subject matter.

On the other hand, the naked prohibition against disclosures is fairly characterized as a regulation of pure speech. Unlike the prohibition against the "use" of the contents of an illegal interception, subsection (c) is not a regulation of conduct. It is true that the delivery of a tape recording might be regarded as conduct, but given that the purpose of such a delivery is to provide the recipient with the text of recorded statements, it is like the delivery of a handbill or a pamphlet, and as such, it is the kind of "speech" that the First Amendment protects.

VI

As a general matter, "state action to punish the publication of truthful information seldom can satisfy constitutional standards." Smith v. Daily Mail Publishing Co. (1979). More specifically, this Court has repeatedly held that "if a newspaper lawfully obtains truthful information about a matter of public significance then state officials may not constitutionally punish publication of the information, absent a need . . . of the highest order." Florida Star v. B.J.F. (1989).

Accordingly, in New York Times Co. v. United States (1971) (per curiam), the Court upheld the right of the press to publish information of great public concern obtained from documents stolen by a third party. In so doing, that decision resolved a conflict between the basic rule against prior restraints on publication and the interest in preserving the secrecy of information that, if disclosed, might seriously impair the security of the Nation. In resolving that conflict, the attention of every Member of this Court was focused on the character of the stolen documents' contents and the consequences of public disclosure. Although the undisputed fact that the newspaper intended to publish information obtained from stolen documents was noted in Justice Harlan's dissent, neither the majority nor the dissenters placed any weight on that fact.

However, New York Times v. United States raised, but did not resolve the question "whether, in cases where information has been acquired unlawfully by a newspaper or by a source, government may ever punish not only the unlawful acquisition, but the ensuing publication as well." The question here, however, is a narrower version of that still-open question. Simply put, the issue here is this: "Where the punished publisher of information has obtained the information in question in a manner lawful in itself but from a source who has obtained it unawfully, may the government punish the ensuing publication of that information based on the defect in a chain?"

Our refusal to construe the issue presented more broadly is consistent with this Court's repeated refusal to answer categorically whether truthful publication may ever be punished consistent with the First Amendment. Rather, "[o]ur cases have carefully eschewed reaching this ultimate question, mindful that the future may bring scenarios which prudence counsels our not resolving anticipatorily. . . . We continue to believe that the sensitivity and significance of the interests presented in clashes between [the] First Amendment and privacy rights counsel relying on limited principles that sweep no more broadly than the appropriate context of the instant case."

The Government identifies two interests served by the statute—first, the interest in removing an incentive for parties to intercept private conversations, and second, the interest in minimizing the harm to persons whose conversations have been illegally intercepted. We assume that those interests adequately justify the prohibition in [the statute] against the interceptor's own use of information that he or she acquired by violating [the law], but it by no means follows that punishing disclosures of lawfully obtained information of public interest by one not involved in the initial illegality is an acceptable means of serving those ends.

The normal method of deterring unlawful conduct is to impose an appropriate punishment on the person who engages in it. If the sanctions that presently attach to a violation of [the statute] do not provide sufficient deterrence, perhaps those sanctions should be made more severe. But it would be quite remarkable to hold that speech by a law-abiding possessor of information can be suppressed in order to deter conduct by a non-law-abiding third party. Although there are some rare occasions in which a law suppressing one party's speech may be justified by an interest in deterring criminal conduct by another, this is not such a case.

The Government also points to two other areas of the law—namely, mail theft and stolen property—in which a ban on the receipt or possession of an item is used to deter some primary illegality. Neither of those examples, though, involve prohibitions on speech. As such, they are not relevant to a First Amendment analysis.

With only a handful of exceptions, the violations of § 2511(1)(a) that have been described in litigated cases have been motivated by either financial gain or domestic disputes. In virtually all of those cases, the identity of the person or persons intercepting the communication has been known. Moreover, petitioners cite no evidence that Congress viewed the prohibition against disclosures as a response to the difficulty of identifying persons making improper use of scanners and other surveillance devices and accordingly of deterring such conduct, and there is no empirical evidence to support the assumption that the prohibition against disclosures reduces the number of illegal interceptions.

Although this case demonstrates that there may be an occasional situation in which an anonymous scanner will risk criminal prosecution by passing on information without any expectation of financial reward or public praise, surely this is the exceptional case. Moreover, there is no basis for assuming that imposing sanctions upon respondents will deter the unidentified scanner from continuing to engage in surreptitious interceptions. Unusual cases fall far short of a showing that there is a "need of the highest order" for a rule supplementing the traditional means of deterring antisocial conduct. The justification for any such novel burden on expression must be "far stronger than mere speculation about serious harms." Accordingly, the Government's first suggested justification for applying § 2511(1)(c) to an otherwise innocent disclosure of public information is plainly insufficient.[1]

---

1. Our holding, of course, does not apply to punishing parties for obtaining the relevant information unlawfully. "It would be frivolous to assert—and no one does in these cases—that the First Amendment, in the interest of securing news or otherwise, confers a license on either the reporter or his news sources to violate valid criminal laws. Although stealing documents or private wiretapping could provide newsworthy information, neither reporter nor source is immune from conviction for such conduct, whatever the impact on the flow of news." Branzburg v. Hayes (1972). [Footnote by the Court.]

The Government's second argument, however, is considerably stronger. Privacy of communication is an important interest, and Title III's restrictions are intended to protect that interest, thereby "encouraging the uninhibited exchange of ideas and information among private parties. . . ." Moreover, the fear of public disclosure of private conversations might well have a chilling effect on private speech.

Accordingly, it seems to us that there are important interests to be considered on both sides of the constitutional calculus. In considering that balance, we acknowledge that some intrusions on privacy are more offensive than others, and that the disclosure of the contents of a private conversation can be an even greater intrusion on privacy than the interception itself. As a result, there is a valid independent justification for prohibiting such disclosures by persons who lawfully obtained access to the contents of an illegally intercepted message, even if that prohibition does not play a significant role in preventing such interceptions from occurring in the first place.

We need not decide whether that interest is strong enough to justify the application of § 2511(c) to disclosures of trade secrets or domestic gossip or other information of purely private concern. In other words, the outcome of the case does not turn on whether § 2511(1)(c) may be enforced with respect to most violations of the statute without offending the First Amendment. The enforcement of that provision in this case, however, implicates the core purposes of the First Amendment because it imposes sanctions on the publication of truthful information of public concern.

In this case, privacy concerns give way when balanced against the interest in publishing matters of public importance. As Warren and Brandeis stated in their classic law review article: "The right of privacy does not prohibit any publication of matter which is of public or general interest." The Right to Privacy, 4 Harv. L. Rev. 193, 214 (1890). One of the costs associated with participation in public affairs is an attendant loss of privacy.

We think it clear that a stranger's illegal conduct does not suffice to remove the First Amendment shield from speech about a matter of public concern. The months of negotiations over the proper level of compensation for teachers at the Wyoming Valley West High School were unquestionably a matter of public concern, and respondents were clearly engaged in debate about that concern.

Justice BREYER, with whom Justice O'CONNOR joins, concurring.

I join the Court's opinion because I agree with its "narrow" holding, limited to the special circumstances present here: (1) the radio broadcasters acted lawfully (up to the time of final public disclosure); and (2) the information publicized involved a matter of unusual public concern, namely a threat of potential physical harm to others. I write separately to explain why, in my view, the Court's holding does not imply a significantly broader constitutional immunity for the media.

As the Court recognizes, the question before us—a question of immunity from statutorily imposed civil liability—implicates competing constitutional concerns. The statutes directly interfere with free expression in that they prevent the media from publishing information. At the same time, they help to protect personal privacy—an interest here that includes not only the "right to be let alone," but also "the interest . . . in fostering private speech." Given these competing interests "on both sides of the equation, the key question becomes one of proper fit."

I would ask whether the statutes strike a reasonable balance between their speech-restricting and speech-enhancing consequences. Or do they instead impose restrictions on speech that are disproportionate when measured against their corresponding privacy and speech-related benefits, taking into account the kind, the importance, and the extent of these benefits, as well as the need for the restrictions in order to secure those benefits? What this Court has called "strict scrutiny"—with its strong presumption against constitutionality—is normally out of place where, as here, important competing constitutional interests are implicated.

The statutory restrictions before us directly enhance private speech. The statutes ensure the privacy of telephone conversations much as a trespass statute ensures privacy within the home. That assurance of privacy helps to overcome our natural reluctance to discuss private matters when we fear that our private conversations may become public. And the statutory restrictions consequently encourage conversations that otherwise might not take place.

At the same time, these statutes restrict public speech directly, deliberately, and of necessity. They include media publication within their scope not simply as a means, say, to deter interception, but also as an end. Media dissemination of an intimate conversation to an entire community will often cause the speakers serious harm over and above the harm caused by an initial disclosure to the person who intercepted the phone call. And the threat of that widespread dissemination can create a far more powerful disincentive to speak privately than the comparatively minor threat of disclosure to an interceptor and perhaps to a handful of others. Insofar as these statutes protect private communications against that widespread dissemination, they resemble laws that would award damages caused through publication of information obtained by theft from a private bedroom.

Nonetheless, looked at more specifically, the statutes, as applied in these circumstances, do not reasonably reconcile the competing constitutional objectives. Rather, they disproportionately interfere with media freedom. For one thing, the broadcasters here engaged in no unlawful activity other than the ultimate publication of the information another had previously obtained. They "neither encouraged nor participated directly or indirectly in the interception." No one claims that they ordered, counseled, encouraged, or otherwise aided or abetted the interception, the later delivery of the tape by the interceptor to an intermediary, or the tape's still later delivery by the intermediary to the media.

And, as the Court points out, the statutes do not forbid the receipt of the tape itself. The Court adds that its holding "does not apply to punishing parties for obtaining the relevant information unlawfully."

For another thing, the speakers had little or no legitimate interest in maintaining the privacy of the particular conversation. That conversation involved a suggestion about "blow[ing] off . . . front porches" and "do[ing] some work on some of these guys," thereby raising a significant concern for the safety of others. Where publication of private information constitutes a wrongful act, the law recognizes a privilege allowing the reporting of threats to public safety. Even where the danger may have passed by the time of publication, that fact cannot legitimize the speaker's earlier privacy expectation. Nor should editors, who must make a publication decision quickly, have to determine present or continued danger before publishing this kind of threat.

Further, the speakers themselves, the president of a teacher's union and the union's chief negotiator, were "limited public figures," for they voluntarily engaged in a public controversy. They thereby subjected themselves to somewhat greater public scrutiny and had a lesser interest in privacy than an individual engaged in purely private affairs.

This is not to say that the Constitution requires anyone, including public figures, to give up entirely the right to private communication, i.e., communication free from telephone taps or interceptions. But the subject matter of the conversation at issue here is far removed from that in situations where the media publicizes truly private matters.

Thus, in finding a constitutional privilege to publish unlawfully intercepted conversations of the kind here at issue, the Court does not create a "public interest" exception that swallows up the statutes' privacy-protecting general rule. Rather, it finds constitutional protection for publication of intercepted information of a special kind. Here, the speakers' legitimate privacy expectations are unusually low, and the public interest in defeating those expectations is unusually high. Given these circumstances, along with the lawful nature of respondents' behavior, the statutes' enforcement would disproportionately harm media freedom.

I emphasize the particular circumstances before us because, in my view, the Constitution permits legislatures to respond flexibly to the challenges future technology may pose to the individual's interest in basic personal privacy. Clandestine and pervasive invasions of privacy, unlike the simple theft of documents from a bedroom, are genuine possibilities as a result of continuously advancing technologies. Eavesdropping on ordinary cellular phone conversations in the street (which many callers seem to tolerate) is a very different matter from eavesdropping on encrypted cellular phone conversations or those carried on in the bedroom. But the technologies that allow the former may come to permit the latter. And statutes that may seem less important in the former context may turn out to have greater importance in the latter. Legislatures also may decide to revisit statutes such as those before us, creating better tailored provisions designed to encourage, for example, more effective privacy-protecting technologies.

For these reasons, we should avoid adopting overly broad or rigid constitutional rules, which would unnecessarily restrict legislative flexibility. I consequently agree with the Court's holding that the statutes as applied here violate the Constitution, but I would not extend that holding beyond these present circumstances.

Chief Justice REHNQUIST, with whom Justice SCALIA and Justice THOMAS join, dissenting.

Technology now permits millions of important and confidential conversations to occur through a vast system of electronic networks. These advances, however, raise significant privacy concerns. We are placed in the uncomfortable position of not knowing who might have access to our personal and business e-mails, our medical and financial records, or our cordless and cellular telephone conversations. In an attempt to prevent some of the most egregious violations of privacy, the United States, the District of Columbia, and 40 States have enacted laws prohibiting the intentional interception and knowing disclosure of electronic communications. The Court holds that all of these statutes violate the First Amendment insofar as the illegally intercepted conversation touches upon a matter of "public concern," an amorphous concept that the Court does not even attempt to define. But the Court's decision diminishes, rather than enhances, the purposes of the First Amendment: chilling the speech of the millions of Americans who rely upon electronic technology to communicate each day.

To effectuate these important privacy and speech interests, Congress and the vast majority of States have proscribed the intentional interception and knowing disclosure of the contents of electronic communications.

The Court correctly observes that these are "content-neutral law[s] of general applicability" which serve recognized interests of the "highest order": "the interest in individual privacy and . . . in fostering private speech." It nonetheless subjects these laws to the strict scrutiny normally reserved for governmental attempts to censor different viewpoints or ideas. There is scant support, either in precedent or in reason, for the Court's tacit application of strict scrutiny.

A content-neutral regulation will be sustained if " 'it furthers an important or substantial governmental interest; if the governmental interest is unrelated to the suppression of free expression; and if the incidental restriction on alleged First Amendment freedoms is no greater than is essential to the furtherance of that interest.' " Turner Broadcasting System, Inc. v. FCC (1994).

Here, Congress and the Pennsylvania Legislature have acted " 'without reference to the content of the regulated speech.' " There is no intimation that these laws seek "to suppress unpopular ideas or information or manipulate the public debate" or that they "distinguish favored speech from disfavored speech on the basis of the ideas or views expressed." The antidisclosure provision is based solely upon the manner in which the conversation was acquired, not the subject matter of the conversation or the viewpoints of the speakers. The same information, if obtained lawfully, could be published with impunity. As the concerns motivating strict scrutiny are absent, these content-neutral restrictions upon speech need pass only intermediate scrutiny.

The Court's attempt to avoid these precedents by reliance upon the *Daily Mail* string of newspaper cases is unpersuasive. In these cases, we held that statutes prohibiting the media from publishing certain truthful information—the name of a rape victim, the confidential proceedings before a state judicial review commission, and the name of a juvenile defendant, violated the First Amendment. In so doing, we stated that "if a newspaper lawfully obtains truthful information about a matter of public significance then state officials may not constitutionally punish publication of the information, absent a need to further a state interest of the highest order." Neither this *Daily Mail* principle nor any other aspect of these cases, however, justifies the Court's imposition of strict scrutiny here.

Each of the laws at issue in the *Daily Mail* cases regulated the content or subject matter of speech. This fact alone was enough to trigger strict scrutiny. But, as our synthesis of these cases in *Florida Star* made clear, three other unique factors also informed the scope of the *Daily Mail* principle.

First, the information published by the newspapers had been lawfully obtained from the government itself. Second, the information in each case was already "publicly available," and punishing further dissemination would not have advanced the purported government interests of confidentiality. Third, these cases were concerned with "the 'timidity and self-censorship' which may result from allowing the media to be punished for publishing certain truthful information." But fear of "timidity and self-censorship" is a basis for upholding, not striking down, these antidisclosure provisions: They allow private conversations to transpire without inhibition. And unlike the statute at issue in *Florida Star*, which had no scienter requirement, these statutes only address those who knowingly disclose an illegally intercepted conversation. They do not impose a duty to inquire into the source of the information and one could negligently disclose the contents of an illegally intercepted communication without liability.

In sum, it is obvious that the *Daily Mail* cases upon which the Court relies do not address the question presented here. Our decisions themselves made this clear: "The *Daily Mail* principle does not settle the issue whether, in cases where information has been acquired unlawfully by a newspaper or by a source, the government may ever punish not only the unlawful acquisition, but the ensuing publication as well."

Undaunted, the Court places an inordinate amount of weight upon the fact that the receipt of an illegally intercepted communication has not been criminalized. But this hardly renders those who knowingly receive and disclose such communications "law-abiding," and it certainly does not bring them under the

Daily Mail principle. The transmission of the intercepted communication from the eavesdropper to the third party is itself illegal; and where, as here, the third party then knowingly discloses that communication, another illegal act has been committed. The third party in this situation cannot be likened to the reporters in the *Daily Mail* cases, who lawfully obtained their information through consensual interviews or public documents.

These laws are content neutral; they only regulate information that was illegally obtained; they do not restrict republication of what is already in the public domain; they impose no special burdens upon the media; they have a scienter requirement to provide fair warning; and they promote the privacy and free speech of those using cellular telephones. It is hard to imagine a more narrowly tailored prohibition of the disclosure of illegally intercepted communications, and it distorts our precedents to review these statutes under the often fatal standard of strict scrutiny. These laws therefore should be upheld if they further a substantial governmental interest unrelated to the suppression of free speech, and they do. Surely "the interest in individual privacy," at its narrowest must embrace the right to be free from surreptitious eavesdropping on, and involuntary broadcast of, our cellular telephone conversations. The Court subordinates that right, not to the claims of those who themselves wish to speak, but to the claims of those who wish to publish the intercepted conversations of others. Congress' effort to balance the above claim to privacy against a marginal claim to speak freely is thereby set at naught.

6. Conduct that Communicates

c. *When May the Government Regulate Conduct that Communicates?*

iii. Spending Money as Political Speech (casebook, p. 1113)

v. The Continuing Distinction Between Contributions and Expenditures (casebook, p. 1121)

Buckley v. Valeo and its progeny draw a distinction between laws restricting contributions, which are allowed, and laws restricting expenditures, which are deemed to violate the First Amendment. In Federal Election Commission v. Colorado Republican Federal Campaign Committee, the Court considered whether restrictions on coordinated expenditures by a political party violate the First Amendment.

FEDERAL ELECTION COMMISSION v. COLORADO
REPUBLICAN FEDERAL CAMPAIGN COMMITTEE
121 S. Ct. 2351 (2001)

Justice SOUTER delivered the opinion of the Court.

In Colorado Republican Federal Campaign Comm. v. Federal Election
Comm'n (1996) (Colorado I), we held that spending limits set by the Federal
Election Campaign Act were unconstitutional as applied to the Colorado Republican Party's independent expenditures in connection with a senatorial campaign. We remanded for consideration of the party's claim that all limits on
expenditures by a political party in connection with congressional campaigns are
facially unconstitutional and thus unenforceable even as to spending coordinated
with a candidate. Today we reject that facial challenge to the limits on parties'
coordinated expenditures.

I

We first examined the Federal Election Campaign Act of 1971 in Buckley v.
Valeo (1976) (per curiam), where we held that the Act's limitations on contributions to a candidate's election campaign were generally constitutional, but
that limitations on election expenditures were not. Later cases have respected
this line between contributing and spending. See, e.g., Nixon v. Shrink Missouri
Government PAC (2000).

The simplicity of the distinction is qualified, however, by the Act's provision
for a functional, not formal, definition of "contribution," which includes "expenditures made by any person in cooperation, consultation, or concert, with, or
at the request or suggestion of, a candidate, his authorized political committees,
or their agents," 2 U.S.C. § 441a(a)(7)(B)(i). Expenditures coordinated with a
candidate, that is, are contributions under the Act.

II

Spending for political ends and contributing to political candidates both fall
within the First Amendment's protection of speech and political association. But
ever since we first reviewed the 1971 Act, we have understood that limits on
political expenditures deserve closer scrutiny than restrictions on political contributions. Restraints on expenditures generally curb more expressive and
associational activity than limits on contributions do. A further reason for the
distinction is that limits on contributions are more clearly justified by a link to
political corruption than limits on other kinds of unlimited political spending are
(corruption being understood not only as quid pro quo agreements, but also as
undue influence on an officerholder's judgment, and the appearance of such
influence). At least this is so where the spending is not coordinated with a
candidate or his campaign.

The First Amendment line between spending and donating is easy to draw when it falls between independent expenditures by individuals or political action committees (PACs) without any candidate's approval (or wink or nod), and contributions in the form of cash gifts to candidates. But facts speak less clearly once the independence of the spending cannot be taken for granted, and money spent by an individual or PAC according to an arrangement with a candidate is therefore harder to classify. As already seen, Congress drew a functional, not a formal, line between contributions and expenditures when it provided that coordinated expenditures by individuals and nonparty groups are subject to the Act's contribution limits. In *Buckley*, the Court acknowledged Congress's functional classification, and observed that treating coordinated expenditures as contributions "prevent[s] attempts to circumvent the Act through prearranged or coordinated expenditures amounting to disguised contributions." *Buckley*, in fact, enhanced the significance of this functional treatment by striking down independent expenditure limits on First Amendment grounds while upholding limitations on contributions (by individuals and nonparty groups), as defined to include coordinated expenditures.

The issue is posed by two questions: does limiting coordinated spending impose a unique burden on parties, and is there reason to think that coordinated spending by a party would raise the risk of corruption posed when others spend in coordination with a candidate?

III

The Party's argument that its coordinated spending, like its independent spending, should be left free from restriction under the *Buckley* line of cases boils down to this: because a party's most important speech is aimed at electing candidates and is itself expressed through those candidates, any limit on party support for a candidate imposes a unique First Amendment burden. The point of organizing a party, the argument goes, is to run a successful candidate who shares the party's policy goals. Therefore, while a campaign contribution is only one of several ways that individuals and nonparty groups speak and associate politically, financial support of candidates is essential to the nature of political parties as we know them. And coordination with a candidate is a party's natural way of operating, not merely an option that can easily be avoided. Limitation of any party expenditure coordinated with a candidate, the Party contends, is therefore a serious, rather than incidental, imposition on the party's speech and associative purpose, and that justifies a stricter level of scrutiny than we have applied to analogous limits on individuals and nonparty groups.

The Government's argument for treating coordinated spending like contributions goes back to *Buckley*. There, the rationale for endorsing Congress's equation of coordinated expenditures and contributions was that the equation "prevent[s] attempts to circumvent the Act through prearranged or coordinated expenditures amounting to disguised contributions." The idea was that coordinated expenditures are as useful to the candidate as cash, and that such "disguised contributions" might be given "as a quid pro quo for improper commitments from the candidate" (in contrast to independent expenditures, which are poor sources of leverage for a spender because they might be duplicative or counterproductive from a candidate's point of view). In effect, therefore, *Buckley* subjected limits on coordinated expenditures by individuals and nonparty groups to the same scrutiny it applied to limits on their cash contributions. The standard of scrutiny requires the limit to be "'closely drawn' to match a 'sufficiently important interest,' . . . though the dollar amount of the limit need not be 'fine tun[ed].'"

The Government develops this rationale a step further in applying it here. Coordinated spending by a party should be limited not only because it is like a party contribution, but for a further reason. A party's right to make unlimited expenditures coordinated with a candidate would induce individual and other nonparty contributors to give to the party in order to finance coordinated spending for a favored candidate beyond the contribution limits binding on them. The Government points out that a degree of circumvention is occurring under present law (which allows unlimited independent spending and some coordinated spending). Individuals and nonparty groups who have reached the limit of direct contributions to a candidate give to a party with the understanding that the contribution to the party will produce increased party spending for the candidate's benefit. The Government argues that if coordinated spending were unlimited, circumvention would increase: because coordinated spending is as effective as direct contributions in supporting a candidate, an increased opportunity for coordinated spending would aggravate the use of a party to funnel money to a candidate from individuals and nonparty groups, who would thus bypass the contribution limits that *Buckley* upheld.

IV

Each of the competing positions is plausible at first blush. Our evaluation of the arguments, however, leads us to reject the Party's claim to suffer a burden unique in any way that should make a categorical difference under the First Amendment. On the other side, the Government's contentions are ultimately borne out by evidence, entitling it to prevail in its characterization of party coordinated spending as the functional equivalent of contributions.

There are two basic arguments here. The first turns on the relationship of a party to a candidate: a coordinated relationship between them so defines a party that it cannot function as such without coordinated spending, the object of which is a candidate's election. We think political history and political reality belie this argument. The second argument turns on the nature of a party as uniquely able to spend in ways that promote candidate success. We think that this argument is a double-edged sword, and one hardly limited to political parties.

The assertion that the party is so joined at the hip to candidates that most of its spending must necessarily be coordinated spending is a statement at odds with the history of nearly 30 years under the Act. It is well to remember that ever since the Act was amended in 1974, coordinated spending by a party committee in a given race has been limited by the provision challenged here (or its predecessor). There is no question about the closeness of candidates to parties and no doubt that the Act affected parties' roles and their exercise of power. But the political scientists who have weighed in on this litigation observe that "there is little evidence to suggest that coordinated party spending limits adopted by Congress have frustrated the ability of political parties to exercise their First Amendment rights to support their candidates," and that "[i]n reality, political parties are dominant players, second only to the candidates themselves, in federal elections." For the Party to claim after all these years of strictly limited coordinated spending that unlimited coordinated spending is essential to the nature and functioning of parties is in reality to assert just that "metaphysical identity" between freespending party and candidate that we could not accept in *Colorado I.*

There is a different weakness in the seemingly unexceptionable premise that parties are organized for the purpose of electing candidates, so that imposing on the way parties serve that function is uniquely burdensome. The fault here is not so much metaphysics as myopia, a refusal to see how the power of money actually works in the political structure. When we look directly at a party's function in getting and spending money, it would ignore reality to think that the party role is adequately described by speaking generally of electing particular candidates. The money parties spend comes from contributors with their own personal interests. PACs, for example, are frequent party contributors who (according to one of the Party's own experts) "do not pursue the same objectives in electoral politics," that parties do. PACs "are most concerned with advancing their narrow interest[s]" and therefore "provide support to candidates who share their views, regardless of party affiliation." In fact, many PACs naturally express their narrow interests by contributing to both parties during the same electoral cycle, and sometimes even directly to two competing candidates in the same election.

Parties are thus necessarily the instruments of some contributors whose object is not to support the party's message or to elect party candidates across the board, but rather to support a specific candidate for the sake of a position on one, narrow issue, or even to support any candidate who will be obliged to the contributors. The FEC's public records confirm that Federal Express's PAC (along with many others) contributed to both major parties in recent elections.

Parties thus perform functions more complex than simply electing candidates; whether they like it or not, they act as agents for spending on behalf of those who seek to produce obligated officeholders. It is this party role, which functionally unites parties with other self-interested political actors, that the Party

Expenditure Provision targets. This party role, accordingly, provides good reason to view limits on coordinated spending by parties through the same lens applied to such spending by donors, like PACs, that can use parties as conduits for contributions meant to place candidates under obligation.

3

Insofar as the Party suggests that its strong working relationship with candidates and its unique ability to speak in coordination with them should be taken into account in the First Amendment analysis, we agree. It is the accepted understanding that a party combines its members' power to speak by aggregating contributions and broadcasting messages more widely than individual contributors generally could afford to do, and the party marshals this power with greater sophistication than individuals generally could, using such mechanisms as speech coordinated with a candidate. In other words, the party is efficient in generating large sums to spend and in pinpointing effective ways to spend them.

It does not, however, follow from a party's efficiency in getting large sums and spending intelligently that limits on a party's coordinated spending should be scrutinized under an unusually high standard, and in fact any argument from sophistication and power would cut both ways. On the one hand, one can seek the benefit of stricter scrutiny of a law capping party coordinated spending by emphasizing the heavy burden imposed by limiting the most effective mechanism of sophisticated spending. And yet it is exactly this efficiency culminating in coordinated spending that (on the Government's view) places a party in a position to be used to circumvent contribution limits that apply to individuals and PACs, and thereby to exacerbate the threat of corruption and apparent corruption that those contribution limits are aimed at reducing. As a consequence, what the Party calls an unusual burden imposed by regulating its spending is not a simple premise for arguing for tighter scrutiny of limits on a party; it is the premise for a question pointing in the opposite direction. If the coordinated spending of other, less efficient and perhaps less practiced political actors can be limited consistently with the Constitution, why would the Constitution forbid regulation aimed at a party whose very efficiency in channeling benefits to candidates threatens to undermine the contribution (and hence coordinated spending) limits to which those others are unquestionably subject?

4

The preceding question assumes that parties enjoy a power and experience that sets them apart from other political spenders. But in fact the assumption is too crude. While parties command bigger spending budgets than most individuals, some individuals could easily rival party committees in spending. Rich political activists crop up, and the United States has known its Citizens Kane. Their money speaks loudly, too, and they are therefore burdened by restrictions on its use just as parties are. And yet they are validly subject to coordinated spending limits, which may amass bigger treasuries than most party members can spare for politics.

Just as rich donors, media executives, and PACs have the means to speak as loudly as parties do, they would also have the capacity to work effectively in tandem with a candidate, just as a party can do. While a candidate has no way of coordinating spending with every contributor, there is nothing hard about coordinating with someone with a fortune to donate, any more than a candidate would have difficulty in coordinating spending with an inner circle of personal political associates or with his own family. Yet all of them are subject to coordinated spending limits upheld in *Buckley*. A party, indeed, is now like some of these political actors in yet another way: in its right under *Colorado I* to spend money in support of a candidate without legal limit so long as it spends independently. A party may spend independently every cent it can raise wherever it thinks its candidate will shine, on every subject and any viewpoint.

A party is not, therefore, in a unique position. It is in the same position as some individuals and PACs, as to whom coordinated spending limits have already been held valid and, indeed, a party is better off, for a party has the special privilege the others do not enjoy, of making coordinated expenditures up to the limit of the Party Expenditure Provision.

5

The Party's arguments for being treated differently from other political actors subject to limitation on political spending under the Act do not pan out. Despite decades of limitation on coordinated spending, parties have not been rendered useless. In reality, parties continue to organize to elect candidates, and also function for the benefit of donors whose object is to place candidates under obligation, a fact that parties cannot escape. Indeed, parties' capacity to concentrate power to elect is the very capacity that apparently opens them to exploitation as channels for circumventing contribution and coordinated spending limits binding on other political players. And some of these players could marshal the same power and sophistication for the same electoral objectives as political parties themselves.

We accordingly apply to a party's coordinated spending limitation the same scrutiny we have applied to the other political actors, that is, scrutiny appropriate for a contribution limit, enquiring whether the restriction is "closely drawn" to match what we have recognized as the "sufficiently important" government interest in combating political corruption.

B

Since there is no recent experience with unlimited coordinated spending, the question is whether experience under the present law confirms a serious threat of abuse from the unlimited coordinated party spending as the Government contends. It clearly does. Despite years of enforcement of the challenged limits, substantial evidence demonstrates how candidates, donors, and parties test the limits of the current law, and it shows beyond serious doubt how contribution limits would be eroded if inducement to circumvent them were enhanced by declaring parties' coordinated spending wide open.

We hold that a party's coordinated expenditures, unlike expenditures truly independent, may be restricted to minimize circumvention of contribution limits.

Justice THOMAS, with whom Justice SCALIA and Justice KENNEDY join, and with whom the Chief Justice joins as to Part II, dissenting.

The Party Expenditure Provision severely limits the amount of money that a national or state committee of a political party can spend in coordination with its own candidate for the Senate or House of Representatives. Because this provision sweeps too broadly, interferes with the party-candidate relationship, and has not been proved necessary to combat corruption, I respectfully dissent.

I

As an initial matter, I continue to believe that Buckley v. Valeo (1976) (per curiam), should be overruled. "Political speech is the primary object of First Amendment protection," and it is the lifeblood of a self-governing people. I remain baffled that this Court has extended the most generous First Amendment safeguards to filing lawsuits, wearing profane jackets, and exhibiting drive-in movies with nudity, but has offered only tepid protection to the core speech and associational rights that our Founders sought to defend.

II

We need not, however, overrule *Buckley* and apply strict scrutiny in order to hold the Party Expenditure Provision unconstitutional. Even under *Buckley*, which described the requisite scrutiny as "exacting" and "rigorous," the regulation cannot pass constitutional muster. In practice, *Buckley* scrutiny has meant that restrictions on contributions by individuals and political committees do not violate the First Amendment so long as they are "closely drawn" to match a "sufficiently important" government interest, but that restrictions on independent expenditures are constitutionally invalid. The rationale for this distinction between contributions and independent expenditures has been that, whereas ceilings on contributions by individuals and political committees "entai[l] only a marginal restriction" on First Amendment interests, limitations on independent expenditures "impose significantly more severe restrictions on protected freedoms of political expression and association."

A

The Court notes this existing rationale and attempts simply to treat coordinated expenditures by political parties as equivalent to contributions by individuals and political committees. Thus, at least implicitly, the Court draws two conclusions: coordinated expenditures are no different from contributions, and political parties are no different from individuals and political committees. Both conclusions are flawed.

1

The Court considers a coordinated expenditure to be an "'expenditur[e] made by any person in cooperation, consultation, or concert, with, or at the request or suggestion of, a candidate, his authorized political committees, or their agents.'" This definition covers a broad array of conduct, some of which is akin to an independent expenditure. At one extreme, to be sure, are outlays that are "virtually indistinguishable from simple contributions." An example would be "a donation of money with direct payment of a candidate's media bills." But toward the other end of the spectrum are expenditures that largely resemble, and should be entitled to the same protection as, independent expenditures. Take, for example, a situation in which the party develops a television advertising campaign touting a candidate's record on education, and the party simply "consult[s]" with the candidate on which time slot the advertisement should run for maximum effectiveness. I see no constitutional difference between this expenditure and a purely independent one. In the language of *Buckley*, the advertising campaign is not a mere "general expression of support for the candidate and his views," but a communication of "the underlying basis for the support." It is not just "symbolic expression," but a clear manifestation of the party's most fundamental political views. By restricting such speech, the Party Expenditure Provision undermines parties' "freedom to discuss candidates and issues," and cannot be reconciled with our campaign finance jurisprudence.

2

Even if I were to ignore the breadth of the statutory text, and to assume that all coordinated expenditures are functionally equivalent to contributions, I still would strike down the Party Expenditure Provision. The source of the "contribution" at issue is a political party, not an individual or a political committee, as in *Buckley* and *Shrink Missouri*. Restricting contributions by individuals and political committees may, under *Buckley*, entail only a "marginal restriction," but the same cannot be said about limitations on political parties.

Political parties and their candidates are "inextricably intertwined" in the conduct of an election. A party nominates its candidate; a candidate often is identified by party affiliation throughout the election and on the ballot; and a party's public image is largely defined by what its candidates say and do. Most importantly, a party's success or failure depends in large part on whether its candidates get elected. Because of this unity of interest, it is natural for a party and its candidate to work together and consult with one another during the course of the election.

The Court's holding presents an additional First Amendment problem. Because of the close relationship between parties and candidates, lower courts will face a difficult, if not insurmountable, task in trying to determine whether particular party expenditures are in fact coordinated or independent. As the American Civil Liberties Union points out, "[e]ven if such an inquiry is feasible, it inevitably would involve an intrusive and constitutionally troubling investigation of the inner workings of political parties."

B

But even if I were to view parties' coordinated expenditures as akin to contributions by individuals and political committees, I still would hold the Party Expenditure Provision constitutionally invalid. Under *Shrink Missouri*, a contribution limit is constitutional only if the Government demonstrates that the regulation is "closely drawn" to match a "sufficiently important interest." In this case, there is no question that the Government has asserted a sufficient interest, that of preventing corruption. The question is whether the Government has demonstrated both that coordinated expenditures by parties give rise to corruption and that the restriction is "closely drawn" to curb this corruption. I believe it has not. As this Court made clear just last Term, "[w]e have never accepted mere conjecture as adequate to carry a First Amendment burden." *Shrink Missouri*.

Considering that we have never upheld an expenditure limitation against political parties, I would posit that substantial evidence is necessary to justify the infringement of parties' First Amendment interests. But we need not accept this high evidentiary standard to strike down the Party Expenditure Provision for want of evidence. Under the least demanding evidentiary requirement, the Government has failed to carry its burden, for it has presented no evidence at all of corruption or the perception of corruption. The Government does not, and indeed cannot, point to any congressional findings suggesting that the Party Expenditure Provision is necessary, or even helpful, in reducing corruption or the perception of corruption. In fact, this Court has recognized that "Congress wrote the Party Expenditure Provision not so much because of a special concern about the potentially 'corrupting' effect of party expenditures, but rather for the constitutionally insufficient purpose of reducing what it saw as wasteful and excessive campaign spending."

Even if the Government had presented evidence that the Party Expenditure Provision affects corruption, the statute still would be unconstitutional, because there are better tailored alternatives for addressing the corruption. In addition to bribery laws and disclosure laws, the Government has two options that would not entail the restriction of political parties' First Amendment rights. First, the Government could enforce the earmarking rule of 2 U.S.C. § 441a(a)(8), under which contributions that "are in any way earmarked or otherwise directed through an intermediary or conduit to [a] candidate" are treated as contributions to the candidate. Vigilant enforcement of this provision is a precise response to the Court's circumvention concerns.

In any event, there is a second, well-tailored option for combating corruption that does not entail the reduction of parties' First Amendment freedoms. The heart of the Court's circumvention argument is that, whereas individuals can donate only $2,000 to a candidate in a given election cycle, they can donate $20,000 to the national committees of a political party, an amount that is allegedly large enough to corrupt the candidate. If indeed $20,000 is enough to corrupt a candidate (an assumption that seems implausible on its face and is, in any event, unsupported by any evidence), the proper response is to lower the cap. That way, the speech restriction is directed at the source of the alleged corruption—the individual donor—and not the party.

In my view, it makes no sense to contravene a political party's core First Amendment rights because of what a third party might unlawfully try to do. Instead of broadly restricting political parties' speech, the Government should have pursued better-tailored alternatives for combating the alleged corruption.

D. *What Places Are Available for Speech?*

1.   Government Properties and Speech

d.   *Designated (Limited) Public Forums (casebook, p. 1146)*

In Good News Club v. Milford Central School, 121 S. Ct. ___ (June 11, 2001), the Court considered the constitutionality of an elementary school's exclusion of a group's using school property after school for religious activities including prayer and Bible study. The case is presented in Chapter 10.

There were two parts to the Court's holding. First, the Court ruled that excluding the group violated the Speech Clause of the First Amendment. The Court said that the parties in the case had accepted that by opening its facilities the school had created a "limited public forum." The Court said that "[w]hen the State establishes a limited public forum, the State is not required to and does not allow persons to engage in every type of speech. The State may be justified 'in reserving [its forum] for certain groups or for the discussion of certain topics.' The State's power to restrict speech, however, is not without limits. The restriction must not discriminate against speech on the basis of viewpoint, and the restriction must be 'reasonable in light of the purpose served by the forum.'" The Court found that excluding the religious speech was impermissible viewpoint discrimination. Second, the Court concluded that allowing the religious group to use the property on the same terms as other community groups would not violate the Establishment Clause of the First Amendment.

The entire case, both the speech and religion discussions, is presented in Chapter 10.

3. Speech in Authoritarian Environments: Military, Prisons, and Schools

b. *Prisons (casebook, p. 1166)*

SHAW v. MURPHY, 121 S. Ct. 1475 (2001).   Justice THOMAS delivered the opinion of the Court.

Under our decision in Turner v. Safley (1987), restrictions on prisoners' communications to other inmates are constitutional if the restrictions are "reasonably related to legitimate penological interests." In this case, we are asked to decide whether prisoners possess a First Amendment right to provide legal assistance that enhances the protections otherwise available under *Turner*. We hold that they do not.

While respondent Kevin Murphy was incarcerated at the Montana State Prison, he served as an "inmate law clerk," providing legal assistance to fellow prisoners. Upon learning that inmate Pat Tracy had been charged with assaulting Correctional Officer Glen Galle, Murphy decided to assist Tracy with his defense. Prison rules prohibited Murphy's assignment to the case, but he nonetheless investigated the assault [and sent a letter to the inmate containing legal advice].

In accordance with prison policy, prison officials intercepted the letter, and petitioner Robert Shaw, an officer in the maximum-security unit, reviewed it. Based on the accusations against Officer Galle, Shaw cited Murphy for violations of the prison's rules prohibiting insolence, interference with due process hearings, and conduct that disrupts or interferes with the security and orderly operation of the institution. After a hearing, Murphy was found guilty of violating the first two prohibitions. The hearings officer sanctioned him by imposing a suspended sentence of 10 days' detention and issuing demerits that could affect his custody level.

[T]he Court of Appeals [ruled in favor Murphy and ruled] that inmate-to-inmate correspondence that includes legal assistance would receive more First Amendment protection than correspondence without any legal assistance. We conclude that there is no such special right.

Because *Turner* provides the test for evaluating prisoners' First Amendment challenges, the issue before us is whether *Turner* permits an increase in constitutional protection whenever a prisoner's communication includes legal advice. We conclude that it does not. To increase the constitutional protection based upon the content of a communication first requires an assessment of the value of that content. But the *Turner* test, by its terms, simply does not accommodate valuations of content. On the contrary, the *Turner* factors concern only the relationship between the asserted penological interests and the prison regulation.

Moreover, under *Turner* and its predecessors, prison officials are to remain the primary arbiters of the problems that arise in prison management. If courts were permitted to enhance constitutional protection based on their assessments of the content of the particular communications, courts would be in a position to assume a greater role in decisions affecting prison administration. Seeking to avoid "'unnecessarily perpetuat[ing] the involvement of the federal courts in affairs of prison administration,'" we reject an alteration of the *Turner* analysis that would entail additional federal-court oversight.

Finally, even if we were to consider giving special protection to particular kinds of speech based upon content, we would not do so for speech that includes legal advice. Augmenting First Amendment protection for inmate legal advice would undermine prison officials' ability to address the "complex and intractable" problems of prison administration. Although supervised inmate legal assistance programs may serve valuable ends, it is "indisputable" that inmate law clerks "are sometimes a menace to prison discipline" and that prisoners have an "acknowledged propensity . . . to abuse both the giving and the seeking of [legal] assistance." Prisoners have used legal correspondence as a means for passing contraband and communicating instructions on how to manufacture drugs or weapons.

We thus decline to cloak the provision of legal assistance with any First Amendment protection above and beyond the protection normally accorded prisoners' speech. Instead, the proper constitutional test is the one we set forth in *Turner*. Irrespective of whether the correspondence contains legal advice, the constitutional analysis is the same.

Chapter 10

First Amendment: Religion

C. The Establishment Clause

4. Religious Speech and the First Amendment

a. Religious Group Access to School Facilities (casebook, p. 1282)

As the casebook indicates, in a series of cases, the Supreme Court has held that if the government opens its facilities to community or student groups, it cannot exclude religious groups. The Court has held that such an exclusion violates the speech rights of the religious group because it is being denied access entirely based on the religious content of its expression. Moreover, the Court has ruled that allowing a religious group the same access as non-religious groups does not violate the Establishment Clause of the First Amendment. In Good News Club v. Milford, the Court applied this principle to a religious group that wanted to use elementary school facilities immediately after school.

GOOD NEWS CLUB v. MILFORD CENTRAL SCHOOL
121 S. Ct. 2093 (2001)

Justice THOMAS delivered the opinion of the Court.

This case presents two questions. The first question is whether Milford Central School violated the free speech rights of the Good News Club when it excluded the Club from meeting after hours at the school. The second question is whether any such violation is justified by Milford's concern that permitting the Club's activities would violate the Establishment Clause. We conclude that Milford's restriction violates the Club's free speech rights and that no Establishment Clause concern justifies that violation.

I

The State of New York authorizes local school boards to adopt regulations governing the use of their school facilities. In 1992, respondent Milford Central School (Milford) enacted a community use policy adopting seven purposes for which its building could be used after school. Two of the stated purposes are relevant here. First, district residents may use the school for "instruction in any branch of education, learning or the arts." Second, the school is available for "social, civic and recreational meetings and entertainment events, and other uses pertaining to the welfare of the community, provided that such uses shall be nonexclusive and shall be opened to the general public."

Stephen and Darleen Fournier reside within Milford's district and therefore are eligible to use the school's facilities as long as their proposed use is approved by the school. Together they are sponsors of the local Good News Club, a private Christian organization for children ages 6 to 12. Pursuant to Milford's policy, in September 1996 the Fourniers submitted a request to Dr. Robert McGruder, interim superintendent of the district, in which they sought permission to hold the Club's weekly afterschool meetings in the school cafeteria. The next month, McGruder formally denied the Fourniers' request on the ground that the proposed use—to have "a fun time of singing songs, hearing a Bible lesson and memorizing scripture," was "the equivalent of religious worship." According to McGruder, the community use policy, which prohibits use "by any individual or organization for religious purposes," foreclosed the Club's activities. In February 1997, the Milford Board of Education adopted a resolution rejecting the Club's request to use Milford's facilities "for the purpose of conducting religious instruction and Bible study."

II

The standards that we apply to determine whether a State has unconstitutionally excluded a private speaker from use of a public forum depend on the nature of the forum. See Perry Ed. Assn. v. Perry Local Educators' Assn. (1983). If the forum is a traditional or open public forum, the State's restrictions on speech are subject to stricter scrutiny than are restrictions in a limited public forum. Because the parties have agreed that Milford created a limited public forum when it opened its facilities in 1992, we simply will assume that Milford operates a limited public forum.

When the State establishes a limited public forum, the State is not required to and does not allow persons to engage in every type of speech. The State may be justified "in reserving [its forum] for certain groups or for the discussion of certain topics." Rosenberger v. Rector and Visitors of Univ. of Va. (1995). The State's power to restrict speech, however, is not without limits. The restriction must not discriminate against speech on the basis of viewpoint, and the restriction must be "reasonable in light of the purpose served by the forum."

III

Applying this test, we first address whether the exclusion constituted viewpoint discrimination. We are guided in our analysis by two of our prior opinions, *Lamb's Chapel* and *Rosenberger*. In *Lamb's Chapel*, we held that a school district violated the Free Speech Clause of the First Amendment when it excluded a private group from presenting films at the school based solely on the films' discussions of family values from a religious perspective. Likewise, in *Rosenberger*, we held that a university's refusal to fund a student publication because the publication addressed issues from a religious perspective violated the Free Speech Clause. Concluding that Milford's exclusion of the Good News Club based on its religious nature is indistinguishable from the exclusions in these cases, we hold that the exclusion constitutes viewpoint discrimination. Because the restriction is viewpoint discriminatory, we need not decide whether it is unreasonable in light of the purposes served by the forum.

Milford has opened its limited public forum to activities that serve a variety of purposes, including events "pertaining to the welfare of the community." Milford interprets its policy to permit discussions of subjects such as child rearing, and of "the development of character and morals from a religious perspective." For example, this policy would allow someone to use Aesop's Fables to teach children moral values. Additionally, a group could sponsor a debate on whether there should be a constitutional amendment to permit prayer in public schools, and the Boy Scouts could meet "to influence a boy's character, development and spiritual growth." In short, any group that "promote[s] the moral and character development of children" is eligible to use the school building.

Just as there is no question that teaching morals and character development to children is a permissible purpose under Milford's policy, it is clear that the Club teaches morals and character development to children. For example, no one disputes that the Club instructs children to overcome feelings of jealousy, to treat others well regardless of how they treat the children, and to be obedient, even if it does so in a nonsecular way. Nonetheless, because Milford found the Club's activities to be religious in nature—"the equivalent of religious instruction itself," it excluded the Club from use of its facilities.

Applying *Lamb's Chapel*, we find it quite clear that Milford engaged in viewpoint discrimination when it excluded the Club from the afterschool forum. [T]he exclusion of the Good News Club's activities, like the exclusion of Lamb's Chapel's films, constitutes unconstitutional viewpoint discrimination.

IV

Milford argues that, even if its restriction constitutes viewpoint discrimination, its interest in not violating the Establishment Clause outweighs the Club's interest in gaining equal access to the school's facilities. In other words, according to Milford, its restriction was required to avoid violating the Establishment Clause. We disagree.

We have said that a state interest in avoiding an Establishment Clause violation "may be characterized as compelling," and therefore may justify content-based discrimination. Widmar v. Vincent (1981). However, it is not clear whether a State's interest in avoiding an Establishment Clause violation would justify viewpoint discrimination. We need not, however, confront the issue in this case, because we conclude that the school has no valid Establishment Clause interest.

We rejected Establishment Clause defenses similar to Milford's in two previous free speech cases, *Lamb's Chapel* and *Widmar*. In particular, in *Lamb's Chapel*, we explained that "[t]he showing of th[e] film series would not have been during school hours, would not have been sponsored by the school, and would have been open to the public, not just to church members." Accordingly, we found that "there would have been no realistic danger that the community would think that the District was endorsing religion or any particular creed." Likewise, in *Widmar*, where the university's forum was already available to other groups, this Court concluded that there was no Establishment Clause problem.

The Establishment Clause defense fares no better in this case. As in *Lamb's Chapel*, the Club's meetings were held after school hours, not sponsored by the school, and open to any student who obtained parental consent, not just to Club members. As in *Widmar*, Milford made its forum available to other organizations. The Club's activities are materially indistinguishable from those in *Lamb's Chapel* and *Widmar*. Thus, Milford's reliance on the Establishment Clause is unavailing.

Milford attempts to distinguish *Lamb's Chapel* and *Widmar* by emphasizing that Milford's policy involves elementary school children. According to Milford, children will perceive that the school is endorsing the Club and will feel coercive pressure to participate, because the Club's activities take place on school grounds, even though they occur during nonschool hours. This argument is unpersuasive.

First, we have held that "a significant factor in upholding governmental programs in the face of Establishment Clause attack is their neutrality towards religion." Milford's implication that granting access to the Club would do damage to the neutrality principle defies logic. For the "guarantee of neutrality is respected, not offended, when the government, following neutral criteria and evenhanded policies, extends benefits to recipients whose ideologies and viewpoints, including religious ones, are broad and diverse." The Good News Club seeks nothing more than to be treated neutrally and given access to speak about the same topics as are other groups. Because allowing the Club to speak on school grounds would ensure neutrality, not threaten it, Milford faces an uphill battle in arguing that the Establishment Clause compels it to exclude the Good News Club.

Second, to the extent we consider whether the community would feel coercive pressure to engage in the Club's activities, the relevant community would be the parents, not the elementary school children. It is the parents who choose whether their children will attend the Good News Club meetings. Because the children cannot attend without their parents' permission, they cannot be coerced into engaging in the Good News Club's religious activities. Milford does not suggest that the parents of elementary school children would be confused about whether the school was endorsing religion. Nor do we believe that such an argument could be reasonably advanced.

Third, whatever significance we may have assigned in the Establishment Clause context to the suggestion that elementary school children are more impressionable than adults, we have never extended our Establishment Clause jurisprudence to foreclose private religious conduct during nonschool hours merely because it takes place on school premises where elementary school children may be present. Here, where the school facilities are being used for a nonschool function and there is no government sponsorship of the Club's activities, [there is no Establishment Clause violation].

Fourth, even if we were to consider the possible misperceptions by schoolchildren in deciding whether Milford's permitting the Club's activities would violate the Establishment Clause, the facts of this case simply do not support Milford's conclusion. There is no evidence that young children are permitted to loiter outside classrooms after the schoolday has ended. Surely even young children are aware of events for which their parents must sign permission forms. The meetings were held in a combined high school resource room and middle school special education room, not in an elementary school classroom. The instructors are not schoolteachers. And the children in the group are not all the same age as in the normal classroom setting; their ages range from 6 to 12. In sum, these circumstances simply do not support the theory that small children would perceive endorsement here.

Finally, even if we were to inquire into the minds of schoolchildren in this case, we cannot say the danger that children would misperceive the endorsement of religion is any greater than the danger that they would perceive a hostility toward the religious viewpoint if the Club were excluded from the public forum. This concern is particularly acute given the reality that Milford's building is not used only for elementary school children. Students, from kindergarten through the 12th grade, all attend school in the same building. There may be as many, if not more, upperclassmen than elementary school children who occupy the school after hours. For that matter, members of the public writ large are permitted in the school after hours pursuant to the community use policy. Any bystander could conceivably be aware of the school's use policy and its exclusion of the Good News Club, and could suffer as much from viewpoint discrimination as elementary school children could suffer from perceived endorsement.

We cannot operate, as Milford would have us do, under the assumption that any risk that small children would perceive endorsement should counsel in favor of excluding the Club's religious activity. We decline to employ Establishment Clause jurisprudence using a modified heckler's veto, in which a group's religious activity can be proscribed on the basis of what the youngest members of the audience might misperceive. There are countervailing constitutional concerns related to rights of other individuals in the community. In this case, those countervailing concerns are the free speech rights of the Club and its members. And, we have already found that those rights have been violated, not merely perceived to have been violated, by the school's actions toward the Club.

V

When Milford denied the Good News Club access to the school's limited public forum on the ground that the Club was religious in nature, it discriminated against the Club because of its religious viewpoint in violation of the Free Speech Clause of the First Amendment. Because Milford has not raised a valid Establishment Clause claim, we do not address the question whether such a claim could excuse Milford's viewpoint discrimination.

Justice SCALIA, concurring.

I join the Court's opinion but write separately to explain further my views on two issues.

I

First, I join Part IV of the Court's opinion, regarding the Establishment Clause issue, with the understanding that its consideration of coercive pressure, and perceptions of endorsement, "to the extent" that the law makes such factors relevant, is consistent with the belief (which I hold) that in this case that extent is zero. As to coercive pressure: Physical coercion is not at issue here; and so-called "peer pressure," if it can even been considered coercion, is, when it arises from private activities, one of the attendant consequences of a freedom of association that is constitutionally protected. What is at play here is not coercion, but the compulsion of ideas—and the private right to exert and receive that compulsion (or to have one's children receive it) is protected by the Free Speech and Free Exercise Clauses, not banned by the Establishment Clause. A priest has as much liberty to proselytize as a patriot.

As to endorsement, I have previously written that "[r]eligious expression cannot violate the Establishment Clause where it (1) is purely private and (2) occurs in a traditional or designated public forum, publicly announced and open to all on equal terms." The same is true of private speech that occurs in a limited public forum, publicly announced, whose boundaries are not drawn to favor religious groups but instead permit a cross-section of uses. In that context, which is this case, "erroneous conclusions [about endorsement] do not count."

II

Second, since we have rejected the only reason that respondent gave for excluding the Club's speech from a forum that clearly included it (the forum was opened to any "us[e] pertaining to the welfare of the community,") I do not suppose it matters whether the exclusion is characterized as viewpoint or subject-matter discrimination. Lacking any legitimate reason for excluding the Club's speech from its forum—"because it's religious" will not do, respondent would seem to fail First Amendment scrutiny regardless of how its action is characterized. Even subject-matter limits must at least be "reasonable in light of the purpose served by the forum." But I agree, in any event, that respondent did discriminate on the basis of viewpoint.

Justice BREYER, concurring in part.

I agree with the Court's conclusion and join its opinion to the extent that they are consistent with the following three observations. First, the government's "neutrality" in respect to religion is one, but only one, of the considerations relevant to deciding whether a public school's policy violates the Establishment Clause. As this Court previously has indicated, a child's perception that the school has endorsed a particular religion or religion in general may also prove critically important. Today's opinion does not purport to change that legal principle.

Second, the critical Establishment Clause question here may well prove to be whether a child, participating in the Good News Club's activities, could reasonably perceive the school's permission for the club to use its facilities as an endorsement of religion. The time of day, the age of the children, the nature of the meetings, and other specific circumstances are relevant in helping to determine whether, in fact, the Club "so dominate[s]" the "forum" that, in the children's minds, "a formal policy of equal access is transformed into a demonstration of approval."

Third, the Court cannot fully answer the Establishment Clause question this case raises, given its procedural posture. The specific legal action that brought this case to the Court of Appeals was the District Court's decision to grant Milford Central School's motion for summary judgment. The Court of Appeals affirmed the grant of summary judgment. We now hold that the school was not entitled to summary judgment, either in respect to the Free Speech or the Establishment Clause issue. Our holding must mean that, viewing the disputed facts (including facts about the children's perceptions) favorably to the Club (the nonmoving party), the school has not shown an Establishment Clause violation. To deny one party's motion for summary judgment, however, is not to grant summary judgment for the other side. There may be disputed "genuine issue[s]" of "material fact," particularly about how a reasonable child participant would understand the school's role. The Court's invocation of what is missing from the record and its assumptions about what is present in the record only confirm that both parties, if they so desire, should have a fair opportunity to fill the evidentiary gap in light of today's opinion.

Justice STEVENS, dissenting.

The Milford Central School has invited the public to use its facilities for educational and recreational purposes, but not for "religious purposes." Speech for "religious purposes" may reasonably be understood to encompass three different categories. First, there is religious speech that is simply speech about a particular topic from a religious point of view. The film in Lamb's Chapel v. Center Moriches Union Free School Dist. (1993), illustrates this category. Second, there is religious speech that amounts to worship, or its equivalent. Our decision in Widmar v. Vincent (1981), concerned such speech. Third, there is an intermediate category that is aimed principally at proselytizing or inculcating belief in a particular religious faith.

A public entity may not generally exclude even religious worship from an open public forum. Similarly, a public entity that creates a limited public forum for the discussion of certain specified topics may not exclude a speaker simply because she approaches those topics from a religious point of view. But, while a public entity may not censor speech about an authorized topic based on the point of view expressed by the speaker, it has broad discretion to "preserve the property under its control for the use to which it is lawfully dedicated." Greer v. Spock (1976). The novel question that this case presents concerns the constitutionality of a public school's attempt to limit the scope of a public forum it has created. More specifically, the question is whether a school can, consistently with the First Amendment, create a limited public forum that admits the first type of religious speech without allowing the other two.

Distinguishing speech from a religious viewpoint, on the one hand, from religious proselytizing, on the other, is comparable to distinguishing meetings to discuss political issues from meetings whose principal purpose is to recruit new members to join a political organization. If a school decides to authorize after school discussions of current events in its classrooms, it may not exclude people from expressing their views simply because it dislikes their particular political opinions. But must it therefore allow organized political groups—for example, the Democratic Party, the Libertarian Party, or the Ku Klux Klan—to hold meetings, the principal purpose of which is not to discuss the current-events topic from their own unique point of view but rather to recruit others to join their respective groups? I think not. Such recruiting meetings may introduce divisiveness and tend to separate young children into cliques that undermine the school's educational mission.

School officials may reasonably believe that evangelical meetings designed to convert children to a particular religious faith pose the same risk. And, just as a school may allow meetings to discuss current events from a political perspective without also allowing organized political recruitment, so too can a school allow discussion of topics such as moral development from a religious (or nonre-ligious) perspective without thereby opening its forum to religious proselytizing or worship.

The particular limitation of the forum at issue in this case is one that prohibits the use of the school's facilities for "religious purposes." It is clear that, by "re-ligious purposes," the school district did not intend to exclude all speech from a religious point of view. Instead, it sought only to exclude religious speech whose principal goal is to "promote the gospel." In other words, the school sought to allow the first type of religious speech while excluding the second and third types. As long as this is done in an even handed manner, I see no constitutional violation in such an effort. The line between the various categories of religious speech may be difficult to draw, but I think that the distinctions are valid, and that a school, particularly an elementary school, must be permitted to draw them.

Justice SOUTER, with whom Justice GINSBURG joins, dissenting.

I

This case, like *Lamb's Chapel*, properly raises no issue about the reasonableness of Milford's criteria for restricting the scope of its designated public forum. Milford has opened school property for, among other things, "instruction in any branch of education, learning or the arts" and for "social, civic and recreational meetings and entertainment events and other uses pertaining to the welfare of the community, provided that such uses shall be nonexclusive and shall be opened to the general public." But Milford has done this subject to the restric-tion that "[s]chool premises shall not be used . . . for religious purposes." As the District Court stated, Good News did "not object to the reasonableness of [Mil-ford]'s policy that prohibits the use of [its] facilities for religious purposes."

The sole question before the District Court was, therefore, whether, in refusing to allow Good News's intended use, Milford was misapplying its unchallenged restriction in a way that amounted to imposing a viewpoint-based restriction on what could be said or done by a group entitled to use the forum for an educational, civic, or other permitted purpose. The question was whether Good News was being disqualified when it merely sought to use the school property the same way that the Milford Boy and Girl Scouts and the 4-H Club did. The District Court held on the basis of undisputed facts that Good News's activity was essentially unlike the presentation of views on secular issues from a religious standpoint held to be protected in *Lamb's Chapel*, and was instead activity precluded by Milford's unchallenged policy against religious use, even under the narrowest definition of that term.

Good News's classes open and close with prayer. In a sample lesson con-sidered by the District Court, children are instructed that "[t]he Bible tells us how we can have our sins forgiven by receiving the Lord Jesus Christ. It tells us how to live to please Him. . . . If you have received the Lord Jesus as your Saviour from sin, you belong to God's special group—His family." The lesson plan instructs the teacher to "lead a child to Christ," and, when reading a Bible verse, to "[e]mphasize that this verse is from the Bible, God's Word" and is "important—and true—because God said it." The lesson further exhorts the teacher to "[b]e sure to give an opportunity for the 'unsaved' children in your class to respond to the Gospel" and cautions against "neglect[ing] this responsibility."

It is beyond question that Good News intends to use the public school premises not for the mere discussion of a subject from a particular, Christian point of view, but for an evangelical service of worship calling children to commit themselves in an act of Christian conversion. The majority avoids this reality only by resorting to the bland and general characterization of Good News's activity as "teaching of morals and character, from a religious standpoint." If the majority's statement ignores reality, as it surely does, then today's holding may be understood only in equally generic terms. Otherwise, indeed, this case would stand for the remarkable proposition that any public school opened for civic meetings must be opened for use as a church, synagogue, or mosque.

II

I also respectfully dissent from the majority's refusal to remand on all other issues, insisting instead on acting as a court of first instance in reviewing Milford's claim that it would violate the Establishment Clause to grant Good News's application. Milford raised this claim to demonstrate a compelling interest for saying no to Good News, even on the erroneous assumption that *Lamb's Chapel*'s public forum analysis would otherwise require Milford to say yes. Whereas the District Court and Court of Appeals resolved this case entirely on the ground that Milford's actions did not offend the First Amendment's Speech Clause, the majority now sees fit to rule on the application of the Establishment Clause, in derogation of this Court's proper role as a court of review.

The Court's usual insistence on resisting temptations to convert itself into a trial court and on remaining a court of review is not any mere procedural nicety, and my objection to turning us into a district court here does not hinge on a preference for immutable procedural rules. Respect for our role as a reviewing court rests, rather, on recognizing that this Court can often learn a good deal from considering how a district court and a court of appeals have worked their way through a difficult issue. It rests on recognizing that an issue as first conceived may come to be seen differently as a case moves through trial and appeal; we are most likely to contribute something of value if we act with the benefit of whatever refinement may come in the course of litigation. And our customary refusal to become a trial court reflects the simple fact that this Court cannot develop a record as well as a trial court can. If I were a trial judge, for example, I would balk at deciding on summary judgment whether an Establishment Clause violation would occur here without having statements of undisputed facts or uncontradicted affidavits showing, for example, whether Good News conducts its instruction at the same time as school-sponsored extracurricular and athletic activities conducted by school staff and volunteers, whether any other community groups use school facilities immediately after classes end and how many students participate in those groups, and the extent to which Good News, with 28 students in its membership, may "dominate the forum" in a way that heightens the perception of official endorsement. We will never know these facts.

Of course, I am in no better position than the majority to perform an Establishment Clause analysis in the first instance. Like the majority, I lack the benefit that development in the District Court and Court of Appeals might provide, and like the majority I cannot say for sure how complete the record may be. I can, however, speak to the doubtful underpinnings of the majority's conclusion.

This Court has accepted the independent obligation to obey the Establishment Clause as sufficiently compelling to satisfy strict scrutiny under the First Amendment. Milford's actions would offend the Establishment Clause if they carried the message of endorsing religion under the circumstances, as viewed by a reasonable observer. The majority concludes that such an endorsement effect is out of the question in Milford's case, because the context here is "materially indistinguishable" from the facts in *Lamb's Chapel* and *Widmar*. In fact, the majority is in no position to say that, for the principal grounds on which we based our Establishment Clause holdings in those cases are clearly absent here.

In *Widmar*, we held that the Establishment Clause did not bar a religious student group from using a public university's meeting space for worship as well as discussion. As for the reasonable observers who might perceive government endorsement of religion, we pointed out that the forum was used by university students, who "are, of course, young adults," and, as such, "are less impressionable than younger students and should be able to appreciate that the University's policy is one of neutrality toward religion." To the same effect, we remarked that the "large number of groups meeting on campus" negated "any reasonable inference of University support from the mere fact of a campus meeting place." Not only was the forum "available to a broad class of nonreligious as well as religious speakers," but there were, in fact, over 100 recognized student groups at the University, and an "absence of empirical evidence that religious groups [would] dominate [the University's] open forum."

Lamb's Chapel involved an evening film series on child-rearing open to the general public (and, given the subject matter, directed at an adult audience). There, school property "had repeatedly been used by a wide variety of private organizations," and we could say with some assurance that "[u]nder these circumstances . . . there would have been no realistic danger that the community would think that the District was endorsing religion or any particular creed. . . ."

What we know about this case looks very little like *Widmar* or *Lamb's Chapel*. The cohort addressed by Good News is not university students with relative maturity, or even high school pupils, but elementary school children as young as six. The Establishment Clause cases have consistently recognized the particular impressionability of schoolchildren, and the special protection required for those in the elementary grades in the school forum. We have held the difference between college students and grade school pupils to be a "distinction [that] warrants a difference in constitutional results." Nor is Milford's limited forum anything like the sites for wide-ranging intellectual exchange that were home to the challenged activities in *Widmar* and *Lamb's Chapel*. In fact, the temporal and physical continuity of Good News's meetings with the regular school routine seems to be the whole point of using the school.

Even on the summary judgment record, then, a record lacking whatever supplementation the trial process might have led to, and devoid of such insight as the trial and appellate judges might have contributed in addressing the Establishment Clause, we can say this: there is a good case that Good News's exercises blur the line between public classroom instruction and private religious indoctrination, leaving a reasonable elementary school pupil unable to appreciate that the former instruction is the business of the school while the latter evangelism is not. Thus, the facts we know (or think we know) point away from the majority's conclusion, and while the consolation may be that nothing really gets resolved when the judicial process is so truncated, that is not much to recommend today's result.

6. When Can Government Give Aid to Parochial Schools? (casebook, p. 1305)

In Zelman v. Simmons-Harris, below, the Supreme Court upheld the constitutionality of a voucher program that could be used for parochial school education. In reading *Zelman*, consider what constitutional issues remain concerning vouchers. What range of choices must exist for vouchers to be constitutional? Are state laws that prohibit the use of aid for parochial schools constitutionally vulnerable? Are provisions such as Ohio's, which prohibit discrimination by schools receiving vouchers, constitutionally required; are they potentially vulnerable to constitutional challenges?

ZELMAN v. SIMMONS-HARRIS
122 S. Ct. 2460 (2002)

Chief Justice REHNQUIST delivered the opinion of the Court.

The State of Ohio has established a pilot program designed to provide educational choices to families with children who reside in the Cleveland City School

District. The question presented is whether this program offends the Establishment Clause of the United States Constitution. We hold that it does not.

There are more than 75,000 children enrolled in the Cleveland City School District. The majority of these children are from low-income and minority families. Few of these families enjoy the means to send their children to any school other than an inner-city public school. For more than a generation, however, Cleveland's public schools have been among the worst performing public schools in the Nation. In 1995, a Federal District Court declared a "crisis of magnitude" and placed the entire Cleveland school district under state control. Shortly thereafter, the state auditor found that Cleveland's public schools were in the midst of a "crisis that is perhaps unprecedented in the history of American education." The district had failed to meet any of the 18 state standards for minimal acceptable performance. Only 1 in 10 ninth graders could pass a basic proficiency examination, and students at all levels performed at a dismal rate compared with students in other Ohio public schools. More than two-thirds of high school students either dropped or failed out before graduation. Of those students who managed to reach their senior year, one of every four still failed to graduate. Of those students who did graduate, few could read, write, or compute at levels comparable to their counterparts in other cities.

It is against this backdrop that Ohio enacted, among other initiatives, its Pilot Project Scholarship Program. The program provides financial assistance to families in any Ohio school district that is or has been "under federal court order requiring supervision and operational management of the district by the state superintendent." Cleveland is the only Ohio school district to fall within that category.

The program provides two basic kinds of assistance to parents of children in a covered district. First, the program provides tuition aid for students in kindergarten through third grade, expanding each year through eighth grade, to attend a participating public or private school of their parent's choosing. Second, the program provides tutorial aid for students who choose to remain enrolled in public school.

The tuition aid portion of the program is designed to provide educational choices to parents who reside in a covered district. Any private school, whether religious or nonreligious, may participate in the program and accept program students so long as the school is located within the boundaries of a covered district and meets statewide educational standards. Participating private schools must agree not to discriminate on the basis of race, religion, or ethnic background, or to "advocate or foster unlawful behavior or teach hatred of any person or group on the basis of race, ethnicity, national origin, or religion." Any public school located in a school district adjacent to the covered district may also participate in the program. Adjacent public schools are eligible to receive a $2,250 tuition grant for each program student accepted in addition to the full amount of per-pupil state funding attributable to each additional student. All participating schools, whether public or private, are required to accept students in accordance with rules and procedures established by the state superintendent.

Tuition aid is distributed to parents according to financial need. Families with incomes below 200% of the poverty line are given priority and are eligible to receive 90% of private school tuition up to $2,250. For these lowest-income families, participating private schools may not charge a parental co-payment greater than $250. For all other families, the program pays 75% of tuition costs, up to $1,875, with no co-payment cap. These families receive tuition aid only if the number of available scholarships exceeds the number of low-income children who choose to participate. Where tuition aid is spent depends solely upon where parents who receive tuition aid choose to enroll their child. If parents choose a private school, checks are made payable to the parents who then endorse the checks over to the chosen school.

The tutorial aid portion of the program provides tutorial assistance through grants to any student in a covered district who chooses to remain in public school. Parents arrange for registered tutors to provide assistance to their children and then submit bills for those services to the State for payment. Students from low-income families receive 90% of the amount charged for such assistance up to $360. All other students receive 75% of that amount. The number of tutorial assistance grants offered to students in a covered district must equal the number of tuition aid scholarships provided to students enrolled at participating private or adjacent public schools.

The program has been in operation within the Cleveland City School District since the 1996-1997 school year. In the 1999-2000 school year, 56 private schools participated in the program, 46 (or 82%) of which had a religious affiliation. None of the public schools in districts adjacent to Cleveland have elected to participate. More than 3,700 students participated in the scholarship program, most of whom (96%) enrolled in religiously affiliated schools. Sixty percent of these students were from families at or below the poverty line. In the 1998-1999 school year, approximately 1,400 Cleveland public school students received tutorial aid. This number was expected to double during the 1999-2000 school year.

The program is part of a broader undertaking by the State to enhance the educational options of Cleveland's schoolchildren in response to the 1995 takeover. That undertaking includes programs governing community and magnet schools. Community schools are funded under state law but are run by their own school boards, not by local school districts. These schools enjoy academic independence to hire their own teachers and to determine their own curriculum. They can have no religious affiliation and are required to accept students by lottery. During the 1999-2000 school year, there were 10 start-up community schools in the Cleveland City School District with more than 1,900 students enrolled. For each child enrolled in a community school, the school receives state funding of $4,518, twice the funding a participating program school may receive.

Magnet schools are public schools operated by a local school board that emphasize a particular subject area, teaching method, or service to students. For each student enrolled in a magnet school, the school district receives $7,746, including state funding of $4,167, the same amount received per student enrolled at a traditional public school. As of 1999, parents in Cleveland were able to choose from among 23 magnet schools, which together enrolled more than 13,000 students in kindergarten through eighth grade. These schools provide specialized teaching methods, such as Montessori, or a particularized curriculum focus, such as foreign language, computers, or the arts.

The Establishment Clause of the First Amendment, applied to the States through the Fourteenth Amendment, prevents a State from enacting laws that have the "purpose" or "effect" of advancing or inhibiting religion. There is no dispute that the program challenged here was enacted for the valid secular purpose of providing educational assistance to poor children in a demonstrably failing public school system. Thus, the question presented is whether the Ohio program nonetheless has the forbidden "effect" of advancing or inhibiting religion.

To answer that question, our decisions have drawn a consistent distinction between government programs that provide aid directly to religious schools, Mitchell v. Helms (2000) and programs of true private choice, in which government aid reaches religious schools only as a result of the genuine and independent choices of private individuals, Mueller v. Allen (1983); Witters v. Washington Dept. of Servs. for Blind (1986); Zobrest v. Catalina Foothills School Dist. (1993). While our jurisprudence with respect to the constitutionality of direct aid programs has "changed significantly" over the past two decades, our jurisprudence with respect to true private choice programs has remained consistent and unbroken. Three times we have confronted Establishment Clause challenges to neutral government programs that provide aid directly to a broad class of individuals, who, in turn, direct the aid to religious schools or institutions of their own choosing. Three times we have rejected such challenges.

In *Mueller*, we rejected an Establishment Clause challenge to a Minnesota program authorizing tax deductions for various educational expenses, including private school tuition costs, even though the great majority of the program's beneficiaries (96%) were parents of children in religious schools. We began by focusing on the class of beneficiaries, finding that because the class included "all parents," including parents with "children [who] attend nonsectarian private schools or sectarian private schools," the program was "not readily subject to challenge under the Establishment Clause." Then, viewing the program as a whole, we emphasized the principle of private choice, noting that public funds were made available to religious schools "only as a result of numerous, private choices of individual parents of school-age children." This, we said, ensured that " 'no imprimatur of state approval' can be deemed to have been conferred on any particular religion, or on religion generally." We thus found it irrelevant to the constitutional inquiry that the vast majority of beneficiaries were parents of children in religious schools, saying: "We would be loath to adopt a rule grounding the constitutionality of a facially neutral law on annual reports reciting the extent to which various classes of private citizens claimed benefits under the law." That the program was one of true private choice, with no evidence that the State deliberately skewed incentives toward religious schools, was sufficient for the program to survive scrutiny under the Establishment Clause.

In *Witters*, we used identical reasoning to reject an Establishment Clause challenge to a vocational scholarship program that provided tuition aid to a student studying at a religious institution to become a pastor. Looking at the program as a whole, we observed that "[a]ny aid . . . that ultimately flows to religious institutions does so only as a result of the genuinely independent and private choices of aid recipients." We further remarked that, as in *Mueller*, "[the] program is made available generally without regard to the sectarian-nonsectarian, or public-nonpublic nature of the institution benefited." In light of these factors, we held that the program was not inconsistent with the Establishment Clause. Five Members of the Court, in separate opinions, emphasized the general rule from *Mueller* that the amount of government aid channeled to religious institutions by individual aid recipients was not relevant to the constitutional inquiry. Our holding thus rested not on whether few or many recipients chose to expend government aid at a religious school but, rather, on whether recipients generally were empowered to direct the aid to schools or institutions of their own choosing.

Finally, in *Zobrest*, we applied *Mueller* and *Witters* to reject an Establishment Clause challenge to a federal program that permitted sign-language interpreters to assist deaf children enrolled in religious schools. Reviewing our earlier decisions, we stated that "government programs that neutrally provide benefits to a broad class of citizens defined without reference to religion are not readily subject to an Establishment Clause challenge." Looking once again to the challenged program as a whole, we observed that the program "distributes benefits neutrally to any child qualifying as 'disabled.'" Its "primary beneficiaries," we said, were "disabled children, not sectarian schools." We further observed that "[b]y according parents freedom to select a school of their choice, the statute ensures that a government-paid interpreter will be present in a sectarian school only as a result of the private decision of individual parents." Our focus again was on neutrality and the principle of private choice, not on the number of program beneficiaries attending religious schools. Because the program ensured that parents were the ones to select a religious school as the best learning environment for their handicapped child, the circuit between government and religion was broken, and the Establishment Clause was not implicated.

Mueller, *Witters*, and *Zobrest* thus make clear that where a government aid program is neutral with respect to religion, and provides assistance directly to a broad class of citizens who, in turn, direct government aid to religious schools wholly as a result of their own genuine and independent private choice, the program is not readily subject to challenge under the Establishment Clause. A program that shares these features permits government aid to reach religious institutions only by way of the deliberate choices of numerous individual recipients. The incidental advancement of a religious mission, or the perceived endorsement of a religious message, is reasonably attributable to the individual recipient, not to the government, whose role ends with the disbursement of benefits. As a plurality of this Court recently observed: "[I]f numerous private choices, rather than the single choice of a government, determine the distribution of aid, pursuant to neutral eligibility criteria, then a government cannot, or at least cannot easily, grant special favors that might lead to a religious establishment." Mitchell v. Helms (2000).

We believe that the program challenged here is a program of true private choice, consistent with *Mueller*, *Witters*, and *Zobrest*, and thus constitutional. As was true in those cases, the Ohio program is neutral in all respects toward religion. It is part of a general and multifaceted undertaking by the State of Ohio to provide educational opportunities to the children of a failed school district. It confers educational assistance directly to a broad class of individuals defined without reference to religion, i.e., any parent of a school-age child who resides in the Cleveland City School District. The program permits the participation of all schools within the district, religious or nonreligious. Adjacent public schools also may participate and have a financial incentive to do so. Program benefits are available to participating families on neutral terms, with no reference to religion. The only preference stated anywhere in the program is a preference for low-income families, who receive greater assistance and are given priority for admission at participating schools.

There are no "financial incentive[s]" that "ske[w]" the program toward religious schools. Such incentives "[are] not present . . . where the aid is allocated on the basis of neutral, secular criteria that neither favor nor disfavor religion, and is made available to both religious and secular beneficiaries on a nondiscriminatory basis." The program here in fact creates financial disincentives for religious schools, with private schools receiving only half the government assistance given to community schools and one-third the assistance given to magnet schools. Adjacent public schools, should any choose to accept program students, are also eligible to receive two to three times the state funding of a private religious school. Families too have a financial disincentive to choose a private religious school over other schools. Parents that choose to participate in the scholarship program and then to enroll their children in a private school (religious or nonreligious) must copay a portion of the school's tuition. Families that choose a community school, magnet school, or traditional public school pay nothing. Although such features of the program are not necessary to its constitutionality, they clearly dispel the claim that the program "creates . . . financial incentive[s] for parents to choose a sectarian school."[1]

---

1. Justice Souter suggests the program is not "neutral" because program students cannot spend scholarship vouchers at traditional public schools. This objection is mistaken: Public schools in

Respondents suggest that even without a financial incentive for parents to choose a religious school, the program creates a "public perception that the State is endorsing religious practices and beliefs." But we have repeatedly recognized that no reasonable observer would think a neutral program of private choice, where state aid reaches religious schools solely as a result of the numerous independent decisions of private individuals, carries with it the imprimatur of government endorsement. The argument is particularly misplaced here since "the reasonable observer in the endorsement inquiry must be deemed aware" of the "history and context" underlying a challenged program.

There also is no evidence that the program fails to provide genuine opportunities for Cleveland parents to select secular educational options for their school-age children. Cleveland schoolchildren enjoy a range of educational choices: They may remain in public school as before, remain in public school with publicly funded tutoring aid, obtain a scholarship and choose a religious school, obtain a scholarship and choose a nonreligious private school, enroll in a community school, or enroll in a magnet school. That 46 of the 56 private schools now participating in the program are religious schools does not condemn it as a violation of the Establishment Clause. The Establishment Clause question is whether Ohio is coercing parents into sending their children to religious schools, and that question must be answered by evaluating all options Ohio provides Cleveland schoolchildren, only one of which is to obtain a program scholarship and then choose a religious school.

Justice Souter speculates that because more private religious schools currently participate in the program, the program itself must somehow discourage the participation of private nonreligious schools. But Cleveland's preponderance of religiously affiliated private schools certainly did not arise as a result of the program; it is a phenomenon common to many American cities. Indeed, by all accounts the program has captured a remarkable cross-section of private schools, religious and nonreligious. It is true that 82% of Cleveland's participating private schools are religious schools, but it is also true that 81% of private schools in Ohio are religious schools. To attribute constitutional significance to this figure, moreover, would lead to the absurd result that a neutral school-choice program might be permissible in some parts of Ohio, such as Columbus, where a lower percentage of private schools are religious schools, but not in inner-city Cleveland, where Ohio has deemed such programs most sorely needed, but where the preponderance of religious schools happens to be greater. Likewise, an identical private choice program might be constitutional in some States, such as Maine or Utah, where less than 45% of private schools are religious schools,

---

Cleveland already receive $7,097 in public funding per pupil—$4,167 of which is attributable to the State. Program students who receive tutoring aid and remain enrolled in traditional public schools therefore direct almost twice as much state funding to their chosen school as do program students who receive a scholarship and attend a private school. Justice Souter does not seriously claim that the program differentiates based on the religious status of beneficiaries or providers of services, the touchstone of neutrality under the Establishment Clause. [Footnote by the Court.]

but not in other States, such as Nebraska or Kansas, where over 90% of private schools are religious schools.

Respondents and Justice Souter claim that even if we do not focus on the number of participating schools that are religious schools, we should attach constitutional significance to the fact that 96% of scholarship recipients have enrolled in religious schools. They claim that this alone proves parents lack genuine choice, even if no parent has ever said so. We need not consider this argument in detail, since it was flatly rejected in *Mueller,* where we found it irrelevant that 96% of parents taking deductions for tuition expenses paid tuition at religious schools. Indeed, we have recently found it irrelevant even to the constitutionality of a direct aid program that a vast majority of program benefits went to religious schools. The constitutionality of a neutral educational aid program simply does not turn on whether and why, in a particular area, at a particular time, most private schools are run by religious organizations, or most recipients choose to use the aid at a religious school. As we said in *Mueller,* "[s]uch an approach would scarcely provide the certainty that this field stands in need of, nor can we perceive principled standards by which such statistical evidence might be evaluated."

This point is aptly illustrated here. The 96% figure upon which respondents and Justice Souter rely discounts entirely (1) the more than 1,900 Cleveland children enrolled in alternative community schools, (2) the more than 13,000 children enrolled in alternative magnet schools, and (3) the more than 1,400 children enrolled in traditional public schools with tutorial assistance. Including some or all of these children in the denominator of children enrolled in nontraditional schools during the 1999-2000 school year drops the percentage enrolled in religious schools from 96% to under 20%. The 96% figure also represents but a snapshot of one particular school year. In the 1997-1998 school year, by contrast, only 78% of scholarship recipients attended religious schools.

Respondents finally claim that we should look to Committee for Public Ed. & Religious Liberty v. Nyquist (1973), to decide these cases. We disagree for two reasons. First, the program in *Nyquist* was quite different from the program challenged here. *Nyquist* involved a New York program that gave a package of benefits exclusively to private schools and the parents of private school enrollees. Although the program was enacted for ostensibly secular purposes, we found that its "function" was "unmistakably to provide desired financial support for nonpublic, sectarian institutions." Its genesis, we said, was that private religious schools faced "increasingly grave fiscal problems." The program thus provided direct money grants to religious schools. It provided tax benefits "unrelated to the amount of money actually expended by any parent on tuition," ensuring a windfall to parents of children in religious schools. It similarly provided tuition reimbursements designed explicitly to "offe[r] . . . an incentive to parents to send their children to sectarian schools." Indeed, the program flatly prohibited the participation of any public school, or parent of any public school enrollee. Ohio's program shares none of these features.

Second, were there any doubt that the program challenged in *Nyquist* is far removed from the program challenged here, we expressly reserved judgment with respect to "a case involving some form of public assistance (e.g., scholarships) made available generally without regard to the sectarian-nonsectarian, or public-nonpublic nature of the institution benefited." That, of course, is the very question now before us, and it has since been answered, first in *Mueller,* then in *Witters*, and again in *Zobrest*.[2]

In sum, the Ohio program is entirely neutral with respect to religion. It provides benefits directly to a wide spectrum of individuals, defined only by financial need and residence in a particular school district. It permits such individuals to exercise genuine choice among options public and private, secular and religious. The program is therefore a program of true private choice. In keeping with an unbroken line of decisions rejecting challenges to similar programs, we hold that the program does not offend the Establishment Clause.

Justice O'CONNOR, concurring.

While I join the Court's opinion, I write separately for two reasons. First, although the Court takes an important step, I do not believe that today's decision, when considered in light of other longstanding government programs that impact religious organizations and our prior Establishment Clause jurisprudence, marks a dramatic break from the past. Second, given the emphasis the Court places on verifying that parents of voucher students in religious schools have exercised "true private choice," I think it is worth elaborating on the Court's conclusion that this inquiry should consider all reasonable educational alternatives to religious schools that are available to parents. To do otherwise is to ignore how the educational system in Cleveland actually functions.

I

These cases are different from prior indirect aid cases in part because a significant portion of the funds appropriated for the voucher program reach religious schools without restrictions on the use of these funds. The share of public resources that reach religious schools is not, however, as significant as respondents suggest. Data from the 1999-2000 school year indicate that 82 percent of schools participating in the voucher program were religious and that 96 percent of participating students enrolled in religious schools but these data are incomplete. These statistics do not take into account all of the reasonable educational choices that may be available to students in Cleveland public schools.

---

2. Justice Breyer would raise the invisible specters of "divisiveness" and "religious strife" to find the program unconstitutional. It is unclear exactly what sort of principle Justice Breyer has in mind, considering that the program has ignited no "divisiveness" or "strife" other than this litigation. Nor is it clear where Justice Breyer would locate this presumed authority to deprive Cleveland residents of a program that they have chosen but that we subjectively find "divisive." We quite rightly have rejected the claim that some speculative potential for divisiveness bears on the constitutionality of educational aid programs. Mitchell v. Helms.

When one considers the option to attend community schools, the percentage of students enrolled in religious schools falls to 62.1 percent. If magnet schools are included in the mix, this percentage falls to 16.5 percent.

Even these numbers do not paint a complete picture. The Cleveland program provides voucher applicants from low-income families with up to $2,250 in tuition assistance and provides the remaining applicants with up to $1,875 in tuition assistance. In contrast, the State provides community schools $4,518 per pupil and magnet schools, on average, $7,097 per pupil. Even if one assumes that all voucher students came from low-income families and that each voucher student used up the entire $2,250 voucher, at most $8.2 million of public funds flowed to religious schools under the voucher program in 1999-2000. Although just over one-half as many students attended community schools as religious private schools on the state fisc, the State spent over $1 million more—$9.4 million—on students in community schools than on students in religious private schools because per-pupil aid to community schools is more than double the per-pupil aid to private schools under the voucher program. Moreover, the amount spent on religious private schools is minor compared to the $114.8 million the State spent on students in the Cleveland magnet schools.

Although $8.2 million is no small sum, it pales in comparison to the amount of funds that federal, state, and local governments already provide religious institutions. Religious organizations may qualify for exemptions from the federal corporate income tax; the corporate income tax in many States; and property taxes in all 50 States; and clergy qualify for a federal tax break on income used for housing expenses. In addition, the Federal Government provides individuals, corporations, trusts, and estates a tax deduction for charitable contributions to qualified religious groups. Finally, the Federal Government and certain state governments provide tax credits for educational expenses, many of which are spent on education at religious schools. Most of these tax policies are well established, yet confer a significant relative benefit on religious institutions. The state property tax exemptions for religious institutions alone amount to very large sums annually. For example, available data suggest that Colorado's exemption lowers that State's tax revenues by more than $40 million annually; Maryland's exemption lowers revenues by more than $60 million; Wisconsin's exemption lowers revenues by approximately $122 million; and Louisiana's exemption, looking just at the city of New Orleans, lowers revenues by over $36 million. As for the Federal Government, the tax deduction for charitable contributions reduces federal tax revenues by nearly $25 billion annually. Even the relatively minor exemptions lower federal tax receipts by substantial amounts. The parsonage exemption, for example, lowers revenues by around $500 million.

These tax exemptions, which have "much the same effect as [cash grants] . . . of the amount of tax [avoided]," are just part of the picture. Federal dollars also reach religiously affiliated organizations through public health programs such as Medicare and Medicaid, through educational programs such as the Pell Grant program, and the G.I. Bill of Rights, and through child care programs such as the Child Care and Development Block Grant Program. These programs are well-established parts of our social welfare system and can be quite substantial.

A significant portion of the funds appropriated for these programs reach religiously affiliated institutions, typically without restrictions on its subsequent use.

Against this background, the support that the Cleveland voucher program provides religious institutions is neither substantial nor atypical of existing government programs. While this observation is not intended to justify the Cleveland voucher program under the Establishment Clause, it places in broader perspective alarmist claims about implications of the Cleveland program and the Court's decision in these cases.

II

Nor does today's decision signal a major departure from this Court's prior Establishment Clause jurisprudence. A central tool in our analysis of cases in this area has been the *Lemon* test. As originally formulated, a statute passed this test only if it had "a secular legislative purpose," if its "principal or primary effect" was one that "neither advance[d] nor inhibit[ed] religion," and if it did "not foster an excessive government entanglement with religion." Lemon v. Kurtzman (1971). In Agostini v. Felton (1997), we folded the entanglement inquiry into the primary effect inquiry. This made sense because both inquiries rely on the same evidence, and the degree of entanglement has implications for whether a statute advances or inhibits religion. The Court's opinion in these cases focuses on a narrow question related to the *Lemon* test: how to apply the primary effects prong in indirect aid cases? Specifically, it clarifies the basic inquiry when trying to determine whether a program that distributes aid to beneficiaries, rather than directly to service providers, has the primary effect of advancing or inhibiting religion, or, as I have put it, of "endors[ing] or disapprov[ing] . . . religion." Courts are instructed to consider two factors: first, whether the program administers aid in a neutral fashion, without differentiation based on the religious status of beneficiaries or providers of services; second, and more importantly, whether beneficiaries of indirect aid have a genuine choice among religious and nonreligious organizations when determining the organization to which they will direct that aid. If the answer to either query is "no," the program should be struck down under the Establishment Clause.

III

There is little question in my mind that the Cleveland voucher program is neutral as between religious schools and nonreligious schools. Justice Souter rejects the Court's notion of neutrality, proposing that the neutrality of a program should be gauged not by the opportunities it presents but rather by its effects. But Justice Souter's notion of neutrality is inconsistent with that in our case law. As we put it in *Agostini*, government aid must be "made available to both religious and secular beneficiaries on a nondiscriminatory basis."

I do not agree that the nonreligious schools have failed to provide Cleveland parents reasonable alternatives to religious schools in the voucher program. For nonreligious schools to qualify as genuine options for parents, they need not be superior to religious schools in every respect. They need only be adequate substitutes for religious schools in the eyes of parents. The District Court record demonstrates that nonreligious schools were able to compete effectively with Catholic and other religious schools in the Cleveland voucher program. The best evidence of this is that many parents with vouchers selected nonreligious private schools over religious alternatives and an even larger number of parents send their children to community and magnet schools rather than seeking vouchers at all. Moreover, there is no record evidence that any voucher-eligible student was turned away from a nonreligious private school in the voucher program, let alone a community or magnet school.

I find the Court's answer to the question whether parents of students eligible for vouchers have a genuine choice between religious and nonreligious schools persuasive. In looking at the voucher program, all the choices available to potential beneficiaries of the government program should be considered. In these cases, parents who were eligible to apply for a voucher also had the option, at a minimum, to send their children to community schools. Yet the Court of Appeals chose not to look at community schools, let alone magnet schools, when evaluating the Cleveland voucher program. That decision was incorrect. Focusing in these cases only on the program challenged by respondents ignores how the educational system in Cleveland actually functions. The record indicates that, in 1999, two nonreligious private schools that had previously served 15 percent of the students in the voucher program were prompted to convert to community schools because parents were concerned about the litigation surrounding the program, and because a new community schools program provided more per-pupil financial aid. Many of the students that enrolled in the two schools under the voucher program transferred to the community schools program and continued to attend these schools. This incident provides strong evidence that both parents and nonreligious schools view the voucher program and the community schools program as reasonable alternatives.

Considering all the educational options available to parents whose children are eligible for vouchers, including community and magnet schools, the Court finds that parents in the Cleveland schools have an array of nonreligious options.

Based on the reasoning in the Court's opinion, which is consistent with the realities of the Cleveland educational system, I am persuaded that the Cleveland voucher program affords parents of eligible children genuine nonreligious options and is consistent with the Establishment Clause.

Justice THOMAS, concurring.

Frederick Douglass once said that "[e]ducation . . . means emancipation. It means light and liberty. It means the uplifting of the soul of man into the glorious light of truth, the light by which men can only be made free." Today many of our inner-city public schools deny emancipation to urban minority students. Despite this Court's observation nearly 50 years ago in Brown v. Board of Education, that "it is doubtful that any child may reasonably be expected to succeed in life if he is denied the opportunity of an education," urban children have been forced into a system that continually fails them. These cases present an example of such failures. Besieged by escalating financial problems and declining academic achievement, the Cleveland City School District was in the midst of an academic emergency when Ohio enacted its scholarship program.

The dissents and respondents wish to invoke the Establishment Clause of the First Amendment, as incorporated through the Fourteenth, to constrain a State's neutral efforts to provide greater educational opportunity for underprivileged minority students. Today's decision properly upholds the program as constitutional, and I join it in full.

I

This Court has often considered whether efforts to provide children with the best educational resources conflict with constitutional limitations. Attempts to provide aid to religious schools or to allow some degree of religious involvement in public schools have generated significant controversy and litigation as States try to navigate the line between the secular and the religious in education. I agree with the Court that Ohio's program easily passes muster under our stringent test, but, as a matter of first principles, I question whether this test should be applied to the States.

The Establishment Clause of the First Amendment states that "Congress shall make no law respecting an establishment of religion." On its face, this provision places no limit on the States with regard to religion. The Establishment Clause originally protected States, and by extension their citizens, from the imposition of an established religion by the Federal Government. Whether and how this Clause should constrain state action under the Fourteenth Amendment is a more difficult question.

When rights are incorporated against the States through the Fourteenth Amendment they should advance, not constrain, individual liberty. Consequently, in the context of the Establishment Clause, it may well be that state action should be evaluated on different terms than similar action by the Federal Government. "States, while bound to observe strict neutrality, should be freer to experiment with involvement [in religion]—on a neutral basis—than the Federal Government." Thus, while the Federal Government may "make no law respecting an establishment of religion," the States may pass laws that include or touch on religious matters so long as these laws do not impede free exercise rights or any other individual religious liberty interest. By considering the particular religious liberty right alleged to be invaded by a State, federal courts can strike a proper balance between the demands of the Fourteenth Amendment on the one hand and the federalism prerogatives of States on the other.

Whatever the textual and historical merits of incorporating the Establishment Clause, I can accept that the Fourteenth Amendment protects religious liberty rights. But I cannot accept its use to oppose neutral programs of school choice through the incorporation of the Establishment Clause. There would be a tragic irony in converting the Fourteenth Amendment's guarantee of individual liberty into a prohibition on the exercise of educational choice.

II

The wisdom of allowing States greater latitude in dealing with matters of religion and education can be easily appreciated in this context. Respondents advocate using the Fourteenth Amendment to handcuff the State's ability to experiment with education. But without education one can hardly exercise the civic, political, and personal freedoms conferred by the Fourteenth Amendment. Faced with a severe educational crisis, the State of Ohio enacted wide-ranging educational reform that allows voluntary participation of private and religious schools in educating poor urban children otherwise condemned to failing public schools. The program does not force any individual to submit to religious indoctrination or education. It simply gives parents a greater choice as to where and in what manner to educate their children. This is a choice that those with greater means have routinely exercised.

In addition to expanding the reach of the scholarship program, the inclusion of religious schools makes sense given Ohio's purpose of increasing educational performance and opportunities. Religious schools, like other private schools, achieve far better educational results than their public counterparts. For example, the students at Cleveland's Catholic schools score significantly higher on Ohio proficiency tests than students at Cleveland public schools. Of Cleveland eighth graders taking the 1999 Ohio proficiency test, 95 percent in Catholic schools passed the reading test, whereas only 57 percent in public schools passed. And 75 percent of Catholic school students passed the math proficiency test, compared to only 22 percent of public school students. But the success of religious and private schools is in the end beside the point, because the State has a constitutional right to experiment with a variety of different programs to promote educational opportunity. That Ohio's program includes successful schools simply indicates that such reform can in fact provide improved education to underprivileged urban children.

Although one of the purposes of public schools was to promote democracy and a more egalitarian culture, failing urban public schools disproportionately affect minority children most in need of educational opportunity. At the time of Reconstruction, blacks considered public education "a matter of personal liberation and a necessary function of a free society." Today, however, the promise of public school education has failed poor inner-city blacks. While in theory providing education to everyone, the quality of public schools varies significantly across districts. Just as blacks supported public education during Reconstruction, many blacks and other minorities now support school choice programs because they provide the greatest educational opportunities for their children in struggling communities. Opponents of the program raise formalistic concerns about the Establishment Clause but ignore the core purposes of the Fourteenth Amendment.[3]

While the romanticized ideal of universal public education resonates with the cognoscenti who oppose vouchers, poor urban families just want the best education for their children, who will certainly need it to function in our high-tech and advanced society. As Thomas Sowell noted 30 years ago: "Most black people have faced too many grim, concrete problems to be romantics. They want and need certain tangible results, which can be achieved only by developing certain specific abilities." The same is true today. An individual's life prospects increase dramatically with each successfully completed phase of education. For instance, a black high school dropout earns just over $13,500, but with a high school degree the average income is almost $21,000. Blacks with a bachelor's degree have an average annual income of about $37,500, and $75,500 with a professional degree. Staying in school and earning a degree generates real and tangible financial benefits, whereas failure to obtain even a high school degree essentially relegates students to a life of poverty and, all too often, of crime. The failure to provide education to poor urban children perpetuates a vicious cycle of poverty, dependence, criminality, and alienation that continues for the remainder of their lives. If society cannot end racial discrimination, at least it can arm minorities with the education to defend themselves from some of discrimination's effects.

Ten States have enacted some form of publicly funded private school choice as one means of raising the quality of education provided to underprivileged urban children. These programs address the root of the problem with failing urban public schools that disproportionately affect minority students. Society's other solution to these educational failures is often to provide racial preferences in higher education. Such preferences, however, run afoul of the Fourteenth Amendment's prohibition against distinctions based on race. By contrast, school choice programs that involve religious schools appear unconstitutional only to

---

3. Minority and low-income parents express the greatest support for parental choice and are most interested in placing their children in private schools. "[T]he appeal of private schools is especially strong among parents who are low in income, minority, and live in low-performing districts: precisely the parents who are the most disadvantaged under the current system." T. Moe, Schools, Vouchers, and the American Public 164 (2001). Nearly three-fourths of all public school parents with an annual income less than $20,000 support vouchers, compared to 57 percent of public school parents with an annual income of over $60,000. In addition, 75 percent of black public school parents support vouchers, as do 71 percent of Hispanic public school parents. [Footnote by Justice Thomas.]

those who would twist the Fourteenth Amendment against itself by expansively incorporating the Establishment Clause. Converting the Fourteenth Amendment from a guarantee of opportunity to an obstacle against education reform distorts our constitutional values and disserves those in the greatest need. As Frederick Douglass poignantly noted "no greater benefit can be bestowed upon a long be-nighted people, than giving to them, as we are here earnestly this day endeavoring to do, the means of an education."

Justice STEVENS, dissenting.

Is a law that authorizes the use of public funds to pay for the indoctrination of thousands of grammar school children in particular religious faiths a "law respecting an establishment of religion" within the meaning of the First Amendment? In answering that question, I think we should ignore three factual matters that are discussed at length by my colleagues.

First, the severe educational crisis that confronted the Cleveland City School District when Ohio enacted its voucher program is not a matter that should affect our appraisal of its constitutionality. In the 1999-2000 school year, that program provided relief to less than five percent of the students enrolled in the district's schools. The solution to the disastrous conditions that prevented over 90 percent of the student body from meeting basic proficiency standards obviously required massive improvements unrelated to the voucher program. Of course, the emergency may have given some families a powerful motivation to leave the public school system and accept religious indoctrination that they would otherwise have avoided, but that is not a valid reason for upholding the program.

Second, the wide range of choices that have been made available to students within the public school system has no bearing on the question whether the State may pay the tuition for students who wish to reject public education entirely and attend private schools that will provide them with a sectarian education. The fact that the vast majority of the voucher recipients who have entirely rejected public education receive religious indoctrination at state expense does, however, support the claim that the law is one "respecting an establishment of religion." The State may choose to divide up its public schools into a dozen different options and label them magnet schools, community schools, or whatever else it decides to call them, but the State is still required to provide a public education and it is the State's decision to fund private school education over and above its traditional obligation that is at issue in these cases.

Third, the voluntary character of the private choice to prefer a parochial education over an education in the public school system seems to me quite irrelevant to the question whether the government's choice to pay for religious indoctrination is constitutionally permissible. Today, however, the Court seems to have decided that the mere fact that a family that cannot afford a private education wants its children educated in a parochial school is a sufficient justification for this use of public funds.

For the reasons stated by Justice Souter and Justice Breyer, I am convinced that the Court's decision is profoundly misguided. Admittedly, in reaching that conclusion I have been influenced by my understanding of the impact of religious strife on the decisions of our forbears to migrate to this continent, and on the decisions of neighbors in the Balkans, Northern Ireland, and the Middle East to mistrust one another. Whenever we remove a brick from the wall that was designed to separate religion and government, we increase the risk of religious strife and weaken the foundation of our democracy.

Justice SOUTER, with whom Justice STEVENS, Justice GINSBURG, and Justice BREYER join, dissenting.

The Court's majority holds that the Establishment Clause is no bar to Ohio's payment of tuition at private religious elementary and middle schools under a scheme that systematically provides tax money to support the schools' religious missions. The occasion for the legislation thus upheld is the condition of public education in the city of Cleveland. The record indicates that the schools are failing to serve their objective, and the vouchers in issue here are said to be needed to provide adequate alternatives to them. If there were an excuse for giving short shrift to the Establishment Clause, it would probably apply here. But there is no excuse. Constitutional limitations are placed on government to preserve constitutional values in hard cases, like these.

Today, however, the majority holds that the Establishment Clause is not offended by Ohio's Pilot Project Scholarship Program, under which students may be eligible to receive as much as $2,250 in the form of tuition vouchers transferable to religious schools. In the city of Cleveland the overwhelming proportion of large appropriations for voucher money must be spent on religious schools if it is to be spent at all, and will be spent in amounts that cover almost all of tuition. The money will thus pay for eligible students' instruction not only in secular subjects but in religion as well, in schools that can fairly be characterized as founded to teach religious doctrine and to imbue teaching in all subjects with a religious dimension. Public tax money will pay at a systemic level for teaching the covenant with Israel and Mosaic law in Jewish schools, the primacy of the Apostle Peter and the Papacy in Catholic schools, the truth of reformed Christianity in Protestant schools, and the revelation to the Prophet in Muslim schools, to speak only of major religious groupings in the Republic.

II

Although it has taken half a century since *Everson* to reach the majority's twin standards of neutrality and free choice, the facts show that, in the majority's hands, even these criteria cannot convincingly legitimize the Ohio scheme.

A

Consider first the criterion of neutrality. As recently as two Terms ago, a majority of the Court recognized that neutrality conceived of as evenhandedness toward aid recipients had never been treated as alone sufficient to satisfy the Establishment Clause. Today, however, the majority employs the neutrality criterion in a way that renders it impossible to understand.

In order to apply the neutrality test, then, it makes sense to focus on a category of aid that may be directed to religious as well as secular schools, and ask whether the scheme favors a religious direction. Here, one would ask whether the voucher provisions, allowing for as much as $2,250 toward private school tuition (or a grant to a public school in an adjacent district), were written in a way that skewed the scheme toward benefiting religious schools. This, however, is not what the majority asks. The majority looks not to the provisions for tuition vouchers, but to every provision for educational opportunity.

The illogic is patent. If regular, public schools (which can get no voucher payments) "participate" in a voucher scheme with schools that can, and public expenditure is still predominantly on public schools, then the majority's reasoning would find neutrality in a scheme of vouchers available for private tuition in districts with no secular private schools at all. "Neutrality" as the majority employs the term is, literally, verbal and nothing more. This, indeed, is the only way the majority can gloss over the very nonneutral feature of the total scheme covering "all schools": public tutors may receive from the State no more than $324 per child to support extra tutoring (that is, the State's 90% of a total amount of $360), whereas the tuition voucher schools (which turn out to be mostly religious) can receive up to $2,250.

Why the majority does not simply accept the fact that the challenge here is to the more generous voucher scheme and judge its neutrality in relation to religious use of voucher money seems very odd. It seems odd, that is, until one recognizes that comparable schools for applying the criterion of neutrality are also the comparable schools for applying the other majority criterion, whether the immediate recipients of voucher aid have a genuinely free choice of religious and secular schools to receive the voucher money. And in applying this second criterion, the consideration of "all schools" is ostensibly helpful to the majority position.

B

The majority addresses the issue of choice the same way it addresses neutrality, by asking whether recipients or potential recipients of voucher aid have a choice of public schools among secular alternatives to religious schools. Again, however, the majority asks the wrong question and misapplies the criterion. The majority has confused choice in spending scholarships with choice from the entire menu of possible educational placements, most of them open to anyone willing to attend a public school. I say "confused" because the majority's new use of the choice criterion, which it frames negatively as "whether Ohio is coercing parents into sending their children to religious schools," ignores the reason for having a private choice enquiry in the first place. Cases since *Mueller* have found private choice relevant under a rule that aid to religious schools can be permissible so long as it first passes through the hands of students or parents. The majority's view that all educational choices are comparable for purposes of choice thus ignores the whole point of the choice test: it is a criterion for deciding whether indirect aid to a religious school is legitimate because it passes through private hands that can spend or use the aid in a secular school. The question is whether the private hand is genuinely free to send the money in either a secular direction or a religious one. The majority now has transformed this question about private choice in channeling aid into a question about selecting from examples of state spending (on education) including direct spending on magnet and community public schools that goes through no private hands and could never reach a religious school under any circumstance. When the choice test is transformed from where to spend the money to where to go to school, it is cut loose from its very purpose.

Defining choice as choice in spending the money or channeling the aid is, moreover, necessary if the choice criterion is to function as a limiting principle at all. If "choice" is present whenever there is any educational alternative to the religious school to which vouchers can be endorsed, then there will always be a choice and the voucher can always be constitutional, even in a system in which there is not a single private secular school as an alternative to the religious school. And because it is unlikely that any participating private religious school will enroll more pupils than the generally available public system, it will be easy to generate numbers suggesting that aid to religion is not the significant intent or effect of the voucher scheme.

That is, in fact, just the kind of rhetorical argument that the majority accepts in these cases. In addition to secular private schools (129 students), the majority considers public schools with tuition assistance (roughly 1,400 students), magnet schools (13,000 students), and community schools (1,900 students), and concludes that fewer than 20% of pupils receive state vouchers to attend religious schools. Justice O'Connor focuses on how much money is spent on each educational option and notes that at most $8.2 million is spent on vouchers for students attending religious schools, which is only 6% of the State's expenditure if one includes separate funding for Cleveland's community ($9.4 million) and magnet ($114.8 million) public schools. The variations show how results may shift when a judge can pick and choose the alternatives to use in the comparisons, and they also show what dependably comfortable results the choice criterion will yield if the identification of relevant choices is wide open. If the choice of relevant alternatives is an open one, proponents of voucher aid will always win, because they will always be able to find a "choice" somewhere that will show the bulk of public spending to be secular. The choice enquiry will be diluted to the point that it can screen out nothing, and the result will always be determined by selecting the alternatives to be treated as choices.

But once any public school is deemed a relevant object of choice, there is no stopping this progression. For example, both the majority and Justice O'Connor characterize public magnet schools as an independent category of genuine educational options, simply because they are "nontraditional" public schools. But they do not share the "private school" features of community schools, and the only thing that distinguishes them from "traditional" public schools is their thematic focus, which in some cases appears to be nothing more than creative marketing. It is not, of course, that I think even a genuine choice criterion is up to the task of the Establishment Clause when substantial state funds go to religious teaching; the discussion in Part III, infra, shows that it is not. The point is simply that if the majority wishes to claim that choice is a criterion, it must define choice in a way that can function as a criterion with a practical capacity to screen something out.

If, contrary to the majority, we ask the right question about genuine choice to use the vouchers, the answer shows that something is influencing choices in a way that aims the money in a religious direction: of 56 private schools in the district participating in the voucher program (only 53 of which accepted voucher students in 1999-2000), 46 of them are religious; 96.6% of all voucher recipients go to religious schools, only 3.4% to nonreligious ones. Unfortunately for the majority position, there is no explanation for this that suggests the religious direction results simply from free choices by parents. One answer to these statistics, for example, which would be consistent with the genuine choice claimed to be operating, might be that 96.6% of families choosing to avail themselves of vouchers choose to educate their children in schools of their own religion. This would not, in my view, render the scheme constitutional, but it would speak to the majority's choice criterion. Evidence shows, however, that almost two out of three families using vouchers to send their children to religious schools did not embrace the religion of those schools. The families made it clear they had not chosen the schools because they wished their children to be proselytized in a religion not their own, or in any religion, but because of educational opportunity.

Even so, the fact that some 2,270 students chose to apply their vouchers to schools of other religions, might be consistent with true choice if the students "chose" their religious schools over a wide array of private nonreligious options, or if it could be shown generally that Ohio's program had no effect on educational choices and thus no impermissible effect of advancing religious education. But both possibilities are contrary to fact. First, even if all existing nonreligious private schools in Cleveland were willing to accept large numbers of voucher students, only a few more than the 129 currently enrolled in such schools would be able to attend, as the total enrollment at all nonreligious private schools in Cleveland for kindergarten through eighth grade is only 510 children, and there is no indication that these schools have many open seats.

Second, the $2,500 cap that the program places on tuition for participating low-income pupils has the effect of curtailing the participation of nonreligious schools: "nonreligious schools with higher tuition (about $4,000) stated that they could afford to accommodate just a few voucher students." By comparison, the average tuition at participating Catholic schools in Cleveland in 1999-2000 was $1,592, almost $1,000 below the cap.

There is, in any case, no way to interpret the 96.6% of current voucher money going to religious schools as reflecting a free and genuine choice by the families that apply for vouchers. The 96.6% reflects, instead, the fact that too few nonreligious school desks are available and few but religious schools can afford to accept more than a handful of voucher students. And contrary to the majority's assertion, public schools in adjacent districts hardly have a financial incentive to participate in the Ohio voucher program, and none has. For the overwhelming number of children in the voucher scheme, the only alternative to the public schools is religious. And it is entirely irrelevant that the State did not deliberately design the network of private schools for the sake of channeling money into religious institutions. The criterion is one of genuinely free choice on the part of the private individuals who choose, and a Hobson's choice is not a choice, whatever the reason for being Hobsonian.

III

I do not dissent merely because the majority has misapplied its own law, for even if I assumed arguendo that the majority's formal criteria were satisfied on the facts, today's conclusion would be profoundly at odds with the Constitution. Proof of this is clear on two levels. The first is circumstantial, in the now discarded symptom of violation, the substantial dimension of the aid. The second is direct, in the defiance of every objective supposed to be served by the bar against establishment.

The scale of the aid to religious schools approved today is unprecedented, both in the number of dollars and in the proportion of systemic school expenditure supported. Each measure has received attention in previous cases. On one hand, the sheer quantity of aid, when delivered to a class of religious primary and secondary schools, was suspect on the theory that the greater the aid, the greater its proportion to a religious school's existing expenditures, and the greater the likelihood that public money was supporting religious as well as secular instruction. As we said in *Meek,* "it would simply ignore reality to attempt to separate secular educational functions from the predominantly religious role" as the object of aid that comes in "substantial amounts."

The Cleveland voucher program has cost Ohio taxpayers $33 million since its implementation in 1996 ($28 million in voucher payments, $5 million in administrative costs), and its cost was expected to exceed $8 million in the 2001-2002 school year. The gross amounts of public money contributed are symptomatic of the scope of what the taxpayers' money buys for a broad class of religious-school students. In paying for practically the full amount of tuition for thousands of qualifying students, the scholarships purchase everything that tuition purchases, be it instruction in math or indoctrination in faith. The consequences of "substantial" aid hypothesized in *Meek* are realized here: the majority makes no pretense that substantial amounts of tax money are not systematically underwriting religious practice and indoctrination.

It is virtually superfluous to point out that every objective underlying the prohibition of religious establishment is betrayed by this scheme, but something has to be said about the enormity of the violation. I anticipated these objectives earlier, the first being respect for freedom of conscience. Jefferson described it as the idea that no one "shall be compelled to . . . support any religious worship, place, or ministry whatsoever," even a "teacher of his own religious persuasion," ibid., and Madison thought it violated by any " 'authority which can force a citizen to contribute three pence . . . of his property for the support of any . . . establishment.' " Memorial and Remonstrance ¶ 3. "Any tax to establish religion is antithetical to the command that the minds of men always be wholly free." Madison's objection to three pence has simply been lost in the majority's formalism.

As for the second objective, to save religion from its own corruption, Madison wrote of the " 'experience . . . that ecclesiastical establishments, instead of maintaining the purity and efficacy of Religion, have had a contrary operation.' " Memorial and Remonstrance ¶ 7. In Madison's time, the manifestations were "pride and indolence in the Clergy; ignorance and servility in the laity[,] in both, superstition, bigotry and persecution"; in the 21st century, the risk is one of "corrosive secularism" to religious schools, and the specific threat is to the primacy of the schools' mission to educate the children of the faithful according to the unaltered precepts of their faith. Even "[t]he favored religion may be compromised as political figures reshape the religion's beliefs for their own purposes; it may be reformed as government largesse brings government regulation." The risk is already being realized. In Ohio, for example, a condition of receiving government money under the program is that participating religious schools may not "discriminate on the basis of . . . religion," which means the school may not give admission preferences to children who are members of the patron faith; children of a parish are generally consigned to the same admission lotteries as non-believers. For perspective on this foot-in-the-door of religious regulation, it is well to remember that the money has barely begun to flow.

If the divisiveness permitted by today's majority is to be avoided in the short term, it will be avoided only by action of the political branches at the state and national levels. Legislatures not driven to desperation by the problems of public education may be able to see the threat in vouchers negotiable in sectarian schools. Perhaps even cities with problems like Cleveland's will perceive the danger, now that they know a federal court will not save them from it.

My own course as a judge on the Court cannot, however, simply be to hope that the political branches will save us from the consequences of the majority's decision. *Everson*'s statement is still the touchstone of sound law, even though the reality is that in the matter of educational aid the Establishment Clause has largely been read away. True, the majority has not approved vouchers for religious schools alone, or aid earmarked for religious instruction. But no scheme so clumsy will ever get before us, and in the cases that we may see, like these, the Establishment Clause is largely silenced. I do not have the option to leave it silent, and I hope that a future Court will reconsider today's dramatic departure from basic Establishment Clause principle.

Justice BREYER, with whom Justice STEVENS and Justice SOUTER join, dissenting.

I write separately, however, to emphasize the risk that publicly financed voucher programs pose in terms of religiously based social conflict. I do so because I believe that the Establishment Clause concern for protecting the Nation's social fabric from religious conflict poses an overriding obstacle to the implementation of this well-intentioned school voucher program. And by explaining the nature of the concern, I hope to demonstrate why, in my view, "parental choice" cannot significantly alleviate the constitutional problem.

With respect to government aid to private education, did not history show that efforts to obtain equivalent funding for the private education of children whose parents did not hold popular religious beliefs only exacerbated religious strife? As Justice Rutledge recognized: "Public money devoted to payment of religious costs, educational or other, brings the quest for more. It brings too the struggle of sect against sect for the larger share or for any. Here one [religious sect] by numbers [of adherents] alone will benefit most, there another. This is precisely the history of societies which have had an established religion and dissident groups." Everson v. Board of Ed. of Ewing (1947) (dissenting opinion).

The upshot is the development of constitutional doctrine that reads the Establishment Clause as avoiding religious strife, not by providing every religion with an equal opportunity (say, to secure state funding or to pray in the public schools), but by drawing fairly clear lines of separation between church and state—at least where the heartland of religious belief, such as primary religious education, is at issue.

The principle underlying these cases—avoiding religiously based social conflict—remains of great concern. As religiously diverse as America had become when the Court decided its major 20th century Establishment Clause cases, we are exponentially more diverse today. America boasts more than 55 different religious groups and subgroups with a significant number of members.

Under these modern-day circumstances, how is the "equal opportunity" principle to work—without risking the "struggle of sect against sect" against which Justice Rutledge warned? School voucher programs finance the religious education of the young. And, if widely adopted, they may well provide billions of dollars that will do so. Why will different religions not become concerned about, and seek to influence, the criteria used to channel this money to religious schools? Why will they not want to examine the implementation of the programs that provide this money—to determine, for example, whether implementation has biased a program toward or against particular sects, or whether recipient religious schools are adequately fulfilling a program's criteria? If so, just how is the State to resolve the resulting controversies without provoking legitimate fears of the kinds of religious favoritism that, in so religiously diverse a Nation, threaten social dissension?

Consider the voucher program here at issue. That program insists that the religious school accept students of all religions. Does that criterion treat fairly groups whose religion forbids them to do so? The program also insists that no participating school "advocate or foster unlawful behavior or teach hatred of any person or group on the basis of race, ethnicity, national origin, or religion." And it requires the State to "revoke the registration of any school if, after a hearing, the superintendent determines that the school is in violation" of the program's rules. As one amicus argues, "it is difficult to imagine a more divisive activity" than the appointment of state officials as referees to determine whether a particular religious doctrine "teaches hatred or advocates lawlessness." Brief for National Committee For Public Education And Religious Liberty as Amicus Curiae 23.

How are state officials to adjudicate claims that one religion or another is advocating, for example, civil disobedience in response to unjust laws, the use of illegal drugs in a religious ceremony, or resort to force to call attention to what it views as an immoral social practice? What kind of public hearing will there be in response to claims that one religion or another is continuing to teach a view of history that casts members of other religions in the worst possible light? How will the public react to government funding for schools that take controversial religious positions on topics that are of current popular interest— say, the conflict in the Middle East or the war on terrorism? Yet any major funding program for primary religious education will require criteria. And the selection of those criteria, as well as their application, inevitably pose problems that are divisive. Efforts to respond to these problems not only will seriously entangle church and state, but also will promote division among religious groups, as one group or another fears (often legitimately) that it will receive unfair treatment at the hands of the government.

I recognize that other nations, for example Great Britain and France, have in the past reconciled religious school funding and religious freedom without creating serious strife. Yet British and French societies are religiously more homogeneous—and it bears noting that recent waves of immigration have begun to create problems of social division there as well. See, e.g., The Muslims of France, 75 Foreign Affairs 78 (1996) (describing increased religious strife in France, as exemplified by expulsion of teenage girls from school for wearing traditional Muslim scarves); Ahmed, Extreme Prejudice; Muslims in Britain, The Times of London, May 2, 1992, p. 10 (describing religious strife in connection with increased Muslim immigration in Great Britain).

In a society as religiously diverse as ours, the Court has recognized that we must rely on the Religion Clauses of the First Amendment to protect against religious strife, particularly when what is at issue is an area as central to religious belief as the shaping, through primary education, of the next generation's minds and spirits.

I concede that the Establishment Clause currently permits States to channel various forms of assistance to religious schools, for example, transportation costs for students, computers, and secular texts. School voucher programs differ, however, in both kind and degree from aid programs upheld in the past. They differ in kind because they direct financing to a core function of the church: the teaching of religious truths to young children. For that reason the constitutional demand for "separation" is of particular constitutional concern.

Private schools that participate in Ohio's program, for example, recognize the importance of primary religious education, for they pronounce that their goals are to "communicate the gospel," "provide opportunities to . . . experience a faith community," "provide . . . for growth in prayer," and "provide instruction in religious truths and values." History suggests, not that such private school teaching of religion is undesirable, but that government funding of this kind of religious endeavor is far more contentious than providing funding for secular textbooks, computers, vocational training, or even funding for adults who wish to obtain a college education at a religious university.

I do not believe that the "parental choice" aspect of the voucher program sufficiently offsets the concerns I have mentioned. Parental choice cannot help the taxpayer who does not want to finance the religious education of children. It will not always help the parent who may see little real choice between inadequate nonsectarian public education and adequate education at a school whose religious teachings are contrary to his own. It will not satisfy religious minorities unable to participate because they are too few in number to support the creation of their own private schools. It will not satisfy groups whose religious beliefs preclude them from participating in a government-sponsored program, and who may well feel ignored as government funds primarily support the education of children in the doctrines of the dominant religions. And it does little to ameliorate the entanglement problems or the related problems of social division. Consequently, the fact that the parent may choose which school can cash the government's voucher check does not alleviate the Establishment Clause concerns associated with voucher programs.

The Court, in effect, turns the clock back. It adopts, under the name of "neutrality," an interpretation of the Establishment Clause that this Court rejected more than half a century ago. In its view, the parental choice that offers each religious group a kind of equal opportunity to secure government funding overcomes the Establishment Clause concern for social concord. An earlier Court found that "equal opportunity" principle insufficient; it read the Clause as insisting upon greater separation of church and state, at least in respect to primary education. In a society composed of many different religious creeds, I fear that this present departure from the Court's earlier understanding risks creating a form of religiously based conflict potentially harmful to the Nation's social fabric. Because I believe the Establishment Clause was written in part to avoid this kind of conflict, I respectfully dissent.